W9-AQZ-114

DATE DUE

Common Destiny

Our Hope:
Two Diverse Nations Striving
for Popular Contentment,
Conditioned Without Regret
by Open Empathy and
Material Compassion for Others

Common Destiny
Japan and the
United States
in the Global Age

Richard Krooth
and
Hiroshi Fukurai

McFarland & Company, Inc., Publishers
Jefferson, North Carolina, and London

British Library Cataloguing-in-Publication data are available

Library of Congress Cataloguing-in-Publication Data

Krooth, Richard.
    Common destiny : Japan and the United States in the global age /
Richard Krooth, Hiroshi Fukurai.
      p. cm.
    Includes bibliographical references and index.
    ISBN 0-89950-522-8 (lib. bdg. : 50# alkaline paper) ∞
    1. United States—Relations—Japan. 2. Japan—Relations—United
States. I. Fukurai, Hiroshi, 1954– . II. Title.
E183.8.J3K72 1990
303.48'273052—dc20   89-43691
                                                       CIP

Manufactured in the United States of America

McFarland & Company, Inc., Publishers
 Box 611, Jefferson, North Carolina 28640

Contents

Acknowledgments

This study emerged from several years of the authors' cooperative work and discussions with others.

Some parts of the study review historical materials; others present the authors' conjecture from known facts; still others offer a prognosis for the future. Like the subject matter itself, the presentation and conclusions will be controversial. We hope to contribute to the intense debate concerning the present search by Japan and the United States for a common future.

Naturally, a project such as this involves the cooperation, assistance, and expertise of many people to bring it to a successful conclusion. Here we wish to recognize the help and contributions of others.

At various stages of completion, discussions about the manuscript were held with Professor Michihiko Noguchi at Osaka City University; Professor Kokichi Shoji at the University of Tokyo; Tomoji Ishi at the Japan Pacific Research Network, in Berkeley, California; and professors Jon Alston and Letitia Alston of the Sociology Department at Texas A & M University.

We would also like to thank those who contributed their expert knowledge in the period before this particular manuscript took formation. Notable here are history professors William Appleman Williams and Harvey Goldberg; Professor Robert Bellah of the Sociology Department at the University of California, Berkeley; professors Richard Flacks and Richard Appelbaum of the Sociology Department at the University of California, Santa Barbara; Professor William J. Chambliss of the Sociology Department at George Washington University; Hans H. Gerth, who before his death was professor emeritus in the Sociology Department at the University of Wisconsin; history buff Lester Radke; and sociologist Glenda Tellis.

Funding for this study came from several sources. We thank, in particular, the following groups: The College of Liberal Arts, the Center for Urban Affairs, the Institute of Pacific Asia, and the Office of International Coordination at Texas A & M University; the Faculty Senate and the Mexican Data Base Project at the University of California, Riverside; and the Louis M. Rabinowitz Foundation, Inc.

Credits for technical help are due James Ssemakula, Lori Cheatham,

Ella Dempsey, and the office staffs of the Sociology Department and the Computing Services Center at Texas A & M University; Alex Ramirez and Larry Sautter of Computing and Communications, and Wanda Clark, Marge Sauder, and other office staff in the Sociology Department at the University of California, Riverside; and Susan Rivera and other office staff in the Sociology Department at the University of California, Berkeley.

We also appreciate the support, encouragement, and assistance of Professor Troy Duster of the Sociology Department at the University of California, Berkeley; professors Mary Zey, Thomas Glass, Karen Wilson, Jerry Gaston, Gail Thomas, Jim Burk, Howard Kaplan, Rogelio Saenz, and Ben Aguirre of the Sociology Department, Harlow Landphair in the Center for Urban Affairs, and Jaan Laane in the Institute of Pacific Asia at Texas A & M University; Professor Edgar W. Butler of the Sociology Department and Professor James Pick of the Graduate School of Management at the University of California, Riverside; Professor Emeritus Millie Almy of the Education Department at the University of California, Berkeley; Professor John Kitsuse and Professor Dane Archer of the Sociology Department at the University of California, Santa Cruz; Karl Krooth for editing assistance; oral historian and essayist Ann B. Krooth; and, of course, McFarland & Company, Inc., Publishers.

With the aid offered by these colleagues, critics, and friends, we pursued our task of presenting the search of Japan and the United States for a common destiny. So, needless to say, we alone are accountable for the contents, the facts presented, and the conclusions in this book.

Richard Krooth
Hiroshi Fukurai
Berkeley, California
15 May 1990

Preface

This study is designed to elicit the interest of a broad audience. One hopes it will contribute to the search by Japan and the U.S. for a common destiny, with fairness toward one another and to other nations.

The bulk of our research and writing was completed in the summer of 1989. Since then, three earth-shaking events have taken place: Eastern Europe has broken free of Soviet helotry; the Soviet Union appears to be on the brink of internal crisis requiring Western aid, trade, and technology; and Japan and the United States are planning to expand their respective spheres of influence—Nippon in East Asia and Western Europe, the United States in Europe east and west, as well as throughout the Americas.

To take full account of these developments was impossible given the publication date of this study. Nonetheless, the reader will find these matters briefly mentioned in the last chapter. Earlier chapters also provide the framework for understanding as history the unfolding of the present.

Richard Krooth
Hiroshi Fukurai
10 May 1990

Introduction

What happens today between America and Japan has all happened before. Looking back from the closing decades of this century, we find a clear pattern regarding the failings of our nations. America has been economically arrogant, politically testy, socially blind to the self-respect Japan has held for itself and demanded of others. Japan has been inscrutably coy, purposely devious, inexplicably closed to opening its economy, society, and culture, in the way that others have demanded from its leaders.

Both America and Japan have made a fetish of money and the display of wealth. To achieve material goals, the balance of commerce and payments has been made an item of racial prestige. In both nations, too, the drive to best the other has been elevated to a national mania, a popular, seemingly senseless, pathology that takes the social form of clannishness and emphasizes cultural dimensions of superiority. Satisfactory or awkward, friendly or frigid, government relations have frequently come to turn on the moment's exchange rates and central bank policies. National employment figures have also come to be seen as the ruling political party's brilliant insight ... if they are high; and of the other nation's malicious trade policies ... if they are low. Even the exchange of diplomatic missions and the extension of political niceties have come to turn on the relative economic strength and prowess of each country. And whenever economic survival seems jeopardized or cultural ways come under attack, hatred for foreigners flourishes.

We live in an era of competitive nationalism, rationalized in the light of xenophobic fantasy. Hostile racial feelings have become linked to mercantile calculations. Both nations pursue only some of their goals openly; both operate selectively within the frame of their agreements and membership in international organizations; and both follow any means necessary in their desire to achieve greater national autarky at the other's expense.

1

The U.S. and Japan do not operate on the same economic frequencies. Japan produces for export, with a significant proportion of its total production requiring markets abroad. Japan is also critically dependent on access to the U.S. market for her "overproduced" goods, for without this market the Japanese economy would go into a tailspin, with massive unused industrial capacity and an unacceptably large unemployed work force that would press the ruling Liberal Democratic Party into enacting draconian domestic controls and expansionist foreign policies.

In contrast, the United States does not necessarily require access to the Japanese market. The U.S. has perfected techniques for dealing with the lack of adequate markets in Japan, Western Europe, third world nations, and elsewhere: halting excess production at home; creating domestic unemployment that stops the building up of inventories that cannot be sold; exporting production operations abroad; and profitably importing goods produced in American-owned foreign factories to the benefit of corporate capital and the detriment of the U.S. balance of trade. The irony of such U.S. capital accumulation causing the American balance of payments to deteriorate has its counterpart in the addition of this negative trade balance to that derived from trade with all other countries. Meanwhile, the U.S. has repeatedly used its cumulative negative trade position to chastise Japan as an unfair and unequal trading partner, and to demand that Japan promote domestic consumption and import U.S. goods with a monetary value equal to that of Japanese exports to the U.S.

Japan has responded to U.S. demands in three ways: by promising to import more U.S. goods; by exporting more capital for investment and production within America in order to capture specific shares of the U.S. market without being burdened by balance of trade criticisms; and by convincing the Japanese people that the U.S. is again vindictively demanding that Japan do its bidding or suffer under traditional Western tariffs, quotas, and other trade and investment penalties.

Japan has also begun to experience the dilemma long faced by America: as Japanese exports have become uncompetitive in some markets or have been blocked by foreign restrictions, the Japanese export of capital — fueling Nippon-directed production abroad at a lower cost than in Japan — encourages the Japanese import of the output from these Japanese-controlled foreign factories, potentially creating a negative Japanese trade balance with the nation of production. Japan's Ministry of International Trade and Industry periodically attempts to offset such low-price imports with Japanese exports. But this will not stop Japan's long-run accumulation of corporate wealth by the export of production capital, which eventually will lead to massive imports of goods from Japan's own foreign factories and even the potential emergence of a negative trade balance.

Japan's new stance on investments within the U.S. has also drawn a sharp American rebuttal. The Japanese have been accused of using their U.S.-based factories to import components made in Japan or in its foreign branch factories in South Korea, Taiwan, and other nations, to contribute to the unfavorable U.S. balance of trade. Some U.S. critics complain that

Japanese employers pressure their American employees not to join unions, undermine labor solidarity by encouraging worker competition while speeding up assembly lines, and keep the wages of their American workers low, thereby hindering their ability to purchase U.S. goods, purchases that, in turn, would stimulate the domestic economy. And still others worry that Japanese capital is taking over critical U.S. industries and must be stopped.

2

Nonetheless, both Japan and America have repeatedly offered lip service about their common destiny, though each understands that its aspirations turn on how much can be absorbed in physical or material terms from the other — the better to elevate their respective feelings of worldly security, self-worth, and metaphysical superiority.

From time to time both nations have also expressed dismay over the narrowness of such nationalist goals. But this dismay has usually been meditated through saccharine phrases and vague, sanctimonious explanations that mask underlying motives. Displays of "friendship" between national leaders have mostly been fleeting political gestures staged for public consumption. Today's fine feelings become hostile feelings tomorrow, then respectful ones the day after, in an endless round.

The foundations for U.S.-Japanese understanding have been poorly laid by past encounters. Immigration between the two nations had either been based on an early labor transfer from Japan to America or a continuing American attempt to build on its Occupation after World War II by pressuring Japan to acculturate its population to an open-market economy and educate its people to Western ideas and ideals. Neither had worked well. The Japanese had been discriminated against, held in contempt by America, and subjugated both culturally and economically. When they broke free of such controls within America, it was by the cumulative power of their wealth, not because of widespread social acceptance. And when Japan rose economically, its newfound power held America hostage to its own trade and investments — so it merely copied what America had been, and advanced their common destiny not at all.

Not by trade alone did Japan wield its new power, for its positive balance of commerce expressed itself in interest-bearing loans to needy nations, trade tied to economic aid, and vast investments in overseas production facilities, raw materials extraction, and the labor efforts of other people. National self-sufficiency was extended to include global surplus gathering and the export of goods, materials, students, managers, scientific expertise, and capital finance — together becoming the material means to disseminate Japanese control. A nation of small farmers and growing industries had thus become one of the world's most aggressive traders, financiers, and investors.

3

Japanese culture had not been exported in step. But some had gone abroad, only to be refined in the frame of the values of others, returning to Japan as a Westernized abomination of the nation's aesthetic purposes. Yet, globalism Nippon-style had meant more than the vast accumulation of wealth, to again accumulate more. For it now had become a Japanese way of thinking about other people in the world, so that the filial piety of Confucianism, the natural harmony of Zen Buddhism, and the ascetic austerity of Shintoism — values that were still held dear and practiced within Japan — were quickly discarded when dealing in the lingua franca of worldly affairs beyond Japan's borders.

In facing the outside world, the Japanese developed a sense of superiority over Western nations and other peoples. Japan's geographic integrity and cultural hegemony expressed themselves as a racial nationalism linked to powerful means for production, self-described racial uniformity, and social conformity. Japanese confidence was continually elevated by its successes in the global economy. Its leaders expressed racial supremacy in terms of the deficiencies of other economies and peoples. Prime Minister Nakasone, for example, could boldly speak of the racial inferiority of blacks and Hispanics in America as a major factor for its secondary status as a world producing power. His successor Prime Minister Takeshita could propound the notion that American builders would inevitably be unsuccessful in bidding on Japanese construction projects because they were financially and technically inferior, manifesting the deeper notion that they were culturally inferior as well.

It matters little to the Japanese that America is in the process of upgrading the status of its diverse populations or that American construction companies face a cartelized Japanese building industry that keeps out foreigners by allotting contracts to its own members. Nippon's contemporary posturing reflects Japan's attempt to break away from the frame of its previous subservience to Western models of economic, political, legal, and military institutions. Not only economic power, but a new self-image has shaped the current ideological formulations of Japan's leaders. They have stressed neonationalist principles of self-sufficiency in production, vast sources of finance for investment, and power in carving out spheres in the world marketplace; and they have expressed ethnocentric perceptions based on the racial purity and cultural uniformity of their nation. Yet such ideological formulations have been rooted in two false, propagandistic notions: that Japan is somehow self-sufficient without access to the resources, financial centers, and markets of other nations; and that Japan is a unified nation with racial homogeneity, when in fact ethnic, religious, and cultural diversities prevail, and large minorities of Koreans, Chinese, Okinawans, Burakumin and Ainus live in Japan.

America has responded to Nippon's new political ethos and opinions such as those Nakasone voiced regarding the weaknesses of America's social and production system based on the supposed inferiority of blacks and Hispanics. Harboring its own concepts of national independence, economic self-sufficiency, and social integrity, the American public has rallied behind U.S. leaders who have expressed their own neonationalist perceptions of America's place in the world. Industrial and union leaders, lobbyists, members of Congress, and the public have proposed various retaliatory trade and investment restrictions on Japan. Some of America's resentment of Japan can be traced to racist feelings. Congress has moved to prevent Japanese takeovers of U.S. industries to protect national security, essential commerce, and economic welfare. Companies like IBM have given access to their proprietary technologies to U.S. competitors like DEC in an effort to unite against Japanese computer chip–makers in order to prevent the U.S. electronics industry from losing its independence. No one wants the U.S. to become dependent on or to become nothing more than a distribution pipeline for Japanese electronics.

As Japan's outspoken politician, Shintaro Ishihara, has stated, racial discrimination rooted in competitive posturing has reared its ugliness on both sides of the Pacific.

4

The Japan living in the heart of its own people has meanwhile imploded, given way to the march of technology, work-a-day life, and too little time for one's self, family, and friends. Not only has work been transformed from the level of small-scale farming and local trade to the level of centralized massive production, but the new conditions of labor and living — which include crowded housing, overburdened transport, and escalating costs — mean esoteric feelings and beliefs within each person have begun to give way to secret ambitions for self-aggrandizement. Such thoughts of elevating one's material possessions exist at the expense of the old values and concerns for nature, other people, and one's own metaphysical destiny.

Such transformations in thinking fit well with management's concern for excellence and cooperation in the workplace. Playing on each worker's hope for security, the great enterprises view labor as a necessary cost of production, which can be lowered in two ways: either by paying less in wages or by creating job classifications that competitively drive workers to try to become upwardly mobile, by putting in long hours of unpaid overtime — thereby effectively contributing free labor to their employers.

The basis for such unpaid work, and for labor's drive for upward mobility, fits in the broader frame of the employer-structured labor market. The great *zaibatsu* employers like Mitsui, Mitsubishi, Sumitomo, and Yasuda offer the opportunity of lifetime employment to individual workers on the basis of their merit. But two limits are placed on such employment. One limitation is based on the absence of an open labor market that would allow labor to go from one employer to another; with little occupational mobility between firms, each worker must judge future employment advances by looking to the standards set by his or her own employer. The other limit is the employer's power to control the precise steps each worker has to take to meet company standards for upward mobility. Positioned to hire, manage, and judge the quality of each worker, the great employers thus operate on four levels to promote competition in pursuit of maximum labor efficiency and greater work efforts without having to pay incremental wages.

First, a long initiation period is required to win promotions, gain prestige, attain seniority, and reach the status of lifetime employment. The internal labor market within each firm drives individuals to compete by offering maximum work efforts, thereby providing free labor in comparison to their peers and cohorts of like age and educational background in other industrial countries.

Second, management-designated teams within the firm compete for prestige against all other teams by working intense, long hours without receiving overtime or any extra pay for extra labor.

Third, the *zaibatsu* and other great enterprises mobilize their individual companies to build worker solidarity for added labor and output by linking the success of the company to the need to outmaneuver rival firms within Japan.

Fourth, Japan's leaders encourage the population to follow tradition and work hard to make Nippon the most powerful producing nation in the world. Being Japanese is portrayed as sufficient cause to exercise extra effort on the job. For patriotic ends, individual loyalty and commitment is encouraged, transcending the need for monetary rewards. Such neo-nationalist calls to heed traditional religious and cultural beliefs have been used to extract unpaid labor from the entire population, expropriating free labor from every worker in the name of Japan's competitive power.

5

Employers, encouraging longer hours for the same pay, and lowering living standards in order to minimize wage costs, assumed that the workers and their unions did not understand the competitive drives foisted upon them. Yet the ethics of laborers have changed too and they are no longer willing to selflessly work hard for others. Workers also want to gain prestige and rise above a life of austerity.

Great changes in the material frame encompassing traditional Japan have thus created a milieu inducing different ways of thinking about a new society in formation. The natural world has quickly been transformed by the technological one, momentarily producing a sort of mental jet-lag. Yet, even as clear-cut class differences emerged, harmony in society at large retained aspects of solidarity.

In part, this solidarity is the product of an emergent social species never before seen in Japan, also prefiguring future class conflict rooted in economic disparities. For the new Japanese badge of identification is one of self-image as part of an emergent middle class. Yet this imaging is merely a reflection of the extension of opportunities in the domestic market, accentuating the commercial standardization of values that were internalized by an upwardly mobile public and expressed as the conscious needs of an ever enlarging, middle-income sector. The very concept of the new middle class, then, is social standing based on consumptive power—rather than on the underlying socioeconomic relations of ownership, or nonownership, of the nation's apparatus of production, commerce, and finance.

This new conception of belonging to a community of buyers—subsuming personal identity under the commercial standardization of community values and the monetization of worldly goods—has brought 80 percent of the population within the frame of such ideological sameness. Thus traditional values of respect and piety toward others are bound to weaken, especially since they are reformulated under the influence of Western practices and concepts of political rights, social security, economic possessiveness, and hierarchical controls. Quickened steps into the Western commercial world threatens to devastate Japan's internal relations, undermining traditional self-descriptive notions of a holistic, respectful, ascetic people.

6

In promoting regularized commerce with Japan, America historically has been as much a victim as a victimizer. From Perry and his Black Ships that blasted Japan open to Western trade to the struggle to develop spheres of influence, the U.S. has been first a pupil of an imperial and militarized Europe, then a teacher for Japan to emulate. Much later, after World War II, America once again imposed its methods and image of the marketplace and "democracy" on a vanquished Japan; and the emancipation of Nippon again came by following the pressures and rules America itself had learned from the merchants of the Old World.

Thereafter, Japan's economy was vastly strengthened by the U.S. war of opportunity in Korea. As its booming economy cracked the fetters of the past, Japan's conglomerated, *zaibatsu* enterprises were restored. Then in the ensuing decades of prosperity without the burden of its own, costly military forces—all the while living beneath the U.S. security umbrella—Japan's high levels of economic growth were spurred by low levels of personal, domestic consumption. Massive national savings, banked by a poorly secured work force prepared to finance hard times and their own retirement, were then channeled through the banking system into industrial investment. Expansion of industries meanwhile concentrated on exports that remitted revenues far exceeding spending on imports. Then, as a creditor nation, Japan's export capital captured industries and resources abroad, securing profits from an expanding sphere of influence.

America had purposely opened the way for Japan's new expansion in Asia. Not only had the MacArthur administration ensured that Japan would become the workshop of the region, but a resource-poor Japan was freed to seek raw materials and customers through bilateral trade and barter in an Asia historically unaccustomed to holding adequate hard currency reserves. Japan thereby created full employment at home, utilized the labor of Korean and other peoples within its sovereign islands, raised its educational standards, turned out the best technically educated graduates in the world, trained a nation of skilled and dedicated laborers, adapted and improved Western technology, overcame two exacting price extortions by the Organization of Petroleum Exporting Countries, outmaneuvered the U.S. "voluntary" quotas on the export of Japanese cars, overcame the U.S.-imposed cartel that set the price of computer chips in America and elsewhere, offset the devaluation of the dollar by dumping goods at lower prices abroad than those charged at home, maintained its market shares by producing within the protected markets and spheres of other nations, and delayed U.S. and other nations' exports to Japan.

For its part, America in the 1980s was seemingly being pushed up against an impassable wall: a negative trade balance with Japan bred the need to import Japanese capital to offset this balance, to rebuild unproductive industries, and to finance the U.S. Treasury to cover a federal budget deficit, itself caused by living beyond the nation's production levels and acting as the world policeman. Americans were either saving nothing in some years, or a meager share of their income in others, while federal budget deficits were absorbing an equivalent of almost all of what they did save, leaving virtually nothing for private and corporate investment. To fill the gap and make up the government deficit, both Japan and Western Europe loaned dollars and bought hundreds of billions in U.S. securities, thereby providing the U.S. economy with the means to continue payments to import foreign-made goods.

7

Conflict became inevitable. Japan's trade and investment successes seemed irreversible. Yet time was running short for Nippon trading companies, investors, and lenders. For more than a decade Japanese and European goods had undercut U.S. production, employment, and well-being — engendering a massive political reaction in America. The U.S. of the late 1980s and early 1990s was threatening to end free trade, limit Japanese investments in certain industries, and stir xenophobic fears among various segments of the business community, the farmers, and the working class.

The Japanese and other foreigners were meanwhile losing previous capital value invested in America as the dollar depreciated and the valuation of their assets fell. Their investment zeal to accumulate and hold U.S. IOU's was eroding in step with the increasing unwillingness of their own central banks, as leaders of last resort, to remain net purchasers of American dollars to stop collapse. As dollars and dollar assets thereby lost their worth in the international arena, Americans would either be forced to import less because they could not pay, or to create a protected market, beset by tariffs, limited output, and cartel pricing of grain, dairy products, and manufactured goods—just the opposite of the measures needed to build the foundations to generate new capital investments, stimulate the use of full production capacity, and foster trade sufficient to pay off America's vast and growing foreign debt.

Japan was meanwhile careful not to lock itself out of the massive, American market. Nippon's corporate calculations were made to enter the U.S. as a Trojan Horse, so that investment in American manufacturing would have the advantage of marketing output within the fifty states without tariff, quota, currency exchange, or other barriers. Such investments had obvious social implications as well. For now Japanese capital was in part replacing U.S. capital that had taken flight and thereby "hollowed out" the industrial infrastructure of the American economy. And now, too, America's discriminatory frame, so often used for excluding the Japanese, was momentarily suppressed, as when Japanese companies employed U.S. workers; or when Japanese top management, lording over lower-level American managers, created a hierarchical subservience not unlike that American officials once held over Japanese immigrants and Japanese-Americans.

Obviously, Japanese investments in U.S. manufacturing opened up employment opportunities for U.S. managers who sometimes received higher salaries than their Japanese counterparts; and jobs for American workers stimulated local economies, especially retail businesses and service support sectors. Yet, Japanese investments and management's drive for efficiencies and profits stimulated American racism. Offered jobs with worker participation on teams making production decisions, workers at first were delighted with their right to determine the purposes of production, for the Japanese system offered a pleasant change from the U.S. manufacturing system in which workers had few opportunities for initiative. But when Japanese employers incorporated labor-saving technologies and displaced some workers, used the new equipment to impose a worker speedup on those remaining, and effectively lowered the unit cost of labor to guarantee the employer larger profits, the workers began to join unions to gain bargaining power and a greater share of the profits generated by their own greater productivity. "Contented" American workers began to revolt against their once-benevolent Japanese employers; and in pursuing their newly discovered, self-protective mission, they found the AFL-CIO a ready ally. Corporate Japan's benevolent and humanistic management practices had not long succeeded.

8

Racial conflict was different than in the past, however. The Japan within America was "greening" from its earlier, internal colonial status into a species of cultural integrity based on economic might. Yet the Japanese living in the U.S. remained racially isolated, ideologically fragile, socially deprived, and internally fractured into groups of those attempting to assimilate quietly to the American way of life, and those working for and representing the aggressive subsidiaries of Japanese corporations operating in this foreign, American environment. The latter's sharp business practices provided a facile alibi for America to fix its sights on the depredations of the Japanese as a people.

This American pathology combined with new calls for self-sufficiency and security for the nation's economic and geographic integrity — projecting a continuum of earlier xenophobic fears associated with Japanese immigration at the turn of the century and the internment of Japanese-Americans during World War II. These would become ideological weaponry to be used as defensive reactions to the economic successes of Japan and other Asian nations.

Future racial conflicts obviously cannot be predicted. But many Japanese fear that America might become so anti–Japanese that a forced sale of their American assets at low prices, or even confiscation, is not impossible. After all, Americans have not reacted rationally to Japan's successes and the recurrent U.S. crises they blame on Japan. And the self-image of America, as a Caucasian nation entitled to maintain its territorial integrity and hold fast to its supreme economic position in the world, has led to calls of Manifest Destiny and other irrational measures in the past. Indeed, America restricted and prohibited the inflow of Japanese immigrants to the West Coast at the turn of the century, prevented Japanese-Americans from buying California land in the 1930s, confiscated their wealth and properties and put them in concentration camps in the 1940s, and never adequately reimbursed those wrongfully imprisoned through the 1980s. These images of the abuse of Japan's ancestral migrants to a foreign land have become almost ghostlike, haunting today's critics, who remain skeptical of America's resolve to secure their legitimate, proprietary rights as "foreigners." Thus, they believe, massive Japanese investments in America from the late 1980s and 1990s are not invulnerable.

9

The global posturings of these two economic powers have meanwhile determined their cultural and political relations. Aesthetic values have loomed large only through an economic telescope, their slender common ground converging through the "values" of the market, integrating their diverse cultures and beliefs.

The main force linking them together has also continued to remain a material one. Industrialization had spilled over national limitations, so that global intervention was not only on the plane of trade, but of production and finance as well. New internal pressures had led to uncompetitive, expensive production in America in 1971, in Western Europe in 1973 and 1979, and in Japan in 1985, fostering their concurrent dependence on the third world as emplacement centers for manufacturing, resource acquisition, an inexpensive labor force, and revenues in the late 1980s. As the tripartite powers, they all looked to Eastern Europe's emergent economies in 1989 and the early 1990s. Their main similarities were now in market structures, methods of organizing capital, production, and labor. These spelled a common need for open markets and investment opportunities.

Yet, neither was there freer trade nor unfettered technological transfers, acknowledged or paid for. The polity of the developing trilateral powers of America, Japan, and Western Europe was still based on the active role of each state individually seeking competitive advantages and pursuing unequal power alignments. The struggle for the best managers, the most positive work ethic, and overcoming the most feared competitors thus went forward. The common destiny that political leaders said they sought repeatedly broke down in petty grievances, steps toward economic autarky, bilateral trade, massive capital exports, racial scapegoating, and wild claims of being isolated, encircled, and deprived of markets and resources for survival. America's historic, pathological fear of the Japanese was equalled by Japan's traditional claim that America was squeezing its economic lifeline and threatening to cause unemployment and chaos within the Japanese economy.

10

Such fears and accusations called attention to underlying economic conflicts, yet rationalized national motives in language often bordering on racial stereotypes and irrational prejudice. Pressures intensifying in each nation obviously called for release and resolution, but they also were publicly presented in illogical ways that gave renewed life to old emotions, thinly veiled racism, and atavistic hatreds. As strident nationalism was reawakened, popular explanations of political and economic matters held forth a racial justification for inherently contradictory production and trade problems.

To explain these reactions, scholars meanwhile searched for deeper meanings, some propounding theories of different rates of development for Japan and America, which thereby created asymmetrical relations between these core industrial nations. These nations' rates of development had diverged since World War II, because the U.S. at first controlled and confined Japan, setting it up as the workshop of Asia in the 1950s. While the U.S. moved into new technologies in the 1960s, it watched Japan become the leading producer of high-quality consumer products. The U.S. kept its lead in competitive industrial goods in the 1970s, and maintained a significant advantage over Japanese telecommunications during most of the 1980s.

By the late 1980s Japan entered the latest phase of developing high-tech industries that stressed computers linked to robots and telecommunication advances. But competition suddenly intensified as Western transnational conglomerates lobbied, in the name of national security, for government protection in order to secure exclusive control over their latest technological advances, meanwhile building worldwide networks deploying the most advanced machines and methods using the cheapest labor and most up-to-date marketing facilities.

Japan is now at the crossroad of its industrial life, facing U.S. hostility to its attempt to enter the latest stages of high-tech industries, and suffering displacement in the market by newly industrialized countries, or NICs, that concentrate, at far lower costs, on the previous phases of manufacturing. Using the latest technologies and the lowest-price force of highly proficient workers, enterprises in such newly industrialized nations as South Korea, Taiwan, and Hong Kong also offer Japan both competition and the opportunity to move capital to these nations in order to gain the same advantages. And yet the industrial core of Japan is bound to weaken in both old and new technologies. Like the great powers before it, Nippon could be forced to become a major capital exporting and overseas investing nation.

Other analysts have argued that the theories of dependency of one power on another are inapplicable to contemporary American-Japanese relations, because such theories have usually been applied only to the relations of first and third world nations. And still others have prognosticated that class alignments in both nations have pitted the ruling forces in each against one another — allowing each to use the drives of their respective middle classes for security to justify their policies; as well as to whip up the mindless, racial reactions of one another's working populations as political confirmation of moves toward greater economic autarchy and extended spheres of influence.

Increasingly important for Japan are market shares linked to competitive technologies in the production spheres of computer hardware and software, telecommunications and energy transmission, nuclear and alternative sources of power, aircraft and missile development. As Japan advances in these spheres, the U.S. responds with claims that proprietary

U.S. technology is being misappropriated, that Japan is trading unfairly in world markets, and that Japanese attempts to take over U.S. technological industries are jeopardizing American security. Such economically motivated apprehensions, based on inherently contradictory economic goals, are conveniently described as Japan's national arrogance reflecting the racial characteristics of its people — stereotypes designed to switch the focus of popular thinking about the underlying economic dilemmas both nations face.

The inequities of the past are meanwhile again being elevated in the mind's eye to intolerance for the population of the other. Barriers clouding the thoughts of economic power brokers and self-satisfied politicians are again becoming material limits to the realignment of influence and the future prosperity of large populations. The petrified hand of the past is once more moving the pawnlike pieces on the global board, checkmating the aspirations of both the American and Japanese people, who are at times open to compassion and empathy for others.

The leaders of Japan and America's business lobbyists and politicians will shape the ideological outlook of the populations of both nations and the future destiny of the Pacific Rim, Euro-Asia, and the West. This book explains how and why.

JAPANESE REGIONS AND PREFECTURES

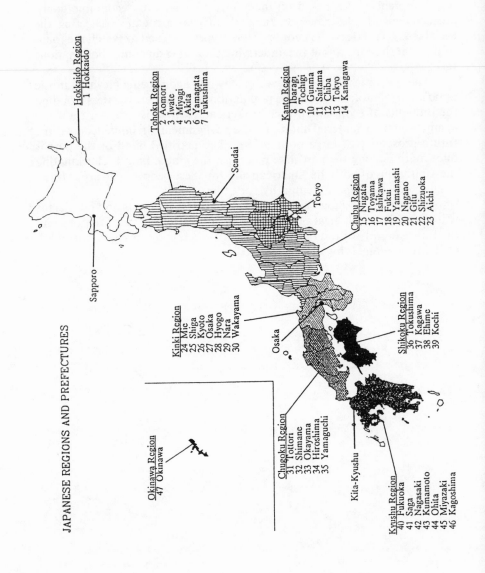

Hokkaido Region
1 Hokkaido

Tohoku Region
2 Aomori
3 Iwate
4 Miyagi
5 Akita
6 Yamagata
7 Fukushima

Kanto Region
8 Ibaragi
9 Tochigi
10 Gunma
11 Saitama
12 Chiba
13 Tokyo
14 Kanagawa

Chubu Region
15 Niigata
16 Toyama
17 Ishikawa
18 Fukui
19 Yamanashi
20 Nagano
21 Gifu
22 Shizuoka
23 Aichi

Kinki Region
24 Mie
25 Shiga
26 Kyoto
27 Osaka
28 Hyogo
29 Nara
30 Wakayama

Chugoku Region
31 Tottori
32 Shimane
33 Okayama
34 Hiroshima
35 Yamaguchi

Shikoku Region
36 Tokushima
37 Kagawa
38 Ehime
39 Kochi

Kyushu Region
40 Fukuoka
41 Saga
42 Nagasaki
43 Kumamoto
44 Ohita
45 Miyazaki
46 Kagoshima

Okinawa Region
47 Okinawa

Sapporo

Sendai

Tokyo

Osaka

Kita-Kyushu

Part 1:
The Metaworld and
the Rise to Power

The soul of Japan cannot be identified by its material successes. Beliefs expressed in traditions, customs, and a national ethos do not clearly manifest themselves on the scale of gross national product or trade balances. But it could be argued that Japan's strong sense of self-determination stems directly from the mythology of its unique creation after the chaotic separation of heaven and earth: the female and male gods *Izanami* and *Izanagi* thrust a halberd into the sea from the Bridge of Heaven, then withdrew it, the droplets trickling off to form an island to which these gods descended to bring forth other islands and other gods. In modern terms, the Japanese see themselves and their islands as heavenly graced, a chosen people in a uniquely divined world.

This myth of Japan's origins was elaborated in the 8th century to strengthen the Imperial House by linking the first Japanese emperor to the gods. *Izanami,* the story goes, burned to death while delivering the god of fire. Seeing her dead body, *Izanagi* purified himself in a river, whereby three more deities were born, one of whom was the sun goddess *Amaterasu Ōmikami,* queen of the divine country Takamagahara. Later she sends her grandson *Ninigi-no-mikoto* down from heaven to the mountain pass Takachiho to rule over the islands of Japan and, through his progeny, begets the first Japanese emperor.[1]

The gods descending to earth used their powers to shape and cast a spirit into all mundane things. *Shinto*—the way of the gods—infused the *kami*—the power of spirits—in humankind and nature, and required that *kami* be worshipped to win its benevolence. The neglect of *kami* might provoke its wrath and even lead to calamity.

Though material structures were not essential for the ancient Japanese to worship nature, the sun, and the moon, today *jinja* shrines are the focal points of worshippers who offer prayers to their deities, who once descended to earth and were crystallized in material beings and things. For believers,

I

there was and is no separation of the metaexistence of the gods and their nature from the vibrant, material world.

This is not usually understood by people in the Western world. From their angle of vision, the myth is taken literally as a contemporary mandate to sustain the spirit of Japan, with the destruction of one god requiring a purification rite that will lead to the creation of a still more powerful god ruler. In this sense, the *Shinto* worship of the *kami* is seen as a reification of the emperor as the descendant of the sun goddess *Amaterasu Omikami* and the living spirits of those who offered their lives to secure the empire.

Chapter 1
Unity of the Shinto State

Shinto

What precisely is the nature of *Shinto,* a religion that shapes the beliefs that direct social life and solidarity in modern Japan? Though its origins are in doubt, Shintoism is probably an indigenous religion whose roots run deep into ancient Japan.

Japanese mythology was first written down with the aid of borrowed Chinese characters. China thereby helped to define Japanese culture. Japan's island isolation made possible adaptation and assimilation. The emergent "Japanese spirit," *wakon,* included much that was Chinese. Modern Shinto is indebted to China's Lao Tzu and Taoism.

Though Japan remained in China's cultural orbit, Japanese preferences in religion, verse, and art helped to maintain indigenous alternatives to the Chinese imports. *Kojiki,* a document published in 712, is the first surviving work to emphasize the divine, mythical origin and absolute power of the Japanese imperial family. Many historians agree that *Kojiki* was written under Shintoist influence, for it stresses magical and mythical religious principles, such as fortune telling, astrology, and geomancy. These magical elements may be traced to Taoism which came to Japan in the sixth century along with Buddhism and Confucianism.[2] The similarities of emphasis on myth and magic make it appear that indigenous religious beliefs and imported Taoist elements were fused to form Shintoism.

Some Taoist gods are found in disguised form in Shintoism, and many Taoist rituals have been incorporated into the Shintoist rites of the imperial household and into Japan's village festivals and rituals. During the construction of a house or building, for example, Japanese hold a ceremony to mark each stage of the construction, such as the ground-breaking, the raising of the framework, and so on. These rituals are conducted by Shinto priests. At Shinto shrines, people can pay to draw sacred lots and secure written oracles (*Omikuji*) or buy copies of an almanac to check their stars and fortunes. Such conduct and rituals are very much part of the Taoistic tradition.

Kojiki gave both a historical origin and an ideological legitimacy to the divinity of the Japanese imperial family. The learned editor of *Kojiki* had no doubt about the cultural superiority of China to Japan. He wrote in his preface that Japanese Emperor Tenmu surpassed both Huang Ti (the ideal Taoist Chinese emperor) and Wen Wang of the Chou Dynasty (the ideal Confucianist emperor) in his ability to command respect and love, whereas Empress Genmei was more famous than Yu, another legendary emperor of China. These scholarly conclusions imply that this sage was reflecting on Japan's feeling of cultural inferiority to an overwhelmingly superior Chinese culture, particularly its Taoist and Confucian elements.

Another important work, *Nihon-shoki* (published in 720), a history of Japan modeled on the Chinese national chronicle, also emphasized the divine origin and absolute power of the imperial family. It is important to realize that these beliefs were recorded in writing only long *after* these ideas had been assimilated. Oral tradition merged myth and fable long before metaphysical accounts of the emperor's origins were "documented" in print. The religious linkage of Japan's emperor to the Shinto shrines and deities operated to assure Japan that it would never ritualistically submit as a Chinese tributary state.

Millions of Shinto-practicing Japanese viewed the emperor as the direct descendant of the gods until recent times. State Shintoism unified Japan's metaphysical origins with nature and the nation's well-being. Those who secured the nation were to be venerated, then, and soldiers who gave their lives for their emperor and nation had their souls enshrined as quasi-deities at the Shinto *honden,* where they are still revered.

Today's true believers in Shintoism still worship the *kami,* regardless of the fact that Emperor Hirohito was forced to renounce his divinity after World War II and that the American-imposed Japanese constitution introduced and institutionalized the Western conception of the separation of church and state, so that Shinto allegedly lost its official protection. They also worship the souls of World War II soldiers, especially at the *Yasukuni Shrine* near the Imperial Palace in Tokyo — an action that many in the West and Asia still equate with a military bent of mind. Here, through prayers and rituals, many thousands of soldiers have had their souls "embodied" within a small piece of wood bearing their names followed by the word for a god, to be kept in the shrine forever.

Buddhism Past and Present

Like Shintoism, Buddhism, the search for truth by reaching the heights of intuitive unconsciousness was not Japanese in origin. Founded by Siddhartha Gautama (ca. 563–483 B.C.) in India, Buddha worship spread with India's Kushan empire into China under the Wei dynasty (A.D. 460). From China, Buddhism spread to the Korean Peninsula, first by land in Koguryo, then passing to Paekche. And from Korea it was carried to Japan by foreign craftsmen who came to live there.

Though conflicts developed between the conservative followers of Shinto and the new believers in Buddhism, Buddhist teachings continued to filter throughout Japanese society. Temples were erected and the manufacture of Buddhist images expanded (A.D. 596–606), eventually leading to a unique Japanese art tradition. Yet Buddhism and its artistic images were later to change under the influence of Chinese Zen Buddhists' emphasis on mental discipline.[3]

In Mongolian times, Buddhist abbots traveled to Japan to bring the teachings of Zen; and in the Manchu era, Confucian scholars also made their way to Japan. As Chinese Zen Masters and Japanese Zen Monks carried on a dialogue and visited one another's monasteries in the 12th and 13th centuries, the new doctrine which opposed the worship of holy images spread, leading to the displacement of earlier forms of Buddhism in the religious loyalties of ruling families and the military class. In Kamakura and Kyoto new temples were built, each having five leading Zen monasteries called Five Mountains *(gozan)* in Chinese fashion. With emphasis on imagery and the legendary Arhats—the forerunners of Zen, who realized enlightenment by their own exertion—Zen Buddhists did not promote representative arts.[4]

Rather, spiritual enlightenment came through meditation, stilling the mind to grasp the truth of the universal nothingness of the absolute. In the pursuit of truth, Zen taught that verity transcends the limits set by rational thought, so one must grasp the truth directly through meditation, not by the word of humankind. Through meditation, human intuitive power itself could be released to reach its highest unconscious, involuntary state.

As Buddhism evolved from complex dogma to teachings understandable to all, it was both internalized and "Japanized." It remained the only serious alternative to Confucian philosophy until the 18th century. And the spirit of Zen survives to the present as a preference for meditative silence. The Zen spirit in Japan expresses itself in the harmonizing culture of stone gardens, ink paintings, the tea ceremony, and flower arrangement.[5] In these ways, skills, aspirations and frustrations were channelled when pressures threatened from the outside world.

Confucianism and the Japanese Ethos

With Buddhism and Shintoism, Confucianism represents another important religion that has had a significant influence upon the formation of the Japanese ethos. Ethical principles such as loyalty, the work ethic, and filial piety that characterize Japanese beliefs today are largely indebted to the virtues of Chinese Confucianism.

Confucianism originating in China in the early 6th century B.C. came to Japan from China via Korea along with Buddhism and Taoism in the 6th century A.D. Partly because of Japan's geographic distance from

China and partly due to indigenous Japanese cultures that prevailed prior to the importation of superior Chinese ways, Chinese Confucianism was modified in the course of its assimilation by the Japanese. While Chinese Confucianism stressed *benevolence* and *individual liberty,* Japanese Confucianism emphasized *loyalty* and *filial piety.*

Confucius (550–478 B.C.) advocated the principle of virtuous government, suggesting a method of government that would strengthen the people as a collective by means of a strong sense of morality and would serve to bring about order by raising their levels of virtues. Confucius regarded benevolence *(jen),* justice *(i),* ceremony *(li),* knowledge *(chih),* and faith *(hsin)* as the most important virtues, but believed that of these benevolence was the essential virtue.

Confucius believed that man's nature was fundamentally good, and considered that the natural affection existing within one's family and between one's relatives was the cornerstone of social morality. Yet Confucius thought that the practice of morality should not be confined only within one's family, but should be extended beyond the family circle to the general community, even to complete strangers. When human nature and human affection have reached perfection, he philosophized, social order would be appropriately maintained. On a broader plane, Confucius recognized that even in a society where people acted virtuously, some deeper bond was essential. Confucius considered this deeper tie as *"li"* or ceremony, meaning norms established by custom, that were less rigid than laws. Confucius' maxim was "guidance by morality, control by ceremony." Social solidarity was a function of these two simple rules.

Another important feature of Confucianism was the precise meaning of loyalty—revealing different interpretations in China and Japan. The Chinese meaning of loyalty suggested being true to one's own conscience. But the Japanese meaning stressed the notion of sincerity and complete devotion to one's lord. In times of war and feudal conflict such loyalty required service to one's lord to the point of sacrificing oneself.

The difference between Japanese and Chinese Confucianism grew greater with the passage of time, especially following the establishment of *Meiji* government in 1868, when the old caste system was abolished and the warrior class lost its privileges. In the Tokugawa era the Chinese literary heritage became increasingly important to the Japanese. Refugees from the Manchu conquest in China arrived in Japan, bringing Chinese books and stimulating Japanese appreciation of Confucian teachings. Confucianism became the core subject matter in elite schools established by feudal authorities and urban private academies. A literati of amateur artists styled themselves after the scholar-artists of late Ming times. Confucianists looked to the benefits of Chinese civilization and its sages, but scorned China's barbaric political history and its tradition of centralizing imperial administrative control over feudal domains. Yet, thereafter in Japan itself, the obligation of national defense fell to the general male population as a whole, whose members might be enlisted as tomorrow's soldiers. Such conscription was implemented in 1882, when an *Imperial Injunction* issued to soldiers and sailors of the Japanese armed forces stressed five Confucian virtues: loyalty, ceremony, bravery, faith, and frugality. No special consideration was given to *benevolence,* the central virtue in Chinese Confucianism.

Militarism accentuated the difference between Japanese, Chinese, and also Korean, Confucian virtues. Soldiers of the ancient Silla dynasty of Korea, *Hwa-rang-do,* the Korean equivalent to Japanese *Bushido,* stressed loyalty, filial piety, faith, *benevolence,* and bravery. In Chiang Kai-shek's Chinese army, the major elements for a soldierly spirit were wisdom, faith, *benevolence,* bravery, and strictness. But *benevolence* was not a value stressed in the Japanese army. While faith and bravery were virtuous elements common to all three, the neglect of benevolence and the emphasis placed on loyalty must be regarded as central characteristics unique to Japanese Confucianism.[6]

One explanation for Japanese divergence from Chinese Confucianism might rest on a critical analysis of two historical periods during which an encounter with superior foreign cultures posed a great threat to the integrity of Japanese society as a whole. According to Morishima Michio, an economist in the London School of Economics, those periods are *Taika-no-Kaishin* (or the *Taika Reform,* 645–649) and *Meiji Restoration* (or *Meiji Revolution,* 1867–68).

When faced by the overwhelmingly superior culture of China, Prince Shotoku Taishi (574–622) had recognized the necessity of building a strong state structure. As heir apparent and regent to Empress Suiko, he moved powerfully to modernize the imperial government, introducing the more advanced Chinese administrative and judicial system. In 603 Taishi applied the Twelve-Cap-Rank System that stressed governmental appointments according ot one's ability, rather than by genealogical links; and in 604, he promulgated a seventeen-article constitution that called for loyalty to the imperial family and the conduct of worldly affairs according to Confucian principles. Though a shared sense of nationalism was not strong during this period, these declarations forwarded the ideological consensus needed to establish a strong national identity surrounding the imperial family.

Morishima also argues that Shotoku Taishi coined the term, *"tenno"* (heavenly emperor), changed from the previous title of *"o-kimi"* (great king). The designation had a far-reaching effect because it suggested the emperor as a Manifest God *(Arabito-gami)* identified with the heavenly God. Thus there could be no conflict between emperor and God.

Faced with the overwhelmingly powerful Chinese influence in early 7th-century Japan, Shotoku Taishi thus attempted to raise the level of national identification around the imperial family. In a sense, he promoted conservatism and loyalism. With the legitimate power of the Manifest God, that thereafter would repeatedly appear in periods of national emergency (as during World War II), was stressed a strong sense of loyalty to the imperial family. The Confucian virtues that reappeared in Taishi's works thus gave new life to the reification of the concept of loyalty.

The *Meiji Revolution,* or *Restoration,* also marks an era in which the commitment of loyalty to the imperial family was raised to a higher level. During the latter part of the Tokugawa period (1600–1868), when Western nations were threatening a still-feudal society and demanding entry to Japan's virgin economic domain, there was a great debate as to whether the policy of *sakoku* (isolationism) should be continued or Japan should open her doors *(kaikoku).* The majority of the progressive and realisitc supporters of the *kaikoku* policy were not internationalists, but urged opening the country simply as an expedient for the present, foreseeing that Japan would eventually become a powerful, global leader.

When Japan came face to face with the West in the 19th century, its leaders acknowledged a gap in technologies, believing they could fuse the "Japanese spirit with Western ability," stressing Japan's nationalists sentiments. And as far as understanding the technological gap between Japan and the West, the feudal lords already knew of Western advancements before the 16th century. Oda Nobunaga (1533–82) had, for instance, capitalized on the Western advancement in arms, science, and technology. He skillfully mastered firearm strategy and established a high-speed mobile naval force. His mastery of Western technologies and methods was so superior in his era that sailing warships fitted with cannons in Osaka Bay blockaded the city of Osaka from the sea.

Though he also favored Christianity, he wanted to keep the West at bay by ideologically fortifying Japan. Reasoning that the Buddhists had become totally corrupted by clinging to traditional forms of power that did not bring with it any valuable technology, Nobunaga destroyed the Enryakuji Temple on Mt. Hiei that had ruled the Buddhist world for almost eight hundred years. And he crucified all 20,000 believers during the Ikko Sect Uprising (a Buddhist sect of *Jodo-shinshu*). No surprise, his harsh personality appeared inappropriate to the times, leading to his assassination by his retainers led by Akechi Mitsuhide in 1582. The latter was also assassinated by another retainer, Toyotomi Hideyoshi (1536–98), a son of a poor peasant, who became the eventual ruler of the country.

Hideyoshi adopted an active posture of acceptance toward China's Ming Dynasty, Korea, and Taiwan, but did not welcome contact with the West. He was alarmed by two prospects: (1) the Western invasion of the Orient (the Spanish had conquered the Philippines at this time), and (2) other feudal *daimyo* (lords) taking advantage of Western technologies to revolt against him just as Nobunaga, his former lord, has done. He thus prohibited the propagation of Christianity in 1587 and crucified Christians in Nagasaki in 1594.

After the death of Hideyoshi, the Tokugawa unified the country and adopted an *isolationist policy* with the clear intention that he would maintain a permanent lead in the arms-import race to keep his dominance. The Tokugawa suppressed Christianity and in 1639 prohibited the entry of all Westerners, except for a few Dutch merchants under the strict control of the Tokugawa Bakufu at the small man-made island of Deshima in Nagasaki Bay.

This *Sakoku policy* lasted two hundred years until 1859 when the Tokugawa Bakufu committed itself to the opening of the three ports of Kanagawa, Nagasaki, and Hakodate to Russia, Britain, France, Holland, and the United States.

Social Bonding in Japan

The Tokugawa Bakufu thus exercised a near-perfect protective trade policy, shielding its internal industries and keeping Japan from becoming a purely agricultural exporting country economically subjugated by the West. Such isolation functioned as a protective shield for Japan's traditional industries.

With Japan secured, the nation strengthened its cultural homogeneity by the standardization of language, the acceptance of common ways of thinking and acting by peoples of different provinces, and consequent similarities in beliefs and social rules. Confucianism, in particular, permeated every sphere of cultural and societal life. Confucian education, against a background of more than two hundred years of bureaucratic control, had trained the warriors to be efficient bureaucrats by the end of the Tokugawa era. They were equipped with the discipline needed by soldiers of a modern army or workers in a modern factory.

Another facet of Confucianism that contributed to its appeal in the Tokugawa period was its emphasis on intellectual and rationalistic thinking. It rejected mysticism, magic, and ghosts. Each of the intellectual traditions of Japan made its contribution to the volatile politics of the 1850s and 1860s, with Confucianism emphasizing duty and loyalty, and Shintoism teaching veneration of the emperor and the sacredness of Japan.[7] Fifteen years after Perry opened Japan to the West, the shogun left office. The country's new leadership promoted reform in the name of a young emperor. Without tradition's fetters to impede them, the Western sciences were quickly digested by Japanese scientists. Japan had entered the industrial age, yet maintained the Confucian virtues bequeathed by its Imperial ancestors: loyalty and filiality as the fundamental character of the empire and the source of national education — as the Imperial Rescript on Education provided in 1890.[8]

What broad conclusions can we draw about Confucianism in the Tokugawa period, then? First, it stimulated a *national consciousness* of being Japanese and created the ancillary ideologies, called *kokugaku* (national learning) and *shinkoku shiso* (gods' land doctrine). As Confucianism was inseparably related to "China as a center of the world" (*Chuka* or *Chugoku* means the center of culture or the world), the study of Confucianism pushed forward the consciousness of being a nation. But the concept of *"chu"* (loyalty) did not legitimate the Tokugawa structure. Certainly, warriors owed their loyalty to their feudal lords, feudal lords to the shogun, and the shogun to the emperor. But at each tier of the hierarchical order up to shogun, the member owed only an indirect loyalty to the emperor. Thus the consistency of one's relationship to the emperor through the shogun was disrupted, and one was forced to select loyalty between them. So, eventually, when loyalty to the Tokugawa Bakufu collapsed, the young Meiji emperor was legitimized as the ruler of the nation.

Confucianism was understood in Japan as an ethical system rather than a religion and taught the Japanese that frugal behavior was noble behavior. Japanese Confucianism stressed loyalty to the lord or state, filial piety to one's parents, faith toward friends, and respect toward one's elders. And from a rationalistic standpoint, it appears natural that a nationalistic, capitalist economy was later developed from its principles based on a seniority system and lifetime employment. Feudal lords would later be replaced by the great employers and the Japanese people would become slavishly loyal to the imperial family during the post–Meiji Restoration era of Taisho, Showa, and Heisei.

Chapter 2

The Tension of
Warrior and Noble

Like its religions, Japan's methods of production and warfare also developed over several centuries. The nobles, *daimyo,* who had once been dominant and attended by the *samurai,* or knights, temporarily lost place and regained it only through cooperation and merger with these military forces. For example, just as the *samurai* had once served, guarded, and fought for the lords, the lords in the 12th and 13th centuries began to take a minor role, retreating to a life of luxury at Kyoto, losing control to successive waves of powerful clans under military leaders. Internecine wars thus led to the emergence of two societies: the elegant, graceful, and refined society established by the nobles in Kyoto, and the rugged, virile, and self-valorous society of the Kamakura military.

By 1192, Minamoto Yoritomo had established a *military government* in Kamakura that eventually ushered in an era centered on the warrior class rather than the nobility.[1] Yet military readiness, pride of power, and ruggedness could not alone centralize authority. In both 1274 and 1281 Mongol forces invaded Japan. The fatal blow struck against the invader was leveled not by military power but by typhoons that struck in the midst of each battle — convincing the faithful that the *kami* (godly) *kaze* (wind) provided divine protection for Japan.[2] The 200 years of relative peace that followed were unsettled from the late 1400s to the early 1600s, as the great feudal lords again made war to dominate one another and built castles to make enemy attack difficult. After 250 years of this internal warfare, Tokugawa Ieyasu broke the last resistance of the opposing lords in 1615 and ushered in the era of the centralized authority of the Tokugawa Shogunate.[3]

Old castles became the symbol of power of the *daimyo* who resided there, administrative hubs to govern their territories, and the center of communications through the emerging castle towns.[4] From the latter half of the 16th century to the turn of the 17th, three great cities — Edo, Osaka, and Kyoto — emerged under the control of the central government. Kyoto was the center for a resplendent court culture, its 400,000 people also excelling in the production of high-grade weaving and crafts. Edo, with one million people, became the largest city in the world, housing the government, the warrior class, merchants catering to their needs. And Osaka, with its 350,000 people, was the center for tax collections, active money-lending, and clearinghouse for cargoes of cotton, oil, vinegar, and sake, which was moved through the terminus at the mouth of the Aji River by great shipping activity between Edo and Osaka, creating scores of business tycoons.[5]

The commerce in goods, food, and labor, and the support for the new merchants, the government's tax collectors and customs officers, *samurai* armies, and sumptuous court life rested on the back of the nation's main producers, the peasantry. Landlords' exactions for rents and taxes pressured the peasants to work long and hard for bare subsistence on their small plots. In the Edo era, which lasted from the 17th to the 19th centuries, 80 percent of the people tilled the land as helots for the warrior class that demanded annual taxes amounting to 50 or 60 percent of their harvests. In good times the government directed edicts at the peasants advising them to live simply and to shun luxuries, to "rise early, work late." In hard times, when there was no rice to eat, the authorities made and distributed gruel. But sometimes peasants demanded reductions in the rice tax and townspeople plundered rice shops in retaliation for the merchants' exorbitant prices.[6]

Merchants in the feudal Japanese state were subject to central control. Because the "outside lords" *(tozama daimyo)* were excluded from the inner sanctum of government participation by the ruling Tokugawa, they sought other professions. Some of the eighty-six *tazama* became merchants, the most eminent being the Satsuma in southern Kyushu.[7] Both urban and rural merchants emerged. They made loans to the Bakufu, knowing that the money and in-kind commodities advanced would not be returned, and lived under strict government regulation of their activities, their mode of dress, their choice of names (which could not resemble a *daimyo* name), and their places of residence outside the *samurai* district.[8]

The Tokugawa fear of an alliance of discontented *tozama* merchants and *samurai* was based on a knowledge of their fixation on accumulated wealth and power. "In fact," says the scholar Herbert Norman, "no feudal aristocracy could express greater distaste for money-making and moneymakers than the Tokugawa moralists and legislators."[9]

The Quest to Accumulate

In Japan, then, the quest for wealth and its accumulation waxed and waned throughout the feudal era. It was controlled by taxes and levies to cover expenditures for arms and armor and the costs of a required *daimyo* presence at Edo. Once Tokugawa Ieyasu quelled all opponents, unified most of the country, and established his central government in Edo, the 265-year reign (1603–1868) of his shogunate heirs was prolonged by preventing the *daimyo* from accumulating sufficient wealth and power to oppose the shogun.

Concerned with stability and security, the politically brilliant shogun Tokugawa Ieyasu imposed a unique state Confucianism on the population, developed a bureaucratic authoritarianism, and fostered a self-enforced, self-perpetuating, social conformity by defining the place of each person within society. Conformity was enforced by both the expectations of others and bureaucratic mandates that delimited the bounds of conformity — backed up by material threats.[10]

The authorities restricted access to foreign goods and weapons, thereby controlling the trade and the accumulation of Japanese merchant wealth that could rival the shogun's power. This virtually closed Japan to foreign trade and influence. For a century Catholic missionaries had already shown their power to convert the *daimyo* and promote subversion. And though imported guns that were soon copied and produced in Japan had speeded unification under the Tokugawa, once the nation was at peace, these gunsmiths threatened the status and superiority of the *samurai* and their lords. Feudal lords were summoned by the shogun to put down the 1637 rebellion of Christians in southern Japan. Thereafter, in the name of proscribing Christianity, the shogunate interfered in the affairs of every region, continuing to post notices in every village forbidding the "religion of Jesus" until the 1870s.

Seclusion Edicts powerfully renounced foreign interests, especially China's Manchus who were perceived as threats to east Asian stability after their 1644 conquests consolidated regions never before under close Chinese rule. Japanese traders and pirates had been in frequent contact with the China coast since the 1400s, and China's traders had been everywhere, even to the Americas. The Manchus feared regional autonomy and foreign trade as much as did Japan's shogun, so both nations moved to stop foreign commerce, resulting in an interregnum that lasted for nearly two centuries. "No Japanese ship," one of Japan's edicts warned, "may leave for foreign countries. No Japanese may go abroad secretly. If anybody tries to do this, he will be killed.... Any Japanese now living abroad who tries to return to Japan will be put to death." The Manchus spent half a century trying to gain control over China's southern coast, closing and evacuating the seaports until capturing Taiwan in 1683. Nagasaki became the only port where a few South China traders were allowed to maintain a small commerce with Japan. Here, too, the Portuguese Catholics and the Protestant Dutch who replaced them were kept at arm's length to stop their corrupting influence on the Japanese.[11]

The three hundred lords and their fiefs were meanwhile kept disunified in the Japan of the shogunates, and the *daimyos* were put to the expense of spending every other year in residence in Edo and leaving their wives and children there at all times as virtual hostages. Because each *daimyo* had to spend huge sums on travel and the maintenance of two estates, he was unable to accumulate the economic wherewithal to raise an army to attempt to set up a new center of governing authority. Lacking independent military forces, the *daimyo* periodically expressed their authority by huge processions of vassals during the way to and from Edo; and the vassals demonstrated their loyalty to their lords by cultivation of their minds, their attitude toward the sword and bow — rather than prowess in using them — and, in cases where the lord died of illness or the vassal fell into disfavor, *harakiri,* fulfilling a moral code of loyalty and honor *(bushido). Harakiri* was only prohibited by the shogunate after many *samurai* performed the rite.[12] But the system of shogunate control continued.

Consolidation of the national domain also had to race potential disruption by outsiders in the 16th century. In 1543 a Chinese ship carrying Portuguese had been shipwrecked in southern Kyushu. Portuguese and Spanish ships were soon anchoring on Japan's coasts to solicit trade. The Portuguese brought muskets bought by the feudal lords, changing their mode of warfare, castle construction, and military training. As commerce within Japan was extended and reached outwards to Southeast Asia and Europe, Japan began to fear the territorial ambitions of others, especially when trade accompanied the Christian faith (introduced by Saint Francis Xavier in 1549) and some trade-minded *daimyo* protected its spread, while others became converts.[13]

Toyotomi Hideyoshi, the ruler in the 16th century, reacted in 1596 by banning Christianity and crucifying twenty-six Catholic converts and missionaries. The Shogun's bureaucratic functionaries also went into action. The Temple Registry was used to record names of the faithful; those unlisted were suspected of being Christians and arrested. But the Shogunate also permitted Christianity to spread, because its bearers promoted trade in sought-for European goods. Jealous of one another's trade positions in the East, however, the English and Dutch Protestants began to warn Japan's government about the territorial ambitions of Spanish and Portuguese Catholics. These warnings led the Shogunate to secure the nation against foreign invaders in 1641 by severing relations with all countries except China and Holland, whose trading stations were confined to Nagasaki. Thereafter, for more than two centuries, from the tiny man-made islet of Deshima in Nagasaki harbor, the Dutch carried on a vigorous trade, but were forbidden to enter the city.[14]

Such measures were initiated by a central, military government that successfully transformed the *samurai* into civilian bureaucrats, and encouraged popular education, literacy, and culture based on Chinese learning. Two centuries of peace and tranquility followed.

From Rebellion to Unified Empire

The Dutch made the initial intellectual challenge to Japan's reliance on Chinese knowledge and science. Later other Western nations threatened.

The United States had a thriving oriental trade by the mid–19th century, fostered partly by the development of steam navigation and partly by the discovery of gold in California. Dispatching two war vessels under Commodore Biddle, an initial unsuccessful attempt was made by the U.S. government to break down Japan's system of exclusion. Biddle's mission was followed by the Perry mission in early 1853 when President Fillmore sent Commodore Perry with a squadron of four vessels to present a letter from the president to the emperor of Japan, and asked consent for negotiation of a treaty of friendship and commerce between the two governments. Steaming into Edo harbor on 7 July, Perry fired his largest guns, was officially received and allowed to leave the president's letter with the emperor for consideration by the Japanese government, and promised to return the next spring for an answer.

The appearance of a foreign naval force had long been anticipated. Nonviolent political discussions broke out, accompanied by the threat of civil war. Until then, the Shogun had wielded the powers of the impotent emperor. But now two parties disputed who was to succeed him, using the arrival of the American squadron as a pretext for grasping at the reins of power. One party was headed by Ii Naosuke Kamon-no-kami, leader of the Fudai *daimyo,* who by line of authority was to be appointed regent in case of an emergency. The other party was led by the prince of Mito, one of the three leading family clans, who was the hereditary vice-shogun in Edo and connected by marriage with the family of the emperor and with the wealthiest *daimyo.* To decide, letters were sent to all the *daimyos* and *Ometsukes,* requesting their opinions concerning the reception to be given to the Americans. The majority wanted to use force to oppose any foreign interference in the affairs of Japan. But it was agreed that an open declaration of war had best be deferred until Japan's defenseless shores could be strengthened and sea forts erected. Orders were then sent to the *daimyos* to muster the full strength of their retainers and munitions of war, warning that "if Japan does not conquer, it will be a great disgrace."[15]

Perry returned in June 1857, to find the emperor at first refusing to accede to the treaty of commerce with the U.S., then being persuaded by his old minister, the Taiko, to let his commissioners sign the Treaty of Kanagawa with Townsend Harris on behalf of the United States. The Shogun thus violated Japanese traditions of acceding to the wishes of the *daimyos.* He explained in his official capacity that a war and likely defeat threatened from the Western world: "some Russian and American men-of-war came here, bringing the news that in a short time English and French men-of-war would arrive here; that these two nations had fought and won many battles in China; that they would come here in the same warlike spirit, and it would be difficult for us to negotiate with them. The American ambassador offered to us, that if we would make a temporary treaty with him, as soon as we should have signed and given him that treaty he would act as mediator between us and the French and the English, and could save us from all difficulties."[16]

The door had been opened to the West. Similar treaties were quickly imposed by Holland, Russia, Great Britain, and France. Dissatisfied with the Shogun's explanations, the *daimyos* were infuriated. Popular remonstrance to the emperor was issued in the capital: "Since the time of Tensho Dai Jin the country has been to the present time sublime and flourishing; but friendship with foreigners will be a stain upon it, and an insult to the first Emperor *(Jinmu)*. . . . If foreigners come to our country they will loudly proclaim the mutual benefits that trade will produce; but when we shall refuse to comply with all their wishes, they will threaten us with their artillery and warships. The Shogun thus disturbs the peace."[17]

A revolution was impending, based on the drive for self-protective security, set off by a forged Imperial Edict criticizing the Shogun and commanding his immediate appearance for conference at Kyoto: "Your duty is to act as Shogun; and yet you who have been appointed as Commander-in-Chief to quell the barbarians, do not perform your duties. You should know what the duties of your office are, and yet you are unable to punish our foreign enemies."[18]

This command reached the Shogun on 29 December 1857. All the great *daimyo* assembled that night until two in the morning in the Throne Room at Edo Castle, expressing a spirit of revolution.[19]

By the following spring the revolution was underway. The leader of one party, Ii Naosuke Kamon-no-kami, appointed regent to replace the Shogun under the emergency line of authority, planned to bring forward a *new order* to deal with the Western invaders. But he was opposed by the leader of the *daimyos,* the Mito and Hitotsubashi branches of the Tokugawa family, who vigorously refused any accommodation with the foreigners. Military calculations and court intrigues ensued. Nariaki of Mito planned a coup d'etat with the senior councillor, Manabe. The Regent ordered the arrest of Nariaki and his principal supporters, and deprived them of their revenues. Nariaki then sought to have his son proclaimed regent, claiming that the Shogun had died; the Regent Kami then had Moto-ko's principal retainers arrested and brought to trial, though the judges refused to convict them and were themselves degraded. The empress intrigued with the regent to marry the emperor's younger sister to the boy Shogun. Nariaki of Mito lost all his offices; his son was ousted as the governor of Osaka and, as heir, was commanded to keep guard on his father. Mito-ko's chief retainer was ordered to commit *harakiri;* some of his other retainers took refuge at the British Legation in Tozenji; and other opponents of the regent were similarly harassed, with many lesser chieftains executed or banished to outlying islands. With the new Shogunate's position secured, Manabe was forced to withdraw, and conniving members of the imperial household were banned from meddling in the regent's realm of authority. And that authority was then used to open the country to foreign trade.[20]

The great *daimyo* then conspired to destroy the regent's power, to isolate the Shogun, embattle the emperor — and keep out the foreigners. Nariaki was joined by the Owari, Tosa, and Echizen *daimyo*. The rebels successfully mobilized their *samurai* and beheaded the regent on 3 March 1860, at the Shogun's court "Festival of the Dolls." The regent's head was impaled on a pole inscribed with the words: "Let us take and hoist the silken standard of Japan and fight the battles of the Emperor." If the emperor would not fight his own battles, the great *daimyo* would fight in his name without him and without the regent and the Shogun!

Government orders issued to arrest the suspected followers of Nariaki brought his taunting reply: "How can I, a poor *daimyo,* arrest these men, when you, the Shogun, are unable to do so? If you wish to seize my men, send your officers and let them try."

The revolt was now out in the open.

Shortly after the regent's assassination, his son-in-law was murdered in bed. The Shogun in terror barricaded his castle at Edo. Military escorts accompanied the imperial ministers on their duties. The emperor issued orders that the higher *daimyos* were now to visit Edo only once every seven years, but the edict was not applied to those *daimyo* who held the ear of the emperor in the interest of the Shogun. Meanwhile, Nariaki in disguise traveled the empire to study the feelings of the people, rather than come forward to carry out his own policy. And the agitation against foreigners grew in force.[21]

Under threat, the foreign ministers moved their legations from Edo to Yokohama in the spring of 1862, demanding that fortified legation buildings be furnished by the Japanese government. For that purpose the great councillor Ando Nobumasa provided the city's recreation ground. But a Japanese mob burned down the new buildings, and Ando barely escaped an assassination attempt with the loss of an ear. Meanwhile, Nariaki's men had failed to win the Shogun over to their side, and now were determined to embroil the government with some foreign nation. An English merchant was murdered, the British minister's demands for redress were treated with contempt, and the vessels of foreigners were fired upon by the *daimyo* Choshu, using as pretext the letter of his commission as guardian of the Straits of Shimonoseki. A squadron of English, French, and Dutch warships then levied a heavy indemnity from one of Choshu's relatives whom they mistook for the *daimyo*.

Although the Shogun disavowed Choshu's acts and undertook to punish him to satisfy foreign demands, he found it next to impossible to punish Choshu because the soldiers and the people at large regarded Choshu as a patriot. The Shogun was forced to come to terms with the *daimyo,* leading British warships to punitively reduce the city of Kago-shima nearly to ashes and force Satsuma to pay a heavy indemnity.[22]

Satsuma, the most powerful trading clan that had made alliances with merchant centers in the major cities, was to become the cause célèbre for opening Japan to the West. He and other great merchant *daimyo* understood the benefits of foreign commerce and the ways in which the shopkeepers and merchants of Edo and Osaka could act as the conveyor of goods into and out of Japan. The great *chonin* in Osaka, who had concentrated 70 percent of Japan's liquid wealth, were now ready to supply funds to finance a commercial revolution to overthrow the Shogun and his *régime*.[23]

Realizing the self-destructive influences of internal strife and Japan's lack of knowledge of European methods of warfare and strategic advances, Choshu tried to reconcile the two great factions, calling for an end to internal struggle.

> The closing or opening of Japan was a matter of the greatest moment. That which cannot be shut again should not have been opened. The closing of Japan can never be a real closing until the country has established its own independence. Since unity is force and strength, and discord is weakness, it would be imprudent to go to war against powerful and brave enemies with discord among them [the Shogun and his allies and the other *daimyo*]. I think the only way to bring about national union is by a solid union between the Shogun and Emperor, acting together as one man.
>
> After the Emperor is firmly established on his throne, the dominant soul of Japan will awaken. Then we will be united in power and independence. Once our independence is restored, we must reform our military, our navy, as well as all branches of industry. The whole nation must devote life and soul to the benefit of our State, and we must learn and study the interior arrangements and the development of arts and sciences in foreign lands.[24]

More than four years later, unity of the Imperial family and the Shogun had still not been established, and it remained unsettled who was the real ruler of the empire: the Shogun or the Emperor. When Tokugawa Iemochi, the Shogun who had seized the reins of power in 1859, died childless, his rival Hitotsubashi demanded his position. But the most powerful *daimyo* withheld their allegiance. Even when a new Shogun, Yoshinobu, attempted to assume the powers wielded by his ancestors, he could not overcome the armed resistance of the *daimyo* to the emperor. The revolution thus became a civil war.[25]

By the fall of 1867 the civil war reached a turning point. The new Shogun, lacking sufficient supporting forces, abdicated his office and withdrew, practically ending the civil war. Shortly afterwards, the 38-year-old Komei emperor died, leaving a young boy, Mutsuhito, heir to the throne with the backing of the clans led by Satsuma and Choshu, Tosa, Echizen, and others. Once the Shogun's unqualified submission was accepted by the emperor, a general amnesty was proclaimed for those who had fought for the Shogun's cause, excepting only the still rebellious *daimyo*. And though the wealthy *daimyo* of the north still held out, further resistance soon became hopeless.[26]

An edict was then issued in the name of the young emperor, abolishing the office of Shogun, expelling all followers of the Tokugawa family from Edo, and ending the Shogunate's two and one-half century reign. But the deposed Shogun suddenly retracted his resignation and led a large force to Kyoto to reassert his authority — only to be routed by imperial troops after a three-day battle, forcing him to take refuge in his castle, and announcing he would never again take arms against the emperor.[27] All vestiges of the great rebellion had ceased, the emperor's party was triumphant, and a centrally controlled empire uniting emperor and *daimyo* had at last become a reality.

The Meiji Restoration and Beyond

Such central control was a critical factor in the Meiji Restoration (1868–89), the alliance of feudal classes with merchant and banking interests to establish the Imperial state as a national unifying force, advancing feudalism to modern production in a few years, with an eye on learning from and emulating the West.

The Western powers, keeping up their pressures on Japan, offered material rewards to soften the blows of their military diplomacy. The Dutch gave the Japanese steam-driven warships in 1854, the British soon matched this gift, and the U.S. in 1868 traded a large warship for Japanese goods — just in time to help swing Japan's political forces in favor of a pro-Western faction. Thereafter the first Japanese naval academies were established and staffed by Dutch, French, British, Italian and American military experts, who taught the Japanese how to organize and run a navy.[28]

Aid from other European nations also came in the forms of mines, arms factories, and cotton-spinning mills — complete with foreign experts, technicians, and skilled workmen to assist in the construction and operation of Western-modeled facilities. Japanese shipyards were also set up by technical engineers from Holland and France.[29] And further steps to *the new order of things* under the young emperor was guided by Choshu's prescient memorial and the other great *daimyo,* who understood the need to liquidate the old forms of production and government in order to institute the new.

The center of government was also made more accessible, with the young emperor beginning the era of innovations by departing from Kyoto, for many centuries the Imperial city, to Edo, thereafter called Tokyo, his new capital. The *daimyo* voluntarily surrendered part of their most cherished feudal rights in the fall of 1869. Four of the greatest among them addressed a memorial to the throne, offering to release their clansmen and to restore their fiefs to the imperial crown.[30]

Two years later, in September 1871, the *daimyo* met in Tokyo to arrange for their retirement to private life under an imperial order that dissolved all the *daimiates,* providing that each *ex-daimyo* as well as the lesser chieftains should receive one-tenth of the income which they had drawn from their fiefs and that they should be appointed prefects, though not for life. Feudalism was thereby formally abolished, but the government paid the *daimyo* for their land rights with government bonds and assumed their debts to merchants and money-lenders. The feudal lord now ceased to be a *territorial* magnate drawing his income from the peasant and became instead, by virtue of the commutation of his pension, a *financial* magnate who could, and did, invest his freshly capitalized wealth in banks, stocks, industries, or landed estates—thereby joining the still small financial oligarchy.

As some money returned to landed estates, there was a renewed basis for exploitation of three-quarters of the population still bound to the soil, producing both life-giving food and the nation's social surplus.[31] Ownership continued in the form of a class of *jinushi* (landlords), with the share of output going to the peasantry falling from 39 percent before the Meiji agrarian reform to 32 percent thereafter.[32]

The Imperial government not only assumed and paid interest on the once-worthless *daimyo* debts, but undertook to enroll the *samurai* in the Imperial army or to recompense them with regular money stipends. The government's assumption of this burden forced it to contract a loan in interest-bearing bonds of $165,000,000. Many of the *samurai* who were paid off squandered their money and fell into poverty.[33] And thereafter they were no longer a force in Japan's hierarchical order, as the enlightened *ex-daimyo* extended the social and cultural revolution to meet the Western challenge.

Pariah peoples were also given status, new social rights were fostered, education promoted, and the old classes were reformed and integrated into the emerging social order. Fearing the uprising of the peasant class, the warlords sought to divide the common people by turning the farmers and townspeople against the *Eta/Hinin* (today called *Burakumin*), who from time immemorial had held traditional occupations in slaughtering cattle and tanning hides. Introducing a new status system in the fall of 1871, the authorities formally removed the ancient disqualifications on the rights of the *Eta.* But rather than taking steps to eliminate prejudice against them, the government further isolated the *Eta* by forcing them to help the military execute criminals and suppress revolts by the farmers. The farmers and townspeople thus learned to hate the *Eta,* keeping them a class apart, not because of their traditional occupations but due to their role as henchmen for the warlords.[34] By the spring of 1872 religious persecution was officially discountenanced and the education system was reorganized. The empire was divided into eight educational districts, each with a university, to be graced with two hundred secondary schools of foreign languages. Law schools were also established, extending the system of jurisprudence so that a thorough revision of imperial statutes and legal processes was begun. Foreigners were still permitted to bring their cases in their respective consular courts, preserving extraterritoriality. But within Japan torture was abolished, the list of capital crimes was reduced, and criminal defendants could now have counsel.

Japan began to interact with the Western world. Students, carefully chosen on the basis of their knowledge and capabilities, were sent abroad to study Western ways. With equal scrutiny, the government selected the nations where the students would be sent to study those Western arts and sciences. Soon Japanese students were traveling to England to study the Imperial Navy; to Germany to examine the structures of the Army and the schools of medicine; to France to learn the laws of bourgeois justice; and to the United States to absorb the practical wisdom of business methods. With their acquired knowledge of Western capitalism and education, the Japanese quickly established their own systems of general and technical education, and a modern banking apparatus.[35]

Banking that had roots in the precapitalist merchant era had meanwhile been bolstered by the government issue of bonds backing up the pension funds issued to the *samurai* and *daimyo* in 1876. It was again strengthened with each new government loan by the Treasury, for the latter exchanged bonds for its own notes, which were the legal and financial basis to establish national banks. The Treasury also came to rely on leading banks like Mitsui, Yasuda, Shimada, Konoike, and Ono for marketing their bonds. In the five years from 1875 to 1880 the nation's aggregate bank capital enlarged more than sixteen times from 2,450,000 yen to 43,040,000 yen.

With this growing financial base and aspirations to move into the commercial world, Japan set up legations and consulates in other nations. News of happenings around the globe also began to filter into once provincial Japan. Daily and weekly newspapers and other periodicals made Japanese journalism the flood gate for information set in the latest metal type and run off on modern printing presses. Railroads soon united all parts of the country.[36] By 1885, some 250 miles of track were being operated by native engineers, with 300 more miles in process of construction. Electric lights and telephones were now used in the large cities, and four submarine cables established telegraphic communications with the rest of the world. A modern postal department had also been set up and handled nearly one million letters and packages a year. And the Japan Mail Shipping Company ran a large fleet of passenger steamers and merchantmen.[37]

The Japanese Implosion

The new "revolution" that fostered knowledge, production, communications, and trade was a hierarchical and bureaucratic undertaking that created a new alliance of forces. It promoted commerce benefiting the merchants; finance enhancing banking wealth; semifeudal institutions empowering the great landowners and nobles at the expense of a peasantry burdened by high rents, taxes, and usury; and industrial development, directed by these same merchants, bankers, and landowners, yet without creating a distinct class of new owners.

Some peasants, impoverished *samurai* now without masters, and various town and city dwellers in jeopardy tried to protect their place in the old order, yet were unable to prevent the pace of change.[38] The reason was evident, as the imperial state now stood between the old and newly emergent social classes and groupings, undermining some to promote the advancing commercial order, and pacifying others by making still others pay.

Such reorganization of the state led to several thousand officeholders being discharged after the abolition of two administrative departments. Taxes levied on land and farmers pushed the peasantry into poverty. Former *samurai* who had spent their state stipends and were idle, hoped to return to the securities of the past, but faced an unyielding central government.[39]

Impoverished groups tried to organize. The last great challenge by discontented peasants and *samurai* broke out early in 1877. Led by Saigo Takamori, formerly a marshall of the empire, and manned largely by discharged officeholders, the bloody campaign lasted several months, and caused several thousand deaths. But the government eventually routed the rebels. Saigo requested a friend to take his head and 38,000 prisoners were arrested for treason. The emperor, showing leniency, pardoned most of the rebels, confined one thousand leading men in government fortresses, and shot twenty leaders. To redress the grievances of the peasants and farmers, the government then quickly reduced the national land tax from 3 to 2½ percent and cut the local tax to one-fifth, covering losses to the treasury by reducing the salaries of nearly all government officials.[40] Thereby the central government also reduced local political power.

Thereafter, the imperial state tightened its control and set its sights on building infrastructure to widen the market and industrialize the nation. The stipends to the *samurai* were legally ended, and freed government revenues were used to subsidize or guaranty investors. The state not only fostered the integration of all forms of land, industrial, and financial ownership, but the expansion of commerce brought new revenue flows that helped to capitalize and expand their industries, extending the tax base. With steady tax resources on hand, the state then made investments in means of transport, communications, and finance, as well as in experimental enterprises that, when built up, the private owners were allowed to purchase from the state at extremely low prices. Factories were sold for 15 to 30 percent of the amounts they had cost the government; and buyers were permitted to pay the purchase price over a period as long as two or three decades.[41]

These new industries now required a work force, a market in which to sell output, a military body to maintain law and order, and an imperial army to protect the nation against foreign inroads while acquiring essential production materials abroad.

Countdown to a Constitution

The threat to Japan's internal markets meanwhile grew. Western-imposed unequal treaties had led to the flooding of Japanese markets with high-quality, low-price manufactures. Competitive Japanese industries were not only essential, but an integrated industrial structure would need a core of ironmaking, shipbuilding, and armament factories—all to be fostered by the newly emergent state.

To reach this goal, Japan had meanwhile imploded. The acquisitive drive of the landlords for high rents, of the bankers for usurious loans, and of the state for exorbitant land taxes to forward the new order again led to an impoverished peasantry, the dispossession of former landowning peasants, the return of some to semifeudal tenancy and, for others, pressure to seek their fortunes in the cities, where they emerged as the nation's initial work force. It was this labor force that made possible an initial 10 percent surge of goods produced in the nation from 1878–82, and that later elevated manufacturing to 21 percent of the nation's entire output between 1908 and 1912.[42]

This *new social order* was created through a realignment of political forces. The *daimyo* who supported the young emperor recognized the critical need to emulate not only the economic advances but the democratic political structures of the Western world. Thus the emperor, promising in Kyoto in 1868 to introduce provincial controls, made good on this promise a decade later on 27 July 1878, by an Imperial Edict convoking provincial assemblies to sit once a year in each Ken, to dispose of questions affecting local taxation and provincial government.[43] But the underlying goal was to centralize power on a national level. Hence, three years later, in October 1881, the emperor proclaimed that a Parliament would be established to meet in 1890, and toward that end the provincial Senate and annual assembly of Ken prefects were adjourned *sine die.*

Toward such consolidation, a new constitution was also offered, vesting the rights of sovereignty and executive power in the person of the emperor, who was declared inviolable. The emperor's ministers were to be accountable to him alone. Certain expenditures for the realm, specified in the constitution, were assigned to the Imperial government in perpetuity. A *Bill of Rights* modeled on the French *Rights of Man* and the first ten U.S. *Constitutional Amendments* confirmed trial by jury, freedom from search, and the rights of religious belief, of free speech and free press, and of public meetings within the limits of civic ordinances.

A parliament was created to meet once a year—to be opened, prorogued, closed, or dissolved by the emperor. It was to be a bicameral legislature, with lords sitting in the upper house, or Chamber of Peers, and taxpayers with limited terms occupying the lower House of Representatives. The upper house was composed of three classes: hereditary peers, nominated peers, and elected members, with the last two classes never to exceed the number of hereditary members. By contrast, the House of Representatives was composed of three hundred members, each a national taxpayer paying at least $15 annually, each to serve four years, thereby building discontinuity into the power of the lower house to contest the veto rights of the hereditary upper house.[44]

In June 1884 the emperor issued an order readjusting the system of nobility, creating new nobles to make up the upper house. In the newly created orders of princes, marquises, counts, viscounts, and barons were the names of three hundred men, including several *daimyos* and former *samurai* who had distinguished themselves in the course of the Restoration.[45]

The next consolidating step in late 1885 was to sweep away the old "triple government" of ministers, privy council, and premiership, replacing them with a Western-style cabinet of ministers presided over by a minister-president. With Ito Hirobumi and Inouye Kowashi assuming charge, the old government board was drastically reorganized, and many thousand officeholders were immediately discharged.[46]

Finally, on 11 February 1889, the long-awaited constitution was at last proclaimed. The Emperor Mutsuhito took a solemn oath to maintain the government according to the constitution, confirmed Kuroda Kiyotaka as prime minister, and kept Ito as president of the privy council.[47]

A modern, centralized state had now emerged, seemingly under tight control. Yet, at the first great national election to the new Parliament and provincial assemblies in July 1890, a new balance of power was struck. Nearly 85 percent of the eligible voters used the franchise, repudiating almost all of the candidates who had in any way received government employment. Few of the old party leaders were chosen as standard-bearers of the new factions. From the very start the government found itself confronted by a powerful opponent on the floor of the new Parliament. And a new civil code of laws and procedures were immediately passed.[48]

The people's basic rights were being extended, framed by the emergent commercial order and the interests of diverse and divergent social classes. Japan had not only emulated Western economies, but had now grafted aspects of their hereditary and democratic institutions onto an imperial, hierarchical order. And this composite system of social privilege and parliamentary debate fed into the nation's advancing economy—and need to expand abroad.

Industrial Aspirations

Japan had not been invidiously subjugated by the Western powers, in large part because of the jealousies of each seeking an advantage by trade treaties and fears that any one in occupation of Japan could use it as a springboard to gain a stronger position in China. This had freed Japan to develop internally, though even in the 1880s capital finance for Japanese industry was still relatively small, machinery crude, and wages abysmally low, so that the workers with their low purchasing power could not enhance the *domestic market* for manufactures. But the working class did require food. And overseas markets grew as the inroads of foreign merchants made an impact, fueling domestic production and the search for raw materials abroad.[49]

Domestic production and control moved in tandem in the late 1880s. By the early 1890s the Japanese centralization of capital and control over factories, finance, and commerce had strengthened. The leading capitalist groups — called *zaibatsu,* or *monied cliques* — began to monopolize an ever-growing list of industries. One of the leading *zaibatsu,* the Mitsui, came to control some 90 percent of the output of Japan's iron, 50 percent of the petroleum and paper, 30 percent of the coal, 25 percent of the silk, 15 percent of the cement, 10 percent of the wool and alcohol, and 5 percent of the gold. By 1900 another *zaibatsu* group, Mitsubishi, controlled 40 percent of the nation's shipbuilding and maritime transport, 30 percent of the trade in wheat, 25 percent of the brewing of beer, and 15 percent of the output of sugar.[50]

The near-encompassing control in Japan was accompanied by an expansion of the *zaibatsu*'s manufacturing and export business. Thus, during the late 19th and early 20th centuries, the cotton textile industry remained the nation's most important manufacturing endeavor, and both production and exports surged. The number of spindles in the Japanese cotton industry increased from 13,000 in 1880 to 2,287,000 in 1913; in even fewer years, 1890–1913, the production of yarn increased sixteenfold, while in even less time (1900–13) the export of yarn increased 2.2 times and that of cloth 7.6 times. By 1897 the value of cotton yarn exports had surpassed imports, and by 1909 the value of cotton fabric exports also exceeded imports. Thus, in textiles at least, the Western mills were confronted with, and sometimes outdone by, Japanese competition.[51]

With production in basic industries rising, Japan's exports started to go beyond cotton goods. A Second Industrial Revolution was underway, comparable to England's switch from Manchester (a textile center) to Birmingham (an iron and steel complex), resulting in Japan's 1913 production of about one-quarter of a million tons of pig iron and a similar quantity of steel. Now able to produce its own industrial plant and machinery, the framework for Japanese commerce was broadened, with trade expanding about 7.5 percent each year over the three decades 1880–1913.[52]

But Japan was still at a competitive disadvantage. Lacking its own essential materials for production, suffering from a food supply inadequate to feed its quickly urbanized populations, but possessing the armaments to win both raw materials and food from other peoples, the Japanese state followed the West by embarking on expansion. For such overseas adventures, the ruling oligarchy drew on the traditional warrior class now become noblemen, as well as on the financial and industrial resources of landowners and entrepreneurs. They upgraded military skills with Prussian teachers. The newly formed state also secured needed armaments by promoting the arms industries, developing their potential, and, later, turning them over to the private hands of the emerging *zaibatsu,* so that state debts and tax revenues were effectively transformed into ownership capital of the chosen.

Imperial Way

Planning to take charge of the resources needed at home but found in Korea, the Kurile Islands, Manchuria, North China, and Formosa, Japan went to war with China in 1894, Russia in 1905, and again with China during World War I.[53]

The step abroad began in the fall of 1874. Japan charged that Formosa "savages" had outraged their shipping; the emperor warned the Chinese rulers in Peking; and Japan sent an expedition of 1,300 soldiers to occupy the eastern end of Formosa. The Japanese refused to withdraw until the emphatic protests of the Chinese government almost led to war, and finally withdrew only after China agreed to pay a $700,000 indemnity.[54]

Lines of demarcation with tsarist Russia were also drawn. An autumn 1875 convention signed at St. Petersburg awarded the Russians the Island of Sakhalin but Japan all of the Kurile Islands.[55]

In 1872 Japan had also demanded tribute from Korea. But Korea later refused further payments, and in the summer of 1882 a Korean mob attacked the Japanese and Chinese legations at Seoul, murdering several occupants and forcing the rest to flee. To exact reparations, both Japan and China dispatched expeditions, effecting a temporary accommodation — then keeping their troops in the disputed territory.[56]

Two years later, in December 1884, Koreans aided by Chinese soldiers again attacked the Japanese legation in Seoul, putting the occupants to flight. Japan's government again extracted reparations, but this time dispatched Count Ito to Peking to make permanent arrangements to secure rights in Korea.[57] Each imperial overlord meanwhile looked jealously at the other. Though China held a much stronger position in Korea than Japan, Japan tied China's military hands by a compact signed on 18 April 1885, whereby China acknowledged Japan's right to equal control and each placed restrictions on the other. This treaty provided that, first, both countries should recall their troops from Korea; second, no more officers would be sent by either country to drill Korean soldiers; and third, neither country should send forces to Korea in the future without previously informing the other party.[58]

But a decade later, in the summer of 1894, Japan broke the pact by dispatching an expedition after the outbreak of disturbances, attacking the king of Korea's palace at Seoul, and then refusing to withdraw its forces simultaneously with those of China. Battling for control of Korea and her seaways, Japan and China then went for one another's jugular, each asserting the independence of their charge. Japan's emperor immediately issued a formal, if hypocritical, declaration of war: "Korea is an independent country, which was first induced by Japan to open its doors to foreign intercourse, and to take its place among the nations of the world. Yet China has always described it as her tributary, and has both openly and secretly interfered with its internal affairs."[59]

Japan then won a naval contest by superior mobility, concerted action, and better gunnery. The Chinese fleet withdrew to Port Arthur and Japan sent troopships to the Chinese mainland for an attack on Port Arthur on 24 October 1894.[60]

Japan was now moving forward on two fronts, taking undisputed possession of Korea to reorganize the country and threatening the traditional Western strongholds in China. Rejecting British mediation and Chinese overtures for peace, the Japanese Parliament then unanimously passed a war budget of 150,000,000 yen. Japanese troops took the offensive, overran Kein-Lien-Tchong, won the battle of Hushan, and took over the Chinese strongholds at Kinchow and Talienwan. Avowing China's impotence to withstand the Japanese attack, China's Prince Kung invited the foreign powers to intervene on 3 November. Meanwhile, the Japanese proceeded to advance, taking Port Arthur and its naval base, docks, and workshops. Outflanked, China was forced to sue for peace.[61]

Yet Japan only intensified her advance, won a string of unprecedented victories, attacked the Pescadores Islands between Formosa and the mainland, and finally was ordered by the emperor to establish an unconditional armistice. On 15 April 1895, China ceded the Liao-Tung Peninsula, Formosa, and the Pescadores; agreed to pay an indemnity of 33,000,000 pounds sterling; and made other important concessions of suzerainty and freedom of island trade.[62]

The other great European concession-holders heatedly protested. Having had long since divided up the "Chinese melon," as they arrogantly called it, they moved quickly to limit Japan's winnings. Yet Japan was no longer a small player in the military drama, ranking among the five colossi battling for a share of the world's armories and treasuries. Krupp, Schneider, Armstrong, and Vickers in Europe had now been joined by Japan's Mitsui and Czechoslovakia's Skoda Works.[63] Under pressure from Germany, Russia, and France, a new power balance was then established: Japan renounced definite annexation of the Liao-Tung Peninsula and Port

Arthur — momentarily being content to occupy Weihai and to subdue and annex Formosa (after the Chinese viceroy refused to withdraw as commanded and proclaimed the island an independent republic).

The other Great Powers then seized the opportunity to extract more concessions from a weakened China. Britain immediately moved to secure its concession in Whasang; and France through a treaty with China took special advantages in the southern Chinese provinces.[64] On the basis of alleged anti–Christian atrocities in China in the summer of 1896, Russia moved in and concluded a treaty with China, forcing the Chinese government to concede a right-of-way across Manchuria to connect Port Arthur with the Trans-Siberian Railway.[65]

Then five years later, in June 1900, the Chinese Boxers rebelled, attacked Tien-tsin, and were met by a determined invasion by the troops of the Great Powers. A handful of 400 Russians, 130 American marines, and 1,000 British marines were soon relieved by 12,000 Japanese, 3,000 Russians, 3,000 British, 2,800 Americans, and 1,000 French. Japanese forces, numerically superior and better handled, took Peking, looted the city, and put the empress dowager and the emperor in flight, while Viceroy Li Hung-chang at Canton was appointed peace commissioner to grant concessions to the invaders.[66]

Japan was becoming an industrial and imperial player in her own right, demanding a status equal to that of the other imperial nations and threatening to remove the privileges given to other countries in Japan unless they granted her demand. In 1894 Japan forced the British to surrender their rights of *extraterritoriality,* thus undermining the right exercised by most Western governments throughout Asia to have their nationals tried in courts of their own natives, rather than by Asian laws. Other Western Powers were soon compelled to follow the British concession, so that by 1899 Japan had become the first Asian country to free itself from this foreign imposition.

To meet the high costs of becoming an industrial and military power in East Asia, however, Japan was forced to cast aside earlier fears about foreign debts and turn to overseas capital markets, thereby enlarging her foreign indebtedness from 40,000,000 yen (4,000,000 pounds) in 1897 to nearly 200,000,000 yen (20,000,000 pounds) in 1913. The loans were mobilized to build China's South Manchurian Railroad, for the construction of Japan's own railways and utilities, and for the manufacture of domestic iron and steel. Though Japan's heavy industries were manufacturing iron and steel, however, the import of Western tools and machinery combined with foreign finance to keep Japan a debtor nation.

And the debt could not be paid from tax revenues on an already over-burdened population. Japan's wealth was only one-fourteenth that of the United States, but her foreign debt was fourteen times as heavy; and the average income per person was only equal to about thirty dollars a year, or about one-fifth the average income in the United States at that time. Yet, domestic taxes had more than doubled after the 1905 war with Russia, and equaled $165 million in 1913 — an average of about 30 percent of the total income of business and property holders. The peasantry was also overburdened. And Japan's waterpower and a few mines, her only large domestic resources, were still underdeveloped and could not provide the means to pay off her foreign debt. It looked as if Japan might fall under control of her foreign creditors. But then came war.[67]

Seeking a wider commerce and empire while Europe was embroiled in World War I required little effort. Orders for textiles began pouring into Japan from all the Allied Powers, with price no barrier to what they would buy. Neutral markets the world over, and especially in Asia, were also turning to the Japanese for those goods that the English textile mills and the Western industrial nations could no longer supply. Suddenly Japanese exports jumped by 40 percent in bulk and 300 percent in value, with the figures reflecting profiteering in the context of a tight world supply.

To meet new demands, Japan expanded both the range and volume of production, enlarging the number of factory workers by 70 percent. To ship its output, the merchant marine was doubled in size, resulting in a tenfold increase in its earnings.

War soon made Japan a creditor by virtue of her trade. Her international accounts gained a credit of more than three billion yen between 1914 and 1919, empowering her to use two-thirds of the surplus to pay off past debts and oblige other nations for the balance.[68]

Meanwhile, with England as her ally, Japan declared war on Germany. Distance kept her from becoming embroiled in the European carnage. In 1915 she presented China with the infamous *Twenty-One Demands,* which would have transformed China into a virtual Japanese colony — to which the other Great Powers naturally objected. Yet Japan proceeded to pick up the German colonies, Tsingtao, the German interests adjoining China, and the German islands in the North Pacific — the Marianas, the Carolines, and the Marshalls — all of which were later given her in the form of a mandate by the peace treaty at Versailles.[69]

Japan had gained much, but spent little during the war. She had secured additional colonies, wealth, and a place in global trade. But Japan had mobilized only 800,000 men and suffered only 1,210 killed, wounded, and missing — less than any other contestant. The war had cost Japan only $1 billion — a fraction of the $122 billion spent by other Allied nations.[70] Yet she was now transformed into one of the Big Five military and industrial powers in the world, taking a seat at the 1919 peace conference. In contrast to the eve of World War I when Japan had considered raising foreign loans to pay interest on her heavy international debt, Japan was now a creditor nation and the world owed her more than a billion yen.[71]

Chapter 3
Japan's New Empire

*The hallowed spirits of our imperial ancestors
... give us confidence.* —Emperor Hirohito
on the attack on Pearl Harbor

*Of course we shall take Burma back. It's part
of the British Empire.* —General Harold
R.L.G. Alexander, May 1942[1]

After World War I Japan began to plan to replace Great Britain as the leading "commercial overlord" in the Far East and China.

By 1915 she had already begun to make Manchuria a protectorate on the model of the French and British protectorates in the Indies.[2] As we have seen, her power was not unbridled. She could not yet seize and control China's seaports and other industrial and commercial centers. But by the early 1930s it was obvious that China was Japan's most valuable potential asset and market. China had as many as 450 million possible customers for British wares; and England had invested more than a billion dollars in Chinese factories, mines, railroads, and other establishments. Could these not become Japanese customers and Japanese investments?

As Japan flexed its military muscle, Britain worried that if it "lost face" to Japan in China, India and the other Far East colonies it held might also be prompted to resist its domination.[3]

Backup for Arms and Empire

In 1919 Japan appeared almost unstoppable in East Asia. With the new confidence won from the successes of World War I, with foreign markets momentarily growing and profits surging, there seemed no limit to its great enterprises. The *zaibatsu* groups had entered one field after another, until the Big Four—Mitsubishi, Mitsui, Sumitomo, and Yasuda—held controlling interests in Japan's primary sectors. By the 1930s these *zaibatsu* groups held control of 50 percent of the nation's output of coal, 69 percent of the railways, 60 percent of the shipping, 50 percent of the machine tool

30

industry, 85 percent of all financial trust operations, and 50 percent of all banks in the nation.[4]

As Japan's industries grew and recruited more former peasants as factory workers, who thereafter no longer produced their own food, the population competed for an insufficient supply of rice, soybeans, and other staples. And as the Japanese population continued to grow, food had to be imported at a heavy cost in foreign exchange. With industry expanding, moreover, the raw materials that Japan lacked also had to be imported for manufacturing; and, with the low wages and traditional frugality that bred a limited domestic market, a substantial portion of Japan's finished goods needed to be marketed abroad. Industrialization thus necessitated Japanese access to raw materials on the Asian mainland, in Manchuria and the Yangtze, in India, and the East Indies. And Japan's market requirements included the raw silk trade in the United States, and the textile and hardware commerce throughout Africa and the East, especially in China and India.

But Japan's entrance into the latter two nations could only lead to conflicts. For in these two most heavily populated nations economic nationalism was growing. And the types of goods manufactured by the Japanese were sure to be excluded by protective measures — for these goods could be made, and not always less efficiently, by the nations in question. "Thus," one reporter predicted, "Japan will find herself in a position similar to that of Great Britain, obliged to rely upon the export of services and high grade goods and other methods of avoiding tariff barriers, or to control markets such as Manchuria by political force."[5]

In the 1920s, however, Japanese businessmen still believed that economic expansion by building up a great export trade and acquiring economic concessions abroad through diplomacy would cost less and gain more profit than military colonial expansion involving high taxes. This seemed particularly true in China, the chief field for Japanese expansion.[6]

Exports, and later arms, thus loomed large in Japan's industrial beehive. The output of manufactured goods increased fivefold between 1914 and 1926; and, with a military boot in Manchuria, Japan's factory production rose by almost half from 1934 to 1940. Technical efficiency also improved: by 1937 Japanese factories were able to produce almost all the machinery and machine tools necessary for any modern industrial system. Moreover, as Japanese owners focused on China and Manchuria — both as a market for their goods and as a source for raw materials — the volume of exports actually rose, going up 20 percent in the crisis years from 1929 to 1936.[7]

Besides exporting goods to and importing raw materials and foodstuffs from China, Japan also exported capital equipment, building hundreds of factories and hiring inexpensive Chinese workers — rather than employing comparatively high-cost labor at home. Japan's holdings rose steadily, to the point where it held almost as large a share of foreign investment capital in China and Manchuria (35.1 percent) as did the British (36.7 percent).[8] Yet, by the early 1930s, Japan's ruling circles already feared that a united and industrialized China in the following decade would produce goods in competition with those of Japan, leading to a loss of markets and a decline in access to inexpensive Chinese labor.

China also promised Japan a way out of its global dilemma. Of all Japan's imports, raw materials and food comprised more than 67 percent in 1929 and 60 percent in 1937; but only a little more than 40 percent (43 percent in 1928 and 41 percent in 1938) of the total came from Asia. Still, Japan was more dependent on Asia than on the U.S. or any other area.[9] So it was logical that if Japan were to expand her imports of key resources, Manchuria and Mongolia would be obvious sources.[10]

Conquering Hawks and Free-Trade Doves

One important wing of the big business community, the Mitsui *zaibatsu,* favored outright military expansion in Manchuria and Mongolia. The Mitsui hawks maintained the largest Japanese monopoly over petroleum, iron, and coal — resources found abundantly in these sections of China. So the Mitsui used its political arm, the Seiyukai party, to lay out its program for military imperialism. The president of the Seiyukai, General Tanaka Giichi, summarized these policies in a memorial given to the emperor in 1927.[11] This memorial distinguishes the Seiyukai program from that of the Minseito party, which was controlled by the Mitsubishi *zaibatsu* and promoted the policy of free, peaceful trade. The memorial argued that the Western powers had won the upper hand in controlling Japan's armaments through the Nine-Power Treaty of 1922, thereby making it impossible for Japan to conquer China and absorb China's resources or wealth. The Minseito party had fallen into this English and United States trap by continuing to advocate *free trade,* when it was clear that Japan could not enter China on this basis. "And yet the Minseito party made the Nine-Power Treaty the important thing and emphasized our TRADE rather than our RIGHTS in China," Tanaka complained. "This is a mistaken policy — a policy of national suicide."

For Tanaka the differences in foreign policy between Minseito and Seiyukai — Japan's two major parties in the Diet — had to be considered in the light of Japan's place in the world. England, he said, could afford to talk about *trade relations* between nations because she held India and Australia to supply herself with foodstuffs and other materials. America could also speak deftly of *free trade* because South America and Canada supplied U.S. needs. What strength these powers did not use in their other spheres of influence they could devote to developing trade with China, to further enrich themselves. Japan was not so lucky, Tanaka argued. For Japan's population was growing, and her food and raw material supply was too small to accommodate the nation's needs. Through trade alone Japan could never defeat England and America in China to get what she had to have to prosper.

And what if the people of China began to produce more goods and then displaced Japanese wares sold in China? "When we remember that the Chinese are our sole customers, we must beware lest one day China becomes unified and her industries become prosperous." In the outlook of this learned military politician, Japan was being hemmed in by the other powers: "Americans and Europeans will compete with us; our trade in China will be wrecked."

His solution was equally clear: the Minseito proposal for trade under the Nine-Power Treaty in Manchuria was a suicide policy for Japan. Japan had to march into China to secure its rights and privileges, to prevent the penetration of European powers, and to forestall China's own industrial development.[12]

With Manchuria and Mongolia under its belt, Tanaka thought, Japan would have the resources for industrialization, national defense, and empire. Extensive Japanese surveys had been made of China's resources since the close of the 19th century, allowing Tanaka to cite the precise figures and the savings in foreign exchange that would come with conquest. "The iron deposits in Manchuria and Mongolia," he said, "are estimated at 1,200,000,000 tons and coal deposits [at] 2,500,000,000 tons," stressing, "We shall save the expense of 120,000,000 yen which we pay for the importation of steel each year." Moreover: "Another important commmodity which we lack is petroleum. It is essential to the existence of a nation. Fortunately, there lie in the Fusham Coal Mines 5,200,000 tons of shale oil from every hundred catties of which six catties of crude may be extracted." Such petroleum and iron, Tanaka said, would be the basis of Japan's national wealth and national defense, drawing an analogy: "That Manchuria and Mongolia are the heart and liver of our empire is a truthful saying."[13] These would become the springboard of Japan's new empire, Tanaka advised:

> The way to gain actual rights in Manchuria and Mongolia is to use this region as a base, and under the pretense of trade and commerce, penetrate the rest of China. Armed by the rights already secured, we shall seize the resources all over the country. Having China's entire resources at our disposal, we shall proceed to conquer India, the Archipelago, Asia Minor, Central Asia, and even Europe. Final success belongs to the country having raw materials; the full growth of national strength belongs to the country having extensive territory. If we pursue a positive policy to enlarge our rights in Manchuria and China, all these prerequisites of a powerful nation will constitute no problem. Furthermore, our surplus population of 700,000 each year will be taken care of.[14]

Some declared this document was a Western hoax or a way to distort Japanese party politics.[15] But, once elected to the premiership, Tanaka was as good as his word, secretly scheming to move abroad by arms. Premature planning forced him to choose in July 1929 between resigning or allowing the Mitsubishi *zaibatsu*'s Minseito party to expose his plans to use the Kwantung Japanese Army to seize the Manchurian city of Mukden, and thereafter take over a large section of southern Manchuria. Since economic crisis had just begun to whipsaw the nation, it was obvious that if Tanaka's plan became publicly known, millions would have opposed the heavy cost in lives and taxes. So Tanaka reluctantly stepped down, only to be replaced by a new premier and cabinet representing the Mitsubishi, their Minseito party, and this party's policy of *peaceful economic expansion*.

What now was Mitsubishi's motive? It aimed to enlarge its income and Japan's empire by freely expanding trade and using the Minseito party to open markets. The goods Mitsubishi made were less dependent on foreign raw materials and foodstuffs than those made by Mitsui. Mitsubishi produced transport equipment and owned extensive means of transportation, while also making or growing wheat, alcohol, beer, sugar, glassware, artificial silk, and a wide variety of other items for consumption. Under the banner of *free trade,* these items could readily be sold both in Japan and abroad.

As the two leading *zaibatsu* controlling Nippon's two major parties, Mitsui and Mitsubishi handed control over cabinets and Diets back and forth, trying to sculpt their different imperial policies.[16] Then the balance tipped, as keen global competition for markets and rising quota and tariff barriers blocked a portion of Japan's foreign commerce. Japan's economy went into a tailspin in 1927, and the 1929 worldwide depression made things worse. In two years' time the value of Japan's exports dropped 30 percent, leaving industry and agriculture tottering.[17] Government aid was demanded to stimulate industry and industrial exports. But the gyrating market meant employers laid off some workers and drove their remaining workers harder, overall producing less, though labor demanded higher pay — just as businesses had to sell their goods at ever lower prices and, because of a lower exchange rate for the yen, received less for what they sold. The volume of exports was actually going up, but export earnings to pay for imports of raw materials were going down.[18]

As Western nations closed their markets to Japanese manufactures, raw silk, and other goods, moreover, the farmers faced despair. To avoid starvation, many Japanese peasants dependent on the foreign market now had only two alternatives: to sell a daughter to one of the brokers touring the land on behalf of the teahouses, cafés, and brothels, or to clamor for new markets controlled by the military.[19] Ultimately they chose the latter, then joined and supported the army, calling for Japan to "honor its military commitments" in Manchuria.

The businessmen also came to this stand by half-steps and fear. As the depression bit deeper into the countryside, the farmers' rice price fell, the raw silk market vanished, and hundreds of ultranationalist cliques sprang up in the villages, demanding "Down with the two-party government and capitalism!" Many, as former recruits in the army, had guns, and some were ready to use them. The Imperial Way Faction, an army clique, vented its frustrations by murdering capitalists and party leaders alike in the years 1934–36. Small wonder that businessmen feared that the rural half of the population as well as the entire army would revolt, and to prevent chaos, tied themselves to another army faction, the Control School. The Control School soon gained the upper hand, eliminated the anticapitalist Imperial Way Faction, and united army leaders, *zaibatsu,* and a scheming emperor.[20]

War by Any Other Name

General Tanaka's message haunted a nation whose self-esteem was in jeopardy. Japan had learned its lessons from the Western powers. It had witnessed British commercial, financial, and political domination over the Chinese government, and had concluded that the Chiang Kai-shek regime was a puppet of the U.S. and the other Western powers. It saw no reason why Japan should not replace this government with its own, and, after factional battles within the Japanese army, the Imperial Way coterie was placed under the Control School, leading to plans and preparations for the invasion of Manchuria.

As the army tightened its grip on the state machinery and the Control Faction became firmly entrenched, preparations were rushed forward to put the Japanese economy on a wartime footing. The armed services soon absorbed nearly 50 percent of the state budget, and increased orders for munitions stimulated the development of heavy industry.[21]

The *zaibatsu* also became hopelessly dependent upon the army's expansionist program, for sufficient imports of needed raw materials and foods could not be paid for through the normal channels of global commerce. Japanese businesses operated with the foreign provision of 96 percent of all coal consumed; 100 percent of all raw cotton, bauxite, wood, crude rubber, and phosphate rock; 85.6 percent of all iron ore; 90.8 percent of all crude oil; and 67.5 percent of all raw hides.[22] Worse yet, to feed Japan's growing urban population—and now the desperate peasants as well—Japan was absolutely required to import 67.2 percent of her salt, 96 percent of her sugar, and 64 percent of her soybeans. To continue production and feed its population, the capture of foreign resources seemed the only solution.

Overseas conquest also became increasingly necessary as Japan's population rose. By 1929 more than 60,000,000 Japanese, far more than could be supported by a simple agricultural economy, crowded the land. Some one million persons were born each year; to maintain this expanding population in the narrow islands foreign foods and markets were essential. Moreover, the people feared that an orgy of protectionism and other threats to their export trade would continue. By the early 1930s many Japanese believed that only the resumption of its old program of colonial expansion could win the supplies and markets to make Japan self-sufficient and invulnerable as a world power.[23]

The Japanese described their policy as being one that was equivalent to the U.S. Monroe Doctrine. Whereas the Monroe Doctrine had kept the European powers out of the Americas, they said, it actually made U.S. intervention easy and inevitable, and did not stop the U.S. from making its own territorial acquisitions. Now it was Japan's turn to enforce the same policy in Asia, to create a Co-Prosperity Sphere for East Asia.

To justify these actions, throughout the 1930s rulers focused the attention of the Japanese public on the Asiatic colonial concessions of the British and other European powers. Japanese leaders who coveted these rich territories began to speak of freeing colonial Asiatics from oppression by white races, coining both xenophobic and imperial slogans such as:

> "Asia for the Asiatics"
> "East Asia for the East Asiatics"
> "Pan-Asia"
> "The East Asia Co-Prosperity Sphere"
> "A New Order in East Asia"

Experience taught Far Eastern peoples the lie of this new line of propaganda, but many Japanese accepted it almost completely and came to believe they were the champions of downtrodden Asians.[24] Yet, like the U.S. model, there would be no "co-prosperity" for other peoples covered by the doctrine; but then again, Japan maintained that she had exclusive responsibility for these people and that she would protect her system of law and order, if need be, against domestic insurrection or foreign powers.

Not surprisingly, through diplomacy and firepower, the *zaibatsu* and the army moved in step toward establishment of an exclusive East Asian sphere of interest. Japan's first conquest took political form in the puppet state of Manchukuo and the building of a powerful infrastructure for trade and war.

Japan meanwhile established air and submarine bases on the Kurile and mandatory islands. Foreign Minister Hirota Koki boasted that Japan bore "the entire burden of responsibility" for the peace of East Asia. So on 17 April 1933, as Japanese armies moved in Manchuria, the infamous *Amau Statement* proclaimed the Japanese "Monroe Doctrine" for East Asia and warned foreign nations against giving any kind of military, technological, or financial aid to China:

> We oppose any attempt on the part of China to avail herself of the influence of any country in order to resist Japan: We also oppose any action taken by China, calculated to play one power against another. Any joint operations undertaken by foreign powers even in the name of technical or

financial assistance at this particular moment after the Manchurian and Shanghai Incidents are bound to acquire political significance.... Supplying China and detailing military instructors or military advisers to China or contracting a loan to provide funds for political uses, would obviously tend to alienate the friendly relations between Japan and China and other countries and to disturb the peace in East Asia. Japan will oppose such projects.[25]

Japanese expansion had found its first victim. The army and the *zaibatsu* marched over the body of the Chinese people and turned Manchuria into a puppet state they named Manchukuo in early 1932. They brought under their control a vast area rich in resources and labor—some 30,000,000 Chinese—while steadily maintaining the fiction that there had been no war, and calling the conquest of this extensive area "the Manchurian Incident."

Japan always insisted that her military advances in China and Manchuria were mere "incidents," and that she had liberated the downtrodden Asians suffering under Western-ruled Caucasian empires. But in Manchuria these incidents led to an expanding zone of occupation and the passage of laws to nationalize—and then turn into a *zaibatsu*-owned, state-protected monopoly—mineral deposits, railroads, and commercial and manufacturing enterprises.[26]

Manchuria was thus Japan's way out of its raw material and market dilemma. In 1931 the population was relatively small for such a massive area, leaving plenty of room for Japanese settlers to make their homes. Its resources were not developed, and Japan had the capital to mine Manchurian coal and iron and to create great plantations to supply Japan's textile mills with cotton. Although Manchurian markets were then filled with Western goods, once it was conquered Japan could conveniently provide exclusive outlets for its own wares, using its puppet government under Pu Yi to pass regulations requiring all shops to sell only Japanese products.

With more than one-third of Japan's exports going to Asia and one billion dollars of gold already invested in Manchuria, moreover, the *zaibatsu* planned to secure an exclusive commercial market and investment sphere to consist of Japan, Manchuria, North China, Formosa, and Korea. If they succeeded, they believed they would replace the Asian empires controlled by the United States, Britain, France, and Holland.

Japan's occupation army meanwhile multiplied from 64,900 to 164,100 men between 1931 and 1935.[27] And as the Manchurian effort escalated, the Japanese military budget increased from 31 to 47 percent of total government expenditures from 1931 to 1936. The industrial power backing this war effort was reflected in an 80 percent increase in production between 1929 and 1939. In this period, heavy industry multiplied its output over five times and light industry production went up 20 percent.[28]

While army staff directed these production advances, the *zaibatsu* profited. The general staff meanwhile produced their study, *How Our Industries*

Will Develop in War Time (Tokyo, 1933). "How can we achieve victory in the coming war? This question can be answered correctly only if we bear in mind that the war of the future will be a war between the industries manufacturing the technical means of warfare. Needless to say, it is absolutely impossible to create a war industry on the eve of war. Our present production facilities do not altogether satisfy the requirements of wartime."[29] Considering this warning, the great *zaibatsu* ownership groups, following the mandates of a state they came to control, increased industrial production almost another half between 1934–36 and 1940.[30] But this took place only through the apparatus of government and by a struggle of the army and *zaibatsu* for control of the joined economies of Japan and Manchuria.

A Government of Cartels and Martial Order

Within Japan, the *zaibatsu* faced the military's intention to use their business cartels to enforce state controls to ensure that military requirements would be met by the secular economy. But as the initial purpose of the *zaibatsu* was to use government authority to force independent companies into their conglomerates, they wanted to regulate the economy through their own direction of the Japan Economic Federation.

This plan was presented in May 1940 to the Yonai government and the Japan Economic Federation, and was adopted as a government policy-implementing body, much like today's Ministry of International Trade and Industry (the MITI). The Federation sought to enhance bureaucratic efficiency and uninterrupted production, calling for consolidation of private enterprises and their reorganization into powerful cartels in the major industrial branches. These cartels were to be granted a wider scope of authority for control purposes, so that private interests would be encouraged to display their creative initiative and to "enforce autonomous control on their own responsibility."[31]

The Federation quickly established Cartel Conferences in each major industry, then gained cabinet sanction for their own controls without state interference, and finally won incorporation of the major points of their program in a September 1941 Major Industries Association Ordinance. This provided for Control Associations in each industry (with the Cartel Conferences merging into these) for authority over labor, raw materials, capital investments, production, and distribution. Further consolidations of capital, retraining of small merchants and industrialists, and mobilization of company assets were sanctioned by the government's Renovation of Enterprises Ordinance.

By 1943 the first Japanese losses in the Pacific required still more controls to produce ships and planes. Premier Tojo demanded dictatorial powers to run the ministries, and the *zaibatsu* insisted on central control of the cartels, state agencies, and Cabinet Planning Board in order to direct the wartime economy. From the Cabinet Advisers Council to the Munitions Ministry, the *zaibatsu* made their presence the central force for directing war production, outflanking or dissolving the agencies controlled by the military. Through the cabinet and the Munitions Ministry, moreover, the representatives of the great monopolies came to control 574 munitions companies within Japan, 100 in Korea and Formosa, and the mobilization and merger of dissolved companies and their production resources.[32]

Extending the empire by military means also exacerbated Japan's internal conflicts. Tensions between the army and the *zaibatsu* had existed long before the invasion of Manchuria began in the early 1930s; and with the army on the frontiers of conquest, in many colonies the military held an advantage over the *zaibatsu*. Within Japan, the *zaibatsu* had meanwhile established Control Associations that they hoped to extend through so-called development corporations to gain control of economic activities for nine colonial regions comprising greater East Asia. Yet, after the 1932 invasion of Manchuria, the military leaders held supervisory powers in the newly taken areas, controlling the use of resources and labor, and taking charge of admitting administrators from the *zaibatsu* groups. In Manchuria the militarists planned a *Nationalist Socialist State,* set up special companies with monopolies in each industry, and put them under the charge of the Japanese military through the puppet Manchukuo government of Pu Yi.[33]

This forced the *zaibatsu* to compromise, providing equal investment capital contributions with the state, allowing each development company to set up subsidiaries in various branches of the colonial economies, and *temporarily* cooperating with the army through Control Associations in each area.

Yet the *zaibatsu* soon *integrated* their interests with those of the army, especially after the army became embroiled in a wider war with China and required the support of both old and new sectors of the *zaibatsu*. Under the new arrangement, the Okuro monopoly tightened its grip over its old iron ore and smelting works. As Japan advanced militarily and escalated its invasion in 1937, the Nissan Trust took an equal share with the Manchukuo government of the newly created Manchurian Industrial Development Company, which in turn absorbed the state-developed Manchurian concessions. Within the year, Nissan had won controlling interest of Manchuria's light metal, steel, and auto production, as well as gold and coal mining.

A free-for-all began in 1938, when unfettered state monopolies were granted in the energy-producing industry, the mining of strategic ores for military production, communications, and transportation. The Yasuda Bank was granted a share in the great South Manchurian Railway Company. Sumitomo moved into light metal production. Mitsui and Mitsubishi, former competitors in influencing government parties and policies, divided the spoils of Manchurian oil refining, synthetic fuel production, auto and plane manufacturing, and the Mukden Arsenal — a critical control center of the occupation, surrounded by the armament industry and related industries, including chemicals, cement, factory machinery, autos, planes, and locomotives.[34]

Starting with the formation of the government's Greater East Asia Ministry in November, 1942, however, the power of the army was reduced by absorption of the army's Manchurian Affairs Bureau and China Affairs Board. Under civilian control, the new ministry sidestepped military influence, asserting control over economic activities in Manchuria, Korea, Formosa, Sakhalin, and the newer colonies; and it also acted as the coordinating center for the *zaibatsu* to consolidate their domestic and colonial operations and holdings. Thereunder, viewing Manchuria as the springboard to a Greater East Asia empire, the *zaibatsu* enslaved its population, drained its resources, constructed infrastructures of roads and communications, and built war industries supplying as much as one-third of Japan's total industrial production!

Between the initial Japanese invasion in 1932 and the digestion of the Manchurian economy in 1943, Japanese private investments had escalated from 1.67 billion yen to 7.1 billion yen. A year later, in 1944, 2.9 billion yen was held fast by the Manchurian Industrial Development Company, which by then controlled the largest sections of heavy industry. During 1944–45, moreover, when the U.S. firebombed the Japanese homeland, Japan began transferring plants and production operations to Manchuria, so that by 1945 Japan's total industrial capital in Manchuria was estimated at five billion yen — far in excess of Britain's prewar total and the equivalent of total English private investment in all profit undertakings in its imperial jewel, India.[35]

The War Machine in China

Japanese generals saw China's industrial hinterland as essential to defeat Japan's primary enemy: the United States. Imperial Russia had been Japan's main foe in 1907, but the ruin of the czarist regime, the birth of the Soviet Union, the powerful increase of American influence in the Far East, and the Japanese exclusion movement within the United States put America at the top of the list of Japan's enemies, followed by the USSR and China.[36]

Japan's military machine rolled first against the weakest of her three principal enemies: China. This led to a hot encounter with her second most powerful enemy: the USSR.

As a rear threat to Soviet interference with her operations in China, Japan aligned herself with Germany in the Anti-Comintern Pact of November 1936. But in 1939 the Nazis rejected this scrap of paper and signed a nonaggression pact with the Soviet Union. The first view of this pact, as a betrayal and block to any alliance with Germany, gave way in Japan as Germany showed her strength in the *Blitzkrieg* victories in Europe.[37] By the summer of 1940 Japanese rulers predicted German mastery in Europe. One member of the general staff reflectively described the quest for imperial booty that lay behind the resulting Axis alliance:

> Underlying the conclusion of the Tripartite Pact lurked the fear of "missing the bus," on the part of the High Command, which was dazzled by the brilliant military successes of the German Army at the outset of World War II. An atmosphere of great worry prevailed lest Japan lose her chance if she maintained a cautious policy "with her hands in her pockets," while Germany was stripping the world of its choice treasures. Within the High Command, the feeling rapidly gained sway that Japan should derive great advantage from the Tripartite Pact by carving out her own sphere of influence in East Asia.[38]

The Japanese thereby hoped the *Axis Pact* would defeat Nippon's major enemy in the East: the United States. (Article two provides that "Germany and Italy recognize and respect the leadership of Japan in the establishment of a *new order* in Greater East Asia.") Military projections showed United States power hampered by the division of its forces between Atlantic and Pacific — Germany and Italy would occupy the U.S. in European theaters, while Japan drew American firepower in Southern Pacific Asia.

Meanwhile, the struggle over the body of China had flared up in April 1939 in Tientsin in North China, when Japan blockaded the British Concession as well as the international settlement at Amoy and Swatow. Lacking the means to offer a military response, Britain backed down, Prime Minister Chamberlain strategically recognizing in the House of Commons on 25 July that Japan had "special requirements" in dealing with China.[39] Britain thus chose appeasement — thereby granting Japan free rein to attack the Soviet Union.

As it took up its "special requirements," by the end of 1939, the Sino-Soviet War had already cost Japan almost two billion dollars and hundreds of thousands of dead and wounded. It had depleted the Treasury, shattered the morale of some, and laid the weakened military machine open to attack by Soviet forces.[40] Japan then bolstered its efforts: one million Japanese soldiers with 1,000 tanks and 1,500 aircraft were in occupation by 1942. This was a significant share of Japan's 1,500,000 regulars, backed up by 4,750,000 trained reserves. China also absorbed most of the Japanese air force, with 1,500 to 2,300 first-line planes out of a total fleet of 3,000 and 48,000 men trained for war missions.[41]

From the front on the two thousand–mile Soviet-Manchurian border, one Russian estimated the Japanese were equipped with one-half of all Japanese artillery, nearly two-thirds of Japan's tanks, and three-quarters of its cavalry.[42] From Japan's side, three-fourths of Manchuria's plain were viewed as surrounded by Soviet territory, requiring them to use slave labor and military personnel to accelerate resource extraction and production of armaments to fortify Japanese forces elsewhere, and prepare to withstand an impending Soviet attack.[43]

Japan was now divided on three fronts, facing Kuomintang and Communist forces in China, a powerful Russian tank force on the Sino-Soviet border, and the ever more powerful United States in the Pacific theater. Manchuria was neither completely won nor absolutely secure, requiring the infusion of more and more capital and human resources. Japan sent in more battalions. And Japan meanwhile struggled to achieve a successful termination of the China war in order to pour her full strength into southern aggression. As the United States increased aid to Japan's Asian enemies and as diplomatic maneuvers broke down, Japan and the U.S. took up weapons, both seeking to take or repossess Asian properties, resources, and control.

Japan also relied on Germany to hold off their mutual enemies, hoping this would buy sufficient time to bring China to her knees and build an invulnerable economic and military empire. She relied on the vast expanse of the Pacific and Indian oceans to protect this newfound sphere which contained enormous natural resources and hundreds of millions of people.[44] Japan thus planted its flag in the Pacific colonies and spheres of influence of the European powers bowled over by the German and Italian armies. Japan's map included thrusts against the main Far Eastern bases of the Americans, the British, and the Dutch: the Philippines, Guam, Hong Kong, British Malaya, Burma, Java, Sumatra, the Celebes, Borneo, the Bismarck Islands, Dutch Timor, and most other Pacific territories were marked for Japanese conquest. After this southern campaign was underway, the Japanese army with navy support planned to extirpate American and British influence in China and to hasten the surrender of the Chiang regime by exerting greater military and diplomatic pressure on Chungking. Plans for diverting Japanese forces were prepared to counter potential Soviet probes into Manchuria, with the army of the rising sun scheming about global conquests as well.[45]

Despite military victories, however, Japan's underlying industrial strength was no match for her major capitalist enemy: the United States. But Japan went down swinging, cornered into a smaller sphere of military influence, bombed into submission, and starved into desperation.[46]

U.S.–Enforced Unity of the Postwar State Economy

By the end of World War II Japan's *zaibatsu* controlled the home economy and held title to enterprises throughout East Asia.[47] From this sphere, the former imperial owners in Britain and the U.S., as well as the Chinese capitalists, hoped to repossess their holdings.

By the 1943 Cairo Agreements between the United States, Great Britain, and Chiang Kai-shek's Chinese government, plans had already been made to reapportion the areas under Japanese rule, including Korea, Manchuria, Formosa, the nearby Pescadores, and the Pacific islands. On 26 July 1945 the provisions of the Potsdam Declaration by these same powers (later also adhered to by the USSR) made additional plans to strip Japan of all her colonial property, leaving to Japan Honshu, Hokkaido, Kyushu, Shikoku, and a few minor islands.

The division of the Far East was in process.

From the beginning, the U.S. authorities held the power to determine the way in which most Japanese territories would be allocated. But not so in Manchuria or China. For in Manchuria the Soviet Union pushed forward, defeated, then interned the Kwangtung army; dismantled the remaining war plants and arsenal depots; signed the Sino-Soviet pact to take over ownership and management of the railway system and its enterprises; and established joint supervision of Port Arthur and Dairen. Later, under the Yalta Agreement, the Russians were also given control over the Kurile Islands and southern Sakhalin.

Besides the four main Japanese islands, the U.S. placed the Ryukyu Islands (including Okinawa) directly under its administration. In April 1947 the U.S. became the United Nations trustee for Japan's six hundred and more Pacific islands, which were scattered over three million square miles of ocean. Included were the Marshalls, the Carolines, and the Marianas or Ladrones. And, though these tiny islands had only 829 square miles of land area and a small population of 85,000, they ran 1,200 miles from the Equator and extended 2,500 miles from east to west. They also dominated an expanse of twenty-five million square miles of ocean—a strategic military, if not economic, asset.[48]

President Truman directed the occupation forces under General MacArthur to inventory Japan's external assets in these territories and to hold them for future disposition under Allied mandates. Within Japan's colonies, government enterprises and individual properties were frozen and slated for possible confiscation by the U.S. Food imports from Japan's former empire were cut off. And gold reserves worth $137 million were devoted to reparations. Japan thereby went bankrupt.

Japanese owners in lost parts of Japan's empire lost their businesses. Millions of men, women, and children were sent back to war-stricken, destitute Japan. Countless merchants and financiers who had once lived in luxury lost virtually all of their possessions, save the clothes on their backs and a small sum of money permitted to them by law. Japan was thus returned to where it had been when Commodore Perry opened the door for Western imperialism.

Yet, Japan's rulers had cleverly prepared for possible defeat to protect their assets, to sidestep a Soviet invasion, and to cooperate with the U.S., which it also hoped to prevent from occupying the homeland. Nippon preparations for capital preservation had begun when America's B-29's were still dropping tons of bombs on Japan's cities and it seemed likely that heavy industry would be destroyed. Through a scheme to nationalize their own industries, the *zaibatsu* foresaw state Treasury redemption of war-damaged properties, with the factories effectively put in legal receivership under the Suzuki cabinet and the *zaibatsu* running an "independent" management organization to guarantee profits.

With future indemnity seemingly secured, the next step was to negotiate a final surrender while the Soviet army was still fully engaged with Japan's military machine in Manchuria—thereby preventing a joint occupation of the Japanese islands and allowing the wartime oligarchy to pose as the legitimate governing authority during the period of a now expected American occupation. The U.S. also wanted the Soviets excluded. Seeing the opportunity for postwar hegemony in the Far East, American Secretary of State Byrnes recognized in his critical message of 11 August 1945 the "authority of the Emperor and the Japanese Government to rule the state subject to the Supreme Commander of the Allied Powers [SCAP]."[49]

The U.S. meanwhile moved to implement this policy without opposition. President Truman approved on 6 September 1945 the joint directive of the departments of State, War, and Navy to consult with and constitute appropriate "advisory bodies" in Japan for making policies satisfactory to the other Allied powers, yet insisting that differences of opinion would result in the governing supremacy of the policies of the United States.[50]

The American Occupation was thereby to be secured, even without the advice or consultation of others.

The president meanwhile directed the Occupation forces under General MacArthur to give U.S. companies preference in Japan's home economy, under a U.S. mandate entitled "Equality of Opportunity for Foreign Enterprise within Japan." The directive effectively offered the U.S. occupiers an advantage, providing that: "The Japanese authorities shall not give, or permit any Japanese business organization to give, exclusive or preferential opportunity or terms to the enterprise of any foreign country, or cede to such enterprise control of any important branch of economic activity."[51]

Through victory and occupation, then, America again established its traditional *Open Door Policy*. Britain, the imperial giant in the Far East before the war, lost place. The joint representation of the British, Chinese, and Soviet Union on the Allied Control Council and the Far Eastern Commission were advisory at best, with the U.S. retaining the controlling position to make and enforce policy in Japan and its former colonies.

President Truman's directive also effectively established a dual system for governing, not unlike the *Dual Mandate* used in the British colonies, "to use the existing form of government in Japan, not to support it." Though the Japanese state would exercise its "normal powers of government," the American supreme commander would be the power behind the throne, able to "exercise his authority through Japanese governmental machinery and agencies."⁵²

With U.S. authority thus secured, how could it be used to regenerate production, self-sufficiency, and commerce without the rehabilitation of the old *zaibatsu* government stripped of its military arm? There was no simple answer, for now new, critical problems required immediate attention. Japan's population had doubled and, without a viable economy to provide work, had to be fed, clothed, and housed by the labor of others. The war and the U.S. Occupation were also fostering an extensive black market that subverted the ancient Japanese traditions of frugality and equity. Yet, the dilemma the Occupation faced was how to eliminate the base for war, conquest, and imperialism and at the same time stimulate enough production and employment to lift Japan into self-sufficiency.

At first, the U.S. was determined to use its supreme authority to eliminate the monopolistic base for the fascist state apparatus that had fueled Japan's war imperialism. The Reparations Commission headed by Edwin E. Pauley thus outlined a program of economic repression for Japan that was so severe that any attempts by the people to raise their standards of living were doomed in advance. Following the Pauley Commission recommendations, the U.S. began to remove what was intended to amount to about three-fourths of Japan's key iron, steel, and machine tool industries and to reduce Japan's once-powerful merchant fleet to the bare 1,500,000 tons needed for Far Eastern trading. Japan's commercial voyages to other world ports were stopped, and her competitive export industry was destroyed. All industrial growth was suppressed; the Occupation goal was to remove as reparations all those factories and equipment above the low-level production scale prevailing in 1930–32, before Manchuria became a colony for Japanese enrichment.

The U.S. also cut the Japanese people's food ration, lowered industrial employment, and wrote and published a new constitution designed to impose its vision of a future democratic balance of power to prevail between the emperor, business organizations, armed forces, and people. The emperor was now merely the titular head of the nation, stripped of his metaphysical lineage and lacking political power. Japanese troops were demobilized and the nation's remaining military equipment and stores were destroyed in just two months' time. Japan's industries were meanwhile kept operating at scarcely one-third of their prewar levels, while millions went homeless and the entire population was reduced to near-starvation.

But as the cold war intensified and the political lines of demarcation tightened in both Asia and Europe, the Occupation authorities had second thoughts. General MacArthur, wanting to stop Japanese labor and the Left from espousing radical solutions, implemented a sharp about-face in U.S. policy. The Occupation authorities now planned a different future, as MacArthur indicated in 1947:

Since the surrender, trade and financial intercourse with the rest of the world is by our decree so prohibited as to constitute economic strangulation. Cut off from our own projected relief supplies in these circumstances, countless Japanese would face starvation—and starvation breeds mass unrest, disorder and violence. Worse still it renders a people an easy prey to any ideology, however evil, which bears with it life-sustaining food.[53]

The new emphasis was on rebuilding Japan as a strong capitalist nation and political ally—a bulwark, so to speak, of the U.S. sphere of influence in Asia, and a U.S. military base to be fortified in anticipation of a series of confrontations with the Soviet Union. As early as May 1947, U.S. Under Secretary of State Dean Acheson was already suggesting that Japan become the industrial base for the Asian market. Then, in spring 1948, various U.S. missions to Japan advocated establishment of a strong industrial Japan, recommending a halt in further transfers of industrial machinery under the Pauley formulation or as reparations. And so by early 1948 the Occupation began to promote Japanese trade and a fast recovery of Japanese production.

A new SCAP scenario followed: doing away with its program to dissolve the great *zaibatsu* conglomerates; complacently watching the reappearance of "purged" political and business leaders in public life; terminating reparations; and allowing Japan to resume trading with foreign nations.

The plans to dissolve the *zaibatsu* were simply reversed. On 6 November 1945 General MacArthur ordered the government to "democratize" industry. By then the least vulnerable personnel of the major *zaibatsu* companies had already been repositioned, putting their most moderate foot forward and keeping whatever secrets they could from the Occupation authorities. The Shidehara cabinet also took pains to explain that these internal company changes were voluntary and that the *zaibatsu* had actually solicited help from the cabinet to decree dissolution of their own holding companies! By early 1948, moreover, SCAP had openly aligned with Japan's conservative politicians and the executives of the leading *zaibatsu* groups in an effort to upgrade production and centralize controls.

The U.S. policy change had broad implications. In the early days of the Occupation the government had preserved the financial base of Japan's wealthiest by issuing ten-year interest-bearing bonds in exchange for the common stocks of the *Big Four Zaibatsu* companies. The government was to hold these old *zaibatsu* stocks for the "public," with the supreme commander acting as the final arbiter to decide under "inter–Allied policy" how liquidation would take place.[54]

It was not then known if foreign capital would be allowed to buy the shares. There had been a long prewar history of U.S. investments in Japan, including those directly placed in subsidiaries, shares of Japanese companies, and agencies of the Japanese government. These had amounted to nearly $500 million, and a few U.S./Japanese cartels had been created to divide production and markets and supply Japan with critical materials available in the U.S.[55] Yet few of the postwar government shares were ever purchased by United States companies.

Rather, SCAP had set a new framework by handpicking a government integrating *zaibatsu* representatives, backing up *zaibatsu* administrators managing the operation of most large factories. Then, in 1947–48, the Japanese government-held shares were sold to the public through leading brokers, allowing the leading *zaibatsu* banks and corporations to buy back their own securities and thereby recreate the economic foundation of their prewar power. The results were predictable. A March 1951 survey indicated that only 8.32 percent of all stockholders in the nation already owned 68.13 percent of all shares. Many of these stockholders were the old *zaibatsu* companies themselves, the only groups with extensive capital to buy and accumulate these securities. The centralization of control had again been put in motion, with corporations holding 15.5 percent of all stocks in 1949 and increasing their holdings over ten years to 48.27 percent in 1959.[56] Once they retrieved their securities, the *zaibatsu* were back on their feet, ready to reconstruct their business empires.

The New System of Control

A different formulation for control also emerged from the ashes of wartime state Shintoism, along with a new species of government/*zaibatsu* domination over the economy.

The official U.S. plan to use the existing Japanese government to enforce American policy had required that the militarists and colonial adventurists be separated from those kept in place as the nominal ruling authorities, including the emperor and so-called moderate leaders, political parties, and their business backers. This American plan to eliminate the military extremists was viewed as the path to create a peaceful, self-contained nation, put the economy on track, and maintain U.S. military hegemony in East Asia. In part this was a new mythology, designed by the U.S. and Britain to rebuild future Pacific commerce and secure vital economic and geopolitical interests. But part was factual: Japan could not have been reinstated as a component of the capitalist sphere unless the leading figures of the state and the *zaibatsu* were rehabilitated.[57]

Japan was defeated militarily, but was not lacking in capital. The war had brought great wealth to both the imperial household and the *zaibatsu,* partly as a natural extension of an expanding wartime economy. Japan's government reported to Allied headquarters that the emperor held some 1.6 billion yen in twenty-nine companies and banks, as well as the imperial household possessions consisting of gold and silver bullion, art objects, jewelry, the wealth holdings of fourteen princes and a vast landed domain.[58]

Allied headquarters also reported that the Mitsui, Sumitomo, Yasuda, and Mitsubishi *zaibatsu* together owned 320 industrial firms, were linked as partners in many others, and had financial and bank assets of 123 billion yen — equivalent to thirty billion dollars at prewar exchange rates.[59] Other estimates double these figures. And the largest *zaibatsu,* Mitsui, ran twenty-two affiliates, 173 companies, and hundreds of subsidiaries in both light and heavy industries. Some plants had been damaged by U.S. bombers, but most heavy industries were in operating condition, only lacking raw materials and a labor force. "In steel machine tools and other machinery made from steel, Japan's own figures show how she still has in working condition more than twice the facilities she had when she invaded Manchuria in 1931," U.S. Reparations Commissioner Edwin W. Pauley reported. Japan held the capacity to produce eleven million tons of steel a year, with large potential output in other strategic industries if raw materials were made available.[60]

There were also renewable sources of investment capital. Once conquered, Japan's former military expenditures ceased, future financial and material resources were freed for fixed investments in rebuilt industry, and the SCAP created agencies to sustain private investments, then switch the instruments of government control to traditional rulers to burden or benefit the Japanese people.

Yet, postwar Japan switched not from guns to butter, but, under central authority, from arms to private capital investment. Japanese military expenditures in 1940 had represented 63.8 percent of all central and local government outlays on goods and services. Throughout the war period average military expenditures were 50 percent of these government outlays. But fifteen years later they had fallen to 5.9 percent, the switch in government spending for investments and civilian purposes representing the balance.[61]

The government was central in this switch, with the U.S. directing matters until the official surrender was completed in 1952, then handing control authority to willing Japanese state officials. From January 1947 to 1949 the SCAP had controlled the basic industries, using its Reconstruction Finance Bank for essential funds to rehabilitate coal mining, electric power production, and shipping. For this, until April 1949 the U.S. aid "Counterpart Fund" (the "Foreign Trade Account") used invisible export and import subsidies to stimulate trade. After 1949, the proceeds from the Japanese sale of U.S.–provided materials were deposited in the "Counterpart Fund" to support *private ownership* by allocating the proceeds for financing private investments in fixed capital — amounting to 19.4 percent of all proceeds in 1949 and 17.3 percent in 1950. When the peace treaty took effect in 1952 the financing was taken over by the Japanese Development Bank, with funds for private investment in fixed capital as a percentage of total state funds amounting to 25.3 percent in 1952, 18.2 percent in 1956, and 13.5 percent in 1960.[62]

The core for Japanese production was thereby resurrected, with outlays for private fixed investments as a share of the nation's total output (GNP) moving up from 8.8 percent in the period 1946–51 to 16.1 percent in the years 1956–59.[63] Thereby, too, the nation was put back to work, with more people leaving the land and joining the rest of the population in the growing cities.

A momentary rise in the prewar agricultural population of sixteen million occurred as starving populations attempted to return to their country roots to find food immediately after the war. But by 1950 there had been only a small increase (to 16,100,000) of farmers tilling the soil. Then a gradual decline set in. By 1955 the number of farmers dropped to 14,890,000 and by 1960 to 13,220,000, as more disinherited females and even sons with too few hectors left the land for the cities, seeking a better life than could be had on Japan's tiny two and one-half–acre farms. And taking account of those tied to agriculture, forestry, and fisheries, the march to the urban areas was clear: about half of the Japanese population worked in rural areas at the start of World War II, 42 percent remained in the immediate postwar years, 38 percent were left when the U.S. Occupation ended, and less than 30 percent remained in the early 1960s.[64]

Faced with massive unemployment and desperation, immediately after the war SCAP had successfully empowered labor to organize for improved conditions and a larger share of the value of the nation's output. To put the labor system back into the frame of tranquility and create wages high enough to cover the cost of necessities, SCAP took steps to ensure that the new labor unions would secure *economic, not political, demands.* Labor's share rose from the prewar level of 30 percent of the nation's output to above 50 percent in 1950 and over 55 percent in 1960.[65]

There was still poverty, but as the 1960s got under way most adults had work. The large urban underclass was usually hidden away by the quiet of tight living quarters, low wages, subsistence or "modest" incomes, and low offerings of public welfare. One official 1963 report cites occupation figures of five persons per dwelling and 4.5 million families "badly housed."[66] In Tokyo, another report notes, 630,000 families were living in 100-square-foot, *tatami* homes.[67] In 1965 the Ministry of Health reported more than 20 percent of Japanese households were then surviving at a subsistence level — meaning at the extreme edge of poverty. Some 1.5 million families had less than modest incomes. And public assistance to 640,000 families covered only a fraction of the families in difficulties.[68] Even by 1968, Japan seemingly lacked the means to upgrade the condition of all its people, per capita income being less than one-third of that in the U.S.[69]

Nor was it only the impoverished who faced deprivation. Overall in the period 1955–1972, urban area land prices had gone up 2,557 percent, and the cost of housing began to exceed that in Western nations. With little social security, workers relied on individual savings withheld from wages for their own retirement. Japan's social security benefits were a bare 6 percent of national income compared with about 7 percent in the U.S., 15 percent in Italy, 19 percent in France, and some 20 percent in West Germany.[70] Wages lagged far behind living costs and adequate retirement savings. The traditions of work relations and the authoritarian state kept the labor force at a social disadvantage. These in part were some of the roots of Japan's emerging successes.

Part 2:
Roots of Japan's Successes

Japan's postwar economic successes rest on an expanding foundation of production. Production has itself been put in motion by a centralized system of capital ownership groups acting through, and in conjunction with, innumerable government agencies.

Japan's expansion has appeared limitless. Like America's once-dominant economy, Japan's economy has known no boundary or limitation since the 1950s boom fueled by the Korean War. Even pressures on the wage scale have been regulated. As new labor recruits from rural Japan were drawn toward urban factory work in the 1950s and 1960s, and only partly satisfied the employers' growing demand for labor, the employers kept average wages in line by their lifetime system of employment — an apparatus that had been put in place in the first half of the 20th century, and was thereafter continued by employers who offered job security and fixed wages on the basis of their workers' diligence and seniority.

Labor charges impacting each unit of output were also cut. In the expanding market of the late 1950s and the 1960s, lifetime employees were driven to produce more for the same, relatively *fixed wage payments,* in sharp contrast with the labor market of Western capitalist nations — economies that treated *labor as a variable cost,* setting wages by time spent on the job or by the level of output in a given workday. The Western rate of pay by time (per hour) or by output (per piece produced) was often set below the minimum standard of consumption essential to keep the worker in a condition to return to work and support the family. And by holding forth the incentive to better one's condition, a speed-up or a longer workday could be imposed on labor, as was also done in Japan using other incentives.

From the Japanese employers' point of view, though, there has been still another difference. For those employers have allocated *fixed wage outlays* over the number of products made, so that when more are produced, in effect each worker spends less labor time on each item — or each worker spends nearly the same time, but works overtime to produce more without added pay. With unit labor costs thus reduced, each item can be sold at a lower price without cutting into the employer's profit margin. If price is not lowered, moreover, the employer's total profit tends to rise based on the workers' speeded-up output or unremunerated labor time.[1]

This labor system has gone through two stages so far as overseas marketing is concerned.

First, during the 1960s and 1970s unit fixed labor costs became the basis for Japanese "dumping" of commodities in overseas markets — which itself was a response to Japan's changing methods of social control, production for export markets, and global position. As the major focus of Japan's control centers gradually shifted from emphasis on national self-sufficiency to production for exports, "dumping" was based on treating labor as a fixed production cost.

Second, another change of focus occurred in the 1980s, based on several intertwined processes. Western nations had begun to break down the barriers to Japan's closed, monopsonistic market, so Japan sought to shield itself by upgrading its technological base for production and reassembling its work force. By the late 1980s and early 1990s, Japanese workers had also secured greater wages; currency revaluation further raised the fixed cost of labor relative to labor costs elsewhere. Since these fixed costs had traditionally been impacted and absorbed in the high price of goods sold at home, making possible low-price dumping of identical goods produced for foreign markets, the price of domestic goods was gradually being pushed upwards. And this encouraged both Japanese and indigenous producers in newly industrialized Asian nations to export lower-price goods to conquer the Japanese domestic market.

By the late 1980s and the start of the 1990s, then, Japan's high-price domestic market was teetering off balance, putting its great enterprises and government under unrelenting pressure to promote *the export of production operations using technological methods previously developed for Japanese factories.* Obviously, these enterprises sought to escape high-priced labor at home, as well as the possibility that rising domestic living costs would put pressure on the work force, lead to demands for higher wages, and thereby further increase the price of labor. Their motive, in part, was to export production capital for operations in those Western nations that threatened to impose tariffs and had lower labor costs than in Japan. And Japanese capital was also vigorously sent to the newly industrialized and other developing countries, such as Mexico, Brazil, and especially East Asia, to take advantage of even lower labor costs, with the possibilities of exporting to the West, back to Japan, and to other nations.

Japan entered its third technological revolution at home — made possible by Nippon's well-trained population that was adept in the skills necessary to adopt Western technologies and adapt them to Japanese production methods. The West, especially the United States, accused Japan of appropriating its technological advantages. But by the late 1980s consortiums comprised of Japanese industries, the state, and the universities were already drawing on Western scientists, knowledge, and techniques developed for the most advanced microtechnologies, robotics, energy sources, and composite materials, with the goal of production applications.

Rather than decay at the core of Japanese industry, a new resurgence was supplementing and replacing its old technological base; and previous sectors of displaced industrial workers were being transferred directly by employers, or through the expanded market, to lesser-paying, lesser-skilled jobs. The reorganization of capital and the reassembly of the labor force was thus going forward at a pace unknown in Western societies.

Chapter 4

Life, Labor, and Competitive Posturing

In the competitive, global milieu of the 1970s and 1980s the context of daily life and labor changed in both the United States and Japan. At the very time the U.S. economy weakened, "decayed," and experienced a crisis in the accumulation of capital at home, Japan extended its industrial base, created full employment, kept wages and consumption at moderate levels, maintained high domestic prices, and profitably dumped manufactured goods in overseas markets.

Though Japanese output had grown at a rate exceeding 11 percent annually in the 1950s and the 1960s, in the early 1970s it slowed and by 1974 showed an absolute decline. Workers put on part time or receiving reduced wages then cut their demands for services, so that, in turn, hundreds of thousands of retail stores, tea shops, restaurants, bars, *pachinko* halls, and *geisha* houses had less business, trimmed their staff, cut wages, and made those remaining work harder.[2]

As foreign fuel and raw material prices continued to rise and pushed up costs and prices in 1973–74, Japan's market losses and recession were also relayed to Asia in terms of their reduced exports to Japan. Without markets in which to sell their raw materials, textiles, or oil, the nations of East Asia, Southeast Asia, and the Pacific Basin received secondhand from Japan the crisis in production, employment, and consumption.

And yet Japan overcame these momentary downturns by relying on the economic weaponry of its system of company towns, fixed wage payments, and worldwide dumping at prices below those charged at home.

The Company Town and Dumping

Perhaps the best way to understand Japan is to view it as one great company town, where management's methods of external control are united with labor's own motivations to exert one's best efforts and maximum endurance in producing high-quality output for sale abroad.

Both technological means and management styles have been fused with the Japanese work ethic and ideological apparatus in furthering such labor efficiency and production. Management and government set the framework by regulating production, controlling labor's living conditions on and off the job, setting market prices, and defining the rules and standards the population must respect in their work and personal lives to ensure the stability, security, and success of Japan in the global arena. The population's strong belief in the work ethic falls under this ideological framing, emphasizing strong commitment and exertion from the individual worker. And protest surrounding conditions on the job, like discord in the community, is largely restricted by government institutions and corporatized control over the opportunity to work and prosper.

Starting in 1971 intense competition for markets led Japanese companies to further emphasize low production costs, labor efficiency, productivity rises in excess of wage increments, and controlled levels of popular consumption and leisure time—in turn reflected in limitations on personal or family expenditures of money and energy. Toyota and other major firms carried this formula to an extreme by minimizing their workers' standard of living and personal freedom in order to maximize labor efforts, reduce production costs, and thereby dump manufactured goods at low prices in world markets.

The lion's share of manufacturing costs were meanwhile absorbed by propping up domestic prices, so that consumption within Japan was also regulated and, for working-class families, limited. And the process was extended, when labor was treated by the great, lifetime employers as a fixed cost.

Labor as a Fixed Cost

In Japan's production milieu the starting point remains the employers' control over labor. As noted earlier, in contrast to the Western practice of paying labor by the hour or by the task, large Japanese employers pay labor a given sum based on the position they hold in the production process, thereby turing labor into a *fixed cost* of production, not unlike the cost of machinery or the cost of the factory itself. The more production hours worked each day or the more rapid labor can be made to work to produce additional units of output in a given time—and the more adept and willing workers are to commit themselves—the lower will be the *unit-product cost* of labor as well as of machines and other fixed outlays.

The longer workday or sped-up labor effort is an *external standard* determined by upper-level management, who set all production goals. By demanding that the job be finished by working longer hours or by speeding up the production line, a hierarchical system of enforcement is put in place. The workers meanwhile follow an *inner compulsion* to meet management demands, a compulsion bred from rigid control over the scholastic training of the young and a Confucian tradition of respect for, and submission to, external authority. Labor unions actively participate in maintaining low production costs by aligning themselves with company needs in hopes of making "their" company successful and returning national glory to Japan. The resulting fusion of nationalistic, often Shintoist, sentiments with Confucian elements of unquestioning loyalty to the firm has become an important feature of Japanese production. Because management sets such production norms and targets, the employers are able to secure labor's best effort — maximum endurance.

Inner Compulsion and the Speedup

In accepting the speedup, the inner compulsion of the Japanese worker is thus a critical element. Japanese labor, in the past and today, has proved to be one of the most hard-working forces in the world. But while the effectiveness of management and the quality of industrial output continue to be maintained, there has been both a gradual reduction of working hours since the turn of this century and a growing dissatisfaction with the content of labor among the work force.

Working hours represent the time turned over to the employer at the cost of one's personal time. They are a gauge to levels of production and to levels of contentment among workers. In the 1920s during the intermediary stage of the development of Japanese capitalism, for example, the average Japanese worker put in more than 3,000 hours of labor per year, while today an average Japanese worker exercises his or her productive capacity in little more than 2,100 hours. Government and union regulations enacted to protect the work force, and changes in life-styles and concepts of work itself, have brought about a significant reduction in daily labor hours from 10.21 in 1920 to 8.3 in 1980.

Compared with the West, however, Japanese workers still rank high in labor hours on the job. [See Tables 4.1 A and B.] The Japanese worker devotes a greater number of total labor hours to his job per year than any other worker in the industrialized world. Japanese workers outwork English, American, French, and West German workers. [See Table 4.1 B.] This is also an expression of unpaid labor time in Japan, fixed salaries being paid periodically for a particular lifetime job place, not for the number of hours the workers put in to perform the management-defined job.

Table 4.1 A
Total Labor Hour Per Capita:
Japanese Labor

Year	Yearly Labor Hours	Daily Labor Hours	Monthly Labor Hours
1920	3,080	10.21	24.8
1930	2,094	9.08	26.5

Year	Yearly Labor Hours	Daily Labor Hours	Monthly Labor Hours
1940	2,948	9.04	27.1
1950	2,270	8.03	23.5
1960	2,435	8.23	24.2
1970	2,108	8.01	21.9
1980	2,116	8.03	21.9

Source: Sogo-Kenkyu Kaihatsu Kiko, *Seikatsu-suijun no Rekishi,* March 1985.

Table 4.1 B
Total Labor Hour Per Capita:
International Comparisons

Year	Japan	U.S.A.	England	W. Ger.	France
1981	2,146	1,888	1,950	1,656	1,717
1982	2,136	1,841	1,915	1,626	1,683
1983	2,152	1,898	1,938	1,613	1,657

Source: Economic Planning Agency (Keizai Kikaku-cho), *Kokumin Seikatsu-hen: Jinsei 80-nen jidai-ni Okeru Rodo-to Yoka,* 1988.

Paying fixed wages regardless of the speedup of production or the lengthening of hours might be one reason for the growing *dissatisfaction* with the content of labor among the work force. In any case, an ironic aspect of the Japanese labor force is the incongruity between the worker's strong sense of commitment and loyalty to the firm and the relatively high level of negative feelings regarding work satisfaction. The material relationships of employment call for one's strong commitment to work and a bond of loyalty to the firm; but such commitment and loyalty often override inner feelings and aspirations, lowering the level of work satisfaction. Because of pressures demanding the loyalty, commitment, and obligation of each worker, the individual's personal feelings and dissatisfactions are usually secondary considerations.[3]

Hence work satisfaction among the Japanese does not necessarily score high, especially when compared with that of Western workers. One survey shows that on a scale of 1 to 10, in which 1 indicates the least satisfied and 10 the most satisfied workers, the Japanese work force scored an average of 6.42, whereas U.S. workers scored 7.68 and workers in other countries ranked higher as well (France: 6.83; West Germany: 7.06; Italy: 7.33; England: 7.72; Canada: 8.04).[4]

The strong ideological obligation toward and simultaneous dislike of work also appears to reflect deeper feelings of frustration shared by many workers, stemming from hierarchical, structural constraints imposed upon them to regulate their work. A 1988 survey asked Japanese workers whether ten years hence, envisioning Japan's life-style (including the conditions involving work and human relations in the firm), they thought power and authority should be respected. More than three-quarters (76.4 percent) of Japanese workers did not want such respect to be offered, while only 6.4 percent of Japanese workers said they respected such hierarchical authority structures. By contrast, 84.8 percent of American workers acquiesced to such overriding controls.[5]

Though Japanese workers feel a powerful obligation to work, they also want to exercise their individual talent and ingenuity with fewer constraints placed on them by their employers. Over 88 percent of Japanese workers surveyed in 1987–88 emphasized the importance of work — a much higher level than prevails in the West. But 70.5 percent felt that their employers should emphasize developing individual talent — similar to the percentage of workers feeling this way in England and West Germany, though far below such workers' sentiments in Canada, France, the U.S., and Italy. In Japan, as in all these other nations, about three-fifths of all workers thought their employers should emphasize research and development. Clearly, Japanese workers are as much concerned about learning and challenge on the job as the workers in the Western nations.

Table 4.2
View Toward Future Life-styles:
International Comparisons

Questions:
  (1) Work is not so important.
  (2) Power and authority are respected.
  (3) Developing individual talent should be emphasized.
  (4) Research and development (R&D) should be emphasized.

Response	Japan	England	France	W. Ger.	Italy	U.S.A.	Canada
(1) Agree	4.1	25.7	56.8	29.7	23.2	22.1	25.2
Disagree	88.3	56.2	20.3	53.0	65.2	66.3	60.3
(2) Agree	6.4	73.4	55.6	43.7	63.7	84.8	76.1
Disagree	76.4	5.4	13.9	34.1	8.5	4.9	6.9
(3) Agree	70.5	70.1	84.3	76.5	91.3	85.8	82.7
Disagree	7.3	3.4	1.5	5.1	1.2	3.9	4.6
(4) Agree	63.2	60.9	60.7	55.5	61.5	65.8	58.6
Disagree	10.9	11.0	8.8	19.9	14.6	10.8	14.2

Source: Economic Planning Agency (Keizai Kikaku-cho), *Kokumin Seikatsu-Kyoku-Hen: Jinsei 80-nen jidai ni Okeru Rodo-to Yoka,* 1988, 144.

Maintaining the Work Force and the Basis of Dumping

From the employer point of view, labor costs have meanwhile been established at relatively fixed sums by setting the level of labor's cost of personal and family maintenance, as well as by regulating labor's personal life conditions. The great employers have controlled this equilibrium by setting wages equal to a certain level of consumption and awarding what they determine is sufficient time for rest and leisure. The workers' on-the-job exhaustion has thereby been reinstated in the personal, off-the-job sphere, so labor appeared undiminished for the next day of work.[6]

As for the actual condition of the Japanese work force, Japan's economy replicates England's 19th-century classical designs. The cost of the sustenance and reinstatement of labor is the foundation of the labor cost of factory production. But here the analogy ends. For in Japan's largest companies labor is a *fixed charge.* And the only costs that vary with production are those for raw materials, energy, and supplies keyed to the volume of production.

The division of production costs into fixed and variable charges holds critical importance for global marketing, too, as most Japanese companies use two alternating methods to allocate costs as an offset to sales revenue: (1) either the fixed costs of labor and technology are attributed to the units of output sold at a high price *within Japan,* so that goods sold *in the world market* absorb relatively no charges for labor or technical capital; or (2) all fixed and variable costs are attributed to the units of output sold at a high price *within Japan,* so that goods sold *in the world market* absorb absolutely no charges and can be profitably sold at any price above zero.

There are variations in these two cost allocation methods, but the essential factor is maintenance of monopoly prices within Japan, so that revenue from domestic sales covers some or all of these costs and those not covered are made up in the price of goods sold in overseas markets. The more costs covered by domestic sales revenue, the fewer costs need to be covered by overseas sales revenue, and the more Japanese prices can be cut in foreign markets.

In the 1960s, 1970s, and 1980s, there was also a significant difference between the Japanese and Western styles of dumping. Japan treated labor as a fixed cost to be offset against high-priced, domestic sales, while Western manufacturers viewed labor as a variable charge to be allocated equally to each unit produced. And this meant that every item Japan sold abroad carried almost no labor cost, while that sold by U.S. or other Western manufacturers did. Japan could thus lower its dumping prices below those of Western nations to capture market shares and, so long as the overseas price covered variable costs of energy and materials, still make a profit.[7]

The System of Captive Enterprises

Japanese dumping was, and today still is, facilitated by the unequal hierarchical relations between enterprises, allowing the largest firms to relay the burden of any fall in domestic and foreign market prices in the form of lower wages in, and profits awarded to, smaller companies that act as their subcontractors. In such vertical interfirm relations in the manufacturing sector, *Ko-gaisha* (children-firms) and *Mago-gaisha* (grandchildren-firms) are stretched to perform more labor and are drained of potential profit to meet challenges imposed by their *Oya-gaisha* (parental firms).

In the post–World War II period, such vertical corporate relationships have been characterized by their economic and symbiotic proximity in production and sometimes by management personnel moving from parental to subordinate firms (such interfirm mobility is called *Amakudari*). Based on the availability of markets, such communities of enterprises are bound together by a common fate and common interests; in extreme cases they are communities that also share a communal philosophy.

Lesser firms are captives of the great enterprises, and compete against one another for the favors of becoming the chosen firm for such a relationship. Two-thirds of medium and small firms in manufacturing sectors belong to the vertical paternalistic enterprise relationship (i.e., they are either *Ko-gaisha* or *Mago-gaisha,* or both).[8] Because of a relative lack of personnel and access to capital resources through the market, medium and small enterprises are forced to compete against each other for market shares. In 1987, 86.6 percent of them concentrated on competing against each other for markets in the same industry. And only 4.9 percent of medium and small enterprises competed against *Oya-gaisha* for expanding their market.[9]

The smaller subcontractors thereby rely on one or more parent firms. A 1988 Ministry of Finance report indicates that 17.3 percent of all minor enterprises were linked to a single parental company, 20.3 percent to two parental companies, etc. — but 68.2 percent had *never* changed parent companies, 15.2 percent had changed only once, and 10 percent had changed twice. The vast majority of minor enterprises had been locked into place by subcontracts that operated as their only, monopsonistic market and determined what they produced.

They were not independent suppliers, but were satellized by the larger firms, being hired to process materials, produce parts, and perform in-plant production functions. In processing and parts production, minor enterprises were thus largely bound to one, two, or three parent firms; for in-plant subcontracting, the smaller firms hired out to six or more parents.[10]

There seemed to be no escape from this satellite system. Generally speaking, the longer the relationship a small enterprise held with a larger one, the less chance of changing parent companies. At least this was so for more than 20-year links, comprising 34.6 percent of all minor enterprises, 47.8 percent of which had *never changed* parent companies. The 15-to-19 year category included 17.9 percent of all enterprises, 19.7 percent of which had *never changed* parents; and of the 31.5 percent of all firms that had a 10-to-14 year relationship with a parent, 24.5 percent had *never changed* parents. Those small enterprises with a shorter term relationship had changed parents more often, but even here the change from one parent to another still replicated the paternalistic linkage.[11]

Without a way out of the hierarchical ordering of firms and the subcontracting system, the smaller firms became the shock absorbers of the ups and downs of the Japanese economy. They either lost orders in a lax market or had their subcontract fees cut — forcing them to relay the malaise to their own workers by wage cuts, sped-up work, and a longer workday.

The Wages System, Japanese-Style

The workers' relative condition was shaped by such top-to-bottom relationships, with the workers in the smallest enterprises having their pay scale and working conditions hurt by the relay of the cost/price squeeze from the linkages between firms — so that the extraction of wages from workers in companies at the lower reaches effectively remunerated workers in firms at the apex of the hierarchical order.

Not only were Japanese enterprises divided by size, but the workers were paid distinctly different wages based on the size of the enterprise that employed them. Large firms of over five hundred workers were considered major enterprises that paid the highest wages; those with less than one hundred workers were considered minor enterprises that paid the lowest wages; and the others with more than one hundred but less than five hundred workers paid middling wage scales.

The fact that most firms in Japan are relatively small with less than one hundred workers means that between 77.5 and 87 percent of all job openings from 1985 to 1987 occurred in these minor enterprises.[12]

The large corporations examine the qualities of potential workers before hiring — calculating the time, energy, and investment required to train them to become efficient managers or productive workers who, in time, might be paid relatively higher wages. By initially offering higher wages and more satisfactory terms of work, the large corporations have the best chance to absorb the most talented prospects just out of school and entering the labor market. Small and medium enterprises (called *Chu-sho-kigyo*) are left to search for potential employees in the pool of leftovers.

Today, graduating students from colleges and universities have only one chance to win employment with the large firms. If they fail that opportunity, another chance will never be given, and they then fall into the next lower labor reserve from which the small and medium enterprises choose.

This inequality in hiring and wages effectively creates two labor markets, with the following wage differentials paid according to firm sizes. In 1951, employees in small firms (5–29 workers) received only 38 percent of the wages paid to workers in firms with five hundred and more employees. While such wage differentials have been reduced in recent years, going up to 61 percent in 1978, there still exist substantial disparities between large, medium, and small enterprises. For medium-size firms with

Table 4.3
Intergenerational Mobility of Occupation 1975

| | | Initial Employment | | | | | | | |
| | | Major Enterprises | | | Minor Enterprises | | | | |
		Admin.*	White Collar	Blue Collar	Admin.	White Collar	Blue Collar	Agri-culture	Self-Emp.
MAJOR	1. Professional — 75*	—**	—	—	—	—	—	—	—
	2. Admin.† —	100	9	—	—	—	—	—	—
	3. White Collar —	—	54	7	—	—	—	—	—
	4. Blue Collar —	—	—	37	—	—	9	—	—
MINOR	5. Admin.* —	—	—	—	75	9	—	—	—
	6. White Collar —	—	8	10	—	40	8	—	5
	7. Blue Collar —	—	5	15	—	13	50	18	13
EMP.	Agriculture —	—	—	8	13	—	5	62	—
	Self-Employed 7	—	14	14	13	24	22	10	72

* The figure in percentage.
** Indicates a figure of less than 4.5%. The total sample numbered 2,514.
† Administration.
Source: Table 7, in *Why Has Japan "Succeeded"?* by Michio Morishima (London: Cambridge University Press, 1982), 179. Morishima indicated that the table was prepared with the cooperation of Professor Hara Junsuke from the results of a survey on social mobility carried out in 1975 under the leadership of Tominaga Kin'ichi. See also Tominaga, *Nihon no Kaiso Kozo* (The social structure of Japan) (Tokyo: Tokyo University Press, 1979).

100–499 workers, for example, the disparity in wages was 75 percent of those of workers in firms with five hundred or more employees in 1951, but 83 percent in 1978.

This paternalistic/dependent relation among *Oya-gaisha, Ko-gaisha,* and *Mago-gaisha* is illustrated in Table 4.4.[13]

Table 4.4
Incorporation of Five Working Days Schedule

Scale of Enterprise

	Medium/Small Firms (30–99)				Large Firms (1,000 plus)			
Year	Every Week	3 Times a Month	Once a Month	Never	Every Week	3 Times a Month	Once a Month	Never
1975	2.8	1.1	12.7	63.2	28.5	9.0	13.0	14.1
1980	2.5	2.3	16.5	56.9	30.6	10.8	15.1	8.0
1985	3.0	2.3	18.6	57.6	35.5	11.3	14.8	7.9
1986	3.1	3.2	18.5	55.2	35.5	16.4	9.5	6.9

Source: Ministry of Labor, *Chingin rodo jikanseido-to sogo chosa* (Survey of incorporated systems of working hours).

The difference large and medium to small firms also impacts the time off and quality-of-life for their respective employees. In 1975 some 28.5 percent of large enterprises operated on a five-days work schedule; by 1986 35.5 percent of large enterprises used a five-day work schedule. But in 1975 only 2.8 percent of medium and small firms had a five-day work week; and the figure barely rose, to 3.1 percent, by 1986. In 1975 63.2 percent of small and medium firms still worked six full days per week; the figure was 55.2 percent as recently as 1986.[14]

Despite inequalities between and within firms, Japanese workers can not simply leave one job and find another one. For there is no labor market as such, only a closed system that provides for lifetime employment with limited upward mobility, and downward mobility for those who displease their employers.

One 1975 survey, for example, revealed a powerful downward bias for occupational mobility.[15]

Categorizing occupations into nine sections, the figures in each column show the proportional distribution of those still working who initially were hired in a particular job category and either moved down or up. While there was low upward mobility from the lower- to the upper-strata jobs (except for 9 percent of workers originally employed in blue-collar, minor enterprises who switched to blue-collar jobs in major enterprises), mobility from the upper strata into the lower was quite common. This was especially so for those in the self-employed category.

The Misunderstood Labor System

Fixed job categories with little opportunity for upward mobility also locked wages in place. In turn, this made possible Japan's system of labor-as-a-fixed-cost, that enabled export dumping in the 1960s through the late 1980s.

Japan's share of the world's gross national product had risen from a mere 2.8 percent in 1950 to 7.7 percent in 1974, then to an estimated 8.5 percent by 1987–88. This was made possible by top corporate executives concentrating on strict, army-like control of production, with subordinates led to make the precise decisions their superiors would make, and line positions relaying the orders to the factory floor.[16] These top-down orders superficially appeared to be the decisions of on-line workers — with bottom-up, quality-circles of workers motivating each member to act as his or her own quality inspector to ensure "defect-free" output. And by encouraging supposed high levels of trust across the hierarchical and functional boundaries, the factory was said to be using bottom-up consensual decision making.[17] Such paternalistic management of the affairs of the "whole worker" was described in terms of supervisors taking care of the personal as well as work needs of subordinates; employing people for life; promoting participatory worker involvement with the success of the employer company and the national economy.[18]

But in truth, Japanese managers *demanded* such responsibility from each worker and ensured it by so-called quality circles that periodically brought together ten or so workers from the same production division.[19] At Toyota, production line workers were *compelled* to attend such gatherings without pay, were often tired or bored, and listened with half-hearted attention at best, yet felt pressured to chant unrealistic company slogans.[20]

The ideal goal as set by upper-level management was for the workers themselves to take responsibility for improving the quality of output; but in practice the orders were only partly followed, as the rank-and-file saw through the superficial attempts by upper-echelon managers to put workers of unequal rank and pay in discussion groups to improve the production process, quality of work, and working environment.

At Toyota, worker complaints usually did not go beyond the immediate supervisor of the discussion groups.[21] Yet there was no doubt that, within each great company, every worker felt compelled by the organization's rules and "culture" to follow upper management's strategy as relayed through its structure and laid down in its systemized methods of output.[22]

The results appeared as low costs, defect-free products, and dependable delivery.[23] The rank-and-file may not have gone gently into that factory setting, but go they did.[24]

Japan's population had meanwhile received only partial recompense. Work speedups and minimized consumption had together driven the population harder and exhausted labor's energy for nonwork pursuit. The working-class family was neither enriched, nor even made financially secure by its labor. And the middle sector, or middle class, was based less on asset accumulation than the buying of high-price consumer goods.

The terrible economic situation immediately after World War II had made the population grateful for such work, income, and the availability of housing and food. From 1950 to 1986 Japanese employers were positioned to institute a near-replay of their wartime formulation of "subsistence wages."[25] Wage levels in Japan were just sufficient to cover a modest level of consumption to rebuild the laborer's spent energy and support his family; to provide a little leisure; and to allow some savings for retirement. These benefits, though limited, prepared labor and the family to offer almost unquestioning support for the success of the system they were part of—to both build up the employers' capital and to compliantly function in the frame of a powerful nation.

"We know that the Japanese government and managerial elite have fashioned a workplace environment and a social support system that favors the development of feelings of loyalty instead of alienation," anthropologist Marvin Harris wrote in 1981. "In the largest firms, workers enjoy lifetime security, pensions at fifty-five, and comprehensive company-subsidized medical and social services. And on the factory floor, Japanese workers are organized into small production teams whose members have collective responsibility for product quality and are rewarded with semi-annual bonuses based on the team's performance."[26]

Whether the population became conscious of the social implications of this basic extraction of its energy, labor, and savings that were channelled into new industrial investments, this system became the basis of Japan's fabulous accumulation of wealth after World War II. And today, the core of this accumulation is still Japan's labor system. From a Western viewpoint, Japanese workers might appear to be sped-up carbon units operating in a great technical machine directed from above by a rising hierarchy of managers. But the reality of Japanese relations between managers and workers is different: cooperation among workers is based on respect for on-line managers, who work themselves and judge the ability of their charges to perform the tasks handed down from the upper reaches of the management hierarchy. Labor may grumble about the difficulty of work, speedups, unpaid labor time, and wages that are insufficient to cover all their needs; yet they go on working diligently under the hierarchical ordering of the factory. The authority mandated from the apex of this pyramidal structure is spontaneously, if reluctantly, followed by those beneath.[27]

Such a response is based on a cultural milieu unlike anything known in the West. For in Japan personal and social obligations are not only recognized as essential to one's temporal existence, but respect for others and particularly those in authority is an essential component of beliefs concerning Japan's *metaexistence* and destiny. Traditional values of respect and piety toward others have also remained key forces in the system of hierarchical controls. And even Japan's bold steps into the Western commercial world have not yet devastated Japan's internal relations, or undermined traditional self-descriptive notions of a holistic, respectful, and ascetic people.

In the workplace, opposition to authority from rank-and-file workers definitely occurs. But it is largely symbolic, consisting of complaints about speedups and involving the annual "strike" of parading workers every spring. The reality of work life is different, based on a twofold system of authority, with the managers representing the company's line for giving orders and the unions helping to enforce them.

At the Toyota assembly line, for example, the speedup is resented by the on-line assembly workers. Upper-level management sets the pace of the assembly line, and the team chiefs often encourage the members to accept every extra burden. "Here, at this position, we have five unused seconds," says a team chief, looking at his stop-watch. When one worker cannot handle a job in the unused seconds, the task is shifted to another, and so on, even down to forcing it on the inspectors at the end of the line.[28] The team chief keeps the workers at their job places, and the pace of the machines does the rest. "There's no need to shout at or berate workers to make them work," said a production hand. "Just start the conveyor and keep it going: that's enough. The conveyor belt forces the worker into submission."[29]

If the team by itself cannot bear the work place, the on-line manager may assume part of the burden. And together, the teams, their heads, and on-line managers rationalize how the work shall be done, with the maximum safety, in the sped-up work environment. Workers may not have job-time to have their injuries attended to, and they may be pushed to the limit of physical endurance, but the speedup goes on.[30]

Using the speedup, the employers also seize every advantage to increase their market shares by enlarging production during periods of tight world supply. In 1987 Japanese companies already accounted for 70 percent of the $2.6 billion in revenues from the (dynamic random access) memory chip market. But in the spring and summer of 1988 a shortage in the world memory chip market led seven Hitachi semiconductor plants, as well as Fujitsu and Mitsubishi Electric Corporation, to push to capture an even larger market share. Pushing their employees to work longer hours, they even cancelled vacations and used the unions to pressure the workers to skip their mid–August week off.[31] And to such employer demands both the unions and the rank-and-file were compliant.

Western writers explain such rank-and-file subordination as something bred of "self-respect" in a system of unchallengeable hierarchical authority. They see this as part of the need of Japanese men to stay emotionally in tune with one another, so that even managers are part of the work groups that share a collective responsibility for getting the job done without interruptions or accidents — whether by helping out slower workers or taking on a heavier responsibility in case of accidents.[32]

Their view is shaped by Western experience, though for the Japanese a sharing of work burdens goes beyond the Western drive of lower-echelon managers to push their underlings faster. Rather, the great majority of Japanese people live in a milieu of fulfilling the expectations of others, and fearing censure, shame, and punishment by their neighbors.[33] One Western expert even posits that superiors, too, are expected to have the Confucian virtue of *benevolence,* to act as responsible guardians of the welfare of their charges, thereby also limiting their own claim to the lion's share of the benefits of production.[34] Yet such benevolence has never been part of the Confucian system in Japan. At least this was true in Japan's high-growth era before 1986, when Japanese companies prospered by using external threats and the workers' inner compulsion to respect authority to drive them to perform the same tasks — only better and cheaper. "In the past, we didn't need strong commanders," says a retired dean of the Nomura School of Advanced Management, "The whole trench moved itself."[35]

In this past, top management was in charge, but the socially induced need to be accepted by others led the individual worker to succumb to community pressures, to accept censure and bow to authority.[36] From the worker's point of view, a sense of belonging to the organization created an esprit d' corps that tied the worker to other workers and to the managers at all levels. Production decision making took place from the "bottom-up," so to speak, with consensus being established on each level in incremental steps that finally reached upper management. "Most of the Japanese companies have the bottom-up style," offered Kawamura Shigekuni, president of Dai Nippon Ink and Chemicals. "The people in the middle ranks make the decisions. But gradually this is changing. It's getting very difficult to get unanimous consensus. Responsibility is being transferred to the president, even though he doesn't like it. He's being pushed to the corner."[37]

There is, moreover, a difference of opinion on how the decision-making process should operate in corporate Japan. Masuda Yoshihisa, the "black sheep" president of Settsu Corporation, does *not* agree with most Japanese executives. Head of a powerful paperboard manufacturer, Masuda contends that senior Japanese management *is already in charge,* but lacks foresight, is lazy, and cries for help from the government when something goes wrong. Such management has the double financial advantage of access to low-cost funds and cooperation from related firms through placement of large chunks of the corporation's stock with linked or friendly companies. Top management rarely has problems with normally docile labor unions; yet engages in cartel-like activities to gain the edge over competitors. Japanese top management also refuses to respond to change, he says, and resorts to procrastination that causes friction between Japan and other nations. Preferring U.S. management styles, Masuda strives to teach his Japanese employees about the strength of the U.S., "that when individuals have different personalities, they achieve some unity with the same object or value and that becomes a very strong power."[38]

The power of individual diversity that is unified with others for the common purpose of production, then, might provide for both maximum production and personal expression, raising work satisfaction. It is this system that Japan might be pressured to emulate in its factories in the United States and perhaps even in Japan itself in the new economic regime in the 1990s.

Unions, Living Standards, and the Nexus of Production

Under the pre–1986 system, the union that operated at each large factory facilitated an interlinked consensus. Unlike union and management production relations in the West, the Japanese unions usually acceded to upper-level management's decisions to introduce new technology, intensify the pace of work, impose overtime and holiday work, and the like. Rather than acting as an independent force that represented its workers' essential interests, the Japanese unions kept the rank-and-file in line, as a reaffirmation of the employer's policies and thus the alliance of capital and labor for a seemingly common purpose.[39] Because the nexus of production relations is the workplace, this alliance of labor and management was expressed in the division of the values produced between the work force, the managers, and the stockholders. The motives of each differed, for stockholders sought returns on their investment and market appreciation of their securities, while workers and managers were work-oriented with a goal of achieving upward mobility and personal security, including the acquisition of one's own home, and acquiring a rising level of consumer goods and residential amenities.

No longer building and supplying homes for its workers, by the early 1970s Toyota had set the frame for such consumer spending. Toyota asked married workers who had lived in company houses for ten years to leave and advised them to buy their own homes. To facilitate home purchases, the company provided two plans: a monthly plan whereby the workers who had been with the company five years were entitled to a $6,700 loan at 4.5 percent, repayable in twelve years; and a maximum $33,000 loan at 5.5 percent, payable to the Long-Term Credit Bank in a cooperative arrangement with the company. "Approximately 4,000 workers have supposedly bought houses built with the help of these two types of loans," factory hand Kamata reported, "and in a very real sense these young married men are tied to the company—that is, to the assembly line—by their loan payments until the day they retire."[40]

This aspiration for a qualitatively better life (called "my-home-ism") began to spiral upwards in the mid–1960s, and significantly affected the condition of the work force on the job.[41] Great firms like Toyota attempted to build company-town environments, in order to lower the workers' living costs, as well as to keep workers in competition with each other to promote a speedup, extract free labor by offering workers the possibility for job security, and thereby exhaust labor — leaving less time and energy for personal needs.[42]

During the early 1980s labor militancy was still largely symbolic — a periodic, rhetorical ritual through which all the elements of the work force reestablished their social compact with the great employers in an industrial frame that was premised on a supposed acknowledgment of equity, job security, and participation as linked to corporate goals. "Workers ... understand that their fates are tied to the profitability and competitiveness of their firms," management professor Robert Reich wrote in 1983, just as many basic Japanese industries began their competitive decline in a global frame. "They therefore bargain for change and adaptability — retraining programs; relocation assistance; new investment in plant and equipment."[43]

Within these relations, however, the traditional consensus of the rank-and-file workers with those at the higher reaches was also being weakened, for the avenues of communication had broken down about conditions of work and production speedups beyond human capacity. Even in the early 1970s, workers on the production line had already begun to think about their personal need for a fair day's work at a fair day's pay that would enable them to leave work in less than an exhausted state, have free time for themselves, and receive sufficient wages to buy the personal amenities they were convinced would provide a decent life for themselves and their families.[44]

Japan was slowly beginning to follow the path America had once taken *away* from a work ethic based on capitalist enterprise, thrift, and industry that would lead to supposed material success and spiritual fulfillment. The social texture and pressures were certainly different in Japan. For, unlike Japan, in the first three centuries of U.S. history, the work ethic had constantly changed its meaning, yet, one social critic says, "these vicissitudes, often imperceptible at the time, foreshadowed its eventual transformation into an ethic of personal survival."[45]

Nonetheless, a comparable ethic had developed in Japan by the late 1980s. "People over 40 do not work for themselves, but for the good of their company and their family," explained one 23-year-old employee of a Japanese import company of fashionable, foreign-designed clothes in early 1988. "Now we work for ourselves. We think of ourselves first, and that's a big difference between us."

"I am loyal to my job, but not to my company," offered Kishida Hirokazu, another *shinjinrui,* or new breed, a 26-year-old account executive. "I think that the people who helped Japan to grow rapidly in the 1960s created a good foundation for society, but now our society needs independent professionals. We don't forget our debt to those people, but we can do the same things they did independently."

These attitudes in the late 1980s were widespread among Japan's young people, calling into question continuation of familiar images of Japanese as somber, unrelenting workers.[46] Yet, the critical questions were how and why such work attitudes had changed in two decades, and if such attitudes would be generalized among Japan's work force.

Fighting to Keep the Young Compliant

Regimentation of attitudes toward compliance and personal aspirations in Japan begins not in the workplace, but in the home and school. Respect within the family and community has powerful religious foundations that have promoted obligatory relations for hundreds of years. But discipline in the schools weakened after World War II and led to a brief outbreak of protest in the 1960s and to juvenile delinquency and school violence in the early 1980s.

In the 1960s the Japanese student movement grew under the influence of U.S. student opposition to America's involvement in Vietnam and the French student/labor strike against educational and state bureaucracy in 1968. Japanese students and the socialist-leaning railway workers opposed shipping U.S.- and Japanese-made armaments to Vietnam. The students also opposed the rigid hierarchical educational apparatus, taking over and closing several Japanese universities, one of them for eight months. Free universities that charged no fees to students or workers were set up. And because the university had always been considered a sanctuary off-limits to the police, communities kept the police from raiding the student quarters.

But the student movement did not have the critical political backing it required to last into the 1970s. The ruling Liberal Democratic Party (LDP) sought to crush it. The Japanese Communist Party claimed that Japan was oppressed by the West, and that the Japanese people, including students, must not protest and divide, but unify their efforts against Western imperial designs on Japan itself. And the various gradations of Socialists vacillated about whether to cooperate with the LDP in parliamentary parry and riposte. Only the farmer-student alliance designed to stop the expansion of Tokyo's Narita Airport onto agricultural land continued through the 1970s into the late 1980s; and only the Buraku Liberation Movement lasted from before World War II to advocate full social, economic, and political rights for the Burakumin people, Japan's untouchables.[47]

In the 1980s individualism and rebellion were literally snuffed out in the school system, ending a fivefold rise in attacks on junior high school teachers between 1978 and 1983. School rules not only demanded uniform dress and conduct in the classroom, but conformity outside of school as well. School-dictated curfews were enacted and enforced by teachers patrolling neighborhoods. Corporal punishment was reinstituted. Instilling obedience became a main function of both lower-level and high schools.

Overly authoritarian teachers and administrators were so strict their actions actually led to the death of a handful of nonconformist students in the 1980s. And most student infractions were nominal, even trivial, by Western standards.

"The students just learn to be obedient to rules from above," reported Oka Shin'ichi, attorney for a young woman expelled from high school because she permed her bangs and once before had violated school rules by qualifying for a driving license!

Public polls in the late 1980s nonetheless reported that the vast majority of teachers and many parents supported strict academic rules. Tsujimura Tetsuo, director of the Education Ministry's junior high school division, agreed, calling for strict adherence to basic rules, but enough leeway to allow students to learn by themselves. Yet, Kojima Isamu, a junior high school teacher in Saitama prefecture, north of Tokyo, said that many teachers believed they had to immediately root out any signs of rebellion to prevent a return to the violence of the early 1980s — and that society expected teachers to perform the role of parents as well.

They were to use corporal punishment, the traditional "whip of love," to keep the students in line. Self-assertion of students by nonuniform dress was seen as leading to poor school attendance and thus to the abandonment of ties with other classmates and the school. The core values of community and discipline were thereby reinforced, producing adults who would conform and could *not* think for themselves. Thus were community standards of acceptable practice raised above individual expression and ingenuity.[48]

Advanced education was still largely financed through parental support. This system worked to the advantage of the already well-to-do, who could afford the cost and wanted to see their own children succeed in the world of prestige and work. In 1982, on average, almost 79 percent of the expense of a Japanese college education was paid by students' parents, while another 12.8 percent was partly paid from parental resources. These figures were vastly higher than in the leading Western nations, indicating the great importance Japanese society places on college as a way station for upward mobility, and also reflecting high parental expectations for their children to succeed in their careers.[49]

Yet college in Japan is a playground, a time for fun, games, and sports teams, with little serious study taking place. Even in hiring, college students are judged by their potential qualities as team players who willingly follow the orders of their elder leaders. College sports clubs establish norms for living with the expectations of an organization and training by means of a system of formal relations in which older members *(senpai)* guide the younger members *(kohai)*. Junior members learn to be subservient.

Many companies seek to hire students who are members of sports clubs, reasoning that such students have already learned good discipline, teamwork, and good manners. "To be a member of a baseball team is worth 100 A's to company recruiters, and the mountain climbing team is worth

50 A's," said Tominaga Nobuhiro, a junior at the prestigious Keio University in Tokyo. "In Japanese colleges, many students spend four years without doing much of anything," noted a spokesman for the Sumitomo Bank in describing his company's recruiting process. "So it is a plus for a student if he can say he did something with devotion. If a student was a captain of the [sport] club, then he is likely to be trained in harmonizing the team to produce good teamwork and to work under pressure. We don't require them to submit grades. Even if grades are bad, it does not necessarily mean that we don't want a student. We stress personal characteristics."[50]

Japanese society in the 1980s was thus organized to encourage individuals to conform to community and organizational values, beliefs, and ways. What others thought as a group was more important than the thinking and ways of the individual. Some people rebelled against rigid conformities and subservience, of course, but their voices were rarely heeded. Settsu's president Masuda Yoshihisa continued to call for the rights of individualism on the job in order to promote unity in production. And the 22-year-old rebel author Hayashi Takeshi urges in his two bestselling books that students should fight back against teachers who dominate them, treating them as subhuman and not permitting them to make the mistakes from which they might also learn. Some college students rebelled against organized sports, wanting a four-year moratorium on team-imposed rigor, in preparation for what they expected as a lifetime of obligatory, perhaps drudging, work. And there were dropouts from the labor market who were considered useless by the general populace.

And yet these are not the dominant trends. The emotional implosions students feel in school and workers experience on the job usually do not manifest themselves as protest against those in charge. A school overheated by strict corporal punishment for rule-breakers might give in to parents and outraged students by allowing students to participate in setting new rules. Workers on the job might feel dissatisfied because they work without the slightest control over the policies of the factories that employ them. But there are amenities provided by the employers to assuage their emotive rhythms; and the violence displayed in the sex books that are Japan's animated comics might provide an outlet for the stored-up rage many men may feel. By such means Japan has cooled the ardor of those who might protest. Production has not been interrupted by its managers, new recruits, or seasoned workers. Accumulation has gone forward as never before.

Disaccumulation, Wages, and Investments Abroad

Under new market pressures, times nonetheless changed a little in the late 1980s. The difference in wage structure maintained through the status hierarchy among firms and by Japan's unique hiring system had created a dual labor market. Any rise of costs or lowering of prices at the largest firms in order to secure markets was immediately relayed to the smaller firms in the form of reduced revenues. These smaller firms then tried to protect their profit margins by making their already lesser paid employees work harder, longer, and for less pay. But this linked-firm system came under added pressure in the late 1980s as Japan's largest companies were forced to compete with cheaper manufactured goods coming from low-wage, newly industrialized nations.

In a sense, Japan's reduction in wage differentials between large and medium/small size firms indicated the workers had organized and won more gains than was common in the past. But in another sense, it was a warning to the big employers that the general rise in the wage scale had reduced their ability to squeeze the wages of workers in smaller firms — by pressuring the smaller employers to absorb the losses the large firms experience in production and marketing. And it indicated one reason why the great employers began deserting domestic industries and investing abroad where greater profits could be won in the late 1980s and 1990s.

The entire Japanese production apparatus had long depended on sustaining a relatively closed home market in which high, monopoly prices could be maintained to effectively absorb all fixed production costs, including labor. As noted earlier, excess output was sold abroad at a "dumping" price that covered only the variable costs of raw materials, energy, transportation and, in some cases, a portion of administrative overhead. In the late 1970s and early 1980s, Japanese companies still followed the "10 percent rule" — if a foreign competitor lowered prices to equal or undercut the Japanese price, the latter would be slashed 10 percent in the overseas market by raising the domestic price of the same goods in Japan to cover all overhead costs, all energy costs, and, in extreme cases, all transport and raw material costs! In other words, the goods dumped on foreign markets conceivably could carry no costs at all. This was done to capture market shares, with the hope that competitors would be forced to retire from the field and would be replaced by the Japanese, who in turn would eventually raise the price of their goods.

Yet such cost allocation and dumping methods were reformulated in 1985–86. The United States, recognizing that it was turning large sections of key U.S. markets over to the Japanese dumpers, forced the upward valuation of the yen against the dollar and the currencies of all Western powers that used the dollar as their reserve currency. Within these Western nations, the purchasing power of their domestic currencies did not much change. But the ability to buy imported Japanese goods was sharply undermined — falling by 32 percent in the U.S., 13 percent in Great Britain, and 3–4 percent in West Germany, Austria, and France.[51]

Japan's Economic Planning Agency immediately moved to analyze which major importing nations could either sustain the continued pace of

Japanese exports or, failing this, were prime areas to export Japanese capital for production and marketing back to Japan or to third nations.

These nations were categorized along the lines of Japan's own production sectors: farming and fishing, textile manufacturing, heavy industry, light manufacturing, and the latest technologies, such as medical products. It was clear that Japanese import expenditures on products in these areas were rising even before the sharp rise of the yen. And Japan's goal was to take advantage of the new situation — not only by traditional dumping, but by the export of capital and production facilities themselves.[52]

As we shall see, once the newly industrialized countries (NICs) broke into Nippon's market with their own manufactures; once Japanese factory subsidiaries in these NICs sought a mass market for inexpensive, high-quality goods in Japan; and once the United States developed its own system with a high-price, protected domestic market that financed U.S. dumping in Japan, Japan's old methods of dumping and securing foreign market shares had to change. How this happened is the subject of the following chapters.

Chapter 5

Tradition, the Middle Class, and Upward Mobility

Part of the source of capital accumulation in Japan has been the disparity between the value of output and the allocation of wages as a share or proportion of the sales proceeds going to the labor force. Another source has been the expansion of the high-price domestic market, itself fueled by the drive for upward mobility—induced by the massive availability of goods, especially after an inpouring of inexpensive, high-quality manufactures from Asia's newly industrialized nations in the late 1980s.

By the first measure of wealth accumulation, wages can be viewed as a component of the value of output, which obviously covers all costs of production. Production volume might rise, but how hard labor works for a given wage or salary determines not just productivity calculated by labor time, but the relation—and difference—between new values created and the level of the workers' remuneration. By prefiguring the level of wages in relation to the value of output using different scenarios for production volume, Japanese management can calculate in advance the various levels of revenue that can be generated from domestic and overseas sales to cover other costs and leave a surplus.

Through use of a speedup, longer workday, or wage cut, upper-level management is able to assign given work tasks involving both *paid* and *unpaid labor time,* as well as to concentrate on the relation of the value of output and the workers' pay. This calculation involves more than just the size of the new values that wage workers create in a certain period of time. For the other element is *unremunerated labor,* which, in Japan at least, is a measure of pure value returned to the employers.

In the West, by contrast, economists looking at productivity in terms of output by *paid labor time* tend to concentrate on the volume of production. Their concern with increased output is often a function of labor time and its compensation without an explicit calculation of unpaid labor or other measures or surplus value, instead redefining the difference between wages (with or without other costs) and priced inventory as "value added" in production.

75

Two Routes to Lower the Cost of Labor

In large Japanese companies, lowering the overall and unit cost of labor is a major task of management in preplanning and prognosticating profit margins. Managers view labor as a necessary cost of production, which can be lowered in two ways: first, by cutting the workers' living costs in company towns like those owned by Toyota so that the company can pay less in wages; then second, by creating job classifications that competitively drive workers to strive for promotion by putting in long hours of *unpaid overtime,* thereby effectively contributing "free labor" to their employers.[1]

Cutting the workers' costs of living and their families' cost of maintenance and reproduction in order to keep wages low follows classic lines that had been used earlier in Great Britain, the United States, and Germany.[2]

There are differences, of course, for in Japan the basic requirements for the survival of the workers and their families have been shaped by the population's modest economic expectations, themselves based on traditions including Buddhist renunciation of worldly goods and the Confucian belief in the value of sharing. Though these in turn have been contoured by the prevision the employers embody in wage and benefits awarded their workers, competition underlies the aspiration of each worker for economic improvements and more personal freedom. Workers might feel committed to the output and quality goals of a particular employer, yet recognize the competitive strivings the employer has built into the job. Discontent has often accompanied hard, unrelenting work; and striving for standing in a sped-up or an unaccommodating job environment is not alien to wanting the most secure position, the highest wages, and the best amenities the employers might offer.[3]

Understanding these drives and aspirations, the employers have foreseen the opportunity to lower the workers' cost of living to hold down their wage demands — giving rise to the company town, Japanese-style, in the form of the "castle town," which vaguely replicates the spatial design and circular patterns of the castles and walls of the *daimyo* feudal estates that surrounded Edo in the precapitalist era. Toyota has created Toyota City, developed amenities and housing for its workers to rent or buy, thereby binding their work force to the company by means of low-interest mortgages and property rights. The company's almost free health and welfare benefits for workers had the same effect. Holding a permanent place provided the worker with security, no matter how little time he had for family or personal affairs. A permanent, upwardly mobile worker stuck to his job because his wages paid the company-financed mortgage and welfare programs. In the United States, at Homestead, Pennsylvania, Andrew Carnegie had created a similar system in 1886–92. Toyota added little to the technique.[4]

When it came to wage scales, though, Toyota had a slightly different method of allocation, continuing to make distinctions based on Japan's reverence for age, seniority, skill, and relative permanence of employment. Wage scales differed for those in lifetime positions, as distinguished from workers employed under short-term contracts. Generally, wage differences for regular workers were based on seniority and skill levels, rather than the higher, seasonal scales paid for time and overtime to relatively unskilled assembly-line workers.[5]

Management functions, skills, and levels of remuneration were also different. Positions in upper management were based on the merit earned from attending a university, but this in turn was usually based on social class position and ability to pay and succeed. Thus Japan's educational system remained a powerful factor in legitimizing the hierarchy of authority in the Japanese corporation.[6]

Even today managers expect to work just as hard as manual workers, though in different ways. The functions of managers are to keep the mechanical production line and its workers operating efficiently without interruptions.[7] Most feel no need to defend their superior status, and some even earn less than older, production-line workers with seniority. Of course, the production-line worker will never have an opportunity to enter the ranks of management or to enjoy the benefits that accrue to a manager.

Females, if they work at all, are likely to end up on the production line. Though professional women are qualified to be managers, and though nearly three-quarters of Japanese women were university-educated by 1987, only one in four worked after graduation and over half of all Japanese companies provided absolutely no opportunities for their advancement.[8] Working beside less-educated males on the production line and often taking orders from less-educated managers is a woman's lot.

Unpaid work on the production line and labor's drive for upward mobility combined to fit the expectations of the employer-structured labor market from the 1960s to the mid–1980s. The great *zaibatsu* employers, Mitsui, Mitsubishi, Sumitomo, and Yasuda, as well as other major enterprises offered the opportunity of lifetime employment to individual workers on the basis of their merits. Yet two limits were placed on such employment. One was the total absence of an open labor market that would allow labor to move from one employer to another in search of the best possible job. With little occupational mobility each worker judged future employment advances by looking to the standards set by his or her own employer.

The other limit was the employer's position to control the *precise steps* each worker had to take to meet company standards for upward mobility. Each worker's merit was examined in the context of the employer's structured organization of the labor process, with exerted labor-energy calculated by time whether paid or not. "At 6:00 a.m. the conveyor belt starts," Kamata reported from the Toyota plant. "From then on we enter a time without freedom, from this moment until 11:00 a.m.: five hours of work without a break."[9]

The lowest level in the organizational structure of work was membership on a labor team, run by a team leader, under the direction of the job foreman. Camaraderie was to prevail between these individuals, with all of them working under company-set quality norms and production and work-safety targets.[10] No doubt the workers felt an obligation to one another to keep the production line going at a steady pace in order to avoid overtime for everyone—as Kamata said, "we do our job in a hell of a hurry to keep our fellow workers from suffering. That is how Toyota raises output."[11]

But rather than viewing the company-set production pace as simply an external, coercive point of authority, the workers operated with an inner compulsion that in part reflected their desire to win security within the firm, and their drive for attaining seniority, a better job, and more pay and benefits. So long as the team members viewed the success of the company as a sign of their own success, logic dictated conformity to sped-up conditions and responsibility for uninterrupted production.[12] The workers helped one another on the assembly line, through team work and by performing one another's functional tasks. And as one Toyota worker reported: "The foreman was absent, so we had to work harder to make up for him."[13]

Positioned to hire, manage, and judge the quality of each worker, the great employers thus operated on several levels to promote competition in pursuit of maximum labor efficiency and greater work efforts *without having to pay incremental wages*. For this goal, following production schedules, the employers aligned the workers into three strata within each plant, shifted workers within the company and to suppliers, and relied on at least one unskilled, outside source of rural labor. At Toyota, at any rate, the system functioned in the following fashion.

The Job Ladder

For overall production operations, the company initially balanced its needs for labor in its main plants and through its subcontractors who practiced just-in-time parts inventory deliveries. This system aligned production schedules of "in-house" and outside suppliers through advance planning, so that weeks in advance deliveries of parts were synchronized to meet the requirements of final product assembly. Parts arrivals were timed for immediate use in overall production, with little or no storage required. At Toyota's assembly plants, inventories arrived between two hours and two days before use, so the number of workers needed for continuous assembly was known in advance. If there were changes in parts delivery schedules, workers could even be shifted to the supplying plants or subcontractors, or the required work hours at the Toyota assembly lines could be altered.[14]

For advanced, four-months' scheduling, part-time, temporary workers were recruited from rural areas after the growing season was over and the crops were brought in. Toyota recruited heavily during the farmers' off-season, when incomes dropped. "It's fall, and farmers all over the country are starting to go out and get winter jobs to tide them over until spring," Kamata pointed out.[15] As a residual, "discardable" labor source, these unskilled laborers had no job security and received no promise of future reemployment. They were, however, paid a premium wage above that of other workers, as well as a bonus for completing the work season.[16] Many were anxious to please Toyota's goal-oriented managers, hoping for momentary security by showing job fortitude under oppressive, competitive conditions. Rural workers eager to receive high wages were easy targets for recruitment, and, from a management perspective, could be used to displace militant workers who protested or who went on strike, as had actually happened in 1950.[17]

With this seasonal labor pool waiting in reserve, Toyota designed an employment ladder, with promotions leading toward job security. Newly initiated male and female workers tended to be young, compliant, and willing to work hard at the most unskilled production-line jobs. Through their conformity to the rules management periodically set down, they could gain additional pay, more job security, and eventually enter a labor pool that was different from, and superior to, that at the lower organizational reaches. But above them, calling for harder work and more unpaid labor time, were other workers who had already attained greater skills either on the job or by special training. These workers had shown their zeal for efficiency and donated long, unpaid hours of overtime. The result was a clear segmentation of Toyota's internal labor market.

This was elaborated by management-designated teams within the firm, with each team competing for prestige against the others by working intense, long hours without receiving extra pay for their extra labor. With team-work then drawing on the inculcated drives of team-oriented sports and Confucian respect for authority, it was a simple psychological extrapolation to expect individual workers to view their assigned team membership as their reference group, submerging their individual aspirations (and muffling their complaints) and giving full effort to overcome other competitive groups.[18]

Globalism and the New Alliances

The great and lesser enterprises also mobilized the resources of their individual companies to build worker solidarity for added labor and output by linking the success of the company to the need to outmaneuver rival firms within Japan.

Such calls to harder efforts for the same pay were also put in motion by global, competitive pressures. Japan's leaders called on the population to follow tradition's work ethic to make Nippon the most powerful producing nation in the world. Being Japanese was portrayed as sufficient cause in itself to exercise such extra effort on the job; and for such a patriotic end, individual loyalty and commitments often transcended the need for monetary rewards.

Japan's transnational enterprises meanwhile assumed the posture of England's nineteenth-century Birmingham Alliances, not only exporting goods, but capital and production operations as well. Japanese enterprise effectively promised its domestic workers that they would receive a portion of the enlarged revenue flow earned in overseas markets, but also warned that employees would suffer a partial loss of wages if the foreign market turned sour.[19] Yet the employers mentioned nothing about the consequences of transferring capital and jobs abroad.

Management professor Reich argues that by 1984, there were already two distinct types of multinational enterprises: the U.S. and British type, which owed its allegiance to no particular nation, with managers, directors, creditors, shareholders, and employees from many nations; and the Japanese and continental European type, which though it spread its operations globally, maintained a primary orientation to the citizens of a particular nation. "Regardless of how many of its managers, directors, creditors, shareholders, or employees lie outside the nation," he says, "the enterprise nevertheless is pledged to promote the welfare of its home country's citizens ... [to] seek to increase the real incomes of ... [the] home country's citizens over time. They are agents of their national economies."[20]

In the U.S. at least, Japanese-affiliated manufacturers were mostly majority owned, the proportion of such ownership slightly declining as the number of U.S.–based operations enlarged more than two times between 1981/83 and 1987.[21]

Within the U.S., Japanese management often failed abysmally in its efforts to direct American workers. Problems occurred most often when Japanese companies bought preexisting U.S. operations, and did not know how to handle their workers whose work rules and attitudes shackled the new Japanese owners. Conditions were different in start-up facilities in which Japanese investors began from scratch with new technology and malleable, young, nonunion employees. "Much of the success we attribute to the Japanese mystique reflects green-field investment and a young work force," concludes labor expert and University of California professor Harley Shaiken. But when taking over old plants, discord was common between previously happy unions and new management.[22]

In contrast, in Japan labor could be treated another way. And in the late 1980s, Japan's neonationalists called attention to traditional religious and cultural beliefs, powerfully using them to speed production and extend the workday without an equivalent increment in pay, thereby promoting the extraction of unpaid labor from every worker in the name of Japan's competitive power.[23]

It was this power that shaped Japan's growing national output, mass marketing, and the emergence of a middle class.

Part 3:
The Contours of Neonationalism: Speedup, Mass Marketing, and the Middle-Class Bulge

Japan's competitive position in global markets had changed by the mid–1960s. No longer bound by U.S. economic strictures, Japanese production had surged, and a speedup in the workplace moved in lockstep with a common belief that Japan could make its way in the world beyond its shores. Earlier calls for emancipation and protection from foreigners by military operations in Manchuria and East Asia were no longer germane to Japan's global trade and investments.[1]

Rather, Japan's new self-identity was based on its industrial expansion, modernization, and exports. These were now explained as a collective enterprise, which was suffused by a spiritual climate *(fudo)*, knit together by interdependent personal and human relationships, and necessitated by collective work, conformity, and a linkage of the individual person to others through associative groups.[2] This network of human relations was also the foundation of social connections between individuals (called *Ie*), so that the individual functioned and survived only through the network as a positive force of society and production.[3]

But could such collectivist relations and ideological beliefs make everyone equal, so that a standardized, egalitarian distribution of income and wealth would be possible? Some intellectuals rationalized the emergence of middle-class society in this way.[4] But others argued that, through Japan's affluence, the emergent middle class represented a half-way point between cooperative, collectivist relations and individualist perspectives and drives.[5] Still others said that Japan's middle class emerged with the extension of Japanese inroads into overseas markets and investment spheres, reifying its class structure to include a middle segment or mass with a rising standard of living and a self-satisfying, yet distorted, image of national homogeneity that other nations supposedly lacked.[6]

These views did not necessarily offer a holistic portrayal of Japan's massive emergence of individual aspirations to better one's condition, attain material rewards, and elevate one's self to the rank of the middle class. Yet, self-consciousness regarding a sense of belonging to this middle element, or middle class, was itself a new awareness, so that the idea of a "new middle class" emerged as one that spoke of one's material, social condition, rather than one's metaphysical status.[7] Thus the material foundation for the individual acquisition of goods and services had been laid.

Chapter 6
Changes in the Material Frame

Great changes in the material frame encompassing traditional Japan had created a milieu that induced different ways of thinking about the new society in formation. In part, this was the product of an emergent social species never before seen in Japan. For the new Japanese badge of identification was one of self-image as part of an emergent "middle class." Yet this imaging was merely a reflection of the extension of opportunities in the domestic market, accentuating the commercial standardization of values that were internalized by an upwardly mobile public and expressed as the conscious needs of an ever-enlarging, middle-income sector. The defining feature of the new middle class was social standing based on consumptive power — rather than on the underlying socioeconomic relations of ownership, or nonownership, of the nation's apparatus of production, commerce, and finance.

This new conception of belonging to a community of buyers — subsuming personal identity under the commercial standardization of community values and the monetization of worldly goods — brought 80–90 percent of the population within the frame of such ideological sameness.[8] Employees of Toyota thus aspired to buy their own color television sets and other equipment for their company dormitory rooms, or to own the product of their labor — to own a Toyota to park in the company parking lot and drive to the job and to freedom away from the plant. "One out of every two workers has a car," one factory worker reported, "of which he made a part or two himself."[9]

In the face of the simultaneous availability of wages and goods to buy, Japanese society was being preprogrammed. Emerging relationships and markets, not yet fully socially described, were assigning functional roles and transforming every person into a part of the new order. As the system of work for wages was generalized and the mass production of goods filled domestic markets, a price was placed on every person's labor on the job as well as on the objects they created. The units of pay for work now had to be equated with the price these objects commanded. And it was assumed that life would be better under the new market ordering — that the market itself would act as the best of guards for personal security and tranquility.[10]

For this exercise, there would be no need for intervention by traditional values and calculations for distribution of the nation's bounty. And toward those falling outside the new reference frame, respect and piety were thus bound to weaken, once reformulated in the light of Western practices and concepts of political rights, social security, economic possessiveness, and hierarchical controls. These were the quickened steps into the Western commercial world undermining Japan's traditional self-descriptive notions of a holistic, respectful, ascetic people.[11]

In four decades Japan moved from being reliant on others for work and goods to becoming the provisioner to others, and then to reliance again, but this time within a different reference frame. These changes transformed the nature and organization of capital, the quality of production and work, and the functions and condition of labor.

Reliance on America had lasted from the close of World War II to the mid-1950s. Japan as the provider began in earnest with the Korean War and, extended to markets worldwide, lasted until 1985. And Japan's new reliance, this time on Asia's newly industrialized nations emerged in 1986 and is expected to intensify during the rest of the 20th century.

In all three periods, filling and extending the market Nippon held was elevated to a high point in the nation's consciousness. Trade became one of the nation's demigods; and the material condition of the nation was filtered through traditional beliefs, with worshippers bowing down to the liturgy of unrelenting work, uninterrupted production, and expanding commerce. Survival was posited as the nation's base, economic security its expression.[12] So far this was science of value, prices, and profits carried that the success of Japanese companies came to depend, not on the home market, but on selling output in the global marketplace. And, eventually, even Nippon itself could be "hollowed out"—deprived of production facilities and jobs while Japanese companies hired foreign workers to produce goods for export to Japan. These patterns emerged in the following ways.

Industrial Upgrade, Foreign Markets, and Financial Dependency

By the late 1950s the U.S. Occupation's plans to break up the *zaibatsu* had been completely reversed and Japanese industry was again moving toward concentration, with control centralized in the hands of a relatively few companies.

Thus, in 1958, 2.5 percent of all incorporated industrial, commercial, and trading firms each had ten billion yen ($27.7 million) or more in capital and accounted for 73 percent of all company assets, employed 42 percent of all workers, and made 58 percent of the nation's sales. The two hundred largest Japanese firms accounted for 39 percent of total company assets and 33 percent of total net profits. And when the U.S. demanded an *Open Door* for American capital investments in Japan, one Nipponese company after another redoubled its efforts to build plants, centralize control, enlarge its scale of operations, and otherwise improve its competitive position. Large firms became still larger and more powerful.

Yet, in the early 1960s, Japanese industry was still relatively small-scale by comparison with foreign firms. The leader of the Japanese automobile industry, Toyota, was producing one-twelfth the output of General Motors, which then accounted for one-half of all U.S. automobiles produced. Each of Japan's four largest chemical concerns averaged only one-sixth the average sales of each of the eleven largest American companies and one-eighth those of the nine largest European firms.[13]

Nonetheless, Japanese firms were growing and seeking out foreign markets, and momentarily held the advantage of lower labor costs, and thus lower selling prices, for products similar to American and European products. As Japanese production drove forward, however, a point was reached where expansion and the demand for labor temporarily met an insufficient supply of available workers, pushing up wages in both small and middling companies and making them more equal to those paid in the great firms that offered lifetime employment. Thus from 1960 to 1970 wages in firms with five to twenty-nine workers rose from 46 to 62 percent of those in large firms with five hundred or more workers; wages in firms with thirty to ninety-nine workers rose from 59 to 70 percent of those in these giant companies; and wages in firms with one to five hundred workers increased from 71 to 81 percent of those in the larger enterprises.

Higher wages bred higher fixed production costs, squeezed profits, and pressured businesses to seek tariff protection against competitive foreign goods, as well as government financial subsidies and credits to lower export prices to undersell competitors in foreign markets.

Western nations moved in step to competitively lower their production costs, financed with superior capital resources, to capture markets throughout the world. The resources and connections of giant Western concerns also permitted them to take over markets, from which the Japanese were then excluded. But Japan's Ministry of International Trade and Industry (MITI) responded to this problem by openly demanding that the government promote the centralization and cartelization of the nation's industry. Decrying excessive domestic competition, Japan's largest concerns also called for government curbs on such competition in the interest of efficient, low-cost production. They contended that only with government controls and subsidies could Japanese businessmen succeed against their competitors abroad.[14]

By the mid-1960s, moreover, the business community was moving to amend the Occupation-imposed Antimonopoly Law, and a growing list of industries were soon exempted by statute. During the next five years government power was used to centralize still more Japanese industries and subsidize more exports to meet competitors. Within the decade Japan's five largest banks held almost 40 percent of all Japanese bank deposits. And the great business complexes controlled chains of banks, which held the population's savings, and used these resources to finance conglomerated industrial and commercial firms, as they had before the war.[15]

In fact, the twelve great city banks each had hundreds of their own branches, drawing savings from over 12.5 million people in Tokyo alone[16] — feeding capital into industries that became increasingly dependent on outside finance, so much so that where businesses were 42 percent dependent in 1934, by 1974 they were 90 percent dependent.[17]

Japan's Growing Needs

Japan as the provider of manufactured goods, the identity that began powerfully with the Korean War, was extended to markets worldwide until the close of 1985. Large-scale manufacturing bred the need to import vast quantities of raw materials to feed the nation's production machine and foods to sustain the urbanized work force, with the composition of Japan's imports indicating this historical overriding dependence.[18]

Expanding production thus meant a growth on reliance on other nations and other peoples for raw materials and foods — as distinguished from needing their *manufactured goods*. It also revealed Japan's vulnerability. For obviously Japan's total industrial strength could not outlast her stores of oil imported from the Middle East, her access to iron ore mined in Australia, or her need for other essential foreign resources. Access to these raw materials and to overseas markets to sell Japanese manufactures became equivalent in the minds of Japan's leading politicians. Foreign Minister Fukuda Takeo referred to both in the mid-1970s, proclaiming that "The Japanese government must use all its power to protect these overseas sources of profit."

As Japan's industrial base expanded, moreover, the importation of raw materials increased proportionally and more foreign exchange earned by exports was required to pay for resources and foodstuffs. And because Japanese held no overseas territories, there was also no doubt that the nation's growing hunger for raw materials would have to be met by both economic and political measures.

Planning to sidestep Western controls over the old colonial world and spheres of influence, Japan had thus initiated her reentrance to South and Southeast Asia in 1954, by supporting the Colombo Plan. Between fiscal years 1954–55 and 1961–62, Japan provided 2,233 million yen for technical cooperation, sent 347 experts to Colombo Plan countries, and received 646 trainees for study in Japan under technical cooperation schemes. By 30

June 1961 Japan had committed itself to 107,922 million yen in economic assistance to the region, under agreements for cooperation and loans and lines of credit through the Export-Import Bank of Japan.[19] Japan also signed long-term contracts running for as long as a decade and a half to secure iron supplies and other materials.

Futurists such as Herman Kahn foretold the new era of Japan's new reliance on others.[20] Nor was this a static need. As the business cycle periodically swept Japan and companies pressured their workers to enlarge output, the momentary overproduction of goods and capital called for outlets for both. Tremendous sources of unused capital thus jelled with the need to invest in foreign facilities in order to produce raw materials and foods for import, renewing both production and sustaining the population.

Production Myths and Export Successes

Despite the Western myth of Japan's unimpeded successes, Japanese production was periodically cut back as export markets failed or were blocked by Western limitations. During 1961-62 only 79-87 percent of the capacity of Japan's manufacturing facilities were in use; in 1971-72 capacity utilization was 78-84 percent; in 1974-75, 73-82 percent. The myth of undiminished industrial use was meanwhile kept in place by the rise in labor productivity, with the workers increasing output by an annual average of 6.9 percent in the period 1950-60, 10.2 percent between 1960 and 1964, 14.2 percent between 1965 and 1970, and 6-7 percent between 1971 and 1975.

But increased productivity that accompanied periodic idle plant capacity meant that the generation of revenue was not fully utilized for new domestic investment, thereby building up financial resources that required alternative uses. The amount of this available finance had risen from 10,585 billion yen in the fiscal year 1969 to 12,370 billion yen in fiscal 1970, to 14,400 billion yen in fiscal 1971, and to an estimated 29,000 billion yen in fiscal 1975.

Much of this capital was exported, and a growing share was invested in raw material production. Thus between 1951 and 1967 almost 43 percent of all overseas investments were made for the purpose of securing raw materials to be exported to factories located in Japan; and from 1968 to 1974 an estimated 59 percent were made for this purpose. Nations such as Indonesia, Thailand, South Korea, and Taiwan were the destination for this capital, where the cost of production was not only lower than in Japan, but comparable Nippon production of raw materials, food products and light manufactures were not possible, or were not being duplicated, within Japan.[21]

Thus had the first stage of Japan's new entrance to Asia begun.

Capital Dispersion and a Balanced Economy

The next stage was capital dispersion by balancing overseas investments in many geographic areas. Dispersion was designed to act as a
vent for Japan's growing financial surpluses as well as a way to continue
accumulation without fostering an internal crisis within Japan by
overinvestment and, thereby, overproduction.

Japan's internal conundrums had come to the fore. With the combined
pressure of a domestic labor shortage forcing up wages at home and the
growing need to export manufactures to mobilize foreign exchange to pay
for imported raw materials, the leading investors had the resources and the
determination to export up to $2.5 billion a year in long-term capital.
Cheaper labor in Asia was as much their drawing card as the possibility of
importing raw materials and goods manufactured by low-wage workers in
overseas subsidiaries. Thus the domestic labor shortage not only fueled investments in low-wage Pacific Asian nations, but became the basis to create
a new sphere of influence with 200–300 million people to act as both
workers and customers, promising to resolve the question of both too few
workers and too few customers for Japan's production capacity.

With the relative cost of Asian labor at only one-tenth or one-twelfth
the price of labor in Japan, the higher cost of Japanese production was obvious. No doubt, Pacific Asia's potential customer market might be limited.
But, then again, increasing Japanese wages within Japan's high-price
monopsonistic market promised only a small expansion in home consumption. Still, averaging the profits and incomes of the well-to-do with the
small incomes of peasants and workers, relative incomes of the Japanese
were expected to rise faster than those in the non–Communist nations of
Pacific Asia, so that, together, a combination of an expanded market
within Japan and in other Asian markets would provide additional
customers.[22]

Table 6.1
Per Capita and Relative Per Capital Income

Year	Per Capita Income (I) All Non-Communist Pacific Asia	(II) Australia & New Zealand	Relative Per Capita Income (III) Japan	(III) ÷ (I)	(III) ÷ (II)
1970	200	3,000	1,950	9.75	0.65
1980	400	4,500	5,000	12.50	1.11
1990*	800	7,000	10,000	12.50	1.43
2000*	1,600	10,000	20,000	12.50	2.00

* Estimates.

The Genre of Capital Exports

Japan had again learned from the West, this time that capital exports for investment heralded a higher stage of capitalist development than the mere export of commodities or the extension of credit to buyers to pay for them. Historically, such capital outflows represented domestic surplus capital that faced increased costs, taxes, and other disadvantages at home, and sought improved security and/or higher rates of return elsewhere. And facing more powerful capital exporters, weaker nations and their companies had often purchased stock as portfolio investments in the overseas companies of the more powerful.

In part, Japan followed this script, first plowing capital into loans and the companies of others, then setting up their own firms and subsidiaries abroad—the scenario advancing from an emphasis on portfolio investments in the companies of others (1951–55), to an emphasis on both portfolio investments and loans (1956–67), and finally to direct investments abroad (1968–74).[23]

By March 1974 Japan held over ten billion dollars in direct investments abroad, the largest share, 24 percent, being in the United States.

These comprised a new genre of capital exports, concentrated in geographies and spheres compatible with Japan's expansion. From 1951 to 1967 the largest portion of Japan's overseas investments had been placed in the dollar zone in the Americas, with the next largest share in the sterling and franc areas in East and South Asia. By 1969/70 emphasis on North America declined slightly, almost a quarter of Japanese investments going to so-called developing nations, most of them to East and Southeast Asia. These patterns continued into the mid–1970s, with countries on Japan's doorstep becoming an increasingly important domain for investments.[24]

Throughout this quarter century (1951–75), Japan was reestablishing its position as a global power. At first Japan paid for her raw material imports with the excess proceeds of exports that in part were tied to war reparations, then to foreign aid paid in yen, as well as yen-dominated loans and credits. As exports tied to aid were regularized and the Foreign Office *(Gaimusho)* urged Japan to increase to 70 percent the share of foreign aid going to Southeast Asia, Japan reestablished her position in Asia.

Japanese aid rose sharply from $360.7 million in 1964 to $669 million in 1966, $1,049.3 million in 1968, and an estimated $1,400 million in 1970. By mid–1967, Japanese aid to Southeast Asia was nearly on a par with the U.S. aid program (33.5 percent as against the U.S. 35.3 percent of all aid to the region, excluding South Vietnam). Even in the mid–1970s, Japan planned that by the end of the next decade she would enlarge her exports to Southeast Asia by directing 1 percent of her total output—some $5,000 million a year—into economic aid.[25]

Capital Export, Decay, and Accumulation

For lack of a better phrase, Japanese politicians and militarists have traditionally described such redirection of the nation's resources as establishing a *new order.*

By the mid–1970s the chairman of Japan's Economic Council was again emphasizing that "a new order is needed to cope with the changing world economic scene. America has been maintaining world order up till now, but henceforth West Germany and Japan should also participate in the creation of the new order."[26]

The meaning of "the new order" was given content within the next decade as Japan's climb to success began in the late 1970s, reached a momentary high in 1986, and seemed poised to continue to the end of the century.

Japan had entered the stage of its Third Industrial Revolution, advancing beyond the First Revolution of using factory machine tools equipped with the cam system to deliver energy, and the Second Revolution based on a management hierarchy directing the operation of the high-efficiency assembly line, to the next stage requiring a new division of labor and emphasis on R&D — in microelectronics, robotics, new power sources, compound materials, and even bioengineering.

From at least 1980 Japan's basic industries that relied on early stages of industrialization had come under fire from competitors in the NICs, threats by Western nations to close markets to Nippon's goods, and workers' demands for higher wages and lower prices at home. Some critics foretold that, like the United States and Western Europe, Japan would enter a historical stage of "deindustrialization" and "decay," with the decline reflected in massive unemployment, an eroding high-price home market, and pockets of poverty-stricken people the government would have to subsidize. Unlike the situation in the United States, however, Japan's "decay" of old industries was fostered by the government itself! Since the mid–1970s Japan's planners at MITI had foreseen that a new struggle for technological excellence, altered labor functions, advanced raw materials and energy sources, and then-unknown means of transport would change the face of the world economy.

To lay Japan's foundation for the new era, from 1975 to 1988 the MITI put up substantial shares of the development costs for consortia studying ceramics, giant integrated circuits and software applications, robotics, communications using fiber optics, new steel technologies, laser and nuclear energy, bullet train and supersonic transport, engine and thermo-dynamic missile systems, superconductive compound materials, and a whole range of other high-tech materials.[27]

The lead time to transform these investments into commercial products varied, but the plans laid by MITI were designed to turn Japan into a high-tech nation at the same time old, basic industries and their technologies were operated at lower capacity levels within Japan *and* were exported to other nations, especially to the third world. What would suddenly appear as "decay" of these old industries within Japan would thus be the planned realignment of Japan's technical capital on a global scale, and the reorganization of the division of labor between high-tech Japanese workers and lower-level production workers outside of Japan. Japan would either export the previous stages of industrial technology to buyers elsewhere, or invest in the latest technical equipment at home or in wholly-owned Japanese subsidiaries abroad. In each case, the export of Japanese-produced technology would increase, creating the base for extended domestic employment that, in turn, would be added to the employment of high-tech workers in Japan's newest industries.[28] Or, Japan would use other nations on the technological cutting edge as the jump-off point for production and global marketing.

Japan's New Domestic Underclass

Large sums of Japanese investment capital might be used to upgrade domestic technology or be sent abroad to employ workers elsewhere. Yet there were still manual, physically dirty, jobs in Japan that Japanese workers shunned, but foreign workers sought at higher wages than they could earn in their own, native countries.

For decades, Thai and Philippine women had been sent to Japan to work in sleazy nightclubs, for example. And in 1987 the majority of illegal immigrants were still young Philippine women who were exploited by the operators of the sex and entertainment industries. The flow of illegal immigrant *Japayuki-san* — or "Japan-bound people" — remained about 76 percent of the total inflow in the 1980s. But the overall inflow enlarged as Japan became a nation of high wages, labor shortages, and a strong currency. In 1987 wages in Japan were ten times those in the Philippines for unskilled work. Thus, foreign, darker-skinned workers sought work in small factories, restaurants, construction jobs, shipyards, kitchens, and bars. They became an underclass, fitting into the ideological prescriptions of Japan's sense of racial superiority. "We don't like to see our social conditions — our working-class conditions — filled with particular foreigners as we see in some European countries," said Ishigaki Yasuji, a senior official in the Justice Ministry's Immigration Bureau, referring to Asian immigrants as well as Pakistanis, Bengalis, and others. "We learned lessons from the European experience."[29]

Yet the inflow of foreigners was sometimes tolerated by officialdom. Service and construction industries already faced a labor shortage of about 7 percent in 1986, a shortfall that foreign workers helped relieve. And in 1988 some 100,000 illegal aliens were in Japan washing dishes, sweeping streets, collecting garbage, packing seafood — and threatening local labor markets. "Japanese don't want to do this kind of work anymore," explained a small employer worried about work continuity in packing clams for local distribution. "They won't work on holidays. But I still have clams to deliver." Older Japanese cast blame on the nation's new wealth and claimed that it was eroding the value placed on hard work, discipline, company loyalty, and proud labor. More accurately, though, some policy makers contended that if Japan was to avoid the social costs of bringing in foreign labor, Japanese employers would have to pay higher wages to induce more Japanese workers to perform the menial jobs taken by the foreigners.[30]

For money was *the issue* among small-business employers, who viewed inexpensive foreign workers as their only hope of staying afloat. While big employers could move plants to Taiwan, Singapore, Thailand, or the Philippines to take advantage of cheaper labor, small businesses were immobile and locked into paying higher Japanese wages. "If small businesses can't hire foreign workers, they will go out of business," reported Kawano Yoshihisa, president if KSP, a small printing company in Tokyo.

To the small firms, the government's plan to shut out unskilled foreign workers thus appeared as blatantly pro-big business. The immigration authorities stepped up deportations of alleged violators, who in 1987 increased 33.6 percent to 14,129 from the previous year. Japan's Labor Ministry obliquely argued that Japan should increase aid to developing nations to relieve the pressure on unskilled workers to seek jobs in Japan. Others wanted to shift the penalties from the illegal workers to the hiring employer, as was done in the U.S. in 1987-88.[31]

But the basic need for cheap foreign labor, both within and outside Japan, was the only way in which certain firms and capitals would survive the state-designed reorganization of the nation's infrastructure, work force, and consumer markets.

Japan's Global Division of Labor

The central issue was the government's planned destruction of small businesses by supporting a wage floor that would: (1) promote the new demand-led domestic economy; (2) ultimately systematize big capital and cheap labor in the abandoned or partially vacant industries; (3) maintain Japan's so-called cultural homogeneity and social harmony; and (4) keep Japan at a high level of skills, while capital requiring lesser skilled jobs were sent abroad — not enlarged in Japan proper.

Within Japan, old skills were being undermined by advancing technologies that impacted what once were human functions. At the lower reaches of marketing, technology was being mobilized to run every conceivable kind of vending machine — from distributing candy and soda to computer software, condoms, pearls, and pornography — thereby replacing unskilled labor. Capital had organized handyman agencies to provide services such as shopping, detective work, shooting home movies of sexual encounters, or playing soccer with a client's children.[32]

The era of Japan's technical, global investments had also been driven forward with its accompanying functional division of labor. Export capital was certainly not new to Nippon. But in both purpose and scale the new export was different — designed, for example, to secure manufactured consumer goods and steel from the NICs in Asia; crude resources and markets from Latin America, Pacific nations, and the rest of Asia; and raw materials, market shares, and financial returns from the United States and Western Europe.

Treating the world as its investment sphere, Japan's policies were now on a par with those of the U.S. and Western Europe in fostering a new allotment of work roles, a new division of labor, and, consequently, a new third world dilemma.[33]

In the second half of the 1970s Nippon also began what England had accomplished in the 19th century and the U.S. and Germany copied in the early 20th: to export an increasing proportion of its wares in the form of technology and means of production as distinguished from the export of consumer manufactures. Britain's classic shift in the core of industrial capitalism from Manchester (a textile center) to Birmingham (a steel complex) was reflective of maintaining textiles as its largest single export, yet adding to the outgo of Birmingham steel products the export of machines and factories, themselves representing the means of production.[34] Japan's shift of production was less spatially oriented within Japan and more designed for global operations. True enough, the main thrust of exports from production facilities within Japan would likely continue to be consumer manufactures in the late 1980s and early 1990s. But there would also be a significant rise in the export of Japanese-made machines for working metal products or constructing motor vehicles, and the components of factories or the whole factories themselves.

Machine technology, representing an inferior stage to that used within Japan, would continue to be exported as the basis of Japanese investment capital to the third world, especially to nations of the Pacific Basin, Southeast Asia, and Latin America. By the late 1970s Japan already concentrated over half of its exports of machines to third world nations, outstripping the U.S. orientation to export less than a third to such countries — because American creditors believed that these countries were unreliable debtors. By the late 1980s Japan's largest companies focused on such markets as more important than barrier-ridden America.

Yet, toward the U.S., Japan remained flexible. "It is a strategy of the Japanese to enter corporate alliances [with U.S. companies] to head off protectionism," Nomura Research Institute vice-president Takahashi Yoshindo bluntly said in August 1986. And so long as the threat of more tariff and investment barriers persisted, Japanese companies would likely maintain this posture.[35]

Yet, like U.S. corporate capital exports used to set up wholly owned subsidiaries in the 1960s and 1970s, Japanese capital exports in the 1980s stressed *direct controls* over the production operations of its subsidiaries.[36] Such exports had several dimensions, one being the high cost of operating basic industries within Japan, leading to the move to offshore facilities at a rate faster than the U.S. had moved its production overseas during 1971–86. Japanese investments in the U.S. from 1962 to 1987 were more than 90 percent majority interests.

Consumer markets in some third world nations were also expanding more rapidly than in the U.S. or Western Europe during the early 1980s, and Japan's export of manufactures, machines, and whole factories set the frame to fill these markets. Not only did Japan maintain full employment by producing older technologies for sale to, say, Mexico, but in some cases large Japanese companies owned these foreign-based production facilities, serviced local markets, and exported the balance to other nations, including the United States and Western Europe.[37]

Shunto, Wages, and the New Consumerism

By the late 1980s Japan also began to accelerate the export of heavy industrial equipment and newer technologies. The motive was obvious. Western protectionism blocked its commodity exports, and Japan's escalating home prices had increased the cost of living to the point where labor's demand for higher wages increased the basic cost of production above that of competitor nations.

Thanks to the strong yen, by the end of 1987 Japan's organized labor unions' thirty-three-year-old focus on higher wages had essentially been achieved, making Japanese hourly wages the industrial world's highest in dollar terms. Since its initiation in the mid–1950s, the slogan of the labor unions' *shunto* spring offensive had been "Win Western-Level Wages." Yet *shunto* under the leadership of the unions in the wealthiest industries meant simultaneous negotiations in all industries for high wages, neglecting the complaints at the local level concerning speedups, unpaid labor time, delayed wage payments, unjust firing, and similar concerns. Manual workers at the plant level were the most neglected.[38] Nonetheless, the gap between wages in the small and middle-size firms compared with the great companies had been narrowed.

In 1986, before the yen began its ethereal climb, Japanese manual workers had an average wage per hour of 1,480 yen ($11.37 at February 1988 exchange rates) as compared with 1,640 yen ($12.59) for U.S. workers. But by February 1988 the tables had turned: the *Nikkeiren,* or Japan Federation of Employers Associations, reported that U.S. hourly workers were earning only 83 percent of those of Japanese workers and 89 percent of the wages of West Germans.[39]

Such relatively higher wages meant in part that Japanese industries lost competitiveness, becoming a force of investment export that forwarded deindustrialization, and "hollowed out" key sectors in steel, shipbuilding, and consumer electronics. Companies like Matsushita, the world's largest electronics producer, exporting heavily to the West under brand names like National and Panasonic, now took the path of most of America's five hundred largest corporations: exporting production operations, shipping direct to customers in the United States, in other markets, and even back in Japan.

Japan thereby joined the leading Western nations in building an exogenous economy dependent on making investments in production operations abroad. By the early 1980s about 70 percent of manufacturing income in Japan, like that in West Germany, Britain, and the United States, was already being generated by their respective transnational enterprises that *simultaneously* operated at home and abroad.[40] Matsushita's offshore production provided a prime example, comprising about 12 percent of its total output in 1985, but surging to an estimated 25 percent by the close of 1987! A similar path was being followed by other companies: they closed operations within Japan, began manufacturing abroad under indigenous nationalist-titled companies using new brand names, and exported from these locations to markets in many places.

Japanese transnationals maintained tight control of their overseas operations, though these were named in the script and expression of the locale of operations and thus outwardly appeared to be owned and controlled by, say, South Koreans or Taiwanese nationals. These Nippon enterprises quickly acquired the savvy needed to use many points on the compass as planning, designing, producing, distributing, and marketing zones. "The auto marques that had the most robust growth in the 1986 U.S. markets were Honda and Hyundai's Excel," wrote management consultant Peter F. Drucker, who then pointed out the forces behind Japan's capital export boom:

> The Excel, although made in South Korea with domestic labor, is Japanese-designed, has a Japanese engine, and is made by an affiliate of Japan's Mitsubishi. Honda's entire additional U.S. volume was supplied by its plant in Marysville, Ohio. The minicompact that Ford is planning to introduce this year in the U.S. market as its answer to Honda and Hyundai was designed by Mazda's Japanese engineers. But it is being made for Mazda in South Korea. Planners in many other companies expect Japanese-owned plants inside the Common Market, primarily in Spain, to supply half their companies' sales in Western Europe within five or six years.[41]

It was in part Japan's emplacement in many centers that determined its competitive lead. Japanese automakers appeared to be fragmented, moving with hell-to-leather competitive determination at home and toughened for competitiveness abroad. But it was illusory to think that determination and not scale of production was the primary quotient of success.[42] For Japanese firms, scale of production represented technological power, worker resources, and marketing strength—not the shifting of pieces of paper representing mere ownership or control.

MITI had also pushed large companies into consortium that together incorporated third world markets, supply centers, and labor forces into a planned prosperity sphere for Japan. Framed by this emergent sphere of influence, just as fast as Nippon firms found their costs rising and their old technologies becoming unprofitable at home, they moved these same technologies to production bases in South Korea or Hong Kong, while simultaneously turning to the latest technical methods and highest work skills for production within Japan.[43] Obviously, workers in industrial nations were no longer the only ones capable of operating and repairing the sophisticated equipment in modern factories. That skill had spread to many developing nations, where wages were far lower than in the United States, Western Europe, and Japan.[44]

By the late 1980s, high costs of materials, energy, and labor in Japan—and the high prices of its exports—had fueled the export of production operations. Drucker noted that the fall in the dollar to about 160 yen in early 1987 meant that already Honda's costs in Ohio were probably below costs in Japan. Similarly, Matsushita's semiconductor plant in Texas and its huge TV and VCR plant in Hamburg, West Germany, likely had lower costs than the company's plants near Osaka.[45]

Planned by MITI in collaboration with the great companies, the export of production had not taken on life without a projected model of the future. Negotiations were made by great companies like Fujitsu using their own in-house attorneys. Foreign attorneys were consulted on ways to expand overseas markets and real estate holdings. U.S. lawyers permitted by Japan's new 1987 law to advise clients on the laws of their home states of New York, California, Hawaii, Michigan, and the District of Columbia, immediately received attention from the elite of corporate Japan including major banks, life insurance companies, and manufacturers of cars, computers, and televisions such as Fujitsu, N.E.C., Dai Ichi Life Insurance, Japan Air Lines, Orient Leasing, Nissan, Bank of Tokyo, Sony, Nippon Life, and Sumitomo Trust Bank.

"Often, these companies need foreign expertise on technical money matters or trade problems, like how to deal with an antidumping suit brought in the United States," one 1988 report noted. "More and more, however, attention is being focused on real estate, especially in the United States, where in the last year alone [1987] Japanese investors increased their property portfolios by an estimated $12.5 billion." And though they had done relatively little to help U.S. companies increase their access to Japanese markets and were not permitted to even discuss Japanese law, U.S. attorneys were willing charges. "As the world shifts toward Asia, we must shift as well," said Japan-based Robert T. Greig, a partner of New York's Cleary, Gottlieb, Steen, and Hamilton. "How can you be a preeminent international law firm in 1988 and not have an office in Tokyo?"[46]

As the steady drive to export capital continued, Japan's corporate accumulation was gradually being balanced and stabilized. New pressures were also building up, as the export of financial resources and production bred the repatriation of profits and the accumulation of additional sums of capital. In 1987 alone, Japan's big investors stepped up their buying of foreign stocks and bonds, and overseas assets climbed more than $300 billion — to make up a more than $1 trillion total, $240 billion of which was net of foreign debts. Looser overseas regulations on raising money abroad also made Japan a heavier borrower of $250 billion in 1987, so that the year's net difference of investment and borrowing was about $50–60 billion. But with profits repatriated or reinvested abroad, these extended Japan's overseas infrastructure and fed further capital exports — as well as conspicuous consumption within Japan and an overly inflated stock market.

Then in fiscal 1988 Japanese direct investment overseas surged another 50 percent to $33.36 billion. The U.S. and Canada accounted for the lion's share, with 46 percent, followed by Europe with 20 percent, Asia with 14.6 percent, and Central and Latin America with 14.4 percent.[47]

Corporate Japan was doing well in its new spheres of influence, as exogenous accumulation went forward and, from within the nation and without, big Japanese industries laid the foundation for new employment and social relations — regardless of the consequence for other industries, workers, and consumers within Japan.

Chapter 7

The Dynamics of Capital Exports

*When [Japan's] Bridgestone buys Firestone
and Sony buys part of CBS, Japan calls it "internationalization."*
*I recently asked a senior Japanese official
what they would call it if Firestone were buying Bridgestone and CBS were buying Sony.
And, remembering back to his youth, he said,
"Well, I guess that would be a lot like the
[U.S.] Occupation."* — Clyde Prestowitz,
author of *Trading Places*[1]

The export of capital by any nation presupposes the financial resources to
send this capital elsewhere. Classical theory assumed that capital export
would take place when there was a "glut" of domestic financial resources
or when great economic institutions, such as trusts and monopolies, sought
greater rates of return by sending capital to low-wage areas or regions
where certain essential resources could be found (or products fabricated)
and then sold at high prices in the metropole.

Japan's drive to export financial resources has followed this theoretical
scenario, and, in addition, balanced capital outflows with the degree to
which world markets could or were willing to absorb commodity exports
that themselves were a direct consequence of reinvestment of capital in
Japan's domestic production facilities. There was one difference in the
Japanese dynamic of capital exports, however: deindustrialization that
fostered domestic decay of technical capital and unemployment was
directed by the state, which meanwhile promoted a new stage of technology
and its corresponding skills.

The 1980s were the critical years for Japan's overseas investments.
Rather than being a mere commodity exporter, Japan had become a capital
exporter by mobilizing the vast financial resources that it had not needed
to pay for imports and would not make available to the nation's working
population for consumption.

Between 1978 and 1986 the number of Japanese enterprises investing
abroad enlarged from 887 to 1,419. Even smaller companies saw an oppor-

tunity to invest abroad. Capitalized at less than 100 million yen ($769,000 at the exchange rate of $1 = Y130) or with less than three hundred workers, the number of minor companies investing abroad increased more than threefold from 306 (accounting for 34 percent of all investments) in 1978 to 599 (42.2 percent) in 1986—then surged to 1,063 in 1987.[2]

Table 7.1
History of Japanese Enterprise Overseas Investment: 1978-87

Years	All Enterprises	Minor Enterprises	Minor Manufacturing Enterprises
1978	887*	306 (36.4%)**	112 (12.6%)
1979	990	437 (44.1)	133 (13.4)
1980	790	326 (41.2)	99 (12.5)
1981	748	336 (44.9)	108 (14.4)
1982	765	247 (32.2)	86 (11.2)
1983	868	306 (35.2)	94 (11.3)
1984	828	312 (37.6)	109 (13.1)
1985	1,023	318 (31.0)	137 (13.3)
1986	1,419	599 (42.2)	279 (19.6)
1987	— —	1,063 (— —)	469 (— —)

* Number of investments.
** Percentage with respect to all investments for the same year.
Source: Figure 2-1-24, *White Paper on Small and Medium Enterprises,* edited by Small and Medium Enterprises Agency, published by Ministry of Finance, 1988.

By the mid-1980s the focus of Japan's overseas investments was still maximizing earnings on foreign bonds, rather than direct investments, loans, portfolio stocks, or other forms of securities. At least this was so in 1985 and 1986.

Table 7.2
The Content and Transitions of Long-term Capital Investments

Types of Investment	1985	1986	1987	Increase 85–86	Increase[1] 86–87
Balance of Long-term Capital Payments*	73,177	144,680	32,208	97%	69%
Japanese Capital Investment	92,390	144,461	37,515	56	49
(1) Direct Investment	7,592	15,196	3,136	100	29
(2) Long-term Credit	2,063	1,369	736	-33	-5
(3) Loan	8,631	12,211	4,481	41	188
(4) Securities Investment	71,023	110,099	27,716	55	41

Types of Investment	1985	1986	1987	Increase 85–86	Increase[1] 86–87
a. Stocks	1,748	10,755	4,539	515	445
b. Bonds	63,493	98,965	23,202	55	34
c. Foreign Loans	5,782	379	199	93	– 87
(5) Others	3,081	5,586	1,800	81	132

[1] Comparisons of first quarter differences for both 1986 and 1987.
* In million dollars.
Source: Tables I–2–15, *White Paper on Japanese Economy,* published by Economic Planning Agency, 1988.

Geographically, from 1980 to 1986 Japan had first concentrated its investments in North America, then the newly industrialized Asian nations, and finally Europe. But the smaller enterprises that invested abroad switched their focus from North America to the NICs between 1980 and 1987 — lessening their interests in Hong Kong and emphasizing Taiwan and suddenly South Korea.[3]

Table 7.3
Content of Japanese Overseas Investments

Areas	All Enterprises			Minor Enterprises		
	1980	1985	1986	1980	1985	1987[1]
Asian NICs +	19.7%	13.7%	16.8%	30.1%	45.6%	44.6%
1. South Korea	– –	– –	– –	1.8	9.7	10.8
2. Hong Kong	– –	– –	– –	8.5	4.7	6.0
3. Taiwan	– –	– –	– –	8.6	3.8	11.2
ASEAN Nations*	9.7	7.0	5.7	11.3	27.4	16.6
Other Asian Nations	0.9	4.5	3.1	– –	– –	– –
North America	41.2	36.8	40.2	54.3	44.3	42.8
Europe	14.9	12.0	12.6	8.0	5.7	4.9
Other Areas	17.4**	25.0	21.6	7.7	4.4	7.7

+ The breakdown for three NICs nations.
* The figures for minor enterprises preclude the investment in other Asian Nations.
** The total does not add up to 100 percent due to rounding errors.
[1] Comparisons of first-quarter differences for both 1986 and 1987.

Source: Tables 2–1–26, *White Paper on Small and Medium Enterprises,* edited by Small and Medium Enterprises Agency, published by Ministry of Finance, 1988.

The managers of Japanese companies also verbalized their reasons for investing abroad. The greatest concern among both major and minor enterprises for investments in Asia, North America, and the European Common

Market was to market within the target nation or in surrounding nations. Japan not only feared that U.S. and Common Market tariffs and restrictions would eventually block their exports, but in Asia too the logic of production outside Japan was that it would facilitate marketing in the country of production and contiguous areas.

The minor enterprises that concentrated on the NICs and Asia placed greater emphasis on a cheaper labor force than the major enterprises. Marketing to meet consumer needs was also a significant item on the agenda of both major and minor Japanese companies, considered almost twice as important for dealing in the North American and European markets as the Asian one. Minor enterprises were more concerned than the majors about centralizing overseas information, especially in the industrialized West. And meeting business partner or parental company requests drew more major than minor companies to invest in the West and to a lesser degree Asia.

There were other reasons for investments abroad, particularly in Asia: the cultivation of overseas markets; cheap raw materials; evading the risk of changing exchange rates; and tax law advantages. Large companies were more concerned than small ones with trade frictions, strengthening their financial organizations, and acquiring technical know-how, particularly in the West.[4]

Table 7.4
Reasons for Japanese Overseas Investment

Reasons	Major Enterprises	Minor Enterprises	All Asia	N. America* & EC
1. Marketability in Target or Surrounding Nations	54.3%	51.5%	60.0%	53.8%
2. Cheap Labor Force	22.3	39.4	50.0	7.7
3. Greater Consumer Needs	33.0	30.3	22.0	41.5
4. Centralization of Overseas Information	23.4	27.3	20.0	27.7
5. Invitation from the Investing Nation	8.0	18.2	10.0	6.2
6. Business Partners' or Parental Company's Request	21.3	15.2	16.0	26.2
7. Cultivation of Overseas Markets	12.8	15.2	18.0	12.3
8. Cheap Raw Materials	12.8	12.1	14.0	10.8
9. Risk-Evasion of Changing Exchange Rates	17.0	9.1	18.0	13.8

Reasons	Major Enterprises	Minor Enterprises	All Asia	N. America* & EC
10. Advantages in Tax Laws	5.3%	9.1%	8.0%	4.6%
11. Strengthen Financial Organization	11.7	9.1	6.0	12.3
12. Trade Frictions	16.0	6.1	14.0	15.4
13. Technical Know-How	5.3	6.1	0.0	9.2
14. Others	4.3	12.1	10.0	3.1

* North America.
Source: Tables 2–1–25, *White Paper on Small and Medium Enterprises,* edited by Small and Medium Enterprises Agency, published by Ministry of Finance, 1988.

The timing of overseas investments was also closely entwined with changes in exchange rates starting in 1985. As the yen sharply appreciated against the dollar and European currencies, Japanese investments that could now be made cheaply surged in these areas. Third world currencies that were meanwhile depreciated against the dollar were now doubly depreciated against the yen, so that by April 1987, for example, the Mexican peso collapsed to 17 percent of its February 1985 value, making Japanese investments in Mexican *maquiladora* plants very inexpensive.[5]

At first, the currencies of the NICs were kept in line with the dollar, giving the Japanese with their appreciated yen a new advantage to cheaply buy production facilities and assets. But during 1987 the United States realigned these currencies to stimulate the NICs imports of U.S.-made goods, also increasing the cost of U.S. and, to a lesser degree, Japanese investments in this region.

Japan now held a relative advantage for exporting capital to the NICs, the rest of Asia, and the West. It also held the resources to export investment capital to the collapsing wing of Communist nations in Eastern Europe, as a potential locale for production using the world's cheapest skilled labor and within reach of a massive market in Europe both east and west.

Part 4:
Technology and the End
of American Self-Sufficiency

America faces a technological dilemma: it invents, but does not always first use what it invents; it fosters the scientific breakthrough, but it frequently does not finance the mass production of this breakthrough that could mobilize equipment and materials and sustain armies of technical, production, and service workers.

Unlike past scientific advantages that reached the production line and electrified the economy, the present U.S. lag in basic technological applications is holding back production. This is reflected in the decline of agriculture, mining, and basic industries, as well as in high-tech and service sectors; and it is relayed in the gyrations of the nation's employment, the quality of methods of work, and a downward trend in the general scale of wages.

What exactly is the source of America's dilemma? Is it inherent to the present stage of its development? And, if a cure is feasible, will it be used under the constraints of high production costs, intense world competition, and extension of the global economy?

Chapter 8
High-Tech in Crisis: Decay as an Historical Dilemma

One answer hinges on the fact that the nonsocialist world is undergoing a transformation of the foundations for competition, as earlier methods offering security to leading nations in production and trade have given way to the unhindered acquisition and use of the most modern technology by other nations who are able to lower costs and realign production relations. In trying to protect their competitive position, leading nations have moved to reorganize capital, relocate production, reassemble the technical methods of production, restructure and segment the labor force, and reallot and expand markets.

All these changes are phases of the same process: global competition breeds advances in technical means of production and changes in the spatial location of investment assets, the methods of production, and realization of profits.

Microwhiz on Back Burner

Like all technical revolutions driven by competition and unequal advantages, today's transformations in microtechnology require *intensive* research, trial and error using previously untested techniques, and new or enhanced materials and energy sources. These are inextricably linked to experimental methods and skills, as well as to costly investments and the application of materials that may possibly become the source of still unknown processes and products.

"Advanced materials, specialty polymers, ceramics, are the absolute core to advanced technologies in the future," testifies Massachusetts Institute of Technology professor Ken Brown. "Whoever wins the game has the jobs, sells the cars, the machinery, the electronics, because they can design far beyond people who have only plain vanilla materials."[1]

At the heart of the microtechnological surge are the prospects for reducing competitive production costs. Not only does the present miniaturization of applied science hold the potential to cut costs of materials, energy, labor, but reduced scales will likely facilitate quality controls that in turn may speed production and enhance the uniformity of output, cutting costs again. And yet American industry tends to stall at the point of *applying inventive breakthroughs* to mass production and the formulation of new tasks of manufacturing, shaping and expanding the market, and serving customers.

"There is altogether no more reliable early warning of a company's imminent decline than a sharp and persistent drop in its standing as a successful innovator," writes management expert Peter F. Drucker. "And equally dangerous is a deterioration in innovative lead-time, that is, in the time between the inception of an innovation and its introduction as a successful product or service in the market."[2]

In the heat of intense foreign competition, America has tried to synchronize its industrial planning for both innovation and lead time. The present reassembly of U.S. capital has taken place by means of long-term investment in automation using robots driven by computers, as well as by the segmentation of the remaining labor force into high-paid experts on one side and functionally trained, lesser-paid employees on the other. The results are seen in more than just technological advance and a new division of labor.

One example: managers at Black and Decker transformed their relations with the factory work force by using automated machines to speed up the introduction of new product lines, reducing the time cycle from initial development to production from about five years to less than three—thereby cutting costs, lowering prices, and shielding profit margins. Similarly, Xerox Corporation managers cut the time between research product development and market introduction from more than five years to two, used the new technology and processes to speed up production, and offered line-workers incentives to cut the defect rate from 8,000 to 1,300 units per one million.[3]

Beyond the individual company, when an industry or an entire economy suffers deterioration in basic research, experimentation, and innovative lead-time, such deterioration signals competitive decline, neglect of fields of output, and the erosion of the foundation for the accumulation of profit.[4]

U.S. industries have fallen further behind by not stressing R&D in agriculture, steel, and other basic industries. The overview for America is this: the research explosion pushed up spending from $20.1 billion in 1965 to $35.2 billion in 1975, and to an estimated $108.8 billion in 1985. Yet the funds devoted to U.S. *basic research* have perennially been the smallest (1965: $2.6 billion; 1975: $4.6 billion; 1985: $13.3 billion), followed by *applied research* (1965: $4.3 billion; 1975: $7.9 billion; 1985: $23.9 billion), with the lion's share going to *product development* (1965: $13.2 billion; 1975: $22.7 billion; 1985: $71.6 billion). That is, in 1965 funds allocated for production-line development of variations of existing technology were more than twice as much as those allocated for basic and applied research; and in both 1975 and 1985 the first was still far greater than, though less than twice, the second and third.[5]

Commercial R&D concerns that neglect basic research and concentrate on product development receive far more funding than scientific, academic research efforts. The American university system has traditionally concentrated on *basic research* and its *experimental application,* rather than its *commercial form,* the respective allocation of university R&D funding being percentages of 67, 27, and 6 in 1986.[6]

Yet academicians have had to learn fast and hard that their research results will be appropriated by universities and industries for profit goals, and that grant money is available to them for marketable work on the ratio of something like one dollar in grants producing forty dollars in basic research value. University researchers are thus low-price labor. They either accept this status in their desperation for research funds, or reject the tension of being driven by grantors demanding rapid development for on-line production that is out of step with the process and ethos of thorough intellectual investigation.[7]

Indeed, industry looks for research that can be applied experimentally, then put on the production line as soon as possible. So the priorities are different in the sphere of production for markets, where the 1986 R&D budgetary allocations were spent 4 percent on basic research, 20 percent on applied experimentation, and 76 percent on development of marketable products. Government R&D funds are allocated similarly, mostly development and applied trial and error, not basic research—the 1986 estimated figures being respectively 64, 22 and 14 percent.

It follows that industrial application is also greatest where government foots the bill: for military aircraft and missiles (where the state funded 78 percent in 1975 and 76 percent a decade later in 1985); for electrical equipment (45 percent and 40 percent respectively); for machinery (16 percent and 14 percent); for motor vehicles and equipment (14 percent for both years); and for chemicals and related products (9 percent and 3 percent).

The overall results have been an economy skewed toward military production and subsidized more for on-line production of previously known technologies, rather than basic research and experimentation application.

Comparative, Competitive, R&D

The flip side of decline caused by such endogenous neglect is relative backwardness bred by *foreign appropriation.* Fact: Japan and West Germany have taken the best technology the U.S. can offer. Scholars and technicians like MIT's Professor Bowen worry that the Japanese are appropriating superior American science and applying it faster than are American companies.[8]

Zeroing in on applying quality American research, experimentation, and development, Japan has added to its own accumulated technical knowledge. With a vastly larger economy and a greater proportion of output devoted to R&D, the U.S. pool of know-how is the largest in the nonsocialist world. Indeed, as a proportion of GNP, U.S. spending gyrated between 2.25 and 3 percent between 1961 and 1985, while only West Germany momentarily exceeded that proportion (reaching over 2.5 percent) of its own, significantly smaller GNP between 1977 and 1982. Looking back to 1961–62, both Japanese and West German spending on R&D was less than 1.5 percent of their respective GNP figures, raising them in 1982 to par with the U.S. (at 2.5 percent), and continuing thereafter at about the same percentage level.

The fact remains that the U.S. economy is larger, so even an equal percentage investment by other nations of their own GNP means America puts far more capital into research, experimentation, and on-line production development. Comparatively, the U.S. is the leading spender on R&D, though its *civilian* research and development expenditures in mid–1988 were about a percentage point *below* those of Germany or Japan (1.8 percent vs. 2.8 percent of their respective GNP). When *military* research was included, the U.S. spent about the same fraction of GNP, but American spin-offs from the military did not compensate for the effects of the extra 1 percent of GNP going directly to civilian R&D in Germany and Japan.[9]

The U.S. was going into the hole for military R&D that did not benefit its *competitive place* in basic understanding, experimentation, or application to civilian-oriented production.

Some Win, Some Lose

Of course, American R&D expenditures have produced significant production breakthroughs.

In the automation of processes that increase speed, cut costs, and displace laborers who once performed functions that have now become technical or mechanical operations, there are unnumbered individual success stories. Affirmation of America's technological strength comes, for instance, from companies that have developed "machine vision" apparatus that can "see" at high speed small changes in the surface of fruit or manufactured parts, where tiny flaws vital to marketing or performance are hard to detect. The machine's practical uses include finding the glitches in catheters, grading beams, and examining everything from fruit surfaces to molded rubber O-rings.

These machines have reached the expanding market for "vision systems" that guide machines and automate inspection. Yet short-term profits must be forthcoming or start-up companies producing such machines do not have the resources to last long.

Because the costs of installing such systems are high, industrial consumers will not buy them unless they can foresee a cost advantage. The still limited market has caused intense competition among equipment makers, moreover, taking the form of large investments to develop the specialized, product-designated computer hardware. Here computers are designed to fit the mathematical descriptions of the vision task (i.e., comparing standard features of objects with the actual items to be judged), so as to predesignate the algorithmic path to be taken. The result is the computerized enhancement of robotic speed, making the operation 9,000 times faster, so it takes one-tenth of a second to analyze images that contain several objects.[10]

In contrast, the breakdown in bringing inventions to the production line shows up clearly among U.S. chemical producers. Though breakthrough technologies may exist, costly development of new materials are initially based on hand labor and, in the short run, often are not returned by sales to industrial users. Ceramics were developed by such firms as W.R. Grace & Co., which then backed out of production in 1972, just as demand for such materials by electronics producers was starting—and later rose to $660 million in annual U.S. sales. Supercomputers produced by firms like Cray Research today rely on advanced ceramics to dissipate heat and speed the flow of data; and tomorrow all-ceramic car engines that can run better than metal motors will likely yield fuel savings up to 30 percent.

Which nation's firms would produce these ceramics was in part decided in 1981, when Japan pushed into the field, moving from the production of low-tech scissors and sushi knives into complicated multilayer capacitors. This advanced ceramic component for computers established a tenfold lead in the number of new patents Japan filed and enabled Nippon to gain control of 50 percent of the $4.1 billion annual worldwide advanced ceramics market.[11]

Because these capacitors are multilayered, they act as the crucial advanced ceramic parts for lightning-fast computers. Not only can ceramic parts run at hotter temperatures than known materials, but they dissipate heat and speed the flow of data that makes possible consecutive machine functions without the intervention of human labor. In the continuous processing from raw materials to manufactured goods, these high-speed computers facilitate the replacement of human labor functions, define the design patterns of commodities, and expedite the mobilization of the technical instruments of production.

Enter the State

In forwarding such technical advances, the state has been mobilized by various forces. In modern times, governments elected by coalitions of various classes have determined the place and role of intervention applied to production, thereby also mediating the ways in which capital and labor resolve questions of on-the-job controls and the division of the workers' new output. The uncertain path from the earliest laboratory bench work and the modern garage research center to market application has been both impeded and accelerated by state policies, which can withdraw or mobilize capital for technical application to mass production. Intellectual passion may be the mother of inventive triumphs, and capital may be the guiding hand for putting it to the test, but state stimulation carries invention more quickly to the commercial product stage.[12]

Today this has been accelerated by state intervention to subsidize new technical methods, so old industries like textiles will not be wiped out by lower-cost imports and can reassert command of domestic and foreign markets. The state effectively links the mobilization of capital to upgrade automated systems and the development of products made by a favored work force. Thereby the resources of the state provide the technological boost to establish a near market-monopoly within which labor is guaranteed secure employment.

The framework is today's global struggle to automate production in order to lower costs and maintain competitive selling prices. Those nations that neglect to advance to the age of computer-directed robots will be outflanked in the market and lose their basic industries. As a 1986 example, governments in the U.S., Western Europe, and Japan all aided automation of the textile industry. The Japanese Ministry of International Trade and Industry planned to spend $8.1 million over eight years to help twenty-nine Japanese spinning, weaving, sewing machine, and electronic firms develop an automated sewing system by 1990. With such aid, from computer design to inspection, robots would run operations, saving Japan's entire industry. "If we can't get automation under our belts, our textile and garment industries will go into decay," concluded Yamaoka Takeo, president of Japan's Tokyo Juki Industrial Co.[13]

The same process of government aid was taking place in the Common Market and the U.S. State national projects were designed to forward robotic production, to turn the latest technology over to national firms, to keep both research and patents secret, and to stop their export—à la England's competitive prohibitions before 1825, when Britain was the workshop of the world.[14]

Yet the U.S. may not be in charge of producing for export the very microtechnology it invents. One cause is the federal government's restrictions on high-tech exports that keep U.S. companies out of foreign markets. Fears that others will obtain military secrets, military technology, or competitive models has worked to the detriment of free trade and a favorable trade balance.

Faced with these limits, companies like America's United Technology have called for aggressive penetration of foreign markets and renewal of the U.S. *Open Door Policy.* "U.S. industry," United Technology says, "has relied too heavily on the huge domestic market. Exports account for only

9% of the U.S. Gross National Product. This compares to 16% for Japan and 22 to 35% for Canada, France, Italy, Britain, and West Germany." United adds that "We must also be alert to U.S. government policies that make it difficult for American companies to grow internationally," especially in forming joint ventures and other partnerships with foreign companies, making the sharing of U.S. technology essential. "Protectionist policies that restrict exports of technology discourage efforts to capitalize on global business opportunities," it says. "Unnecessary restrictions on technology transfer undermine economic growth and weaken national defense."[15] Only in early 1990 did the U.S. government relent a little, freeing up the export of computer technologies to Eastern Europe.

The federal tax policy of 1987 had also refused advantages to financially risky, long-term venture capital designed to promote domestic technical breakthroughs. U.S. tax increases on capital gains, making them pay the same rate as other income (rising from maximum rates of 20 percent from 1981–86 to 28 percent in 1987) pressured many investors to hold bonds to clip "coupon" interest, rather than to invest in venture firms that do not return dividends and hold on to every dime they earn to pay for vital research and development and to finance growth. Yet former Treasury Secretary James A. Baker contended otherwise, saying that there was no need for major changes in the law to stimulate business investment. "We now have the lowest corporate tax rate of any of our major trading partners," he said, "and the second best depreciation schedule of any of our major trading partners."[16]

Meanwhile, Japanese companies had done exactly what U.S. investors were reluctant to do: invest in small U.S. high-tech firms, pursue the latest technology, and pay for dollar-dominated assets with an appreciated yen in the late 1980s and the early 1990s. With such investments, Japanese companies were also using joint ventures with U.S. firms designed to cover costly development technology and long-term gaps before production began, empowering Nippon enterprises to acquire technical know-how for future advances.[17]

And, as we will see, the future role of state subsidies in both Japan and the U.S. is both production- and market-oriented.

Chapter 9

Where Prosperity Appears: Shaping the 1990s

Given the uneasy balance of competitive, nationalist technological development, is it possible that the struggle for markets, scientific breakthroughs,
and investment spheres will follow classical lines, leading to the nurturing
of state attitudes of national autarky? Overproduction and disorientation
in markets? Temporary technological production ventures and cartels?
State-fostered allocation of markets and the setting of prices? A resurgence
of the selfish drive for nationalist accumulation at the expense of others?
And, eventually, the falling apart of cartels and other partnership alliances
due to disagreements over where technical development, production,
employment, distribution, and accumulation of materials, assets, and
profits take place?

Facing the underlying forces of competition, it is fairly apparent that
cutthroat competition breeds joint ventures, cartels, and other alliances, as
well as state tête-à-tête agreements to regulate or allow the introduction of
technology, determine production levels, allocate markets, and set prices.

Corporate links have thereby been established to relocate physical
operations abroad to take advantage of foreign techniques, to discover
diverse sources of supply, and to recruit a variously priced, global labor
force. Selling agreements between nations and enterprises of different states
have opened markets once closed by quotas, tariffs, consumer attitudes,
and a lack of distribution facilities.

Small and Big Changes

Over time, the strategy has changed a little, too. For whereas U.S. corporations through the 1960s specialized in foreign-sited, wholly owned subsidiaries, the next decade witnessed a concurrent rise in joint ventures for
production and cooperative agreements for marketing, resource acquisitions, etc.[1] The 1980s then added a new dimension in the form of ventures
and alliances designed to spread the rising cost of research and development
of high-risk technology, closing the time gap between invention and application.

Thereby the entire spectrum for capital mobilization, labor recruitment, technological development, and cooperative production, storage, shipping, and marketing was in the process of becoming a transnational affair under the control of members of these alliances, joint ventures, and cartels. As the need for a simultaneous presence in dozens of individual markets was becoming essential, it was being regularized and made systemic—forwarding uninterrupted global marketing and accumulation.

In the leading industrial nations, meanwhile, large agglomerations of capital mobilized technologized production, trade, and finance and put parochial production and the division of labor under pressure. These provincial ways, already suffering erosion, were suddenly liquidated, absorbed, and reassembled by the conglomerates, so that production costs were often lowered by introducing high-tech equipment.

For the moment, organizations with large amounts of capital were able to standardize the production and realization process: that is, to set the optimum unit of production, the quantity and quality of labor, the level and versatility of technology, the pace and scale of production, the uniformity and quality of output, and the common desires and "needs" of buyers. These organizations also sought to realize their sales in a currency with value that was not allowed to vary between the time of investment and sale; hence either currencies invested were kept in a fixed ratio to those received on sale, or, to create an equilibrium that approximated the same result, speculation and arbitrage in currencies were pursued.

Within this frame, Japanese and American firms pursued a common goal: to maintain the lowest costs of production and the highest returns. Foreign partners were sometimes needed because of their familiarity with managing local labor, acquiring needed resources, and forwarding distribution. Acquisition and knowledge of production and skill techniques from assorted social milieu were frequently universalized among venture partners. Product defects were avoided by tapping a labor supply more easily shaped to quality controls (for example, Japanese workers employed in Japan by Texas Instruments). And production lines were filled out from the partners' sources of supply, creating a vast shopping list of products available from the joint venture partners for all markets.

These alliances were not always equal, however. For equality would have meant not only equivalent investments, but comparable benefits from production and sale. Yet the complexity of the agreements could not hide the fact that partners were reluctant to, and often did not, reveal to one another the secrets of their own technology, methods of output, and product composition.

The locale of production also awarded an advantage to the partner and nation state that employed a native labor force, used domestic raw materials and energy sources, and sold at home; hence wages and salaries paid, raw materials and machines purchased, and profits taken and spent stimulated further domestic production, consumption, and profits. If the latter were thrown into research and development of new techniques and technology, first knowledge of scientific breakthroughs obviously went to the favored partner. And preferring the trading companies of one partner over another not only utilized existing contacts and connections, but helped establish new ones that the excluded partner might someday lose on the breakup of the once mutually agreeable venture.[2]

One party might gain an initial advantage, another a later one. A Japanese partner might carry forward the main line of production and use the U.S. partner to distribute its products in the American market — the main case criticized by those who have worried that U.S. firms are relinquishing their future in these fields by losing technology, knowledge, and profits earned in production, as well as having their profitability squeezed because, comparatively, distribution and selling do not add as much value to the product as investments in production.[3]

Yet this reasoning fails to account for the practicalities of the partners operating under and policing these joint ventures. For each joint venture awards momentary advantages to each partner; hence they are very much like cartels that have a limited life once the mutuality of benefits erodes.

U.S. firms had initially moved into alliances with Japanese firms to gain an advantage by putting risk capital into a joint fund that sped research and forwarded technological development using Japanese know-how and technicians.

Japanese companies entered comparable ventures to license U.S. technology, to avoid being locked out of the U.S. market by threatened barriers, and to use their U.S. partners' marketing apparatus and resources to capture the maximum number of customers. With a strategic vision to establish a U.S. market share, these companies sacrificed near-term profits, paid substantial royalties on U.S. patents, and played low-key roles in firms in which they held minority interests.

Sometimes, too, Japan took a leading interest. The classic case of Toyota's restructuring of the loss-ridden GM Freemont, California, auto plant was designed to change both the technical production apparatus and worker-management relations. High-speed, automated machinery was introduced, and the labor force was reorganized — with cuts in both management salaries and rank-and-file wages and benefits. The United Automobile Workers union was compelled to allow Toyota to reformulate twenty-six job categories, each with different pay levels, into four broad groupings with similar wages, and thereafter to allow the company to enforce a labor speedup.[4]

Trade Deficits and International Investments

Has any great nation gained an advantage that borders on *control* of other great industrial powers?

Certainly, the division of labor on a geographic basis produces the appearances of trade deficits and surplus on merchandise accounts, service balances, royalty payments, and earnings from globalized production and direct investments. Yet the heart of accumulation is that the corporate bureaucracies directing its gyrations want it to proceed unimpeded, with security for both investments and returns.

The facts of accumulation are that the U.S. has directly exported many billions in capital a year to Japan; U.S. investments in 3,000 wholly owned or substantially owned companies in Japan generated $44 billion of sales in 1984; 1985 U.S. "services" (covering insurance, financial loans, films, television, patent rights, transportation, etc.) represented more than a third of U.S. merchandise sales in Japan; and U.S.-owned subsidiaries in third nations that export oil, resources, and other commodities to Japan have annually sold products in the multibillions. Together in 1984 these resulted in a near equivalency of over $70 billion in U.S. earnings from Japanese consumers to offset the $70 billion American consumers bought from Japanese companies.[5]

Of course, that near-balance is not reflected in formal Japanese-American accounts, nor in Japan's holdings of dollars invested in the U.S., nor in its quest to raid U.S. gold supplies, nor in Japan's takeover of U.S. domestic, high-tech industries.

Obviously, to eliminate the deficit with Japan, the U.S. sphere of trade must be larger than Japan's narrow *consumer market,* as it is unlikely that Japan, with half the U.S. population, will ever absorb what the U.S. consumer market absorbs from Japan. This means that for the rest of the 1990s the U.S. will likely have an annual trade deficit with Nippon. Offsets might appear in the form of $20 billion a year in future legalization of the export to Japan of Alaska's North Slope oil or of timber cut by private companies on U.S. federal lands.[6] Other ways to bring up U.S. strength in production for competitive export and displacement of Japanese products would be more extensive, federally-fostered, cooperative research and development between U.S. companies; selling more high-tech equipment without the barriers of U.S. government export clearance; removing antitrust regulations that now prevent U.S. corporations from centralizing assets, production, and control; and lowering taxes on U.S. corporations. Thereby domestic investments could be fostered, means of production and employment extended, technology rapidly applied to assembly, and output, sales, and profits expanded.

The central factor is to reassert the functional relationship between high-tech applications to production, a reorganized labor force, and a supply line that spells *additional* output, employment, profits, and wages. Within the relations of production in the 1970s, high U.S. labor costs had pushed U.S. investments for production abroad, while in its own domestic sphere Japan broke labor's resistance and kept production wages low.[7] In the 1980s these relationships changed: America's growing reserve of unemployed workers positioned the employers to cut wages sharply, while the yen rose against the dollar and increased Japanese labor costs in comparison with those in the U.S. Thus market strengths were bound to change as both the U.S. and Japan sought low wages in third nations, while trying to mollify their own domestic work force who lacked jobs or were experiencing lower wages.

Meanwhile, third countries able to buy machinery with a high technological base employed low-cost labor to produce inexpensive, high-quality products. Using such competitive technology, leading Korean companies were able to undermine the market position of both U.S. and Japanese firms in the American market. Japanese companies also produced in Korea: the Japanese-owned, South Korean–located Hyundai Motor Co. dumped cheaper vehicles on the U.S. market. The same scenario took place within the U.S. when foreign firms installed the latest technical equipment and outflanked or otherwise undercut high-price union labor.

Picture the global dilemma in the mid-1980s. The U.S. GM Saturn plant, despite its use of the latest technology, could not compete because it continued to use high-price labor to produce small cars. Japan also could not compete because its labor costs were rising, all the more so because of the appreciation of the yen. With the mobility of, and access to, technology, Korea-based Hyundai meanwhile outclassed Japanese-located and U.S.-based automakers in lower-price, small cars—meaning that to maintain their profits, capital from U.S.- and Japanese-based firms would either have to be diversified to change their product mix or invested in comparable plants in Korea![8]

Obviously the Korean invasion of America was *by trade,* with both Japanese and U.S. investors bolstering South Korean production. Rationalists, supporting Japanese interests or otherwise, sometimes argued that U.S. firms should *not* do what Nippon conglomerates have sought to do: to manufacture overseas, because they would somehow spatially separate product development, marketing, and manufacturing, despite the obvious technical wonders of telecommunications that link output sources abroad with decision-making centers at home.[9]

The reason for Japan's willingness to enter export alliances with, and to export capital to, America was obvious. Because Japan exported 35 percent of its total output, it had to export either goods or investment capital—or suffer an accentuated depression because wages, like means of production, were treated by the largest Japanese companies as fixed charges that needed to be allocated over a rising production volume. To stimulate these exports, alliances with U.S. firms positioned Japanese companies to use their U.S. partners to legislatively oppose or sidestep American tariffs, quotas, and nontariff restrictions. And foreseeing eventual restrictions, Japan meanwhile sought to enter joint ventures agreements or find other investment opportunities in America—to produce and distribute *within* the U.S. itself.

Joint Ventures, "Free Trade," and Autarky

Questions about the nature of these joint ventures remain. Will they become egalitarian for all partners in choosing the locale of production, the sharing of markets, and the distribution of profits? Is their allotment of markets based on cartel-like arrangements and state implementation inevitable? What is the social significance? And is a time bomb of autarchical relations and strident nationalist self-sufficiency necessarily built into a future breakup of the latest varieties of joint ventures and other alliances?

The pressure building up in the late 1980s indicated that the great commercial nations had already given up some competitive markets to cartel alliances, state negotiations of bilateral commercial agreements, and the creation of spheres of trade. For thirty years disdain for free trade and a drive for self-sufficiency had been stronger outside the U.S. than within. For, after all, the U.S. had been the most technologically powerful and lowest cost producer and had therefore been able to capture the lion's share in unfettered world markets. No longer in this position, now it was America's turn to renege on free trade, apply tariff and nontariff import restrictions, and move to market abroad through joint ventures with foreign companies.

Protecting American manufacturers, by early 1990 the U.S. government had enforced selective tariffs and "voluntary" export restraints on Japan, keeping out at least five billion dollars each year in extra Japanese goods. In 1986 alone the U.S. had further cut 10 percent of Japan's textile imports to America; and nontariff import restrictions rose from 20 percent of all U.S. imports in 1981 to 35 percent in 1986. By 1988 new U.S. trade legislation empowered the administration to negotiate international trade agreements covering goods and services under the GATT Uruguay round of talks — with power to investigate countries with "pervasive" unfair trade practices and retaliate if their barriers were not eliminated. This legislation was largely aimed at Japan — as the Japanese well knew. And Japan's 1990 concessions to quickly remove barriers on importing certain U.S. technologies and other products promised to enlarge U.S. exports by a nominal five billion dollars — not enough to make a dent in the American fifty billion dollar trade deficit with Japan.

State Policy and Investment Locale

The flip side was the American invasion of Japan with R&D–oriented affiliates, using joint ventures with the Japanese to increase these production and marketing operations from 8 percent of such affiliates in 1973 to 40 percent in 1984.

Despite the increase in these joint ventures, many experts conclude that 60 percent of all international alliances do not involve the purchase of equity in one another, but rather are based on *selling each other's products.*

So such limited-term relations periodically need to be renewed. *Impermanence* is implied by another fact, too: U.S.–Japanese alliances are 70 percent or more negotiated by firms in consumer electronics, areas in which technical advances and breakthroughs are very rapid and jealousy among contact partners runs high.

These studies and figures suggest the relative instability and momentary nature of such business alliances. It is commonly recognized that a deep-seated lack of trust exists between U.S. and Japanese firms; constant changes in political ties, currency realignments, and ever-new attempts to pressure one another's nation state to undermine old alliances and generate new ones contribute to this lack of trust. Production that had gone forward under joint ventures in Japan in 1985 suddenly had to face a near 50 percent appreciation of the yen by August 1986, bringing the yen to its highest level in four decades. This effectively brought the purchase of U.S. assets down to half-price, but also made Japanese factory wages comparatively 12 percent higher than America's. These two changes gave the Japanese a powerful incentive to move factories to the U.S. or to Taiwan, Korea, Hong Kong, and other nations not bedeviled by a high exchange rate. With the latter's currencies in turn linked to an almost fixed dollar, Japanese companies with subsidiary operations there could sell in the U.S. market without facing the instability of a continually appreciating yen.[10]

Then came the competitive reduction of U.S. tax rates on corporate profits that began in 1987. Some U.S. firms immediately planned to return home for production operations; and some Japanese companies schemed to follow or precede them. Then Japan moved to cut its own tax rates by equivalent percentages. The tax advantages were again squarely in Japan's court, given its increased application of automation and robots that enlarged labor's efficiency at home and a cheaper dollar that encouraged investments in America.[11]

What was the social configuration within the U.S.? Bringing capital home to invest in automation upgraded labor efficiency 45 percent or more and eliminated jobs, while exporting capital also undercut the employment base. In the first case the dollar might be strengthened, weakening exports, while in the second case the potentially weakened dollar would bolster commodity exports.[12]

Obviously, the locale of investments for technical output remained in constant flux based on the relative cost of production, marketing, and sales, as well as the switches in power relations between nation states. Whereas the U.S. in February 1985 had used the dollar at its high point to invest in Japanese and European means of production, the Japanese in August 1986 used the yen at its momentary zenith to invest in U.S. factories, real estate ($385 million in 1984, $1.3 billion in 1985, and $5 billion in 1986) and, after the Bank of Japan cut its discount rate to 3 percent, one-third of all new issues of U.S. Treasury bonds.[13] "They are buying [commercial real estate] for the long term," said Simon Shima, vice-president for international accounts at Coldwell Banker in Los Angeles, "And they are only buying in carefully selected markets, mostly in downtowns."[14]

By exporting capital for these varied investments, the Japanese were trying to escape low returns on capital at home, earn the world's highest yields, maintain their market share overseas, and thus position themselves for a future presence abroad.

Investments Abroad and the Struggle for Markets

The declining domestic rate of profit for Japanese firms was based in part on the appreciation of the yen that raised the price of Japanese exports, led to the loss of export revenues, fueled the export of production operations, and forced the Japanese economy to go through its most significant adjustment since World War II.

Of sixteen industries analyzed by Sanwa Bank in 1985, all had returned a profit at the exchange rate of 224 yen to the dollar, but only two (computers and automobiles) were profitable when the exchange rate was 200 yen to the dollar. At 154 yen to the dollar even these two appear to be on the borderline, though Japanese investors in U.S. Treasury securities still maintained a 3 percent yield advantage over investments in Japan. And at 130 yen to the dollar, even this advantage was expected to erode.[15]

Meanwhile, to rebuild its trade offensive, Japanese computers and cars would need to be constructed in Taiwan, South Korea, Singapore, and Hong Kong — countries where both labor costs and the exchange rate for the dollar were relatively fixed and far lower than in Japan. Thus would the locale of production change and the spheres of trade be altered.

Obviously, the weaknesses of basic and technical industries also exist in Japan, so America's decline in technical application, employment, and profit yields cannot be viewed in isolation. As a counterweight to economic stress, the Japanese state has bolstered and subsidized its industries, giving both conservative and liberal thinkers in America the cue to advocate comparable government intervention.

The political lens focusing the fight for survival has meanwhile been altered, not only for U.S. agriculture, raw materials extraction, and heavy industries, but also for microchips and the service sector they sustain. Besides the U.S. microelectronic sector losing technical know-how and sales to Japanese companies, the self-sufficiency of U.S. users of this technology in basic production, services, and the military is now at stake.

Battle in Microchips

The nuances of the battle of the U.S. and Japan over microchip technology, production, marketing, and dominance have become major stumbling blocks to their common destiny.

America's present competitive position is based on the technology of the silicon chip that is crafted with electronic circuits sandwiched atop one another and powered to perform calculations, store information, and retrieve data necessary for all branches of modern industry and services — from operating bank and stock brokerage computers to making video-cassette recorders and other electronic devices to directing radar and missiles.

Here the U.S. has seemingly impossible weaknesses, because American invention has only been applied to U.S.–based production when short-term profits have been likely. With the high U.S. cost of production of microchips relative to competitors in Japan, Taiwan, and Korea, since the late 1970s American firms have continuously exported their technical knowledge for production operations and then imported cheaper chip components.

Moreover, U.S. memory chip exports did not match the changing demand for greater capacity memory chips from 1980 to 1986, during which time storage capacity was upgraded from 16K RAM to 64K RAM, then to 256K RAM, and eventually to the one-mega microchip level. When U.S. factories neglected to switch production quickly enough to these enlarged capacity chips, Japanese firms that did switch were able to take charge of the memory chip market.[16]

One result has been the reallocation of world chip markets in favor of the Japanese. A 1986 study by Congress' Joint Economic Committee indicated that U.S. high-tech imports from Japan had risen 266 percent since 1980, a process not reversed by the near 50 percent decline in the dollar versus the yen from 1985 to 1986. Moreover, half of American high-tech exports in 1985 required a license from the U.S. government, red tape that impeded exports; and foreign preferential procurement barriers either stopped U.S. exports or discouraged them.[17]

The combined loss of the domestic microchip market and the U.S. inability to competitively export caused a fall in U.S. production, jobs, and profits, as well as a decline in the opportunity for future investments. From 1981 to August 1986 some 65,000 jobs were lost in the microchip industry, 17,500 in 1984–85 alone. Profits declined about one-half billion dollars in the two years 1984–85, driving out so many firms that by mid-1986 35 percent of the Silicon Valley's factory and research space was vacant, constituting the highest industrial vacancy rate in the nation.[18]

Compared to U.S. chip makers, Japanese firms meanwhile held important advantages. As part of conglomerate enterprises with huge financial reserves garnered from various sources, they were able to pump capital into R&D, rapidly change the technical composition of capital, and sustain *long-term losses* while their industry reorganized and relocated abroad to establish market shares. Japanese competitors allied with government agencies spent more on research, plant, and equipment than U.S. chip makers and then built the most up-to-date factories, using upscale production methods, and turning out higher quality products.

With many U.S. microtech firms outflanked, they had three alternative ways to stay in business: solicit direct government protection and aid; export their chip-making and chip-using operations to low-cost areas; or join their competitors in joint ventures to share technology, production facilities, and markets. In fact, in the half-decade 1980–86 they tried all three, pragmatically combining them in ingenious ways that ensured a continued presence at the heart of modern technology.

In the battle for self-sufficiency government aid was ultimately solicited by American semiconductor firms. The potential "danger" of U.S. dependence on foreign firms for semiconductors was soon the subject of study groups set up by the U.S. Defense Department, the National Security Council, the Reagan administration, and the Joint Economic Committee. The latter found that the export of U.S. military goods was often conditioned on the U.S. importing foreign-produced military components, thereby fostering the suppliers' acquisition of critical U.S. markets and high-tech expertise.

If government spending of one billion dollars a year could help save the U.S. chip industry, noted a Defense Department report, "it could well be worth the investment." So high were required investments that it was doubtful that a single U.S. corporation alone held the resources to *both* perfect and bring on stream the next generation of chip technologies (like the 16- or 64-megabit dynamic random access memory chip, or a single advanced high-density chip). Yet, with government backing, an advanced line of memory, logic, and custom chips would together link connective capacities of different genre of both micro- and megachips, make computers "talk" to each other, and help synchronize the elements of future robotic power.

By comparison, both studies argued, the Japanese government had already surmounted the problem by fostering joint programs with its conglomerates. And what could be expected if these Japanese firms were to withhold their chips from the American market? The November 1986 National Security Council report noted that the effects would be "dire" because the Japanese would be positioned "to impede the ability of the United States to compete in almost any area of manufacturing."

Cray Research, the leading U.S. producer of supercommuters, suffered because of its reliance on Japan's Hitachi for an essential chip in its most important computer. Cray saw its market slip in the face of 1986 overcapacity in the industry—Hitachi had slowed deliveries of a key part, and some American commentators charged that Hitachi had deliberately given Japanese competitors an advantage. The U.S. Air Force also had to rely on Japanese firms to produce a product Intel Corp. no longer made, the "bubble memory" used in its satellites and fighter jets. Hitachi was meanwhile rumored to be interested in taking over Motorola, a major U.S. military chip maker. And when Japan's Fujitsu tried to absorb 80 percent of a French-run company, Schlumberger, the U.S. government contended national security might be in jeopardy because Schlumberger controlled the U.S. company Fairchild and Fairchild manufactured sophisticated microchips (called high-end bipolar gate-arrays) used to drive the computers that operate certain weapons. These, officials said, must be protected to ensure an adequate supply, to prevent the know-how from falling into unfriendly hands, and to empower the U.S. to control manufacture.

On 30 October 1986 officials at the Defense Department called Fairchild executives to the Pentagon for an informal conference. The U.S. Defense Department, the U.S. Trade Representative's office, and representatives from several U.S. intelligence agencies were meanwhile openly pushing the Reagan administration either to exclude Japan from access to Fairchild's military technology while allowing Fujitsu executives to repatriate company profits, or to split off the firm's defense-oriented operations and put them under control of U.S. citizens.[19]

All this sounded very much like the government's harrowing pre–World War II investigation of I.G. Farbenindustrie's control over U.S. chemical patents, seen as impeding U.S. preparations for military conflict. The U.S. government was now caught between rescuing the American microchip industry and securing the global system of unfettered property rights to advance technology. "National security considerations must come first," United Technologies publicly proposed. "But we must be certain that any technologies we withhold for exclusive American use are critical to our interests and ours alone."[20]

Chapter 10
Almost a State Cartel

Japan's response to the U.S. technological-exclusion movement has been twofold: to lower costs of production by locating within or outside Japan, raising productivity by reorganizing technical capital and the labor force; and to join cartels to reallot markets, until Japan again holds a position in third markets that effectively replaces any lost U.S. market share.

Using the first maneuver Japanese company executives have reduced their own compensation, upgraded production to lower costs, and improved product quality to eliminate all defects in production. They have rotated and retrained employees to cut the total wage bill, produced for contracted sales so they keep no inventory, and pushed up minimum cartel prices about 8–10 percent for the U.S. market — rather than raising them the 50 percent justified by appreciation of the yen over the dollar.

Maneuver two, "freeing world markets," was allegedly introduced by the U.S.–Japanese trade agreement that became effective 30 July 1986, providing for the chip sellers' allocation of the U.S. market limiting supply and the setting of higher prices, effectively limiting U.S. output to ensure U.S. firms remained profitable. Japan agreed that its companies would no longer sell chips in the U.S. or third countries at prices below fair market value or production costs, and that it would make an effort to double within five years the U.S. share of its own chip market from the 8 percent held in 1986. In return, the U.S. administration agreed that American chip makers would not retaliate against alleged dumping by the various Japanese companies; and U.S. semiconductor makers suspended legal proceedings that would have led to retaliation against the Japanese under laws governing unfair trade practices and dumping.

But on 4 August 1986, the *Wall Street Journal* yelled foul. "If you really want to see what this agreement heralds for Yankee high-tech, look at what protection did for the steel and auto industries," it editorialized. "In frank company, this might be called price fixing or a cartel, but to mercantilists it's 'cooperation.'" The *Wall Street Journal* heralded unfettered markets: "In theory, this will help America's 'fair-traders' compete, but in practice it will do the opposite. The biggest winners will be the South Koreans, who suddenly will be able to make and sell chips for $2 to $4 apiece less than the Americans and Japanese."

The agreement was then observed in its breaking. Because Hong Kong, Singapore, and Latin America were not formally covered by its terms, Japanese firms dumped huge quantities of chips on these third markets. There the chips could be bought by U.S. companies that repackaged or inserted them on circuit boards, which were then shipped to the U.S. as so-called subassemblies, not covered in the accord. "The reason for the Japanese increase" in such chip exports, said Hitachi executive Kinbara, "is that more American computer manufacturers are shifting their production to that area." Such redirection of Japanese sales for indirect marketing goals was transparent, too. "Either chips are being diverted," said James Shinn, Tokyo general manager of Micro Devices, "or there is a remarkable computer demand all of a sudden in Latin America."[1]

Other Asian Workshops

Meanwhile other workshops in Asia moved in. Korea's four industrial megaliths — Hyundai, Samsung Co., Lucky Gold Star International Corporation, and Daewoo — entered the personal computer market aided by three powerful factors: the government-funded Korean Advanced Institute of Science and Technology; computer factory costs averaging $1.75 an hour compared to $10 an hour in the U.S. and Japan; and business links with U.S. firms to license patents or foster two-way marketing in the U.S. and Korea. Daewoo led the movement by aligning with Edge Products of Cambridge, Massachusetts, enabling it by 1986 to gain the largest foreign-held share (6 percent) of the American market for personal computers. As Korea's three other giants planned to emulate this success, Daewoo went forward to create an alliance with other U.S. microcomputer makers, to enable it to sell to U.S. consumers of larger computers.[2]

The new apportionment of markets based on high prices would also benefit Japan's chip makers, the *Wall Street Journal* reasoned: "Right now Japanese chip makers are bleeding each other by competing fiercely on price. With prices kept artificially high, their profits will soar; they will invest these profits, in turn, to become more competitive in the more complex chips in which American companies still dominate."

Here was a guaranty for Japanese high prices, high profits, and future competitiveness in a broader line of high-grade technology. Here also was a formula for fostering high-cost operations in the U.S. For after the Japanese raised their prices, cleared in advance through the U.S. Department of Commerce, higher chip makers' costs would be relayed to the users of chips who had to pay as much as 400 percent more. Though high-cost U.S. chip makers could now profitably find domestic consumers and dump the excess in lower-cost areas, the cost of production among chip users would soar, sending price waves through the American economy, encouraging many to close down their U.S. operations and leave to produce elsewhere in order to remain competitive with Japanese firms able to buy cheaper chips at home.

The result was the potential undermining of high-tech production within the U.S. as well as a frontal attack on service industries dependent upon chip-related use. To no one's surprise, chip users in both Europe and the U.S. sharply attacked the cartel agreement. The American Electronic Association, representing one of the principal groups of users, joined U.S. computer manufacturers in complaining to U.S. trade officials that the chip cartel had forced up U.S. prices of everything that directly used chips or the products or services of those who bought their output and had to recover their costs — from cars and toys and radios, to banks, delivery services, and retail stores.

Some chip prices were eased when the Commerce Department revised its calculation of Japanese production costs to allow lower prices for imported chips. But Japanese exporters meanwhile continued dumping on markets outside the U.S. in order to keep up their volume of production, thereby lowering their unit fixed costs. They then used the extra revenue gained in the American market to offset any losses caused by ever-lower prices charged in third markets.

The U.S. chip makers' trade group, the American Semiconductor Industry Association, was outraged. It had agreed to suspend court action for comparable dumping cases as an inducement for the Japanese to sign the original agreement. But the Semiconductor Association now claimed that such dumping at below agreed-upon fair-value pricing levels in Japan, Europe, Asia, and other third-country markets was an "outright violation" of the U.S.–Japan agreement which the Japanese government had failed to adequately police. The Semiconductor Association then urged the U.S. government to identify individual Japanese violators and penalize repeat offenders in a graduated fashion by imposing duties and taking other measures.[3]

Both U.S. and Japanese officials agreed that Japanese chip makers were in fact dumping in third markets. But the Japanese government claimed that it could not legally stop them. In response to the considerable political influence of the U.S. Semiconductor Association, the U.S. Commerce Department then announced stiff new penalties for dumping and an increase in duties on the erasable programmable memory chips (called EPROMs) of specific Japanese chip suppliers, ranging from 60.1 percent for Toshiba to 188 percent for Nippon Electric. Meanwhile, U.S. semiconductor makers made ready to reinstate their cases on dumping.[4]

Then the leaders of Nippon relented, ordering Japanese semiconductor makers to sharply add 10 to 50 percent to the price of various component chips they sold in Europe and Southeast Asia.

It was a great game the Japanese played: dumping continued until the U.S. competitors complained; then a state tête-à-tête cartel set prices and allotted markets. Next Japanese manufacturers violated the cartel by increasing production for dumping in third markets. When this violation was discovered, the Japanese government pleaded helplessness. The U.S. threatened tariffs, and the Japanese Ministry of Trade and Industry finally organized an industry-wide price increase, and pressured chipmakers to comply. "We had no choice," offered a top executive of one of the country's largest semiconductor manufacturers. "We were given specific instructions."

And so the special interests set off another round of bickering. "If we keep prices high, the progress of semiconductor advancement will stop," said Kawanishi Tsuyoshi, senior vice president and head of the Japanese semiconductor group, in reluctantly agreeing to increases that in fact improved sagging profits amid tremendous manufacturing overcapacity. The users of chips in the U.S. meanwhile complained loudly that they would have to move their operations abroad or buy their chips and parts in Hong Kong, Malaysia, or South America. European officials, who saw American muscle strangling their competitiveness, argued that the U.S. was only protecting its own industry by insisting that Japan not sell components at below-market prices to third parties—thereby enforcing a global price increase that made them pay higher prices for components used in computers, video cassette recorders, washing machines, and automobiles. But the U.S. Department of Commerce viewed the cartel agreement as a "fair one in light of the fact that the Japanese were potentially targeting the U.S. semiconductor market" as a dumping ground.[5]

American Alternatives and Government Subsidies

There were possible U.S. alternatives to this policy. Individual firms seeking profits could enter joint ventures to sell Japanese-made chips in the U.S. market; or U.S. companies could carry out production in Japanese subsidiaries to reach both the domestic Japanese and U.S. import markets. Larger U.S. companies could cooperate with Japanese or Korean partners, giving them access to U.S. patent technology, while emphasizing their own engineering and marketing skills—and not worry that the design and manufacture of chips was the foundation stone of electronics, ceramics, laser and other high-tech advances in telecommunications, quality controls, and other military-related computer systems.

United States chip makers had already been weakened by slumping semiconductor sales and increased competition from abroad. Their mounting losses were reflected in declining prices for their own stock shares. With the 1986 yen at an all-time high, these shares were being snapped up as bargains by Japanese companies that feared U.S. trade barriers and sought to buy into or build up manufacturing operations within the U.S. where chip cut-pricing was not restricted, as it was under the state-fostered U.S.-Japanese trade cartel.

The case destined to change the face of American industry occurred when Fujitsu purchased 80 percent of the shares of Fairchild Semiconductor, which had been 100 percent owned by the French conglomerate Schlumberger. Fujitsu was experienced in producing for the U.S. market, and already owned 48 percent of Amdahl Corp., a Sunnyvale, California, maker of large mainframe computer systems. But Fujitsu needed a boost to offset two years of declining sales and losses due to dependence on the narrow range of *memory chips* that many Japanese firms had sold at prices well below their cost of manufacture. To sidestep the U.S.–Japan dumping agreement that might limit Fujitsu from expanding its American market share and prevent its acquisition of *logic chip* technology, it was cheaper to buy into Fairchild.

"For the price of putting up two new factories [in Japan], Fujitsu gets a whole new company," said Otake Osamu, a Tokyo semiconductor analyst for U.S.–run Dataquest Inc. "This merger represents a dramatic consolidation of market share, making Fujitsu number one," in the gate array market, offered the former head of Fairchild, now president of LSI Logic Corp., referring to programmable chips that perform specific mathematical calculations or logical functions.[6]

Could U.S. firms compete against such a consolidated company? Fujitsu might structure its merger more like a joint venture than a takeover, so that on the surface the U.S. company would survive in name to soften American political repercussions. And Fujitsu might sell shares of the company to the U.S. public. But the firm would remain under Japanese control, would use U.S. investors' money as fuel for expansion, and would induce competitor Japanese firms to try the same maneuver. "Imagine what Hitachi and Toshiba are thinking," offered Kidder, Peabody, and Co. analyst Adam Cuhney. "This just pushes them in the direction [of acquiring U.S. chip makers] that much sooner."[7]

Meanwhile, the Fairchild-Fujitsu combination frightened American chip makers. Japan, they said, would now control a U.S.–based company that sold proprietary chips to defense-related industries. They were also alarmed by the growing reliance of defense industries on foreign-made chips. This situation fueled their enthusiasm for a proposed consortium that would be subsidized by the federal government in order to preserve U.S. leadership in semiconductor technology. They envisioned a jointly operated manufacturing facility, funded chiefly by the Department of Defense, which would produce advanced semiconductors at lower prices than would be possible without government help.

It was a warlike proposal to be presented to the Defense Department, pressuring other government agencies to also take a position. For it was clear that, by themselves, *basic U.S. research outlays* of $4.3 billion would not enable educational institutions to build new laboratories, install the latest equipment, adequately subsidize students, or reorient American education toward engineering and science. Such a reorganization of the labor force would have to involve government-subsidized training in new technological fields, and redirection of subsidies to American students from foreign students studying science and engineering. By themselves, moreover, U.S. chipmakers could not remain competitive by investing the necessary one-third or more of their resources in new plant and equipment and another 15–20 percent on R&D. Yet there was no other way U.S. chip makers could stay abreast of, let alone advance, technological knowledge, which quantitatively had already doubled every decade and a half.[8]

And this meant that the U.S. government would have to fill in the vacuum by forming its own Ministry of Technology and Industry, comparable to Japan's MITI and South Korea's Advanced Institute of Science and Technology. The U.S. government would have to move into the subsidy business; to immediately identify and finance short-term production runs for particular companies; to use the tax-supported public universities to carry out research; to forward a consortium of American chip producers; and to make them as powerful as their Japanese and Korean state-financed competitors.

Thus both the Republican administration and the Democratic Congress would be pressured to seek to readjust national priorities toward high-tech production and exports. Officials might fret that technological leakage would take place through the pores of coproduction, joint ventures, and offset agreements, especially those related to overseas procurement of U.S. military goods.[9] But in the end the executive branch and most members of Congress would be forced to see subsidized high-tech production, import restrictions, and export subsidies as a backup for — and counterweight to — the limited purchase constraints of the growing federal budget deficit. Only government protection against foreign high-tech products seemed capable of propping up this sector of the domestic market and fending off a U.S. recession or worse.[10]

Chapter 11

Competition, Decay,
and the Fourth Dimension

In the late 1980s and 1990s the competitive struggle for technology, production, and markets assumed a new dimension, requiring greater capital and resources to be mobilized on the basis of autarchic formulations, as well as the reassembly of the technical work force. State stimulation backed the competitive drive among ever-larger alliances formed by each nation state with its own giant enterprises. Yet of these some would win only because others would lose, so that some economies would see the decline of certain industries which others would expand.

Standard-Gauge Knowledge Instruments

The medium for advance would appear in the form of control of a technical fourth dimension: the mathematical measurement techniques that set a standard gauge for the instruments for the production of knowledge. As all competitive sellers of these instruments attempted to develop their own gauge that made their products unique and interdependent corollaries of each other, they ended up either by establishing a corner over a minimarket or by selling similar products to the same customers in a wider sphere—thus renewing the scale and intensity of competition.

Since the struggle over the development of this standard depended on a series of intertwined scientific developments, the fight between nation states was again linked to the control of the application of technological knowledge to production, market acquisition, and military strength.

In the global computer market until August 1986, there had already been intense struggle to control three essential physical components: *memory chips* that stored information; *logic chips* that processed information on etched circuits that acted as the "brains" of computers and the next generation of robots and electronic products, called microprocessors; and *software,* programs written specifically for a given microprocessor's circuits.

The first had become established as a standard gauge among all competitors, making *memory chips* almost completely interchangeable. The second had functioned as a gauge largely established and controlled by the United States, compelling other users to license U.S. designs—though, nonetheless, *logic chip* manufacturers eventually became reliant on Japanese-made optical "steppers" used to burn the patterns of circuitry on to silicon, as well as on Japanese-produced pure gases to make high-density chips. And the third had been the essential standard that *software* writers used to accommodate U.S.-designed microprocessors.

By mid–1986 Japan had conquered the market in the first arena, making about 90 percent of the world's newest *memory chips*. Japan sought the entire market, too, by further developing British scientist Brian Josephson's 1960s breakthrough in microscopic switches that use less power and are faster than conventional semiconductors. By early 1986 Hitachi had outdistanced IBM, by using different materials and circuit designs to develop a simple Jospheson-junction *logic chip* that performed arithmetic functions and that switched at 210 picoseconds (each comprising one one-trillionth of a second), more than six times faster than the fastest galium-arsenide semiconductor chip used in U.S. production and consuming about 2.6 percent of the power used by conventional silicon.

Moreover, Japan's government-operated Electrotechnical Laboratory designed a circuit that worked twice as fast as IBM's and took up only one-eighth of the space. With the backing of Japan's Ministry of International Trade and Industry, in the 1990s Japan planned to introduce a Josephson-junction supercomputer half the size of a breadbox, that will outperform today's supercomputers, will be competitively priced, and will be available to businesses using general-purpose mainframes.[1]

Controlling Chips and Markets

Meanwhile, U.S. manufacturers fled the memory chip market, leaving Japan in charge to reap the 1984–86 slump in computer sales.[2] In 1986 the U.S. still controlled the bulk of $500 million in *microprocessor sales,* manufacturing and supplying half the world market and licensing the right to manufacture the rest to Japanese and other manufacturers; and the U.S. also was the major producer of *software programs* symbiotic to the gauge of its own microprocessors' apparatus.

U.S. dominance in microprocessors was based on a particular technical gauge called the 32-bit microprocessor. The three American companies which controlled the market were Motorola with 57 percent, Intel Corp. with 30 percent, and National Semiconductor Corp. with 10 percent of sales. To reach this position, Intel alone had spent an estimated $100 million in development outlays. So when Hitachi and Fujitsu began in August 1986 to develop their own standard-gauge, 32-bit microprocessor, the expenditure of hundreds of millions of dollars and the employment of hundreds of Japanese and foreign engineers was envisioned.

This move to free Japanese companies from dependence on U.S. chip design and software was taken after both Intel and Motorola refused to sell Japan their latest designs for 32-bit microprocessors. Japanese firms still hoped to license the old U.S. 32-bit designs. But they also planned to produce their own, new designs in order to participate in the worldwide market for 32-bit chips, which was expected to amount to $320 million annually by 1991. Hitachi and Fujitsu quickly mapped out a battle plan; financed University of Tokyo professor Sakamura Ken to enable him to combine his own chip design and operating software system in a singular chip called "Tron"; and then made ready to offer the Tron system to all takers in order to develop its practical uses for such tasks as regulating robots and establishing linkages between computers.[3]

Once in operation, the users of the Tron gauge will require other memory, controller, and graphic chips — that will almost certainly be made in Japan by Hitachi and Fujitsu. By basing their manufacture of computers on such chips, they will probably induce others to follow suit, creating an export market of Tron users and creating a demand for software linked to this original gauge.[4]

But will U.S. manufacturers of microprocessors take this challenge lying down, especially if a faster version, a 64-bit chip, can be developed by the technological wizards at the University of Tokyo?

Possibly not. In the U.S. basic technical advance is already going forward. Using the "silicon compiler," for instance, it is possible to design new integrated circuits on a computer, creating parallel chips that, in turn, regulate different simultaneous computer functions. These follow a format that an operator can use to solve practical problems by manipulating symbols representing predesignated bodies of information. Taking these three advances together, new standard gauges are being developed based on the technical composite of the silicon compiler, parallel processing, and so-called artificial intelligence systems.[5]

Artificial Intelligence Systems

Has the future arrived in the form of the computerization of intellectual functions, so that less-skilled workers can follow a machine format to automatically approximate human reasoning?

In forwarding such "artificial intelligence," answers to practical questions or dilemmas can be elicited by three sequential machine functions: first, the computer hardware or software has built within it a predesignated knowledge base or data system; second, that data system is divided into logical or other groups, each represented by symbols that an unskilled keyboard operator can manipulate according to preset formulas; and finally, once the symbols are entered, the computer draws together the results in a manner that approximates human reasoning.

It is not what the computer or computer operator "knows" or "understands" in following the program, but the technical steps taken to retrieve a "solution" to instructions presented in symbols. Such expert systems, so-called, polarize labor functions into a relatively few high-pay program-design operations and a great many low-pay keyboard functions. They are directed by a select few high-paid experts and operated by many low-paid technicians—replacing some skilled with unskilled labor, cheapening the overall labor force, and lowering the cost of operations.[6]

Automating Software

To better understand the place of software in the world of computers, it is essential to describe the role of the Japanese labor force.

Japan's industrial strength since the late 19th century has been based on the ability to control and discipline its work force in a more rigid fashion than is common in the West. Though these workers have been unable to initiate new technology due to an education based on tradition and corporate hierarchical rigidities that discourage the genius maverick, they have been successfully *mobilized for specific goals* using the total sum of available Western inventions.

In recent times they have excelled at building products like VCRs and personal computers that operate on their own. But they have not invented complex systems that interact with other systems, and there have been no Japanese counterparts to Bill Gates of Microsoft or Mitch Kapor of Lotus Development Corp., the geniuses behind the two largest U.S. personal computer software houses. So the Japanese government is now looking to a crash program, called the Sigma Project (meaning "total sum") to boost software production development.

Japan envisions the automation of software itself through the standardization of its common components: (1) the manufacture of same-gauge microprocessors that act as high-capacity personal computers able to use all software; (2) the establishment of common standards to write software programs; and (3) the use of a common document base (a module that will in turn become the libraries for all users) and a common computer language (COBOL) to write all programs.

Such an effort to create a *universal gauge* will almost certainly be resisted by each capital investment unit trying to establish its own unique minimonopoly, as well as by each nation trying to forward its own exports and protect domestic markets. But in the long haul, uniformity could emerge, and every aspect of the computer infrastructure could be made uniform. Each firm might fight to secure its own software technology, to specialize its own programs, and to use its own software to capture its own customers. Yet, eventually, it seems probable that all would succumb to standardized work stations, memory chips, logic chips, and software designed to minimize duplication of programmers' efforts by using a standardized module.

Standardization began in Japan in October 1986 when the state-fostered Research Corporation gathered all the big electronics companies in MITI's "Sigma" project, a project intended to use existing technologies to promote labor efficiency in program writing. The plan was to create viable, competitive software and to standardize the program tools used to build other programs, as well as to facilitate the use of reusable parts of some programs to act as the building blocks for others.

Finance for the project was based on government-subsidized research. The state provided half the funds, and participant corporations provided the other half based on their size and their ability to use potential technological advances. The beginning technology was U.S.–made: AT&T's Unix operating system on which all software programs would be designed to run. Unix was the most advanced software-development system that could be employed to use almost any software. It was the only system that competitor Japanese companies would allow to be used as a standard to which the Japanese language and design programs could be fitted, to allow use by any cartel member's respective computers.

The immediate goal? To allow Sigma's system to be tapped by engineers from Sigma's standardized, special work stations, to retrieve library programs as tools and parts of programs as modules—for use by anything from mainframes to personal computers. Thus, rather than wasting valuable time by reinventing a program, a member could draw on the library model, pay a license fee, and adapt it to the specific use sought.[7]

For the future, the goal is to create a global pool of capital and knowledge that will draw in Japanese and foreign companies like DEC, Olivetti, and Data General with units in Japan; to use their capital and engineers to establish a for-profit venture in which members and the Japanese government have a vested interest.[8] Japan hopes to create its own colony of American and European capital and technology, so that these latter nations will pay to provide an advantage Japan could not otherwise acquire.

Chapter 12

The Pressures of
Transcontinental Technologies

Set in a larger milieu, both internal and external pressures have already helped forward the competitive, nationalist struggle in microtechnologies, with each centrally directed corporate enterprise or conglomerate using its power to direct transcontinental operations in several production locations.

The first pressure, to capture domestic and international markets, has led to intense competitive investments, "overcapacity," and the withdrawal and/or nonrenewal of domestic investments in the latest technology. U.S. microtechnology corporations have been the first to reach this stage, followed by European companies, then Japanese conglomerates. U.S. giants such as IBM have not only lost computer markets to Japanese competitors such as Fujitsu, but have transferred production abroad to take advantage of the Japanese development of U.S. technology, low Asian wages, and proximity to untapped markets. Later, giant Japanese firms like Fujitsu faced a similar dilemma: global overcapacity for production of semiconductors and electronic components pushed down sales some 27 percent (to $1.25 billion) from fiscal 1984/85 to fiscal 1985/86, forcing concentration on more profitable computer and data processing equipment, where sales rose 17 percent (to $6.2 billion) in this period.

The second pressure stems from the competitive financial loss experienced by the major conglomerates. To readjust their competitive positions, they have put pressure on their respective governments: intervention has taken place through tête-à-tête government realignment of currencies and private or state-fostered cartels. In the case of Japanese–U.S. trade relations, currency exchange ratios and comparative interest rates were set by state-to-state pacts in 1986. The U.S. pushed for, and exacted, an implicit Japanese agreement to allow the yen to rise vis-à-vis the dollar, thereby increasing the price of Japanese electronic and microchip exports in the U.S. The U.S. also pressured Japan to reduce its interest rates, to stimulate the Japanese economy and, supposedly, to foster the import of U.S. commodities and the further export of Japanese capital to invest in U.S. Treasury bonds to offset the negative U.S. trade balance and fund the federal deficit.

Just as important was the microchip cartel (mentioned above) set up by the two governments in 1986, which empowered the U.S. Department of Commerce to set a fair market price below which Japanese firms could not sell chips in the U.S. market. For companies like Fujitsu, whose prices were already set higher than those of some of its competitors, the new system provided a source of additional revenues to offset losses associated with a general fall in sales in its other product lines. Fujitsu and other Japanese chip makers also suffered the disadvantage of being unable to dump chips at a low price to increase potential market share in the U.S.

The Process of Disinvestment and Decay

The third pressure on domestic producers was exerted by their own high costs of production and government regulations that combined to cause loss of markets and stimulated the export of both capital and the means of production abroad.

U.S. firms exported huge sums of capital after 1971, when President Nixon made the dollar inconvertible to gold. Nixon's act effectively increased the price of U.S. exports and enabled U.S. capital exporters to inexpensively buy global assets with a strong, inflated dollar. Accumulation from, and reinvestment in, foreign operations eventually reduced total U.S. investments in new technological production and employment at home. This fall in investment then led to a form of "deindustrialization," a decaying economy, and the gradual elimination of one domestic industry after another.

From 1971 to today the process of decline in domestic agriculture, raw material production, and basic manufacturing has intensified. The U.S. economy is rapidly disaccumulating. Meanwhile, American subsidiary operations located abroad have vaulted from one profitable venture to another, especially in Asia.

The U.S. is exporting less and importing more high-tech wares. Though in 1980 its high-tech industries had produced a trade surplus of $27 billion, this surplus declined annually, had shrunk to $4 billion by 1985, and moved toward deficit in 1986.[1] The cause was known. "In the case of the Southeast Asian Newly Industrialized Countries," stated a report prepared for the congressional Joint Economic Committee, "much of the deterioration in the U.S. high-tech trade balance is accounted for by American firms making greater use of their subsidiaries or independent contractors located in these areas where labor costs remain low by American standards. Through such arrangements, American-owned corporations remain competitive, while America as a place of production does not."[2]

Certainly the U.S. had lost its technical base to Japan Incorporated — an allegedly private economy consisting of great enterprises, which are guided and subsidized by the state and financed by the savings of the frugal

Japanese people. Nippon firms were encouraged to buy, adapt, and mobilize U.S. technology, a process that required the reassembly of Japan's industrial, job, and social structures. State-supported industries transformed their technical capabilities, this transformation necessitated the reorganization of the work force, and industry promoted the unifying theme of making each factory a model of efficiency and Japan number one in the industrial world.

Can America emulate Japan's use of its own know-how? Even before the 1980s decay in America's "rust belt" revealed a rotten core of dated technology and labor inefficiency. Trade balances indicated that America was losing ground to her competitors. But the signs of failing exports were at first disguised by a large positive outgo in high-technology sectors. This positive flow disappeared after 1981, when U.S. strength in high-tech lost its edge and could no longer offset the deficit in less intensive technical commerce. The trade results of 1984–89 indicated the accelerated decay of U.S. high-tech industries due to high costs and increased imports of cheaper products from Japan, Korea, Taiwan, Hong Kong, and Singapore.

The origins of these imports were in part due to U.S. firms that set up operations abroad by contracting for production or assembly in their own plants. "These firms sought to maintain their cost competitiveness by locating production offshore in the low-labor-cost regions of the world," a congressional report concluded. Indeed, there was no logical reason to continue to produce within the U.S. for export when the dollar, and export prices, remained high in relation to the yen and European currencies.

As the U.S. created an Asian sphere of production, it also built an infrastructure for R&D to promote both production and marketing. Foreign firms were often commissioned by U.S. companies to undertake new product research or development. When these items were put into production, they were often reexported to the U.S., contributing to the U.S. trade deficit. U.S. electronics plants in Asia emerged as the fastest growing high-tech investments, "to take advantage not only of lower labor costs for reassembly," offered Congress' investigators, "but also increasingly the lower overhead costs for technical and engineering support."[3]

The Social Dimension

The social dimension was not fully addressed by technocratic reports stressing production costs and prices in the global milieu, however.

Though 1986 U.S. manufacturing exports comprised a relatively constant 75 percent of America's total outflow of goods, the American labor force was increasingly being displaced by a combination of new high-tech methods of production in U.S. factories and the doubling of imports from 1980 to 1986. As U.S. technological investments abroad increasingly reached Asia to promote the reexport of inexpensive manufactures to the American market, private accumulation also took precedence over employment of United States workers. Asia became America's output launching pad: "For the last two decades, this region has been a primary area for the assembly of electronic components and consumer electronics goods by U.S. firms," offered a congressional report. "These low-labor-cost assembly activities were followed by development of an extensive infrastructure to support high-tech manufacturing — which, in turn, permitted a more sophisticated set of contract assembly and subassembly manufacturing activities to develop."[4]

Moreover, the report continues, "A significant portion of U.S. high-tech exports, especially in electronics, that goes to newly industrialized countries and other low-labor-cost areas (especially Mexico, for instance) is for further assembly and reexport, not for final sale into the local economy."[5] The whole process contributed in a significant fashion to higher unemployment among the American working class and a lowered general wage scale.

U.S. manufacturers could pay low wages to their workers toiling in so-called subassembly and transshipment centers in the third world. The double advantage of paying lower wages to workers abroad while also cutting the wages paid to domestic workers enabled competitive marketing in the U.S. itself. Moreover, countries outside the U.S. had fewer and less stringent regulations regarding safe working conditions and pollution, so that instead of spending money to clean up the factory environment and eliminate pollution, employers could concentrate on further lowering their production costs.

Chapter 13

The End of
American Self-Sufficiency

*There was no literal lallation but the message
was every bit as blatant: Blame Japan for
America's ills. — "*Cowboys and the Japanese"[1]

Over the last two decades U.S. conglomerates and financial monopolies
have gained skill in withholding investments for production at home and
coordinating manufacturing, assembly, and distribution between foreign
nations and national markets, thereby lowering their production costs
abroad and their prices at home. In the late 1980s production of major components abroad and their nominal assembly at home became a doubly
profitable means of capital accumulation.

The Locale of Production and Sale

This process can be illustrated by the actions of the producers of computer clones compatible with the IBM PC. These clones are produced by
U.S. firms that either own, or have subcontracts with, subassembly plants
in Taiwan, Singapore, South Korea, and Mexico. By exporting the clones
to the U.S., the single greatest market in the world, *it appears that the U.S.
trade deficit worsens, when in fact the deficit is a measure of the success of
America's private corporations.*

"By sourcing offshore," congressional researchers noted, "the U.S.-
based firms that distribute the completed PC units have maintained their
competitive position against foreign competition, especially the Japanese,
at the overall finished product level. There is an interesting distribution of
economic returns from this alignment. Of the total retail value of an IBM-
compatible machine, U.S. firms capture approximately half (including final
assembly costs, which represent about 3% of total retail value). But these
firms are performing virtually no manufacturing activity below the major

subassemblies level. Foreign firms provide most, if not all, the major subassemblies and many of the major items such as monitors and disk drives. Ironically, assembly of the overall PC, an activity once usually relegated to an offshore low-labor-cost site, is now predominantly performed in the U.S. since this represents such a small proportion of the total cost of the completed unit."[2]

A point is reached, however, when the foreign producers of clones fall out with the coordinating U.S. corporations, putting the American firms in the double-bind of facing high-cost production at home and the loss of proprietary technology and partners abroad. Indeed, sharing *control* over the basic component level of technology provides a breeding ground for others to buy, adapt, or take this technology with impunity; and U.S. firms may lose control of these along with systems-level technology and distribution channels.

Such a resegmentation of global accumulation might eventually mean that the relatively high proportion of the total value of new output going to firms in the U.S. will be undermined compared to the share going to firms in other nations. U.S. high-tech companies may return to the Silicon Valley and other domestic production centers. But as the costs of U.S. production periodically become too high in selected areas of high tech, output will again be located abroad.

Rising costs in high-tech are systemic, in part based on the high salaries commanded by skilled technical workers, in part based on rapid technical advances that make old discoveries and products — and the firms that make them — obsolete. Most companies that make hard-disk drives have been "one-product successes." Thus, each new generation of microcomputers opens the door to a new leader for the next generation of hard-disk drives. Thus when the newest 1986–88 line of personal computers from IBM, Apple, and other manufacturers began using the *new standard gauge* 3½-inch drive, disk-drive manufacturers that did not quickly switch to the new standard lost their market.

"Their product line is out of date; they are two years late in 3½-inch disk drives," one market research firm concluded of Seagate Technology, then the major U.S. producer of hard-disk drives for personal computers. But in 1988 Seagate was behind the times, still locked into 5¼-inch drives for 90 percent of its production. "One fact of life in the disk-drive business is short product life-cycles."

Because the 32-bit machines, like Apple's *Mac II* and Compaq's *Desk-Pro 386,* all had hard disks, the hard-disk manufacturers had to retool to the new gauge. "It's critical to get in the design-in phase, which lasts just six months to a year," offered a former executive with Seagate. "If you miss that window, it's very difficult to get back in. . . . Seagate has missed the transition from 8 bit to 16. They don't have the products to bridge that gap."

In 1985 Seagate had responded to losses by laying off about 70 percent of its U.S. work force and moving production to Singapore and Thailand to cut costs. In 1988 Seagate again cut its domestic work force and reduced the operations of its offshore plants from seven-day weeks to five.[3]

In sum, technological advance and the relative cost of labor and markets remained critical to the locale of production.

Taking a long-term view, as the cost to maintain the population of workers rose with U.S. price levels from 1957 to 1983 — though rising less slowly thereafter — America as the locale of production had slipped.[4] There was a general rise of the cost of labor to extract relatively inaccessible resources, and a corresponding rise in the cost of agricultural commodities, which are linked to the prices of machinery, petroleum, loan capital, and other farm necessities. Also increasing cost was the refusal of U.S. basic industries to upgrade technical production or to reduce the unproduction burden of their own swollen bureaucratic organizations. Together these and other costs of basic, secondary, and tertiary industries pushed up the general cost of living, wage and salary demands, and production costs in most industries.

America's forces for production thus went into decline, changing the relationship between employers and workers on one side and the relationship between the public and the state on the other. America began to export its latest means of production and technology, undercutting employment, but strengthening its outposts and spheres of foreign influence.

The transmigration of capital had become politically boundless as well. It "sourced" its production and markets without needing to heed the political boundaries of nations, political parties, organized labor's demands, or consumer-protection advocates. Its vanity was reflected in security and accumulation, not the personal needs and hopes of its paid managers, the nation's workers, or millions of consumers worldwide.

The Technical Division of Global Functions

U.S. technical and inventive genius was now marching to a different drummer as its latest products were exported as know-how that changed the technical division for the mobilization of global labor.

Economic thought and analysis lagged behind this great change. Economists continued to emphasize budgets and deficits instead of the social forces that produced them and the situational position of different classes.

Liberal free-traders spoke of trade expansion with gusto. "It creates jobs, economic growth and thus bigger markets for all countries' exports," the *New York Times* editorialized, seemingly tearing a page out of a 19th-century text. "But it also means layoffs in industries that can't compete." Modern market stresses and government resources, it advised, would offset such joblessness by lump-sum payments of unemployment benefits, which would act "as a nest egg for starting a job search or to take a new job at lower pay." The editors also looked to in-house training in new skills and transferability of pension benefits to new employers. They saw increasing unemployment regardless of such government reforms, yet they frowned on protecting jobs in uncompetitive industries.[5]

The fact that those uncompetitive industries included those in the latest technologies, and that high-tech production abroad accelerated during such periods of instability, momentarily escaped the *New York Times* editors. United States deindustrialization represented an historic switch: the export of parts of America's economy. It also portended the move toward private liquidity, as well as the absorption of the costs of decaying, bankrupt industries and unemployment by the state deficit, thereby providing a corporate springboard for extended global operations. The domestic work force was in part deserted, in part left to live on an inadequate government dole, and in part kept in reserve as a lever to keep down the general level of labor's remuneration.

The End of American Self-Sufficiency

The deeper factor shaping Japanese investments in the U.S. was the end of America's self-sufficient apparatus of production. The opening up of the global economy after 1970 had gradually undermined U.S. economic self-reliance and its previous trade pattern of buying relatively few imports and of exporting only a small share of total American output. The new era of international trade meant facing aggressive competition abroad and foreign dumping at home, as well as an increased U.S. reliance on imports of goods once manufactured domestically. Swings in the valuation of the dollar vis-à-vis European and other currencies further weakened America's control over its trade and investment patterns, and eventually led to the weakening of the dollar and massive inflow of foreign investment capital. By the end of 1987 the United States was the world's greatest debtor, owing $265 billion, a status sharply in contrast with the creditor status of Britain's (+ $170 billion) and Japan's (+ $240 billion).[6]

American politicians past and present offered reasoned justifications, of course. "Capital inflows ... tend to increase our productivity" and economic expansion, Federal Reserve Board governor Wayne T. Angell concluded.[7]

But New York Democratic Senator Daniel Patrick Moynihan looked deeper, by offering a plan to reverse decay by preventing budget deficits, keeping interest rates low, stemming capital inflows, devaluing the dollar, and reversing the nation's trade deficit. He believed that America's crisis began when the Reagan administration created a fiscal crisis by cutting revenues without making a matching cut in expenditures. Moynihan sought the simple reversal of the 1981 tax bill, which was based on what he described as the erroneous supply-side theory that a reduction in taxes causes an increase in revenues. This, he said, would reverse the soaring budget and trade deficits, and stop the neglect of important defense and budget programs. "The large lesson is simply this [Moynihan concluded]: President Reagan thought it was possible to weaken American government without weakening American influence. It is not possible. ... The seeming economic collapse of the 1980s has not been the result of 'imperial overstretch' but of internal, somewhat conspiratorial politics."[8]

There was still not much evidence to hope for high long-term domestic savings, investments, and employment. From 1966 to 1970 1.3 million jobs were lost in basic production. The process continued in the 1970s as the number of work places in U.S. industries were cut at the rate of about 800,000 a year.[9] Between January 1981 and January 1986 about 10.8 million workers permanently lost jobs. These included 5.1 million experienced workers with three or more years of tenure.[10] From November 1984 to November 1987 382,000 U.S. manufacturing jobs were lost, largely because of deep inroads made by foreign producers. "The Rust Belt has been clobbered by the type of industry it specializes in — cars and steel and other industries [that are] no longer growth areas," concluded John Godfrey, chief economist for Barnett Banks Inc. of Jacksonville, Florida.[11]

There was a momentary reversal from December 1987 to July 1988, as the dollar continued to weaken, reviving once-doomed companies — from Seventh Avenue, New York, to the Rust Belt. "It's no surprise, of course, to find rich and famous corporations doing well as the weakened greenback pumps up exports, slows imports, and lengthens the already-extended economic expansion," sages at the *Wall Street Journal* reported. "But for many lesser-known businesses, the weaker dollar has been more than a help; it has become the difference between life and death — the catalyst making their last-ditch cost cutting and reorganization work."

The logic of a weakened dollar, less expensive exports, and more expensive imports was a widened market and a chance to make management, technological, and labor changes, as well as to negotiate for lower-cost raw materials. "I doubt we'd be producing as much without the weaker dollar," concluded Joseph A. Cannon, president of Geneva Steel, which had bought a USX Corporation plant that had been idle thirteen months — and which began shipping steel to the Midwest and then (80,000 tons a month) to Japan. "The plant's 2,000 workers know that, too. Joe Six-Pack Steelworkers follow the yen and the dollar very closely," he said.[12]

The Syndrome of Impoverishment and Decline

Yet this might not be a long-lived reversal. The U.S. was enmeshed in a syndrome of impoverishment. The decline of basic industries meant less production, more imports, fewer exports, and greater trade deficits.

It also meant more government expenditures on welfare for the unemployed and subsidies for failing industries, which together increased the budget deficits. Greater unemployment meanwhile fueled more poverty and crime, spiked by the growth of an unruly underground economy in narcotics and an escalation of violent crimes with racial overtones. The response in most communities was more police enforcement, itself reliant on more funding from already pressed taxpayers. All this led to a local and national budgetary squeeze and, for relief without vastly reducing military outlays, a corresponding decline in educational budgets. The consequent decline in the quality of public education created a breeding ground for a new supply of young people without skills or training who ended up in low-paying unskilled work or assembly line production where they rebelled against taking orders and producing quality goods. And for those who could not find work, the system recycled its failings, driving those least able to live with its pressures into underground, crime-related activities.

Japan faced the United States as a trade competitor, not as an empathetic observer able or willing to help solve America's internal dilemma. Japan truthfully criticized that the United States was unable to control its budget and fiscal deficits, and, rather than attempt to solve its own complicated internal problems, was eager to blame Nippon. In Japanese eyes, America was in decline. The editor of the *Japan Economic Journal*, Ishizuka Masahiko, suggested that America's deficits were an "obvious sign of the decline of American power," and that "America's decline is the other side of the coin of Japan's rise."

The Japanese had no wish to import U.S. goods they claimed were inferior in quality. In part this complaint was true, in part a political myth promulgated to keep out lower-price U.S. goods that were blocked by Japan's nationalist-oriented distribution system and market controls. Japanese commentators did not always discern the difference, often making the mistake of confusing political rhetoric and facts. In truth, there had been a disastrous fall in U.S. production of quality commodities, based on the syndrome of impoverishment. But Japanese commentators extracted its racialist overtones, not its essence. A Japanese writer who had lived in the U.S. indicated that the Japanese recognized America's racial heterogeneity as a flaw; he traced America's problem to "a society in which there are a large number of different races and ethnic groups that have to live together." He added: "We suspect this might be reflected in the quality of your products, in the difficulties you have in managing things."[13]

U.S. businesses railed against such an assessment of U.S. manufacturing incompetence. They believed they had "legitimate" complaints about Japanese trade barriers, and were tired of Japanese lectures about quality control and the merits of the Japanese management system. In response, the Japanese saw another symptom of decline in American complaints about Japanese trade practices and the burdens of paying for Japanese defense. "The United States' 'blame thy partner' trade policy is really very costly," said Kuroda Makoto, Japan's former senior Trade Ministry negotiator. "The only possible explanation to us is that maybe the United States is becoming weaker, and that may be the main reason you have become so frustrated."

By the late 1980s Japan saw these U.S. weaknesses as a good reason to realign power in the world, to establish *a new order* in which the might of Nippon would shore up, and in some cases supplant, the failing economic power of the U.S. One Japanese politician coined the new era *Pax Consortis,* set off by Japan's changing image of the U.S. and prompting a foreign policy debate about how Japan could fit into a new order in which the U.S. could no longer dictate policy, but would share power and the economic cost of leadership with a group of nations that included Japan.

Yet ideas concerning the rebalancing of aid to developing nations, with Japan becoming the leading contributor, while leaving expenditures on defense of the free world to the U.S., would not easily resolve more basic structural problems. Japan offered no clear-cut alternative to America reducing its military spending, and the U.S. could not afford to sustain grants to, or forgive debts contracted by, the third world.[14]

Breakdown of Self-Sufficiency

The fundamental source of the U.S. breakdown in self-sufficiency has been inadequate compensation for work combined with an "easy-credit" marketplace that had cut away the foundation for national savings, domestic investment, and extended production.

The resulting low national savings rate of 2 percent in 1988 meant that the other 98 percent of earnings were spent. "This represents less than one-third of the inadequate savings rate we enjoyed prior to 1980," one economist complained, adding that it is only "one-fifth of the average saving rate of the leading industrial nations and one-eighth of the national savings rate in Japan."[15]

Obviously, it is logical to spend today rather than to save for tomorrow so long as inflation means that more money must be spent to buy the same goods in the future. The psychology of buying now is also fueled by the readily available credit lavished on U.S. consumers.

But this hyperextension of credit periodically leads to crisis, for credit institutions themselves get caught in the bind of having to borrow at higher short-term rates than those at which they have loaned for the long term.

Governments, too, tend to spend at higher levels than they earn by the collection of taxes, so they also face a sort of bankruptcy in terms of perennial deficits that must be made up by means of additional borrowing and taxes. The initial break in U.S. self-sufficiency emerged publicly in 1971, when President Nixon attempted to restore America's *status quo ante* by devaluing the dollar and cutting its link with gold. Periodic de facto devaluations thereafter kept a shield around the U.S. market to a minor degree. But the scaling up of America's negative trade balance after 1984 led the Reagan and Bush administrations to again attempt to force down the value of the dollar — with the aim of making imports more expensive and exports cheaper, in the hopes of reducing record trade deficits and empowering America to continue borrowing foreign capital to cover its government deficit and investment needs.

From a nationalist viewpoint, the plan was not necessarily misdirected; it just did not do the job. Dollar devaluation could not stop nations that had already gained a foothold in the American market from protecting their territorial interests by cutting their prices and profits.[16] Japanese companies dumped at prices nearer and nearer to their variable factory costs of raw materials and energy. They were no longer confined to their earlier policy of simply cutting prices 10 percent below those of competitors, and were willing to sell at *zero profit* to maintain their market shares!

At this point, there was no pure, economic way in which U.S. companies could compete on Japan's terms even on their own turf. As the home team on American soil, many retreated to the bullpen and warmed up their political players. By the spring of 1988, Congress had taken on the task of dealing with Japanese competition by moving to curb imports that were undermining U.S. industry and causing the loss of jobs in manufacturing. "The bill really significantly shifts the balance towards protectionism," one former Reagan National Security Council staff member, Henry R. Nau, declared. The bill in question mandated self-sufficiency. It pressured the American president to honor the U.S. International Trade Commission's periodic findings that an industry had been hurt by foreign competition and should be helped by tariffs on the offending foreigners' goods; to respond to foreign industries' dumping by charging the entire nation as an unfair trader and retaliating against all its exports to the U.S.; and to enforce American will by negotiating multinational or bilateral agreements on manufactured goods, agricultural output, intellectual property like computer software, and trade in services such as advertising and finance.[17]

Such a protectionist — and protected — America would become an enclave, building up a tariff wall to ensure a monopolized, domestic market for American goods and to guarantee a high-price structure at home — thereby facilitating the U.S. efforts to dump these same goods, farm output, services, and intellectual property abroad. The logic of keeping competitor products out of the U.S. market to reduce competition also posited low incentives to build more efficient industries, keep down costs and wages, and compete on the basis of price. High prices in the domestic market could then cover these increased costs, so that an enlarged volume of production could in part be sold at lower prices in the foreign market.

The U.S. could thus compete with Japan in three ways: by blocking out its low-price, dumped goods; by dumping U.S.-made goods in Japan; and by selling at dumping prices in competition with Japan in third markets.

Japan, the European Community, and Korea immediately recognized the implications for their own protected, high-price domestic markets, which had enabled them to dump in the U.S. for more than a decade. They naturally resisted Congress' bill. But they were also unwilling to give up very much of their own, similar systems, as we will later show, breeding an uneasy shift of commercial power as nations struggled with the irreconcilable drives for self-sufficiency and unfettered trade.

The Banks Teeter on Bankruptcy

For the United States, at least, the perennial trade and budget deficits not only meant that accumulating debt had to be repaid, but that the assets for repayment would fall into foreign hands. U.S. banks and financial institutions could not simply create and use dollar credits to pay the debt, as they once had done, because in the late 1980s the dollar was fast losing its place as a reserve currency that held the confidence of central banks in Western Europe and Japan.

During the 1980s American accumulation techniques had been switched *from uncompetitive industries to fields of finance at home and then, on the heels of crisis, also abroad.* Still, U.S. interest rates remained higher than in Japan; U.S. equities had lower price/earnings ratios; and American real estate was far less expensive than comparable real estate in Japan. Because the financial markets in the U.S. still remained attractive to *both* U.S. and foreign investors, the volume of investments had surged. U.S. banks and Japanese investment houses were largely financing the American national debt. Yet, U.S. banks were also locked into the foreign domain, and Japanese and West German banks were reaching into the inner sanctum of U.S. high finance. By the end of the 1980s foreign dollar holdings reached an estimated $1 trillion, with Japan holding as much as $500 billion in U.S. government notes and bonds.[18]

The dominant position of U.S. *commercial banks* in the world had meanwhile clearly eroded. In the 1960s and 1970s these U.S. banks had so weakened themselves by lending to third world debtors who could not repay that, when their more responsible corporate customers turned to less costly capital resources, the banks were saddled with less credit-worthy customers and themselves became vulnerable.

The big banks scrambled to shed their unstable loans to the third world; though they had sold, swapped, or otherwise jettisoned only $100 million from 1962 to 1986, they rid themselves of $1.4 billion in the first quarter of 1988, and $2.3 billion in the second. This seemed a drop in the bucket considering the $50 billion or so owed by Latin American nations to major U.S. banks; but the banks had managed to secure themselves by accepting 50 to 85 cents on the dollar for their troubled loans, thereby bolstering their capital (consisting of equity, retained earnings, and reserves against loan losses). As thirteen of the nation's largest banks reduced their portfolio of troubled loans, these loans declined as a percentage of total equity capital, thereby appearing to strengthen the individual banks and the banking system.[19]

Yet, the cost of selling off third world debt at a discount and creating huge reserve losses to offset current bank income was paid for by bank stockholders. Banks that were too slow to reduce third world loan portfolios were punished with lower stock prices, higher financing costs, and uncompetitive positions.[20] Congress' General Accounting Office estimated in 1988 that bank reserves of $21 billion against troubled loans to less developed nations were insufficient to cover the then $49 billion in uncollectible debts.

Such frailties cut at the core of the banks' lending process and their search for maximum profits with minimum risks. Once the highest-quality business borrowers turned to the securities markets to raise funds more cheaply than they could from banks, said Federal Reserve Board Chairman Alan Greenspan, these banks found their remaining customers to be "less credit-worthy than earlier in the postwar period." "The current ability of the nonfinancial corporate sector to cover its debt-serving costs out of earning is low," Greenspan explained, adding that "for many firms it is uncomfortably low."

The loss of income from bad loans would have to be offset by additional income sources for American banks to survive, he said. Bank rates and earning would thus have to rise. And Chairman Greenspan argued that banks would become profitable again only if the overall return on their portfolios was "substantial enough to offset the additional risks that are now a *permanent feature* of the loan structure of banks." Toward this end, he advocated that Congress repeals the Glass-Steagall Act to grant the banks wide securities powers and alternatives, as "products" necessary to keep pace with market innovations and technological change.[21]

Others advocated that the federal budget be tapped in 1990 for $30 billion to bail the banks out of their bad loans to the third world and to troubled real estate ventures in the U.S. The estimated cost to liquidate or force the mergers of insolvent saving institutions was put at $50–100 billion or more in 1988–90. And the number of banks with capital less than assets, or only a slender percentage of assets, was rapidly rising. These banks were either bankrupt or close to the edge.[22]

So the heavy burden of weakened, second-rate corporate borrowers, banks crippled by bad and uncertain loans, and rising interest charges beset

America—opening the way for Japanese and European investors with a surfeit of capital to plow into financing the U.S. government and lending to or buying U.S. businesses and banks. It was now an article of faith to blame Japan for America's ills. But the truth lay elsewhere.

Dollar Demise and Overseas Bank Successes

The dominant role of the American dollar in international finance was rapidly coming to a close. The United States would probably remain a debtor nation for years, possibly decades. It would also have to pay its bills, not with a weakened dollar that foreigners suspected, but in American assets and the nation's remaining gold supplies.

Conceding that the U.S. had until mid-1988 been able to finance its deficits in its *own currency,* one senior Swiss banker warned that foreign investors' appetites for dollar-denominated securities "could end suddenly before anyone realized it."[23] Certainly, the structure for such a switch was already in place in the late 1980s. U.S. investment banks had already dropped away from *underwriting* Eurobonds by attracting dollars held outside America and had retreated to the field of European *takeovers* using London as their base. During most of the 1980s U.S. investment banks had dominated the London-based Eurobond arena, the hub of international capital markets. But by the first six months of 1988, it was evident that foreigners were skittish about holding large chunks of the $650 billion in dollar-denominated, Eurobond securities. After the October 1987 stock market crash, investors scaled back their trades in both stocks and bonds. With profit-potential fast eroding, U.S. investment banks retreated, no longer making up the majority of the top-ten underwriters of Eurobonds in London, *momentarily* leaving leadership in the field to the Japanese, West Germans, Swiss, French, and English—in that order. These American bankers then drifted toward fee-earning corporate finance activities, scaling back their executive staffs to those familiar with deal making, and especially advising clients on takeovers in England—where they even ousted some London merchant banks in the first half of 1988.[24]

The U.S. banks would use their "financing technology" and experience in international mergers to regain their profitability abroad, even if the dollar and the U.S. economy were in trouble. "I don't see the events of the past year bringing in a sea of change for those firms internationally," judged Samuel Hayes III, professor of investment banking at the Harvard Business School, adding that the merchant banks "were enormously overextended, having grown incredibly in London. So there was a lot of fat there—and there's more left to go." "But," he concluded, "the forces of technology, deregulation and the internationalization of business generally that drove them overseas initially remain in place."

"The U.S. firms will not have as big an investor base to tap as the

Japanese, West Germans and Swiss," confirmed Lowell Bryan, a principal for the consulting firm McKinsey and Company. "But the strength of the American investment banks is the know-how and financial engineering skills of their people. So they will have to focus more on value-added areas requiring specialized skills and not on commodity-type products in capital markets."[25]

What might happen, then, in a future when the U.S. is a debtor nation, American industry remains uncompetitive, domestic commercial banks are saddled with unstable second-class borrowers, and U.S. investment banks are profitably making deals abroad? The United States might require the perennial infusion of foreign capital in yen-dominated or European currency–denominated securities, and the terms imposed by the holders of the new reserve currencies might involve greater controls over the American economy.

Perhaps it will never reach the U.S. defensive point of government orders that, "to hold the line we cannot tolerate further increases in general wage or salary rates except where clearly necessary to correct sub-standard rates."[26] But, then again, some sector in America will ultimately have to pay.

Chapter 14
Japan's Script
Almost Like America's

In 1986 Japan began to follow a script comparable to the American plans drawn up in the 1970s and 1980s, inflating its currency to the highest level since World War II, pricing some goods out of world markets, bankrupting basic industries, and forcing a switch to high-tech investments, which also came under pressure from cheaper Asian goods.

Basic industries such as steel and shipbuilding momentarily closed down capacity, rotated layoffs to reduce payrolls and subdue workers' complaints, paid lump-sum outlays for early retirement, and used personnel transfers as a means of eventual layoffs at often-distant subsidiary locations.

But this did not resolve the problems of lower costs and fierce competition from South Korea and other newly industrialized countries that were forcing a shift from Japan's smokestack industries toward high-tech and service industries. As the decline accelerated and the appreciating yen hurt sales in foreign markets, a shadow was cast over seacoast towns and remote areas where basic shipbuilding, steel, and coal mining once thrived. Faced with falling profit returns on capital, some conglomerates in basic industries were forced to sell their undervalued assets in other firms in order to cover their current operating losses.

This reassembly of Japan's basic industries forced the march of jobs to the urban domain and the inland plains as the next step in technological advance. Though Japan needed to lower labor costs and the price of the consumer goods and foods the work force required, the farmers continued to receive prices far in excess of world market levels, and were not uprooted. Rather, the government and its politicians dependent on the farm lobby for their jobs continued to subsidize rice farmers, maintaining the price at $1.50 a pound and keeping cheaper U.S., Thai, and Australian rice out.[1] Consumers at the government rice shops continued to pay Japan's farmers the difference, impacting the cost of living and pushing up labor's demand for higher wages.

As foreign markets were lost as wages went up and the yen appreciated to competitors in South Korea and other nations whose currencies moved in tandem with the U.S. dollar—and as domestic sales fell with the slump in Japan's economy—Japan's five biggest steel companies offset their losses from March to September 1986 by selling securities, and announced continued losses unless Japanese currency that had fallen to 162 yen to the dollar was raised to 180–190 yen. Without this, plans to reduce capacity from 28 million metric tons to 24 by 1991 were to be implemented by Nippon Steel's plan to close at least three of its fourteen blast furnaces; and in any case employment would be cut by thousands of workers for all big steel makers.[2]

Toward this end transitional steps were essential: labor costs were lowered by up to a one-fifth by temporary, rotational layoff of full-time workers at 70 percent of their normal pay, with some of it provided by government as a boost to speed reorganization. Old industries switched redundant employees by setting up new ventures in services and security systems. New and old industries refused to buy expensive coal resources from domestic Japanese mines, leading to cuts in wages, massive layoffs, and the decay of mining towns. Worse still was the immobility of older workers who lacked the skills for technical employment and exceeded the age limit thirty-five that entitled them to higher pay. These "elders" were replaced by younger, cheaper workers; and the towns they lived in were returned to past industries, small-scale farming and fishing, or hoped to become thriving vacation resorts or convention centers, drawing a revenue flow as a final quest to survive.[3]

Nor was high-tech itself insulated from crisis, eliciting a double outflow of Japanese capital. At one level, consumer electronic firms that had lost world markets closed down their Japanese plants and replaced them with low-wage assembly lines in Korea, Taiwan, and other zones where parity with the dollar was relatively constant. Such action enabled them to continue to sell in the U.S. market without the price-increase burden of the inflated yen. At a second level, Japanese manufacturers of memory chips lost their runaway domestic customers, so they too sought to follow their clients and to expand markets by setting up—or buying out—operations abroad.

The computer buying slump from 1984 to 1986 took Japanese memory chip manufacturers by surprise. "The memory chip market has turned out to be Japan's economic Vietnam," offered Andrew Grove, president of Intel Corp. in the Silicon Valley. Japan's technical lead was undeniable, having escalated from producing 80 percent of all 256K chips to a likely future monopoly of the one-megabit device and a four-megabit chip capable of storing four million bits of data. Yet Japan's state-fostered joint research efforts among its electronic giants for very large-scale integrated circuits (VLSI) had hit a dry market and possibly could follow the pattern of the U.S. loss of $600 million in the 1985 memory chip market. "We predicted that the market would go up 20 to 30% a year, just as in the past," said NEC corporate director Matsumura Tomihiro, speaking of his firm, the largest

Japanese producer of microchips. "The mistake is that we believed our own predictions."

The remaining market was meanwhile grabbed by smaller Japanese and South Korean manufacturers able to produce at low costs and to cut their prices. Together these pressures led to a loss of markets for the five largest Japanese electronic firms, resulting in a 50–80 percent fall in their pretax profits for the half-year ended September 1986, and an estimated 21–50 percent fall for the full year ending March, 1987.[4]

This economic situation at home was the catalyst for Fujitsu's move to other production centers in Asia and the U.S. Fujitsu became a transnational enterprise to avoid U.S.–Japanese price restraints by selling Fujitsu's memory chips from production plants located within the U.S. or the U.S. sphere of fixed-currency trade.

Either the U.S. would be pressed to import Japanese chips made by joint-venture U.S.–Japanese operations, or both U.S. and Japanese production subsidiaries would be set up with high-tech in low-wage nations or within the U.S. or Japanese markets. Thus Toshiba and Motorola talked of a possible joint venture in Japan to produce and sell both memory chips and logic chips to be called Nippon Motorola. And NEC and Fujitsu scrapped plans to build new manufacturing plants at home, while all major chip producers (save Toshiba) planned to cut capital spending by up to half. Hitachi executives took 10 percent pay cuts, but talked cautiously about layoffs and a possible move to the U.S. for speciality chip production. And executives from Hitachi, NEC, Fujitsu, and Toshiba planned more profitable ventures in new fields: logic chips, gate-arrays, and semi-custom chips.[5]

Conquest by Gauges and Market Spheres

The conquest of American markets by Japanese subsidiaries was made possible by using the *existing gauge* of production; and their simultaneous expansion in world markets would become so by developing a *new gauge*.

In the case of Fujitsu, the conquest of the U.S. market was sought by the takeover of Fairchild to produce logic semiconductors. Using the U.S. gauge system, Fujitsu had already copied IBM's line of plug compatible computers that use the same programs, operating instructions, and peripheral equipment. But IBM had legally forced Fujitsu to pay for infringing its copyrights and designs, thereby draining some of Fujitsu's revenue and acting as the verification police to see that Fujitsu's systems did not duplicate IBM models. IBM's legal success had effectively hobbled some of Fujitsu's development programs, leading to its plan to extend its product line to new technologies and gauges — such as application-specific integrated circuits; new gate-array chips; an original 32-bit microprocessor (with Hitachi); and corresponding memory chips.[6]

The same held true for Hitachi's 1982 plan to appropriate IBM's plans and software codes for the production of IBM-compatible computers. Hitachi was forced to pay an estimated $1 billion fine plus $3–6 million per month payments for the use of IBM's software, and also was required to give IBM the right of inspection to see that its patents and copyrights were not violated.

In November 1986 a new era dawned with IBM's agreement to reduce Hitachi's payments and stop inspections, but IBM then accused Fujitsu of violating its agreement with IBM through extensive copying of IBM programs.[7]

Playing out the rationale of accumulation, competitive gauges had become the focus. Now owners of each standard gauge moved to secure patents entitling them to royalties from competitors licensing it. The American Telephone and Telegraph Company had been the creator, and royalty-recipient from licensees, of the Unix software standard. But in August 1988 major U.S. computer companies put up $100 million to form the Open Software Foundation consortium to develop their own version of the Unix operating system that could run on a variety of different computers. Using the computer hardware from many member companies to develop software that would work in different computers, their research, development, and technical support services promised to introduce the consortium's key product in January 1990—thereby freeing Unix licensees from ATT forever.[8]

The possibility remained, though, that future production and communications directed toward the same markets would eventually produce excess capacity. IBM and Carnegie Mellon University thus entered the competition in August 1988, with expected development of the *Andrew File System,* a system intended to use a *single software computer application* to permit the high-speed transmission of computer files between personal computers nationwide. By accessing the file system, the data base would itself be moved, the foundation for problem solving would rise, and the coming generation of high-speed computer networks would quickly connect almost all college campuses and businesses nationwide.[9]

Other contradictions might then emerge. The drain of royalty payments might both weaken and saddle smaller licensees, while providing financial sustenance to the licensors to further extend their technological strength. The emergence of an oligopolized industry became increasingly possible.

Thus would appear the dual tendency of lessees trying to break free of royalty payments by creating their own gauges for production and lessors attempting to strengthen their control over technical knowledge put in service. And this likely future would impact the entire field of microtechnologies, robots not excepted.

High-Stake Robots

The stakes were especially high in terms of robotic production, for the introduction of new gauge standards with more complex technological components held the potential to vastly enlarge the dimension of output.

Past industrialization that had bred the assembly line, mass production, and automated controls based on microtechnology had also evolved a fourth dimension: robotic production that did not require the intervention of the traditional forms of human labor. As Japan's large manufacturing firms had shown, extensive investments in automated manufacturing and technology would be rewarded in terms of greater output for each currency unit spent on labor.

This was made possible by the linkage of automated computer controls to robots on the assembly line, following one of two basic system arrangements. The first was directed toward extended production-runs of a few high-quality products, thereby increasing labor productivity and output in a given time frame. The second was directed toward short production-cycles of a large number of specialized parts suited to the needs of a greater number of individual customers.

Costs of operating the two systems reversed the traditional Western expectation of mass production using inanimate energy to power machinery that affixed tools applied to the raw materials being processed. Computer programs that directed robots now allowed for greater flexibility of output at lower cost, once the new technology was scientifically set in motion and regulated.

Because the cost of investment in the new technology was very high, efficiency tended to fall at the point where computers were used to direct robots (i.e., the first basic arrangement) as if they were mere replications of conventional assembly operations stressing mass production of a few product lines. The huge fixed costs allocated over total output produced a higher unit cost than if conventional machinery was used.

Such higher costs in part emerged from the two-tier labor system: expensive engineers were employed to build, install, and maintain the robots, and relatively inexpensive unskilled workers were employed to operate them. Because robots needed to be adjusted, honed, and reoriented as production went forward, it was not yet technically possible for unskilled workers to oversee operations. Rather, it was initially necessary to use engineers and other highly trained personnel to develop and set up automated equipment as well as to operate and oversee production. Moreover, careful training designed to upgrade labor skills was necessary for understanding and controlling the new technology. Only thereby could these technical means be made flexible in varying both production and functions, to expand the scope of existing systems, and to forward uninterrupted operations.[10]

Obviously, if competitor companies and nations followed the same script on a global scale, output might be vastly enlarged, while the labor force would be split into high-price experts, and low-price unskilled hands, and the unemployed. Competition for too few jobs might force down wages, thereby reducing the total labor cost of production. But a lower general wage would also cut down total buying power that impacts on the many dimensions of the market for raw materials, food, manufactured goods, services, industrial equipment, and in the end labor itself. Such a scenario would result in more computers directing more robots to produce more commodities, and would appear side by side with a relatively few high-priced workers and a growing body of low-paid and displaced workers without the means to buy much at all.

Part 5:
Common Markets/
Common Destiny

*America must unite—now. America must
sacrifice—now. America must work—now.*
—Joseph P. Kennedy, 18 January 1941

Banzai! ("Ten thousand years!")—Victory
cry of Japanese warriors

Agreements for equitable bilateral trade and investments, cartels, and
autarchical state consortia to foster home industries may be the only possible common means Japan, the United States, Western and Eastern
Europe have available to work out a mutually satisfactory destiny during
the rest of the 20th century.

There can and will be no common destiny so long as these trilateral
powers pursue their own provincial and regional images of *neomerantilist
trade* and *commercio-financial hegemony*. At best, they will establish a
mechanism to forward their mutual economic successes. At worst, each will
retreat to a regional arena of helotry that for a time secures their respective
interests at the expense of economically less-advanced countries. Between
these two poles, there will be a continuation of their uninterrupted conflicts
over trade, investments, production, employment policies, currency ratios,
interest rates, and the like.

As in the past, these conflicts may be resolved on an ad hoc basis, case-
by-case, product-by-product. Special-interest legislation in each contending nation may favor domestic industries, thereby solidifying their recourse
to political pressures and continued demands for tête-à-tête negotiations
with competitive industries in other nations. Under such arrangements,
Japan's regional system will experience prosperity or lose economically
only because the common markets of America and Western and Eastern
Europe suffer the losses or reap the rewards. The U.S. stands in a similar

situation, as do both Western and Eastern European countries; and the two latter regions, if consolidated economically and politically, might conceivably exclude both U.S. and Japanese goods, services, and investments. Obviously, these partial solutions will not move toward lasting benefits for each of these three regions.

A common ground will escape them so long as economic ratios alone control their underlying relationships. Western, and now Eastern, European, nations simply cannot hold their positions in the economic realm so long as they are deficient in the sociopolitical sphere; and Japan's adoption of Western economic calculations will one day undermine that nation's positive aspects of social responsibility and empathetic understanding. The new-age autarky of a Japan that hopes to sell more, but buy less, or control more production abroad, yet limit foreign control of investments in Japan, is bound to move in the direction of establishing a coprosperity sphere that will rigidify its political system at home in order to combat the demands of other nations for equity. A consolidated Europe cannot hope to follow Japan's example without a centralized structure that creates an exclusive, transcontinental market and paninvestment sphere, and mobilizes populations into narrow visions of exclusiveness. The United States cannot at once be a free-trader and the most protected market in the world, as well as the guardian of the Open Door for U.S. investments abroad and the nationalist protector of the exclusive investment rights of every American industrialist or banker. United States or Japanese xenophobia does not square with an egalitarian, global commercial order.

The central issue in the balance of the 20th century thus will not be whether capitalist nations and the remaining socialist nations will come to live on the same planet without war — for they must, if there is to be a planet to live on. Rather, it is whether the capitalist and market nations can live equitably with one another and uplift their own and third world populations. If they cannot, the commercial sphere will again be segmented and neomercantilism will bear its traditional fruits: autarchical production, oligopolies, cartels, bilateral trade, exchange control, building up bullion supplies, nationalist ideologies, the designing of economic helotries and commercial spheres of influence, possibly new armaments for military preparedness — against the impositions of others.

Chapter 15

New-Age Autarky

Since the early 1960s a new era of autarky has swept the capitalist world. Nation states not only hold an imaged need to be self-sufficient, but actively mobilize government resources and power to construct state and private consortia to foster home industries and geographic common markets, spheres of economic interest, or even informal "empires." Japan and the United States in particular have turned inward to think only in terms of their exclusive, self-sufficient economies. There is a vast chasm in communications between the largest financial and business institutions of both nations. "The misundertandings are as wide as the Delaware Water Gap, and they are permanent," says lawyer Ko-Yung Tung of the Los Angeles firm O'Melveny and Myers, a firm that makes a significant income from clearing the way for deals in real estate, mergers, and international trade for some of the largest Japanese institutions doing business in the United States.[1]

The drive for, and misunderstanding about, proprietary rights in technology have also intensified, especially since the late 1980s. The more grandiose technology has become, and the larger the financial expenditures required to pursue technological research, development, and production, the more intense has become the drive to build state-industry consortia to prevent competitors from entering markets organized on the plane of the nation or within its sphere of influence. Developing supercomputers or modern aircraft requires many millions or even billions in dollar outlays, for example, so that the volume of output placed on relatively limited markets must be both large enough to absorb costs and sufficiently guaranteed to secure profits. Thus the state must aid production and warrant monopsonistic control over the home market for capital-intensive production, also stimulating national production and employment for the suppliers of the great companies — mediating these through the trade and investment balances of other nations.

Balance-of-Payments: Indicia of Historical Stages

Balance of payments act as historical markers setting out the economic terrain a nation has passed over in relation to the terrain crossed by other nations.

In the early stages of the development of any nation, characterized by producing and exporting inexpensive raw materials and importing more costly manufactured goods, the trade equation with other countries usually reads negative. But at a later stage, for those countries that are able to establish their political and economic sovereignty, the manufacturing of higher-price goods for export markets may offset the prices charged by other nations for imports of their manufactured and other goods. Once nations reach the status of general industrialization, moreover, they may allow their own internal raw material extraction industries and agricultural areas to fall into disuse and may even import essential raw materials and foods at a cheaper price than those available at home from other nations with which they maintain a positive trade balance. At a later stage in industrial development, the turn to high-tech output and the sale of services may even lead to neglect of old, basic manufacturing industries, so that these functions are transferred to other nations, leading to the import of manufactures once produced at home, but whose price is more than offset by the export of higher priced services and high-tech products.

But what happens when a nation like the United States does not renew its technological base for industrial production? Does not efficiently or competitively extract its own raw material supplies? Subsidizes agricultural production and exports to break into the protected spheres of others nations? Offers financial services, yet neglects to rapidly apply its own invention of new technologies to the production of the latest high-tech products? The import of the raw materials, manufactured goods, and high-tech products of other nations turns the trade balance negative, and this negative balance is not offset by the export of food, high-tech goods, or invisible services like shipping, licensing, insurance, or banking fees.

On the other side of the trade equation, what takes place when a nation like Japan simultaneously moves to the cutting edge of applying the latest technologies to production for home consumption and exports; sends abroad its investments in previous stages of technological production to be nearer to raw materials, cheap labor, and markets; undertakes foreign investments to capture the latest technological advances, and stimulates domestic demand by importing inexpensive manufactures, most of its raw material needs, and a portion of its food supplies? The export of high-tech products easily covers the cost of imports, leaving a positive trade balance that enables a massive export of capital for loans, joint ventures, and direct investments abroad, as well as aid to other nations — which again stimulates Japanese exports.

Understanding these differences that represent the two different sociohistorical stages of the U.S. and Japanese economies helps to account for their inability to reconcile their disagreements in the late 1980s.

Disregarding this approach, another school of thought effectively rationalizes that an *equitable relationship* has been established through the overlapping historical stages the U.S. and Japan have passed through. By

combining U.S. market access through exports and sales from U.S.–owned
production facilities within Japan, for example, a so-called product-
presence index can be derived that can be compared with Japan's comparable "product presence" in the United States. By such means it is possible to demonstrate a greater U.S. market penetration in Japan than a
Japanese penetration of U.S. domestic markets.

Figures taken in isolation provide the legerdemain to argue the precise
measurement of this mutual penetration of American and Japanese companies in each other's markets. Thus, for instance, 1984 production for
domestic sales in Japan by the largest three hundred U.S. manufacturing
companies totalled $43.9 billion, while all Japanese companies produced
for sale $12.8 billion in the U.S. The net exports from each nation to the
other awarded the U.S. $25.6 billion in exports and Japan $56.8 billion in
exports. Adding these figures, the total accounting of U.S. production
within Japan for sale and U.S. exports to Japan was thus $69.5 billion, and
for Japanese production within the U.S. for sale and Japanese exports to
the U.S. $69.6 billion.[2]

The problem with this numerical method is that it is ahistoric. The
U.S. trade and investment presence in Japan was largely established in the
1950s and 1960s, and this base was built upon in the 1970s and 1980s.
Japanese trade increments were gradually secured from the 1960s through
the 1980s, and its investment presence in the U.S. was mainly established
in the 1980s, especially after 1984.

The internal dynamics contouring these national patterns also mean
that no resolution of the U.S. imbalance of trade and payments will occur
unless Japan takes four major steps: stimulate its domestic consumption to
reduce exports and encourage U.S. imports; encourage the U.S. to produce
competitive, high-quality exports for sale in Japan; open its economy to
new U.S. investments; and increase its export of capital to the United
States.

But Japan only acted out part of this composite scenario, seeking a
further advantage through superficial solutions to the barriers the U.S.
faced. As a major thrust blocking equitable trade, for example, imports
from the U.S. were not adequately encouraged or allowed. Rather, superficial or token programs were repeatedly paraded as examples of what the
future might hold. Thus, when the U.S. bilateral trade deficit was $10
billion in 1979, American exporters who viewed the problem as one of *lack
of Japanese awareness* of U.S. products loaded $10 million in food and
wares on a 30-year-old freighter remodeled as "Boutique America," and
took Japan by storm. Before the ship could get out of its second port of
call in Yokohama Bay, Japanese throngs had snapped up 130 tons of inexpensive beef for $1.4 million. Thirteen cities later, though, only about 20
percent of the rest of the merchandise had been sold, because discerning
Japanese buyers had complained about no meat, the poor quality of U.S.
products, and long lines.

When the U.S. bilateral trade deficit reached about $40 billion in 1985, Prime Minister Nakasone offered the utopian suggestion that each Japanese buy $100 of foreign goods from the lists drawn up by Nippon bureaucrats. And when the U.S. bilateral trade deficit reached $52 billion in 1988, more pie-in-the-sky sales were to emerge from a twelve-car "American Train" to transverse Japan hawking the wares of U.S. corporations — to the benefit of the privatized East Japan Railway and Japanese company sponsors such as Kirin beer, Nikka Whiskey, and TDK recording tape. These firms were to *act as agents of U.S. corporations:* charging $2.5 million each for a train car for a full year to American Express Co., the State of Hawaii, and Hewlett-Packard; renting subdivided train kiosks for $150,000 to Campbell Soup, Eastman Kodak, and Chicago Pacific Corp.'s Hoover Co.; and selling other U.S. companies' goods on consignment, taking 70 percent of the first $300,000 in sales and 50 percent for the balance.

The operation was completely in the hands of Japanese companies, replicating the same complex distribution system that already hindered U.S. companies' products. "It is one of the wackier attempts to ease the trade problem to come down the tracks in some time," the *Wall Street Journal* concluded.[3] "The project provides an excellent opportunity for American enterprises to test-market their products or services in Japan," claimed *The American Train in Japan* Japanese-enterprisers of their service, listing eleven paying clients for pavilions (at $2.5 million each) and sixteen general supporters (at $150,000 each).[4]

Meanwhile, Nippon companies had deeper ambitions for expanded global markets. Despite Japan's 1988 attempts to stimulate domestic consumption, it refused to *guarantee* U.S. market shares within Japan (as noted above), and sought instead to cut domestic production costs to fill the home market *and* stimulate exports. This policy rapidly led to Japan's "local downpour" of exports, especially in the areas of new product technologies, like facsimile machines, which the U.S. did not yet make, and in products which Japan heavily dumped abroad, like semiconductors, switching equipment, automobile parts, and numerically controlled machine tools. When the U.S. complained that the downpour was increasing, Japan dumped more heavily in Western Europe. And when Western Europe also complained, the dumping was shifted elsewhere. Nonetheless, by mid-1988, exports to the U.S. were increasing, those to the rest of the world were growing even faster, and the growth of economies worldwide was enlarging the demand for Japanese exports.

Surveying Japanese manufacturing and trading companies, the MITI predicted that the quantity of exports would enlarge 2 percent and the price in dollars 12.2 percent from 1 April 1988 to 31 March 1989 — offsetting the cost-effect of expected import growth of 17.9 percent.[5] The detailed figures were not as important as the fact that the MITI was positioned to ensure that this growth transpired, and that Japan's future trade surplus would rise—not fall, as short-term trade balances revealed and Western nations were told.

Steps made toward achieving this end involved a steady rise in Japanese exports and a faster rise in imports. Yet Nippon used the global market as an apparatus to lessen exports here to dump them there, or to increase imports from this nation to cut them from that one. Japan thereby appeased the U.S. in part by receiving monthly imports of about $2 billion following the Plaza Accord of 5 September 1985 and the expansion of Japan's 1988 domestic demand; and Japan periodically reduced exports to the U.S. in the face of the appreciation of the yen and threatened U.S. trade barriers. As the U.S. negative trade balance with Japan was reduced, moreover, almost in step with this reduction Japan enlarged its balance of trade with Western Europe and increased its exports to Southeast Asia.

Thus more Japanese exports were dumped on European markets, particularly those whose currencies moved with the German mark and therefore had not appreciated as much as the dollar against the yen. Meanwhile, the U.S.–enforced appreciation of the South Korean won and the "new Taiwan dollar" against the U.S. dollar in 1987–88 not only made their exports more expensive, but allowed Japanese exporters to raise prices, so that Japanese exports to Southeast Asia almost kept pace with the larger volume of still-cheaper imports from the region. The overall result was that while Japan's surplus with the U.S. narrowed slightly, its surplus with Western Europe enlarged and with Southeast Asia shrunk less rapidly.[6] Meanwhile, Japan maintained a surplus with almost all these trade partners, juggling the monthly and annual balances with each of them to fit the overall needs of its expanding economy.

To offset the MITI policy of export downpour by mid-1988 Japan officially advocated the increased export of capital to the U.S., arguing that the U.S. had a savings deficit and thus needed great sums of capital to upgrade its plants to become more competitive. Since the MITI viewed the U.S. economy as consumption-oriented—and argued that in 1986–87 the population had borrowed more than it had saved—American industry would have to turn to Japan for both finance and the essential machinery to upgrade its factories. U.S. consumer debt had hovered between 17 and 23 percent of GNP in the 1980s; home mortgage debt was 41 percent of GNP, the national debt was 43 percent, and 20 percent of the federal budget went for interest on that debt in 1987–88. Foreign capital had thus financed the empty spaces left in capital investment and government budgets.[7]

This also meant that further export of Japanese technology could be expected. And, again, MITI held forth the required gesture, that to stimulate U.S. exports, both Japan and other trade surplus nations would also have to import more of certain kinds of goods.[8]

In other words, under the guidance of the MITI and the new plan for expanded investment and consumption in the 1990s, Japanese overseas trade and investment policy would be closely controlled and exports would probably increase. Japan's positive balance of trade figures might rise and be offset by the export of more Japanese capital—the *economic* posture assumed by great powers in the past.

The Next Steps in Decline

After the foundation of a negative trade balance has been set in place, the next step in the historic pattern of decline has usually been the import of foreign capital to sustain sections of basic production, new industries, and the budget of the state itself. Proud denials that the United States has reached this eclipse of economic power have accompanied its net import of foreign investment capital, but these are nearly as effective as the Roman emperors declaring that their frontiers are impregnable while first the provinces and then Rome itself were sacked by Visgoth invaders.

Americans should be "proud" that foreigners continue to invest in the United States, "cashing in on U.S. growth and adding dramatically to the total net worth" of its citizens, offered U.S. Chamber of Commerce chief economist Richard W. Rhan at the end of June 1988. The U.S. had recorded the third consecutive rise in its *negative investment stake* in the world, going up from $110.7 billion in 1985 to $269.2 billion in 1986 and to $386 billion in 1987.

The once positive net position the U.S. held by offsetting its own foreign investments against the investment of others in the U.S. had been over $100 billion from 1980 to 1982, but it had slipped to about $90 billion in 1983, plummeted to $5 billion in 1984, and then became negative. Meanwhile, *cumulative* foreign investments in the U.S. had steadily grown from about $500 billion in 1980 to $1,540 billion in 1987.

Foreigners in 1987 held about 5 percent of the assets in an economy that turned out more than $4.5 trillion work of goods and services a year. And, seeing no danger, economist Rahn waxed eloquent that the U.S. was "in no sense a debtor nation like Brazil, Argentina or Mexico," which not only had to repay big debts, but had to borrow in currencies other than their own.[9]

From the other side of the Pacific, there was talk of *Pax Amerippon* or *Pax Japonica,* based on the assumption that Japan would overwhelm the U.S. economically or that Japan would become the world financier and America its policeman.[10] Yet none of these formulations rang true in light of the international system of accumulation then in formation.

Japan's corporate or government gains in wealth drawn in dividends and interest from American workers and taxpayers were no different than those drawn by U.S. corporations or government bodies from its own people. The real difference was that *the wealth that left America might not be reinvested to stimulate production, employ labor, and expand the tax base.* The same thing might be said of U.S. investments in government securities, factories, and securities abroad. The difference, though, was that now America was losing wealth. There was a hole in the economic bucket, and eventually the outflow of wealth would grow.

Japan was a trade creditor collecting its debt from America in the form of U.S. dollars which it then used to buy up more U.S. assets. America was a trade debtor, forced to pay in dollars and with relatively fewer resources to buy assets with yen or other currencies abroad if it was not to run up a larger, overall negative balance. It was still unknown how the people and taxpayers in the U.S. would pay for these negative accounts.

U.S. under secretary of commerce Robert Ortner took the traditional pie-chart approach that had been used when the U.S. had held a huge net trade balance that financed tremendous capital investment abroad. He announced that increased 1987 foreign investment in the U.S. would act to raise the productive capacity and efficiency of the U.S. economy, thereby increasing the size of the American economic "pie," even as the slice going to foreigners grew.[11]

It was a fine image. But it masked the dilemma of how America could pay out more than she received without cumulatively enlarging the nation's negative investment status. To reverse America's relative decline, the only alternatives seemed to be a turn to old-time dumping of commodities; autarchical, one-dimensional, self-sufficient production; cartels; and a melange of neomercantilist practices.

Old-Time Dumping

Japanese dumping is a period piece of the postwar world. After the peace, the U.S. had regulated Japanese commerce. In the 1950s, dumping was not needed because the Korean War provided Japan with a ready market as a supplier of U.S. military forces. In the 1960s some dumping took place, but the sale of Japanese goods in overseas markets largely relied on uniqueness of products and design. But in the 1970s volume production of the state-of-the-arts technologies empowered Japanese companies to treat labor as a fixed cost for the purpose of cut-price dumping to outflank competitors abroad. And in the first half of the 1980s Nippon's dumping reached it apogée in the latest microtechnologies and silicon chips.

The reaction of producers in Western Europe and the United States in the second half of the 1980s framed the future struggle between the newly emergent common markets and their ancillary spheres of interest. For these Western cultures determined they could not compete on a price level with Japanese companies that appropriated their technologies, leading them to take protectionist steps to secure their home markets *and simultaneously* export financial or technological capital for investment abroad.

Security of home markets appeared in the forms of antidumping investigations, tariffs, quotas, and nontariff barriers. The European Common

Market opened one investigation after another into Japanese dumping. In many European industries, producers repeatedly complained that they had seen their profits dwindle or were even facing losses because Japanese dumping was forcing prices down. At first complaints came from the microtechnologies, then from autos and building machine makers . . . there seemed no end. On 3 June 1988 the EEC opened investigations into alleged dumping by seventeen Japanese makers of small hydraulic excavators and seven makers of wheeled loaders, machines used in the building industry.[12]

Some strategists argued that American companies should emulate Japanese dumping techniques. Paul R. Sullivan, senior vice president of Harbridge House, Inc., described dumping as "strategic pricing":

> Strategic pricing, where the same product is offered at different prices in different markets, allows global companies to compete in different ways in different markets. Companies can cross-subsidize their divisions by using products developed in one country to help compete aggressively in another. Contrary to American business mythology, every market need not always make a profit.
>
> American companies may be mistakenly lured into raising prices now as rising costs force competitors to do so. Those with a global marketing orientation will resist this tendency to take opportunistic profits and instead use the weak dollar to gain market share while they can.[13]

By keeping short-term profit returns steady, U.S. prices could be kept constant to outflank imports from competitors with higher prices and to outmaneuver them in foreign markets by dumping at even-lower levels and establishing long-lasting market shares.

The Limits of One-Dimensional Solutions

If U.S. companies do this, though, what effect will U.S. pressures on Japan have to either adopt fair trade or quid pro quo policies on a bilateral basis?

Likely they will produce neither free trade nor egalitarian commercial relations. The attitude of many American commentators is the lattice of relationships that bind Japanese in a web of mutual obligations have no meaning outside Japan, that Japan is "very primitive" in dealing with other nations, and that it has never had a foreign policy. The rest of the world is viewed as having different standards than Japan, as playing another "game."[14] Their underlying attitude is that there is no rational way to negotiate policy with Japan—and that America must *force its hand*. At best, these are narrow solutions to a larger dilemma.

Those who present these solutions argue as follows. Western nations are unable to trade to their best ability in the world market because nations like Japan use self-protective and autarchical impediments to free trade. In the case of Asian nations, there is no way to win them over to Western concepts of production and unfettered trade, so Western nations must accept Asian views, and play by Asian rules, of economic activity. Such play involves parry and riposte. If Japan, for example, closes its markets through the use of tariffs, quotas, or nationalist distribution networks that hinder foreign competitors, the U.S. must respond in kind by denying Japan sectors of its markets and demanding access to Japan on an equal basis.

One experienced U.S. Commerce Department trade negotiator with the Japanese, Clyde V. Prestowitz, Jr., even argues that the Japanese, Taiwanese, and South Korean economies are linked to the state in a way that undermines multilateral trade, unfettered commerce, and thus free trade. Not only do their respective governments mobilize revenues to subsidize certain critical and politically influential industries, but they also use tariffs, quotas, and internal distribution networks that accommodate their own goods and restrict those of competitors, and they make concessions that favor their own exporters. Thus Japan's periodic compromises are nothing more than attempts to enlarge *total Japanese sales.* Imports may rise, as they did from 1.5 percent of Nippon's gross national product in 1960 to 1.6 percent of a vastly enlarged GNP in 1986, but U.S. imports rose even more in the same period, from 1 percent of GNP to 4.4 percent. Japan's "industrial policy" is thereby incompatible with America's "fair trade policy."

Even a more than doubling of the value of the yen against the dollar in the thirty months ending in May 1988 was offset by Japanese manufacturers who cut their costs and sent more goods overseas. Japanese double-talk about the periodic drop in monthly trade surplus figures disguised the fact that imports were momentarily enlarging at a faster pace than export volume was *continually raised.* "Export volume has bottomed and Japanese shipments are increasing steadily," said Bank of Tokyo economist Akahane Soichiro in a *newspeak* response to the April 1988 14 percent rise in Japanese exports to $21.94 billion, the third largest figure on record. Looking at the 30 percent rise in April imports to a record $13.46 billion that offset the increases in shipments of Japanese goods, this formulation holds that somehow Japanese exports would be *reduced,* when in fact exports were rising, even if at a slower rate than imports![15]

This situation and these practices Prestowitz finds unacceptable. He suggested remedies including negotiated access to one another's markets through the cartel-like parceling out of quotas on production and market access, emphasizing open markets where price competition persists, bilateral equity, and — in the case of failure — in-kind retaliation.[16] In other words, Prestowitz and like-minded commentators are advocating a return to the neomercantilist, retaliatory polices of the 1930s.

Some of them see no other way out because U.S. companies have mistakenly focused on the high-margin end of the technology and electronics market and ceded the low end in calculators, copiers, automobiles, televisions, and many other products to foreign competitors. Asian companies came in at this low-margin end but have since steadily worked their way up. In the late 1980s the same thing happened in the aircraft industry, with competitors converging from many nations. "One of the most difficult lessons for American business to learn is to avoid focusing only on the high-value-added market segments," says Paul R. Sullivan, vice president of Harbridge House.

Others take a different route but arrive at the same end. They suggest creating cartel-like structures by mating the largest partners in international collaborative agreements to share assets in return for greater access to global markets. They call for strategic alliances to exchange technology, gain market entry, lower production costs, offset exports, and provide uniform quality to customers worldwide by demanding quality assurance from all suppliers of raw materials and component parts. But they implicitly recognize that these alliances may only be temporary, and that the partners are in search of building volume by securing larger market shares to increase their profits at the expense of all competitors.[17]

New Cartels/Old Complaints

Traditionally, cartels were a function of too many producers for too few markets coming together to reduce the volume of production by quotas, to share out markets by allocation, and to set prices by scheduled agreement. Modern cartels between companies of different nations and between nations representing these companies still exist. But in the case of the U.S. and Japan, cartels designed to resolve market shares for hard consumer goods like cars and modern technological products such as computer chips have been short-lived and confrontational at best.

The battle of chips between these two nations is one of postured rights and probable retaliation, for example. After years of competitive price-cutting and dumping, in September 1986 Japan and the U.S. signed an accord in which Japan agreed to curtail alleged dumping of low-priced chips in the U.S., and to buy more chips from foreign makers, with the U.S. to be awarded 12.5 percent of the entire Japanese semiconductor market. By mid-1988, though *direct dumping* had stopped, the U.S. share of the Japanese market hovered at about 10 percent and was *losing ground*.

In new talks with the Japanese, the U.S. industry trade group, called the Semiconductor Industry Association, demanded the agreed access to Japan's chip market measured by *increased market share* as a goal. But the Japanese chip makers only acknowledged the need for competition, not automatic access to a given or growing share of Japan's lucrative semiconductor market—then the world's largest. The cochairman of the Japanese negotiators, Sato Tohri, Hitachi's executive managing director, then decisively broke the cartel accord. "We can't accept the premise that there should be increased market share," he said. "Market share is a result of effort," not a goal to be set ahead of time.

As their second lines of offense and defense, both sides proceeded to rationalize their positions. Japanese chip manufacturers spoke as if they, as part of conglomerated groups, also represented the nation's chip-buying users, arguing that U.S. producers didn't manufacture the consumer electronic chips that Japan needed and could neither meet production schedules nor quality requirements. "Since the conclusion of the U.S.-Japan semiconductor pact, the member firms of the Electronic Industries Association of Japan have taken measures to try to improve the market access of foreign microchip makers," the association said in a position paper in mid-1988, adding that though these efforts were having results, "an increase in market share is not something which can be guaranteed."[18]

The U.S. Semiconductor Industry Association then defended, presenting a study detailing major increases by U.S. chip makers in the staffing and servicing of facilities in Japan — enough to earn a one-half percent market share, yet actually resulting in a 1 percent decline in the first six months of 1988. "We are absolutely incredulous that there is a difference of opinion — that successful [market-access] efforts could lead to anything other than an increase in market share by foreign suppliers," retorted Jon Cornell, leader of the U.S. delegation and senior vice president of Harris Corp. "If you don't know where you're going, you can't talk about how to get there."

Alan Wolff, an attorney for the Semiconductor Association, warned that if the U.S. share of the Japanese semiconductor market did not improve, the group was positioned to demand an increase in the existing U.S. $165 million punitive tariff, a tariff that had been levied against Japanese shipments in April 1987 as compensation for comparable market-share losses of U.S. concerns in Japan's semiconductor market.[19]

Because the cartel of 1986 was now stone dead, the American Electronics Association moved into defensive formation to emulate Japan by creating an alliance of industry and government to develop new consumer electronic technologies like high-definition television. Except in wartime, such technological cooperation was uncommon and in some cases illegal — if market-sharing and price-setting was involved. But by 7 June 1988 federal government officials were working with giant U.S. companies, including the American Telephone and Telegraph, IBM, National Semiconductor, Intel, Advanced Micro Devices, Apple Computer, and Zenith Electronics Corporation, the last significant domestic television manufacturer, in an effort to resurrect America's plan in the multibillion dollar industry dominated by the Japanese.[20]

When they would form an effective state cartel was still unknown. But the process had begun, with the ultimate goal of making this sector of American industry competitive and reversing the nation's negative trade balance in high-tech products.

Chapter 16
Neomercantilist Practices and Free-Trade Utopia

There is not one single provision of this bill that requires the president of the United States to do anything protectionist. Not one. The bill is potentially more confrontational and potentially more contentious with our trading partners. —U.S. Trade Representative Clayton Yeutter[1]

We consider it essential that the dialogue with Japan be lifted to a more comprehensive level. Japan will be one of the major powers of the 21st century. We are becoming more interdependent. The issue is how to deal with the consequences of inter-dependency, not how to reverse or change the relationship. — Henry A. Kissinger and Cyrus R. Vance[2]

If you can't get it done multilaterally, you get it done bilaterally. Why? Because domestic political support for free trade won't accommodate years of delay. —Former Treasury Sec-retary James Baker[3]

Both Japan and Western Europe have perfected state consortia, bilateral trade mechanisms, and cartel allotment of production and markets at preset prices. America has perfected the ideological utopia of "free trade," or at least equitable "fair trade," yet has also practiced highly restrictive trade. America has also been outflanked in global markets so far as exports originating in the U.S. are concerned.

For the purpose of opening these foreign markets, the U.S. has unsuccessfully used threats of economic retaliation to try to reform Western European and Japanese neomercantilist methods. Yet America has fallen into a self-delusory trap of its own making, advocating free trade as an alternative to mercantile calculations, but meanwhile practicing neither free trade nor neomercantilism, and also neglecting to copy the infrastructural systems and trade practices of its Japanese and Western European competitors. The result has been a loss of U.S. economic strength on a world scale.[4]

The Ethos of Nationalist Neomercantilism

America's domestic dilemma is inseparable from the global infrastructure of the neomercantile system. This system rests on vested interests in various nations that directly control or strongly influence various bodies and agencies of the state and direct their policies toward national self-sufficiency in production, internal trade, and regulation of the nation's global commerce. No doubt, the goals of modern day neomercantilism are different from 19th-century megalomanian determinations to build great industrial metropoles through exclusive empires designed to extract raw materials with cheap labor, or the renewed quest in the 1930s for colonies, spheres of influence, bilateral commerce, and a positive trade balance.[5] Today's neomercantilists seek more than the accumulation of surplus, capital assets, and a bullion supply, allegedly for the greater good of the nation state; they seek *global hegemony*. They want to win control over resources, technology, and a geographically disparate, yet skilled, labor force. They seek to acquire the most up-to-date manufacturing techniques and to build the most efficient and far-reaching marketing and financial networks. Yet, their mutual goal of uninterrupted production combined with the promotion of a national, and nationalist, ethos that includes respect for authority, hard work, competence, perseverance, and group loyalty also makes them very unequal.[6]

Japan leads the capitalist powers in sustaining this ethos. Since the early 1950s her traditions of work and belief in the authoritarian state have powerfully reemerged. A new philosophy of national greatness calls upon the Japanese people to fit themselves into the structural frames of hard work, social conformity, and ethical rigidity.[7] Under the reign of the Liberal Democratic Party (LDP), the various government ministries, especially the Ministry of International Trade and Industry, have become the enforcement centers for this ethos, requiring industrial groups to cooperate, promoting critical enterprises and strategic industries, and merging national security with economic policy.[8]

Other traditions are also reemergent. Japan is a "high-context culture," resting on mass literacy, wide-circulation newspapers, magazines, and books, and other sources of information often slanted to favor Japan's corporate structure and environment of business operations.[9] In a replay of the feudal relationship of landholding *daimyo* and warrior *samurai,* the strains of the traditions of the secular *zaibatsu* and the state bureaucrats have merged. The modern version of the *samurai* protectors are the MITI professionals, who serve, guard, and fight for the interests of Japanese large businesses. The attributes of the three outstanding leaders who struggled to gain supremacy and finally unified the nation in 1615 are still "highly admired by today's Japanese top management: [Oda] Nobunaga was of stern temperament, but open to new ideas; [Toyotomi] Hideyoshi was well respected by his men as a student of human nature; [Tokugawa] Ieyasu was commendable for his long suffering and endurance, regardless of the adversity."[10]

Japan has a powerful reverence for ritual themes; the symbolism of nature's form, color, and feeling; arrangement; the group; silence; and the *kamikaze,* too. The American invaders occupied Japan only until the gods again shielded the nation and blew new life into its people. And now that divine wind encloses Japan and seemingly makes it invulnerable to Western influence over Japan's cultural uniqueness and superiority.[11]

The United States has little understanding of Japan's beliefs and determination. American policymakers usually single out one problem area or another to explain why the U.S. has lost its former place and hegemony, yet rarely make a comprehensive analysis or seek an in-depth resolution. The U.S. suffers from a monochronic vision that events, hence their solutions, take place in sequence one at a time.[12] Thus the U.S. has led other Western nations in pressuring Japan to open its agricultural markets, reform its tax system, streamline its complex, distribution apparatus, address soaring land prices that keep foreign firms out, invest additional capital in the West, etc. The result has been an irresolute hodgepodge of economic and political quackery that Japan has exploited as an opportunity to consolidate its own dominance of markets.

Because such neomercantile measures often *appear* as segmented offensive and defensive policies, it is imperative to view the detailed consequences of Japanese and U.S. interdependency as a sort of score card that records a larger game. Here we wish to emphasize several critical encounters: Japan's new gold bug mercantilism, two techniques of the Japanese inner sanctum for wealth accumulation, the context of bilateral trade "wars" and negotiations, and tariff and other barriers.

Gold Bug Mercantilism

Classical mercantilism determined the wealth of nations by adding up their gold supplies, by then subtracting the debts owed to other nations, and by considering how to increase raw material or manufacturing exports while limiting imports to produce a positive trade balance payable in bullion. Accumulation of gold in bulk was the goal, so much so that the nation's bullion supply was usually made equivalent to the king's worth to the court and the nation. A worthless king was one who impeded the nation's accumulation of gold. "Manufactures," France's Colbert advised his king, "will produce returns in money, which is the single aim of commerce and the only means of increasing the greatness and power of the state."[13]

Contemporary neomercantilism also attempts to determine the wealth of the nation and the benefits provided to certain social sectors and classes, but is not so rigid to monetize all accumulated wealth in the form of gold. Nonetheless, paper currencies or securities as stores of accumulated wealth do not provide assurances to faint-hearted investors when these tokens of value suddenly gyrate in response to international monetary arrangements and soar or plunge with the wild fluctuations on world stock exchanges. In the modern world economy, when great enterprises or nations decide on potential alternatives in which to invest, *relative value* is the byword, as well as the *buy* word.

"The most important question for the Bank of Japan is what happens to the dollar," advised Solomon Brothers economist Kermit Schoenholtz. "Generally speaking, it affects domestic policy, and the domestic policy issues occupy center stage in Japan."[14]

Would Japan, though, also switch to accumulating gold during times characterized by an uncertain dollar? Governments worldwide held an estimated 35,000 tons of gold in the late 1980s. Attempting to sidestep instabilities in currencies and securities that might cause relative losses, the nations of Southeast Asia, especially Taiwan and Japan did turn to investing in gold.

Following the model of Japan, Asia's newly industrialized nations had accumulated capital in recent decades and had much to protect from the West's neomercantile manipulations of markets and currencies. These machinations reached a high point in the late 1980s, with the United States leading the attack on Asia's wealth by state-imposed devaluation of the dollar against the yen and other dollar-locked currencies.

Yet, Japan's own investment funds held their own, occupying eight of the ten top spots among 191 world equity funds for five-year profitability performance. Even for the one-year 1987 results, Japanese and British bond funds did best, while U.S. funds generally lagged. And after the October 1987 stock market crash, Japanese equity funds continued through the first quarter of 1988 to be the most consistent performers, scoring a median, or midrange, return of 18.9 percent.[15]

But considering the merits of appreciation of investment funds in Japan and the global improprieties of buying the West's unstable stocks and bonds to offset their positive trade balances, Asia's new interest in investment in gold and platinum held a certain logic.

"The demand for these metals has been accelerated by the diversification out of stock markets," said Ian MacDonald, vice president of Credit Suisse, New York. "The volatility of platinum has been an attractive feature for traders, while for gold it has been the 'stored value syndrome.'"

Because the Japanese stock market showed signs of running out of steam, offered Jeffrey Christian, managing director of the New York commodity consultants Christian, Podleska, and van Musschenbroek, there was a tremendous wealth in Japan that was "looking for a home." In 1988, low prices in terms of yen raised the demand for platinum from Japan, the world's leading consumer for investment and industry.[16] And gold was also a big item on the Japanese shopping list.

"It is one way to build up their asset base," Consolidated Gold Fields PLC reported. Southeast Asian and Japanese buyers purchased 28 percent (570 tons of 2,008 tons) of the gold traded in 1987. Taiwan's central bank had sought security against a rapid devaluation of the dollar. Some Japanese companies also purchased gold as protection against devaluation; some were simply diverting cash from taxable bank deposits to gold; others were buying gold for jewelry or industrial purposes; and still others were calculating the instability of dollar investments. "Investors worldwide are clearly concerned about the stability of present international monetary arrangements, and the outlook for world stock markets," offered Consolidated Gold Fields expert analyst, George Milling-Stanley. Acting on their fears, by the end of the first quarter of 1988 Japan and Taiwan together had already imported 317 metric tons of gold, amounting to 63 percent of the world's quarterly supplies. As these two countries quickly absorbed the world's surplus gold supplies, gold-producing nations whose hard currencies had slipped in value increased their output of gold, because its value was rising. The combined production in the U.S., Canada, and Australia surged to a record 383 tons in 1987 and approximately 400 tons in 1988.[17]

How long would the drive to accumulate gold continue? Gold earns no return for its investment per se, and gold itself must be stored at a cost requiring a cash outlay. But Asian investors held high expectations that the dollar would be driven downwards by Western government policies and speculators, leading in turn to an upward spiral in the price of gold. They also believed that the nations with the greatest bullion supplies would be able to dictate future currency equivalents. This neomercantilist logic was infallible so long as Asian manufactures held sway in world markets. But this became increasingly unlikely in the late 1980s as Japanese capital invested directly in production facilities moved to the NICs, the third world, the U.S., and Western Europe. Japan's drive to stimulate domestic consumption would possibly also reduce exports as a percent of total output, generate imports, reduce the positive trade balance, and wean Japan from many of its neomercantile ways, including the accumulation of gold.

The Inner Sanctum of Wealth Accumulation

Neomercantilism operates through the political power controlled by centralized wealth. The old *zaibatsu* still operate in Japan, but they have been supplemented by hundreds of corporations and many hundreds, perhaps thousands, of accumulation centers that often work at cross-purposes to one another.

Banking had traditionally been the centerpiece of the conglomerated *zaibatsu;* their own banks both secure accumulated assets and act as the storehouses for their wealth. With the expansion of Japanese trade, international finance, and worldwide investments in the 1970s and 1980s, moreover, the old lines of banking were extended, new banks emerged, and Japan's international banks expanded their operations — often by using depositors' savings and extending credit based on a frail and vulnerable equity base. This gave them enormous power to extend credit created without the security Western banks had traditionally required. And because there was no central world banking authority with the power to put limits on Nippon banks, they became the focal points for advancing seemingly unlimited credit to buyers and making real investments with the *phantom capital* they created.

Western banks sharply complained that the lax security requirements in Japan gave their Nippon competitors a tremendous advantage in overseas markets, especially in the area of investments negotiated by credit instruments. Still in charge of paper currencies and the credit deployed as the dominant means of international exchange, these Western banks exerted pressure through the Bank for International Settlements (BIS) to set guidelines for Japan to bring its equity-to-asset ratio in line with the 8 percent ratio common among Western international banks. Since Japanese banks were required to put aside this equity capital by 1992, they redoubled their efforts to use phantom capital to buy domestic and foreign capital assets before that date, yet arrange for the required equity stake on time.

Bank deposits and self-created credit had allowed the banks to build up huge portfolios of stocks and real estate holdings. As these portfolios appreciated on the upscale Japanese stock exchange and as real estate soared in value in the tight urban real estate market, the "value" of their holdings enlarged. The banks then classified this appreciation as a sort of bank "equity" to be used in calculating their own invested risk-capital. The BIS was prepared to permit the banks to count 45 percent of the value of their stocks and real estate in this way. In other words, the banks first created phantom capital, then invested this phantom capital in stocks and real estate to gain speculative appreciation, and then used this appreciated "value" as the basis of bank "equity" to support new rounds of bank-created credit!

Equity potential to meet BIS requirements was meanwhile also built up in the form of financial capital by issuing *new* equity and convertible bonds in Japan's wildly inflated stock market. Stock-convertible bonds were sold in 1988 by the great banks like Dai-Ichi Kangyo (100 billion yen), Sumitomo (125 billion yen), and the Bank of Tokyo (70 billion yen), with the latter also issuing more than 98 billion yen of new equity. Smaller banks, such as the Bank of Yokohama (30 billion yen), Tokai Bank (80 billion yen), and Saitama Bank (870 billion yen), had led the way in raising capital by issuing convertible bonds. By 1992 the five largest city banks and the three long-term credit banks still would need to raise between 400 and 500 billion yen each, with the Ministry of Finance establishing a queuing system to space out the new issues among the banks flooded with new money.

To avoid the danger of a potential fall in stocks, moreover, the BIS required the banks to trim their assets by 1992. Before the cut-off date, many banks prepared to sell at vastly inflated prices — the Nikkei index had already crossed the 28000 mark in June 1988 and was moving upwards. Meanwhile, another scenario was set in motion in mid-1988, as some *financial stocks* lagged behind others in anticipation of a deluge of new shares.[18] If the banks bought Nikkei stocks cheap, then sold their stocks when prices went higher, and used the proceeds to purchase their *own bank stocks* or convertible bonds at potentially lower prices, the banks would reap the double reward of increasing their stock-inflated "equity" on the market and buying back their own stocks at a lower price on the market in the future.

The windfall potential of such accumulated wealth through the stock exchange would again enhance the "equity" of Japanese banks for international operations, so that in a sense phantom-based capital would act as a kind of "reserve currency" for Japanese trade and overseas investments. As most reserve currencies have historically been associated with the relationship of dominant and lesser powers, the mercantile overtones of Japan's position were obvious.

Other forms of generating phantom capital also emerged in various areas of the financial community in the late 1980s. Two principal methods were in vogue: (1) a company's investment banker who acted as its portfolio manager would pass on sensitive information to colleagues before the rest of the stock market's traders were informed; and (2) big brokerage houses would alert their best institutional customers before they gave advice on daily stock purchases to millions of retail customers. In both cases, the large institutions benefited at the expense of smaller holders.

Because most Japanese security houses combined the functions of *investment banker raising funds* and *portfolio manager investing funds,* knowledge of both aspects of a client's operations provided tremendous opportunities for sharing information with trusted colleagues and other clients. "If one person were in charge of Hitachi, for example, he would oversee raising funds for Hitachi, and also investing Hitachi's holdings," explained Miyamoto Yoshihiko, a director of Nomura Securities, Japan's largest securities house. "If Hitachi made a big equipment purchase, or bought a small American company, or refinanced something, that one person would know all the plans." Because of deep-seated ties at security houses, separating the two functions, as Mr. Miyamoto advocated, would not likely interrupt the system whereby colleagues work their way up the employment ladder together from the moment they graduate from college, all the while swapping confidential information with one another. Moreover, trading under assumed stock brokerage account names to avoid taxes is a regularized practice in Japan; thus the insider practice of buying and selling stocks is anonymous.

In the case of new issues of stock — which frequently double or triple in value on the day they are first sold publicly — big security houses like Nomura, Daiwa, Nikko, or Yamaichi Securities instruct branch-office brokers to inform their biggest customers first — either before the issue is marketed or early in the morning of the initial public offering, before recommendations are more widely broadcast to smaller clients.[19]

Established securities companies have joined the insurance companies and the banks in trying to outflank newcomers searching for inexpensive stocks. Insider trading in securities has become one of their principal means to make great speculative profits, set the markets in turmoil, and unhinge smaller investors. Company executives, in the habit of dealing in the securities of their own firms and of receiving payments in stock, were similarly situated to reap great rewards from their decision-making powers and their access to critical information that would affect the prices of the stocks they held.

Such traditions had been regularized in the 1970s. In 1972, for example, several top executives of the food processor Kyodo Shiryo worked with Nikko Securities and Daiwa Securities to manipulate the company's stock price. It took sixteen years for the case to be resolved: Kyodo was only given a small fine and the offending executives were given suspended sentences!

Public exposure of comparable cases of insider trading escalated with the manipulation of stocks and prices in the late 1980s. Stocks of small companies like Sankyo Seiki, a manufacturer of music-boxes, escalated 10 percent just before Nippon Steel, the world's largest steel-maker, bought 18 percent of Sankyo's stock. Hanshin Sogo Bank, one of Tateho Chemical's lead bankers, *miraculously* sold all of its holdings in Tateho just before Tateho's September 1988 announcement that it had lost $210 million in the bonds futures market.

The framework for large securities firms and major investors to exploit the capital invested in stocks by small investors was extended in the late 1980s, as the lure of speculative profits created the illusion of accumulation by appreciation of the price of securities. It appeared as if the Nikkei stock average could only go one way: up. When small investors paid more for their shares than large investors paid for theirs, the opportunities for profits were less — and sometimes nonexistent. Insider trading by the giants of finance ruled the moment. Yet, because there were few regulations to control such activities, in 1987 the public began to put pressure on the Japanese Securities Dealers Association to impose a detailed registration system for security firms' officials who owned large blocks of corporate stock.

The registration system at first applied to their "insider" employees; but it was proposed in July 1988 to also apply it to insurance and banking officials to discourage in-house business dealings with clients or other "insider" sources. Once these financial institutions were required to notify regulatory authorities of the identities and transactions of executives holding more than 10 percent of the shares of a given company, government scrutiny could be leveled at officials who sold shares within six months of purchase.[20] Yet *notice* did not mean *curtailment* in profiteering; and thus the build-up of another form of phantom capital continued.

One scandal followed another, focusing national- and even world-attention on both great and lesser politicians. In 1988 Prime Minister Takeshita, former prime minister Nakasone, and senior governing party official and former foreign minister Abe Shintaro, acknowledged that their "aides" earned profits by obtaining unlisted shares of the real estate firm Recruit-Cosmos — one of the subsidiaries of Recruit Co., Japan's highest-flying service conglomerate, with interests in travel, employment publications, and other fields — and then selling them at huge profits after the company released its shares on the market. Recruit had offered stock to one hundred well-placed people; seventy-six accepted and Recruit even arranged to lend money to fifty-six of them to buy the stock. On selling their Recruit stock in a rising market, Nakasone's two aides had made combined profits of more than one million dollars at current exchange rates; Abe's secretary had made $657,000; and Finance Minister Miyazawa Kiichi's secretary $388,000. As politicians' aides often act on such matters on behalf of their bosses, the finance ministry was called on to determine whether the dealings violated Japan's Security and Exchange law.[21]

Once their scheme was uncovered, the usual practice of penitent resignations was followed. Ezoe Hiromasa, chairman and founder of Recruit, thus apologized in a resignation statement because the sale of Recruit-Cosmos stock had "disturbed society." He himself was particularly disturbed that the scandal had led to the resignation of a "person whom I long respected," Morita Ko, who had bought and sold Recruit shares, and was president and chief executive officer of one of Japan's leading financial newspapers, *Nihon Keizai Shinbun*.[22] The buying of political favors seemingly had no end: successive Japanese prime ministers Nakasone and Takeshita had both received substantial political contributions from Recruit (aides to Takeshita took $1.1 million in payments and $400,000 in loans). Three of Takeshita's cabinet members resigned and more than a dozen businessmen and bureaucrats were arrested before Takeshita himself resigned. Nakasone continued to refuse to testify under oath in Parliament to avoid perjury charges; to compel him to testify the four non–Communist opposition parties boycotted parliamentary proceeding.[23]

Yet no matter how the situation is decided, the practice of offering politicians the opportunity to participate in substantial wealth accumulation will undoubtedly continue. Long-term relationships between representatives of big industries and politicians are in the nature of the Japanese system. Fixed contributions to benefit a faction of the ruling LDP are assessed on each industry, with the funds channeled through the *Keidanren,* Japan's major big business organization. Local political organizations that support particular candidates are also funded by big business to cement political loyalties.

But as the parade of politicians facing election grew larger, and the politicians demanded more money for their particular faction, some business executives complained that the gala fund-raising parties — that could be counted as tax-entertainment expenses and thereby avoid the $750,000 limit on corporate campaign contributions — had reached the upper limits of $200 to $300 per ticket. "If it were only one ticket it wouldn't be that big of a deal, but some companies have to buy 100 or 300 of them," said critic Hanamura, designer of the annual contribution through the *Keidanren.* Though there might be some cut in the imposts, as Japanese politicians relied more on large corporations and less on individual donations, corporate Japan would continue to fund the political system.[24] And LDP policies would continue to ignore the interests of the average voter, leaving him little to get excited about, or little reason to participate in the political process.

Japan also participated in U.S. insider trading through Switzerland. The U.S. General Accounting Office reported that more than one-third (226) of the 609 cases of suspected insider trading referred by the U.S. stock exchanges to the Securities and Exchange Commission in 1986 and 1987 involved foreign-brokerage firms. U.S. brokerage houses facilitated the scam by handling foreign institutional transactions in bulk through an "omnibus account." Switzerland's cumbersome and unwieldy procedures stopped the SEC from prosecuting many foreign cases.[25]

Phantom capital thereby created a certainty that Japan would set the rules for its own domestic accumulation of capital by stock manipulations, insider connections, and a kind of financial wizardry. Huge amounts of capital were being extracted from small investors through the public stock market, by forms of brigandage that owed much to the American forms of manipulation that had caused the 1929 stock market crash and the American methods of insider trading perfected in the 1980s.

The sum total of these and comparable forms of accumulation strengthened the centralization of financial resources in Japan, created a political/business alliance that aided the movement of capital into the international sphere, and helped build the frame for thinking about Japan as a great power able to create its own investment and trading sphere that was invulnerable to the posturing of other nations.

Bilateral Trade Wars and Negotiations

Until at least 1987, Japan had concentrated on maximizing exports and minimizing imports by almost any means. Japan had its own tariffs and quotas; import quality restrictions, standards, and testing procedures; discriminatory marketing practices; exclusive cartel alliances of Japanese industries and trading companies; and government guidance and subsidies to offset competitive handicaps in the scoring of international R&D, technological advantages, and dumping practices. The MITI and other government agencies tried to shape the world's understanding of Nippon by statistical manipulations and calculations of trade balances. Japan also attempted to eliminate all barriers to its own exports, spoke out against the protectionism of others, promoted a new GATT round in the late 1980s, yet also dragged its heels in opening its own markets.

To combat this *neomercantile policy of state-guided monopoly promoting exports but limiting imports,* the United States had operated along many fronts. It has moved to consolidate an exclusive dollar trading zone modeled on the British Sterling Area. As initial partners for a "free trade area" it negotiated *bilateral agreements* with Israel in 1985 and with Canada in 1987. U.S. officials also planned to pursue a free trade zone with Mexico for production, capital movements, and trade. But Japan presented a more difficult problem. "Pervasive trade barriers stretching down through all levels of the Japanese economy make a free trade agreement with Japan like the one concluded with Canada an unrealistic goal in the foreseeable future," concluded Montana Democratic Senator Max Baucus in 1988. As an intermediary step, envisioning a comprehensive, bilateral agreement with Japan – "as the centerpiece of a new trade policy that can reverse the economic decline of the U.S." – he thus introduced a legislative bill in the U.S. Senate in early August 1988.[26]

U.S. industrial decline could only partially be addressed by *bilateral negotiations,* whether with Canada or Japan. Barriers to the search for a common destiny were evident in America's relations not only with Nippon, but also with Europe and third world nations. During the eight-year Reagan administration, the tactical device of "piecemeal protection" had meant, for example, the periodic lodging of complaints designed to protect particular U.S. industries and products. In President Reagan's first four years (1980–84), ten complaints of unfair trading were put forward; these were followed by twenty-two more by mid–May 1988. The Europeans were berated about their pasta, salad oil, airlines, fruits, nuts, and meat. Japan was berated for its unfair trade in computer chips, tobacco, leather, aluminum, beef, oranges, and construction equipment. South Korea was criticized over insurance, cigarettes, and movies. And other countries from China to Argentina were singled out for complaints concerning one or another of their products. In agriculture alone, the U.S. sought to eliminate global farm subsidies amounting to $200 billion a year in 1987/88.[27]

"The results [of such disagreement] is something I call ad hoc protectionism," said Lloyd Bentsen, then chair of the U.S. Senate Finance Committee. Evidence indicates that U.S. import restrictions of some sort affected 9 percent of American imports in 1981, but 15 percent by 1986; this rise largely reflected so-called voluntary restraints on Japanese autos, all foreign steel, and imported textiles.[28]

America faced the dilemma of speaking out for free trade, yet simultaneously erected barriers to the goods of others. The U.S. promoted multilateral trade through the GATT and its periodic conferences such as the Uruguay Round, starting in 1986 to run through 1990. Yet the 1988 Congress empowered the president to impose bilateral strictures on imports. "If the Uruguay Round falters, it is certainly conceivable that we would shift to bilateral gear," offered Clayton Yeutter, the chief United States trade representative.[29] The Washington economic counselor to the Japanese embassy, Nogami Yoshiji, agreed that Asian nations (read: *Japan*) should be prepared to negotiate their own free trade agreements with the U.S. if slow-moving GATT talks did not produce results during 1989/90.[30]

There seemed no way out of the dilemma of national self-sufficiency and prosperity functioning through efforts to maximize exports, control imports, and erect trade barriers. But it was certainly conceivable that U.S. and Japanese national policies pursuing bilateral negotiations between the two countries might sweep away most tariffs and other trade barriers. In 1988 both the U.S. and Japan began separate studies on the advantages and disadvantages of free trade negotiations, as a result of a meeting of Prime Minister Takeshita and Senator Robert C. Byrd. The U.S. envisioned a "managed" relationship with Japan, or so the U.S. International Trade Commission study in September 1988 proposed. The broader bilateral, intergovernmental mechanism called on the corporate pioneers who were ahead of their respective governments to adjust the new revolution in informational-technology, international trade, and global investments. President Bush pursued these matters and succeeded in opening a small aperture in Japan's walled-off market. Yet there were strong apprehensions that a deal cut with Japan would increase the cost of U.S. imports, allow Japan to undercut the products of U.S. industries, and create enormous problems for other countries, especially Japan's low-wage Asian and Pacific neighbors, whose exports to the United States would become more expensive than Japanese goods.

Beefing Up Agricultural Tariffs and Other Barriers

In agriculture, bilateralism is best understood against the backdrop of taxpayer subsidies and financed dumping. In the period 1984–86 the United States and the European Community each spent nearly $60 billion protecting their farmers. Japan spent nearly $40 billion to protect her farmers. On a per capita basis, the 2.5 million U.S. farmers received the most, followed by Japan's 4.4 million farmers, and the European community's 11 million.

The U.S. financed its farmers' control of domestic markets and exports differently than either the European Community or Japan. Direct subsidies from Washington to the farmers were awarded for three measures intended to limit supply and control prices: not planting; storing food produced; and selling at higher-than-market prices to the government. Quotas were imposed to bar imports of dairy products, sugar, cotton, and peanuts under a special provision of the GATT. Hidden subsidies, such as subsidized water and pest control in California and other states, also helped to make their products competitive with imports. The U.S. government also took charge of dumping surplus grains on foreign markets, especially in the Soviet Union, outflanking Canada, France, and Australia.

By contrast, the European Community secured its farmers in two ways: by setting community food prices that were higher than world market prices; and by imposing levies on imports that, in turn, were distributed when European food was "dumped," reimbursing farmers for the difference between the lower world market price and higher domestic prices. Community farmers were thus subsidized to export at competitive rates on world markets.

Nor were such measures confined to agriculture. In the "Great Pasta War" between the U.S. and the EEC, for instance, the U.S. administration imposed 40 percent duties on government-subsidized exports of European spaghetti and fancy pasta sold in U.S. gourmet groceries. The European Community retaliated by imposing duties of U.S. walnuts and lemons. The U.S. then delayed a promised concession on semi-finished steel. Europe next slapped duties on U.S. fertilizer, paper products, and beef tallow. As more industries became embroiled in the exchange of restrictive measures, the Europeans finally backed off by reducing the government subsidies for pasta exports that were undermining U.S. competitors.[31]

Japan's largely part-time but politically powerful, farmers were secured in still another fashion. Japanese consumers paid prices ten times higher than on the world market for rice, so that the rice farmers could produce more rice to be sold through government stores. Foreign rice was kept out by tariffs and quotas; and at times Japan even subsidized overseas rice dumping below world market prices. Other government food subsidies followed a similar pattern. Japan gave way in mid-1988 to some U.S. and Australian demands to end restrictions on imports of beef and citrus but then promised its own farmers subsidies for the difference between the new domestic market price levels and their old, protected prices.

This *tripartite* farming was the basis for government-protected home markets, dumping abroad, and nominal attempts to do away with the emergent spheres of agricultural influence demanded by politically powerful farmers in the 1980s. A complete elimination of subsidies was considered politically impossible by both Europeans and the Japanese. The 1988 U.S. proposal to do away with all farm subsidies within ten years was viewed as being "as realistic as asking for complete worldwide disarmament," judged Sir Roy Denman, head of the European Community delegation in Washington.[32]

This was because the incremental steps to national, agricultural self-sufficiency had been based on special interests, political alliances, and lavish support systems.

After 1983, U.S. subsidies often exceeded the market value of U.S. crops. Federal subsidies totaled over $160 billion between 1980 and 1987. The U.S. government in 1987 provided $60,000 in subsidies to the average U.S. farmer. This $25 billion national outlay combined with export subsidies provided by the U.S. Agricultural Department to inflate domestic prices and make U.S. wheat more expensive in Kansas City than Moscow, and American barley cheaper in Baghdad than in New York. Export subsidies were three times the world price to export butter and sugar and four times the world price to enlarge rice exports.[33]

Between trading partners, such nationalist practices often cut both ways. Looking at the Japanese market for food products, for example, low-cost, often oligopolized, U.S. producers subsidized by the state and practicing dumping have repeatedly been unhinged by the height of Japanese tariffs and the narrow, nationalist view the Japanese have taken toward unfettered, multilateral trade. To protect Japan's politically powerful farmers, the government has also had to bend, maintaining quotas on beef and citric fruit throughout the postwar period. These quotas for the Japanese fiscal year, 1 April 1987–31 March 1988, for example, limited imports to 214,000 tons of beef, 126,000 tons of oranges, and 8,500 tons of orange juice.[34]

U.S. Food Monopolies and Exports

One starting point for analyzing American dumping and defensive Japanese quotas, then, is the U.S. nature of conglomerated and oligopolist control of production and marketing.

The concentration of control in meat slaughtering and packing, for example, had steadily enlarged. In 1920, the big five firms — Armour, Swift, Wilson, Cudahy, and Morris — controlled half the beef-slaughtering business and large interests in related stockyards and railroad businesses. By the early 1980s the big five were no more. Armour and half of Swift had become part of Conagra. In 1987 Monfort, holding a 10 percent market share, was also absorbed by Conagra. By 1988, Conagra held 22 percent of the market, slightly ahead of Excel's 21 percent, but still behind IBP's 30 percent. The Big Three that emerged had tremendous buying power. "[T]hree or four bidders in a market are not as good as five or six," offered the head of the U.S. Agriculture Department's Packers and Stockyards Administration, adding that "they don't have to collude to know what each other is doing."

In grain-fattened cattle, for instance, three-quarters of the U.S. purchase, slaughter, and sale in the late 1980s was controlled by IBP Inc.,

Conagra Inc., and Cargill Inc.'s subsidiary Excel Inc. This troika did not always control its market cost of cattle, though. Up to the mid-1980s, every time the industry leaders enlarged their market share by say 10 percent, the prices paid to the supplying cattlemen dropped ten cents per hundred pounds. But in the period 1986–88, the decline of cattle herds forced packers to pay higher prices in order to keep their plants operating at reasonable levels of efficiency.[35]

To lower such prices, both Conagra and Cargill planned for the future. Both were food conglomerates with tremendous sources of capital. They had no trouble entering the cattle-feeding business to supply themselves with cattle for slaughter. They thereby moved to create vertical minimonopolies, controlling production from the cattle-raisers to the cattle-feeders who fattened young steers for slaughter, then slaughtering and packing meat at market prices they also helped regulate.

Competing with the seller cattlemen by opening their own "feedlots," they raised the weight of each purchased yearling from about 700 pounds to about 1,200 pounds, thereby enlarging the supply and potentially reducing cattle prices in the open market.

IBP, the nation's largest beef packer, buys about 25 percent of the cattle yearly slaughtered in the U.S. But IBP was nonetheless left out of establishing vertical controls in the cattle-feeding business. It was thus forced to pay higher prices and became vulnerable to a drop in the supply of cattle. This occurred because, up until 1988, IBP had devoted its financial resources to developing new brands of beef and new channels to supermarkets. But during the 1988 drought, the number of cattle plunged to a 28-year low, packers were scrambling to find sufficient cattle to keep their plants running efficiently, the smaller packers closed their doors, and IBP was being pressured to buy its own "feed lots" to supply its own cattle at the expense of the middlemen feedlot owners.

With packers also buying forward contracts — that promised cattle from a particular feedlot at a future date for a specific price — Conagra and Excel tied up future beef supplies and prices by hedging forward-contract purchases. Here again, IBP was less experienced, had less capital for such operations, and was upset that it too would have to enter the competition to control future prices.[36]

Together, obviously, the Big Three held the power to set prices of meat at home. They also were positioned to dump abroad, especially as domestic beef demand reached a plateau in the face of changing consumer habits — particularly the increase in poultry consumption stimulated by worries about America's high-fat diet. "The only way to increase demand for our product may be through exports," said Paul Hitch, president of Hitch enterprises, a large Oklahoma cattle concern.[37] "Potentially, it's a very, very large market in Japan," said Mr. Philip Seng, Asian director of the United States Meat Export Federation. "We're talking easily $1.5 billion to $2 billion and by the year 2000 possibly a $3 billion market in Japan." By mid-1988, though, the U.S. was selling Japan only $600 million worth of beef a year and faced Japanese restrictions on imports in the name of protecting its own farmers' livelihood. And Japan sought to reach a sort of bilateral accord with the U.S. to prevent an American appeal to GATT to police the Japanese.[38]

The U.S. remained willing to negotiate some increase in Japan's 1988 25 percent beef tariffs, provided all nontariff barriers were dropped. The U.S. believed that American beef was so much cheaper to produce that it would remain price competitive in Japan even with higher tariffs. Thus the U.S. opposed both surcharges and bans, wanting Japan to pledge that any tariffs would be capped at specified levels and would diminish over time.[39]

Other food products faced similar national barriers. In citric fruit production, the key three locations in the Americas were California, Florida, and Brazil. Brazil had the largest orange groves, largely controlled the U.S. market, and mixed its orange juices with those of Florida. The Asian market was controlled by Sunkist Growers Inc., a cooperative that represented six thousand growers in California and Arizona.

In late May 1988 U.S. Trade Representative Clayton Yeutter, acting on a complaint filed by Florida citrus growers and processors, ordered an investigation of Japan's "unfair" import restrictions on oranges and orange juice. Arguing that 1987 U.S. exports of 134,500 metric tons could be increased to about 300,000 metric tons a year if the restrictions were lifted, and that the price of oranges in Japan would drop by about one-third if the import quotas were removed, Yeutter warned Japan that the U.S. might retaliate under the GATT rules and the 1974 U.S. Trade Act. Competition among U.S. suppliers for the Japanese market only increased the pressure, Florida suppliers arguing that the Japanese market was almost totally supplied by California growers through the Sunkist Marketing Cooperative.[40]

Japan's Shield

Japan's government also secured the interests of its farmers. The liberal Democratic Party [LDP] maintained power only because almost half its members in the Diet represented rural constituents who were guaranteed protection from foreign-grown beef, citrus fruits, nuts, and rice.

The Liberal Democratic Party had come into power and retained its power by carefully balancing government policies that favored both farmers and industrialists. To recruit more workers in boom times, the great employers with the complicity of the LDP had shaped policies to draw temporary rural farm workers into industry. But as the farm population then slipped, the LDP kept the allegiances of a large part of the remaining peasantry by perennially offering farm subsidies which were offset by the higher rice prices charged in government stores and the higher taxes imposed on urban workers.

Though the LDP lost political control in the big cities, where labor was organized and supported liberal and left-leaning parties in the 1960s, the LDP was able to maintain its following among the peasantry. And to make rural districts more important than urban ones, the LDP tried to gerrymander voting districts, meanwhile holding on to about one-third of the big city vote. Nonetheless, small-scale farming and LDP farm support thereafter dwindled, as farmers continued to move to the cities seeking higher wages, as the monopoly groups began to absorb more land, and as the land itself was turned into a giant outdoor factory, with the countryside, like the city, coming under the control of large enterprises.[41]

Because of historical fears of an inadequate staple food supply, most Japanese felt that for national security the nation had to be self-sufficient in rice production. Traditionally, the ban on foreign rice had sustained Japan's rice farmers. The government purchased almost all the rice produced at home at prices several times higher than the international price and then sold the rice to consumers through retail shops at somewhat lower prices — yet still at prices as much as ten times higher than the world market price. Though the U.S. continually pressured Japan to remove the foreign ban and state subsidy system, in both 1980 and 1984 both houses of the Diet "unanimously" adopted a resolution against the lifting of the import ban. "If you take on rice liberalization, then anti–American feelings will definitely rise," advised LDP heavyweight Kato Koichi.[42]

By the late 1980s a new watershed was reached, when added revenues were drawn from the urban domain to support the farmers exposed to foreign competition, requiring a realignment of the forces that supported the LDP. For this the opposition was momentarily silenced: the root-binding *nemawashi* allowed everyone to "let off steam" *(gasu nuki)* in presenting their constituencies' views, but the final decisions were then transferred to a leadership group or committee chairman, and remaining opponents conveniently absented themselves from the final vote. "Because the opposition is thus silenced, it appears from the outside that ultimate decisions are unanimous," advised Mr. Kato.

"Another rule of party policymaking is that once the decision has been made, it is binding. It is a cardinal rule of the party that no LDP member, no matter how unhappy, may vote against it. Those who are unhappy absent themselves from the vote and tell their constituents they fought the best they could, but it was the fault of the bureaucrats."

For this escapade in undemocratic procedure, Kato noted that: "Setting the producer's price for rice is a good example. When this price is negotiated annually, we [LDP members] have daily meetings lasting from early morning until late at night for a week or more. These meetings are attended by close to half of our 440 LDP Diet members. [Given the resulting protective rice tariffs mandated]: It is not surprising, therefore, that agricultural trade issues are so controversial in U.S.–Japan relations."[43]

The same was true for most other agricultural products. Kato, from his position as chairman of the Diet's powerful agricultural committee, indicated that beef imports could not be liberalized without some border barriers such as surcharges or tariffs because, without sticking to these, the LDP "would be defeated very seriously in the next election."[44]

Some concessions on other farm imports were made in 1987 — after the U.S. took the matter to GATT — thereby allowing about $100 million in imports of processed cheese, lactose, dairy products, sugared food preparations, processed beef, tomato juice, tomato sauce, and ketchup. But Japan blocked GATT from requiring it to dismantle all quotas — though the U.S. did gain compensation for Japan's quotas on starch and powdered skim milk.

To retain the support of farmers, the Japanese government had the alternative of increasing farm subsidies.[45] Facing the heat of massive farmer demonstrations against lifting restrictions, in February 1988 Prime Minister Takeshita publicly declared his opposition to lifting the ban, thereby inciting the wrath of the U.S., which insisted that this was a negotiable issue in the face of the 1987 $59.8 billion trade surplus Japan held with the U.S.[46]

Private farm groups then continued to rail against U.S. pressures on Japan to let foreigners have a larger share of its markets for farm products. Though the U.S. held 70 percent of Japan's import of 10.57 million tons of cattle feed grain in 1986/87, the U.S. wanted a greater market share. U.S. greed led Japan's Central Union of Agricultural Cooperatives to decide to buy 500,000 tons of corn and other feed grains elsewhere in 1988, and ultimately to replace the 25 percent of roughly 5,000,000 tons of feed grain its affiliates import from the U.S. by turning to China, Argentina, and Australia.[47]

Yet, just before the June 1988 Toronto Economic Summit, the frame for a compromise agreement on other products was set: Japan's beef and fresh oranges quotas would be eliminated over three years (and over four years on orange juice), would be replaced by declining tariffs over that same term, but would still allow Japan the option to raise the tariff after six years and impose import restraints if the liberalization had too great an impact on the interests of the politically powerful Japanese farmers.[48]

The detailed provisions were complex, but the Japanese concessions would eventually increase U.S. exports in beef and oranges from $600–650 million to more than $1 billion. Since by 1991 America might potentially double its world beef export markets to about 4 percent of production, the draw on the U.S. supply might increase prices 2 or 3 percent for U.S. consumers. By that time, the Japanese tariff would be up to 50 percent, so U.S. beef prices would have to be low enough to undercut competitors.

The agreement came at a time when the number of U.S. beef cattle was at a 26-year low. Cattlemen cut their herds in response to lower prices. And when drought stuck in the summer of 1988, worried bankers demanded repayment of farm loans before any rancher efforts to rebuild their herds.

Given the expected low supplies of U.S. cattle during the late 1980s, then, U.S. beef was not expected by producers to be economical enough to capture a larger Japanese market share.

Japan might also exploit the situation by making big investments in U.S. meat packers, taking advantage of the expanding Nippon market. "If we create a home for [producing] more quantities of beef, they'll move in and make a push into the cattle-packing industry," predicted Charles Levitt, an analyst for Shearson Lehman Hutton.[49]

Under the new agreement, Florida citrus growers would also expand their exports to the Japanese from six million gallons of orange juice to as much as eighty million gallons a year. Competition from orange growers in Brazil, South Africa, and Australia would increase. But there would be no duty reduction for fresh oranges, which would aid California growers' exports, though an additional one million boxes would be added to the seven million yearly sent to Japan. Japanese buyers would simply continue to pay more than twice what an American buyer paid for a Californian orange.

Within Japan, the farmers were stewing. New government subsidies would have to be used to quiet protesting farmers. The declining number of Japan's beef cattle raisers and orange growers, which had already fallen to 600,000 families, comprising just 14 percent of Japan's farm population in 1988, were losing some of their political clout. The rice farmers would temporarily retain their subsidies under the still-sancrosanct belief that Japan needed to be self-sufficient.[50] But change was definitely in the air. The militant farmers, who had once been the core of the Liberal Democratic Party, would eventually be weakened, join the opposition, and become a small voice in a big pond of powerful new industrial interests.

Overall, agricultural interests play comparable roles in the various segments of production in all the leading nations that have entere global markets, with state policies adjusted to secure home markets for domestic agriculture, to aid in dumping surpluses abroad, and to discourage home production to keep prices high. The state subsidizes the farmers and erects tariffs against foreign farm products in the U.S., Japan, and the E.E.C. Not only do farm interests pressure their respective states for aid superior to that received by competitors from other nations, but developed countries' farmers want to keep out third world farm products — thereby keeping prices high in their domestic economies, extracting $100 billion or more a year from consumers.

These are only some of the impedimenta of the war without end among nations using neomercantile methods. At the core of their operations are state planning and implementation at the expense of all other nations and their vested interests. Seeking to ameliorate the intensity of this struggle for markets in the late 1980s, the United States spoke of, and began to negotiate for, free trade areas through bilateral agreements. And understanding the advantages of such bilateral machinations, Japan laid the groundwork for a demand-led, mass market economy for the first time in the nation's history.

Chapter 17

Planning a Demand-Led, Mass-Market Economy: Noah's Ark Construction and Other Ethereal Projects

At home, Japan had traditionally been a nation that limited the consumption of the working population, concentrated on production for exports, and dumped in world markets to outflank competitors and establish market shares. But pressure from the United States and Western Europe signaled change in 1988. Thus, for the first time in its history, Japan planned to promote and consolidate a shift to a domestic "demand-led economy."

The new plan was designed to simultaneously promote "balanced national economic and social development," improve the quality of life for the 122 million Japanese, and lessen export pressures, thereby reducing Japan's trade surplus. This five-year plan for economic development from 1988 to 1992 was implicitly designed to use government budgetary resources to create an internal mass market with a 4.25 percent annual growth in domestic demand, a partial offset by export cuts, and a forecasted overall economic growth rate averaging 3.75 percent annually.[1]

Taxes, Consumption, and Output

In initially pursuing the creation of a demand-led economy, the Economic Planning Agency in 1987 began to concentrate on the perceptions of Japanese consumers in terms of what they might buy at which price. Prices in the domestic market were largely controlled by monopsonistic distributors for particular goods and foods, who set prices high. But as the yen appreciated, the price of many imported goods, including certain foods, natural resources, and consumer goods, had fallen. In the minds of Japanese consumers in early 1987 the prices of specific items had either gone down or remained unchanged — not gone up. Only with textiles and personal luxuries did consumers think prices had sharply risen.[2]

188

When prices had not fallen, consumers offered assorted reasons, the two major ones being that (1) profits were being absorbed in the structural complexities of Japan's distribution system; and (2) prices were already discounted and purchases took place at the reduced price.[3]

The fact that consumers might respond on the basis of price was the clue the Economic Planning Agency required. The mystery of creating a demand-led economy could now easily be solved by lowering prices to the level at which consumers would buy. The problem at hand, though, was to stimulate such buying by releasing money into their hands.

Given the frugality of Japanese households, which had traditionally saved and lived within their means, the way to stimulate consumption in Japan was to reduce prices — via reduced industrial taxes to cut production costs — and to remove barriers that kept consumers from spending their savings. Tax revenues would have to be raised to pay for increased state subsidies to reduce Japan's cost of production and domestic prices for goods. To buy these cheaper goods, consumers needed to be funded. So the first step to reorient the domestic economy was to find a way to enlarge tax revenues to finance the reorganization of technical production *and* to stimulate consumption.

The state lacked sufficient resources for the task. In the fiscal year ending March 1988, Japan's budgetary shortfall was about $86 billion, accounting for about 21 percent of the nation's annual gross national product. This shortfall represented the degree to which production and care for the rapidly aging population was subsidized without the imposition of equivalent taxes. To carry the overage, Japan had enlarged its public debt, which exceeded one trillion dollars by 1988. The stability of the Liberal Democratic Party would have been jeopardized if the debt was again enlarged to launch the planned demand-led economy. So the only alternative that would allow the LDP to provide industries with continued subsidies while lowering their tax payments was to shift the burden to consumers by increasing taxes on both domestic and imported products.

This shift initially involved using the tax structure to reallocate the nation's wealth, thereby imposing greater inequities than in the past. The tradition of *kuroyon,* literally *nine-six-four,* had meant that salaried employees paid 90 percent of the taxes they owed, business owners 60 percent, and farmers 40 percent. This system worked because companies calculated their employees' taxes and withheld them from paychecks, while farmers and self-employed businessmen calculated their own taxes. Moreover, the sale of land and stocks that created Japan's nouveau riche were not taxed either on their asset values or for their capital gains. The only way the LDP could stay in power, moreover, was to promise the farmers, small businessmen, and nouveau riche that the salaried workers would pay any effective tax increase. Because the politicians used stock appreciation profits to help fund their campaigns, they would approve no more than a 20 percent tax on profits from securities sales, even though the

the profits themselves were *predetermined* to be only 5 percent of the sales price. This was a sham tax, of course, for stock prices had been soaring for years and the Finance Ministry had no way to track stock sales because Japanese taxpayers did not have identification numbers.[4]

By June 1988, Premier Takeshita had promised deep cuts in corporate taxes and a 3 percent consumers' tax that, calculated on the basis of each business' internal accounting records, could be passed on in the form of increased prices for goods. The biggest beneficiaries would be the producers of cars and other consumer durables because the new sales tax on consumers would raise the price of these items. These provisions allowed the prime minister to win the support of three out of four major business organizations. The losers would be those at the lower end of the income scale, who had not benefited from tax cuts and would now have to pay higher prices.

The skewed benefits were also reflected in a proposal that would shrink the number of tax brackets from twelve to five, lower the highest income tax rate for individuals from 60 to 50 percent, drop the corporate rate from 42 percent to the competitive U.S. level of 37.5 percent, and barely reduce the lowest rate from 10.5 to 10 percent. Business gained the lion's share of the $45 billion in tax cuts, while consumers were burdened with an additional $43 billion in sales taxes.[5]

For the immediate future, then, the question became how more heavily taxed Japanese consumers could be mobilized to spend what they had already saved. Would savings be freed and credit expanded to stimulate demand and support the rapidly increasing number of elderly people?

There were definite limits to credit-based consumerism within Japan. Due to inadequate social security benefits provided by their government and their employers, the Japanese people had been culturally indoctrinated to save for their own future security. They feared lack of adequate savings to responsibly pay their bills after retirement. In the United States, the problem of expanding consumer demand had been resolved by extending credit; indeed, household debt in the U.S. often far exceeded the market value of personal assets. "They use credit cards a lot," criticized Watanabe Michio, chairman of the Policy Research Council of the LDP, at the party's 1988 annual summer conference. "They have no savings, so they go bankrupt. If Japanese become bankrupt, they think it is serious enough to escape into the night or commit family suicide."[6]

It thus became the government's problem to cajole, induce, and pressure savers and those with wages and salaries to spend.[7] At the exchange rate of 125 yen to the $1, the average Japanese individual income reached $19,000 in 1987, surpassing the average U.S. figure of $18,000. But food prices in Japan remained three times higher than those in the U.S., other everyday consumer products were 80 percent more expensive, and the high rate of personal savings continued to place capital savings and exports first and domestic consumption last.[8]

Because household buying power was the planned foundation for the new demand-led economy, the rules for tax-exempt household savings had to be changed. Moveover, one of the government's early steps was to drain money from speculation in the stock market, and to encourage consumers to spend rather than to invest. Individual investors had entered the market in the late 1980s, heavily relying on margin trading—putting up some cash to buy securities and borrowing the rest at relatively low interest rates. This practice spiked the market, increasing both volume and share prices, but also increasing the vulnerability of small investors to an eventual crash.

To reduce this risk and push small investors toward consumption, the central government used its power to control the Tokyo Stock Exchange. The authorities had the power to regulate the extent to which investors might use credit to buy stocks, thereby inviting in or excluding small-time speculative investors who hoped to make profits. When the authorities were trying to increase investment in September 1987, they reduced the margin level for stock purchases from 70 to 50 percent. When they reversed course, trying to decrease investors' speculative capital, they raised the margin on 16 May 1988, from 50 to 60 percent. When the speculative market continued to surge, on 2 June 1988, they again raised the margin requirements, now from 60 to 70 percent.

The chairman of the Securities and Exchange Commission, David S. Ruder, read the tea leaves, interpreting the Japanese move as "likely to be an indication to dampen speculative activity in the Japanese stock market, which has gone up over its pre–October [crash] highs."[9] But the big investors did not rely on margin, and thus the stock market might escalate further. Only the small Japanese investors got the message: now they were supposed to spend on material things, not ethereal pieces of paper called stocks and bonds.

How Production Responds

The results for the first quarter of 1988 indicated that the plan might be successful: personal spending (which normally accounted for 55 percent of Japan's gross national product) rose 4 percent, housing investments 23.9 percent, industrial equipment investment 10.1 percent—and Japan's growth to an annual rate of 11.3 percent.[10] Greater output thus promised to lead to more work, more wages, and more spending.

Japan was developing two fronts for production and sales: foreign and domestic. The export of machines, other means of production, and direct investment capital would promote production and sales abroad. The rapid investment in technology and facilities within Japan would raise production for domestic sales to an enlarged sector of consumers and workers.

For many large companies, concentration on production in, and sales from, overseas facilities, as well as on Japanese-based production for domestic sales, climbed in relation to all other revenues.[11] "I believe that a domestic demand-driven economy is taking root in this country now," Prime Minister Takeshita told a group of foreign correspondents before the mid-1988 Summit Conference in Toronto.[12]

Dimensions of the Demand-Led Economy

While attempting to create this demand-led economy, Japan did not give up its production advantages over the U.S., however. The change in the immediate balance between savings and spending might reduce Japan's 1987 almost 17 percent private investment in plant and equipment as a share of gross national product (as compared with the 10.2 percent U.S. rate). But more sales and production would eventually create a still larger output, with more revenues and more profits to reinvest.

In the past, larger output had been made possible in part by excellence in production, making each worker put in longer hours on average every year (2,152 versus 1,898 in the U.S.), intensifying the work process to reduce the time between the receipt of orders and shipments (one to two months for machine tools in Japan, but five to six months in the U.S.), and reducing the defective product rate. The nonconformance/rework rate in the electronics industry was 0.5–1 percent in Japan, but 8–10 percent in the United States, for example, the difference reflecting greater attention to detail at every stage of Japanese manufacturing to control cost and ensure product acceptance. Japanese factories were also more flexible than U.S. factories and were able to exploit the commercial application of new technology faster, a 1987 U.S. Department of Defense study showed.[13]

These production advantages meant, now that America was demanding that Japan stimulate domestic consumption, a great consumer revolution was absolutely essential. It was designed in part to replace exports, hopefully narrowing Nippon's large surplus with the U.S. The MITI also proposed that the demand-led economy would have to reward the workers with cash or credit, give them leisure time to spend, and open the way for cheap imports that would also reduce Japan's trade surplus. This meant work life would have to be shortened to offer consumers time to shop, spurring the demand for imported goods. Hence the decision by the MITI to move to a five-day work week, and the decision by the Ministry of Posts and Telecommunications to close branches of the national postal savings system every Saturday, starting early in 1989. Hence too the plan of major banks and brokerage houses to close on weekends, to be followed by a similar closing of the Tokyo Stock Exchange.[14]

At its 1988 semiannual meeting of 302 major corporations, the MITI thus presented the dilemma of the $76.02 billion trade surplus for the fiscal year ending 31 March 1988, the impending close down of U.S. and Western European markets if the surplus was not reduced, and the requirement that these companies step up their imports of manufactured parts, materials, machines, etc., so that the surplus for the fiscal year ending 31 March 1989 would drop to $65 billion. MITI was not satisfied with the companies' own estimates to increase imports of manufactured goods by 17 percent to $52.2 billion, instead insisting on more than a 20 percent rise from the $44.6 billion in the prior fiscal year and a rise in imports from their own foreign affiliates in excess of their own estimates of $2.4 billion.[15]

Also envisioned were measures to promote bilateral trade equity, stabilized exchange rates, and a broader Japanese sphere of influence. Foreign sellers were to win easier access to Japanese markets. Japan would cooperate with other leading industrial nations to coordinate their policies in an effort to stabilize internal currency markets. And Nippon would both increase foreign aid and recycle profits to third world nations, upgrading their production base and giving Japan a leading place in their technological imports, production apparatus, labor system, and exports.[16]

Japan, too, would have an internal mass market and an economic prosperity sphere comparable to the 244 million consumers in the U.S. and the 320 million in the EEC by 1992.

Noah and the Dynamics of Public Works

Imports, though, need not mean a production slowdown in Japan. For the underlying dynamics in the building and operation of public works were that the great construction companies would grow more wealthy while creating essential infrastructure for Japan. This infrastructure of bridges, roads, airports, etc., would allow the national manufacturers to more inexpensively produce and market consumer goods to the very workers who would receive wages and salaries directly or indirectly through the increase in construction and construction employment. Thus construction, like other heavy industry and the new technologies, would promote the expansion of still other industries.

The logic of this expansion might have political implications as well. For intensified consolidation of the economy would likely make the population increasingly beholden for work and consumption to the Liberal Democratic Party. Thus the LDP would increase its political hold over popular will and the Japanese people's submission to disingenuous influences of the elite. The new system might even become a modern version of the exploitive, centralized "hydraulic societies" ruled by despots in ancient Chinese and Asian societies, that Karl August Wittfogel described.[17] And the island nature of Japan's tight-knit political system and conglomerated financial complex held the potential to make its "hydraulic society" more powerful and materially rational, yet more despotic and ideologically irrational.

Meanwhile, the demand-led production system would be spurred by construction, with steel and its modern alloys still the foundation stone for the construction industry. Japan had built up barriers that prevented foreign contractors from winning a share of the market, especially during 1988 when Japan began the greatest infrastructural program in its history. Yet Nippon asked for unrestricted rights to bid on construction projects in the West, revealing the two systems of trade—free and neomercantilist—and the double standards Japan used in dealing with others.

Nippon Steel Co., the world's largest, appeared in the forefront of Japan's brave new world of construction. With other financially powerful, corporate backers, it became part owner of B.B. Consultants Inc., planning to expand Japan's urban dimensions in a new way under the rubric of the Noah Project—to build office buildings accommodating as many as seven hundred office workers and other service enterprises on great 35,000-ton steel ships floating in Tokyo Bay.

The logic of such future cities had been clear to Nippon policymakers for some time. "Japan is running out of land sites," said an official of one consortium. "A ship can have all the functions of a city," added Denda Hisao, vice-president of B.B. Consultants. "Japan is surrounded by ocean, and we're not using it at all." By the late 1980s, there was clearly too little remaining space in Tokyo, where office occupancy rates approached 100 percent. The Noah Project planned to sell office space for about one-tenth of the $7,500 square foot price in the Tokyo financial district.

The modern needs of Japan for urban office space, hotel facilities, power plants, and factories were explained by an appeal to a traditional image. Architect Kurokawa Kisho indicated that: "The idea of floating . . . is related to Buddhist philosophy. The whole city should be changing. It doesn't exist for eternity. . . . For the Japanese, Tokyo has always been a floating city."

Kurokawa had proposed floating factories, military bases, and expositions. Precedents existed, too. In the mid-1970s Westinghouse Electric Corp. built a factory in Florida to make barge-mounted nuclear plants, only scrapping the facility in the mid-1980s after prospective utility company buyers cancelled their orders. Others had dreamt up floating hotels. Nippon Kokan K.K. had designed a flashy floating hotel in 1983 for sale in Southeast Asia; year-round use was planned, the blueprints calling for hotels on barges to be tugged to resorts during the tourist season, and to some far-distant hot spot during the off-season. The contemporary leisure-resort boom in Asia, according to Nippon Kokan logic, "should make [the idea] much more attractive."

By the late 1980s Asian capital took the initial steps to produce model projects. A Singapore shipyard built a model, tugging an actual floating hotel to Australia's Great Barrier Reef. Japanese power companies also resurrected the floating nuclear reactor concept; the Central Research Institute of Electric Power Industry launched a desk-sized model in a shallow tank of water to illustrate how by the early 21st century real ones could be built and towed to protected moorings near power users. The government-backed Foundation for R&D of Ocean City, with thirty Japanese corporations, including giants like IBM's Japanese subsidiary, represented on its board of directors, promoted the floating city concept. The organization produced glossy pamphlets depicting a 21st-century, $200-billion, million-resident quadruple-deck platform twice the size of central Tokyo, enclosing eight golf courses, two baseball stadiums, and an airport for hypersonic planes. In July 1988, the company announced a $2 billion model — a floating city to be constructed within five years, using known technology on a realistic project.

As a competitor bidding for an immediate market, the Noah Project expected to have orders by May 1990, to be sold at one-tenth the price of a comparable Tokyo office tower, and to moor in the calm waters of Tokyo Bay, steam out for office cruises to the Caribbean or Brazil, and head for open sea in order to dodge gale winds and *tsunami* tidal waves following earthquakes.[18]

Should these construction projects succeed, the production of Japanese-made steel, heavy tools, and computerized control systems could conceivably double production, create a labor shortage, force up wages, fuel domestic consumer buying, and push Nippon into further self-sufficiency.

Japan might grant foreign companies the right to bid on construction projects, but the real test would be the number of successful bids allowed. Until that time, the U.S. might be tempted to favorably respond to the request of Japanese construction executives for the U.S. to lift its ban on Japanese bids for U.S. public works projects.

But the prognosis was, and is, that there would be no equality between Nippon and America in the construction trades. The U.S. had not won a single contract with any branch of the Japanese government by the late 1980s, though at the end of May 1988 the U.S. and Japan had signed a Washington accord that provided for increased U.S. penetration of the Japanese construction market. Yet the accord had no mandatory enforcement mechanisms. Japan only promised "to encourage" foreign participation in sizeable public works financed by the Japanese government and other projects carried out by Japanese companies with financing from both the central and local governments. Because the U.S. government had originally threatened to invoke legislation allowing retaliatory trade moves against Japan for what Washington perceived as an unfairly closed construction market, the signing of the accord emboldened the Japanese Federation of Construction Contractors to call on the U.S. to lift its own ban on Japanese bids for U.S. public works projects. "We strongly hope that the United States Trade Representative will immediately reverse its decision to name Japan as one of those countries that should be subject to exclusion from United States–funded construction projects," said the Federation chairman Sako Hajime.[19]

Even before the U.S. could decide, Japan moved forward. Kumagai Gumi Company, one of Japan's largest contractors, ranked among 1986 general contractors as the seventh largest in the world, followed tradition's path by forming an association to explore possible joint ventures with a much smaller, yet industrially critical, U.S. company — the Turner Corporation, the biggest U.S. general contractor for buildings, though ranking 193rd among the world's general contractors.[20]

What was the overall effect of all these demand-led projects for consumers and enterprise? As the entire Japanese business community swung into place by mid-1988, the nation shifted its perspective from exports to domestic demand as its *main* source of *future* economic growth. Due to the combined expansion of domestic demand, increases in export prices, and cost-cutting restructuring steps taken to deal with the upvalued yen, some 648 big manufacturers upgraded their sales and profit estimates. Another seven hundred or so companies, many nonmanufacturers, also held rising expectations; the June 1988 Japan Central Bank index of their business sentiments reached its highest level since 1975.[21]

Even the Bank for International Settlements was impressed with the boost in Japan's expanded domestic demand, seeing it as a harbinger of reduced exports, a narrowed current account gap, and thus an avenue to encourage owners of financial wealth to increase investments in dollar assets to help finance the U.S. current-account gap. Yet, that would have to be supplemented, the BIS thought, by stronger U.S. fiscal restraint to cool strong domestic demand (and thus reduce imports from Japan) and greater West German expansion in domestic demand to encourage capital formation at home.[22]

America's Fantasy of the "Open Door"

Since at least 1890, the American fantasy has been that other nations will accept U.S. investments without barriers and on an equal footing with the investment of other nations and national investors. When the U.S. was the dominant foreign investor, this policy operated to its advantage. But once Nippon investors were backed up by a more powerful state-subsidized production apparatus to stimulate exports and control imports of both goods and capital, there would be neither an open door nor an equitable entry for American investments.

The largest U.S. and other foreign companies might be allowed into Japan in a token way to produce with Japanese workers, be near changing demands, and ensure a reliable supply to Japanese customers. But the state would be ever-present in drawing the lines of how much foreign capital would be allowed to enter and in which fields of production.

By 1985 foreign companies already accounted for about 3 percent of Japanese manufacturing sales. The appreciation of the yen from 1986 to the end of 1987 did not stop 80 percent of foreign companies already manufacturing in Japan from planning to enlarge local production, often by using cheaper imported components and raw materials and earning larger profits when yen-returns were translated back into home currencies. In the year ending 31 March 1988 foreign investments totaled $2.21 billion, with U.S. companies accounting for $938 million or 42.4 percent.

The lines of demarcation already favored substantial foreign companies from the leading nations. "Large incumbent firms, well-entrenched with dollar-denominated product costs and yen revenues, are enriched," said one long-time resident businessman in Japan. "But Yankee traders newly arrived and looking for a toehold need not apply, as the cost of importing dollars to get established prices drives new businesses out of the market. Any American firm not already under roof in Japan probably won't ever be if things [like the high yen-dollar exchange rates and high prices to foreigners] remain as they are."[23] Boosting their 1988 manufacturing or service-sector investments in Japan were such multinational giants as Michelin & Cie., E.I. Du Pont de Nemours & Co., Digital Equipment Corp., Philipps Petroleum Co., AB Volvo, Bayerische Mortoren Werke AG, Daimler-Benz AG, and Volkswagen AG.[24]

Defined patterns were quickly emerging, with autarky, exchange rate ratios, protected investment zones, and closely controlled spheres of influence clearly on the agenda for America and Japan, posing old conundrums and creating new frontiers.

Chapter 18
New Frontiers
and Old Conundrums

*Containment of the Soviet Union has suc-
ceeded. But the containment model doesn't
manage all these new issues: Third World
debt, sub–Saharan Africa. Clearly the
world's more complicated now. In many
areas of competition, it's not the Soviet
Union we have to watch, but Japan, to some
extent Europe, and increasingly the newly industrialized countries, such as South Korea.*

*We need to try to come to some sort of
economic equivalence of the [NATO] alliance
policies. Unlike with NATO, there's no external threat; the rivalries are within. Against
whom are we going to form an economic
alliance with Japan? The Martians?* — Former
U.S. Defense Secretary Harold Brown[1]

*Burden-sharing is more than the number of
troops and planes. We need to consider the
economic factor. For too long in the U.S. we
have thought of it as strictly a national
security-issue, with no economic component.
But those days are gone. You can't argue that
way with a guy in Congress whose urban
grant you're trying to phase out to support re-
positioning of more U.S. troops in South
Korea, when the Koreans are running up a big
trade surplus with us.* — Former Treasury Secretary James Baker[2]

The postwar division of functions between the United States and Japan ensured that America would provide the defense perimeter, manufactured
goods, and food and resource aid to Japan and "free world" Asia, and
Japan would rebuild economically and politically to American specifica-
tions. Japan was not to rearm under its U.S.-imposed constitution.

Theoretically, at least, the U.S. defense umbrella would permit Japan to establish a coprosperity sphere within the Asian Pacific area.

Forty-five years later, the balance of terror in the world had changed and the Nippon-American balance of trade had been transformed. The United States had changed the ordering of its major military enemies from the Communist nations, particularly the Soviet Union and China, to the Libyas of the globe, and no longer viewed Japan as a nation to be aided, but instead as one that should aid others in expanding the general sphere of capitalist, or at least commercial, influence. Japan, now the preeminent world trader and investor, had power thrust upon it by its previous conqueror, so its wealth could help create the framework for a successful global enterprise and marketplace. U.S. resources would continue to provide the military backup to keep that market from being disrupted or narrowed. And as recurrently happened in the previous century and a half, the third world would be the beneficiary of a dual mandate: entitled to receive aid from Japan and the industrialized Western nations; but also obliged to live by the economic, and sometimes political, terms they prescribed.

The New Division of Labor and Revanchism

"Japan can take a much heavier burden of economic aid, and you [Americans] can provide military measures," said Tokyo University professor Sato Seizaburo. He saw the future.

The practical significance and underlying dynamics of this formulation were destined to keep the U.S. budget in perennial deficit and to push Japanese international accounts powerfully into black ink. Such a division of functions led to the following situations:

1. Defending Japan and other Asian nations added to the U.S. military budget and increased the total federal budget. The U.S. taxpayers had to finance these outlays, as well as the interest on bonds sold to raise revenue to pay for America's defense bill.

2. The U.S. increased spending in Japan and Asia to sustain U.S. bases and troops. This spending stimulated sales, and thus production and employment, by Japanese, South Korean, Taiwanese, and other foreign contractors — adding to their *real* balance of trade to be *paid for in dollars.*

3. Japan had no need to pay for the main portion of her own defense or for an Asian military shield. The money saved could be mobilized by the MITI to channel into research and development consortia or as subsidies to giant industries — bootstrapping advanced production and exports, thereby putting U.S. firms at a further technological and competitive disadvantage.

4. Thus the very America that defends Japan and Asia suffers a growing fiscal crisis because it lacks resources for both defense and domestic social spending, and thus makes too few R&D outlays to make U.S.

industry competitive. Meanwhile Japan has shifted her resources into technology and production, and has become more advanced technologically, more competitive internationally, and so wealthy through its trade surplus that it invades and takes over sections of the U.S. economy and even receives federal military contracts.

The resulting patterns between 1950 and 1986 are known. The U.S. share of world exports fell from 17.2 percent to 10.9 percent. The U.S. share of world monetary reserves shrank from 50.1 percent to 8.8 percent. The U.S. share of world gold reserves fell from 68.2 percent to 27.6 percent. Global military power has also changed. The "Big Three" of the U.S., USSR, and U.K. had been the exclusive holders of ballistic missiles in the 1950s, but more than thirty nations had them by 1988. In terms of GNP, the U.S. was still the leader in 1987, followed by Japan and the Soviet Union. And the U.S. had more strategic warheads than the Russians — and Japan had none.[3]

But the United States could not simultaneously be the world policeman and maintain the world's most powerful economy. If America continued to try to be both, the future overall effect might be the increasing outlay of tax funds on arms contracts and military costs by the federal government, worsening its budget deficits; the upgrading of Japan's competitive economic standing, the growth of its positive trade balance, the rapid accumulation of capital and financial strength for foreign takeovers by giant Japanese corporations; and America's resulting double fiscal and foreign account deficits.

Japan's Formula for Accumulation

From the highest reaches of government, Japan had long demanded that American military purchases, Japanese war reparations payments, and any aid and loans made to other nations by Japan should be earmarked to buy Japanese exports or spent for specific projects that involved Japanese business interests. When Western nations had objected to aid programs and particularized infrastructural projects that mandated the purchase of Japanese products or the participation of Japanese businesses, Japan either had not forthrightly responded or had limited its aid and loan outlays without discussion. This relationship, or lack of one, continued more or less until the late 1960s.

By the early 1970s, moreover, Japan was already planning to use its strategic location to economically replace the United States in Asia. Though Japan was not prepared militarily to assume the defense role the United States had played after World War II, America prodded Japan to cooperate militarily, to accelerate her pace of spending on rearmament, to occupy strategic points, even to acquire atomic weaponry.

Japan was unable to take these measures without realigning her fractured social classes and reorganizing her political forces at home. A 1970

White Paper on Defense called on the nation to use its Self-Defense Forces as a "vehicle for people's education, as a place for application of their education, and as an instrument for social experience." It also called for "mutual interdependence" between industry and the military, so as to further production development in the face of what the military foresaw as a likely shortage of labor power, the potential development of science and technology, and the build-up of defense capabilities in the 1970s. The plan posited tighter control of Japanese society in order to pressure an already frugal people to produce more, create new armaments, and enable Japan to expand abroad at some appropriate, future time.[4]

Most of this planning was premature. For the previous two decades Japan's lack of military power had meant that its overseas trade and investments were shielded by the U.S. military network in Pacific Asia. Japan's production depended at that time on access to oil which came from the Persian Gulf through the Malacca Straits and then across the Indian Ocean. Ninety U.S. bases in Japan and hundreds of U.S. military installations throughout Asia provided security against any possible disruptions in the flow of oil or other raw materials to Japan. Japan was neither able, nor sought, to replace U.S. forces. Such a change would have cost the Japanese great sums of capital and caused intense internal conflicts between the factions favoring and those opposing military ventures abroad.

Until the mid-1970s, then, Japan lacked political and military bargaining power to pursue an independent *welt politik,* so much so that in Pacific Asia Japan was still the only super power without nuclear weapons of its own. Facing Japan were the military forces controlled by the Soviet Union and Communist China. These potential enemies had caused an escalation of fear within the ranks of Japan's Liberal Democratic Party. Until at least 1970, the conservative bloc within the LDP had outvoted, pressured, and persuaded the other parties and their backers to concentrate on upgrading Japan economically. The conservative forces were content to shelter under the U.S. nuclear umbrella.

The year 1971 provided the watershed for the reemergence of Japanese "defense" commitments, spurred by the *Nixon Doctrine.* "In the era of American predominance," President Nixon had stated, "we resorted to American prescriptions as well as resources. In the new era, our friends are revitalized and increasingly self-reliant, while the American domestic consensus had been strained by twenty-five years of global responsibilities. Failure to draw upon the growth of partners would have stifled them and exhausted ourselves." Therefore, the president concluded, "Partnership that was always theoretically desirable is now physically and psychologically imperative."[5] Under American pressure, Japan quietly rearmed, with each of four consecutive five-year defense plans doubling the one before. In millions of yen, the Japanese cost for defense spending rose from 1,300,000 during the period 1961–66 to 2,700,000 during the period 1966–72, and to 6,210,000 during the period 1972–77.

Yet the $14 billion available from 1966 to 1972 paled by comparison with the annual U.S. military outlay of over $100 billion; the U.S. spent in Asia alone from two and one-half to three times as much in a single year as Japan spent in five years. Even after Japan boosted her army to almost 300,000 men in 1976, there was still only one soldier for every 360 citizens — hardly the makings of a military power.

Japan's own military-industrial complex was nonetheless being strengthened. Military orders awarded to Japanese industry had grown. Manufacturers were soon striving to make Japan the chief supplier of arms for Asia. By 1975 Japan's arms industry viewed the military governments in South Korea, Taiwan, and elsewhere in Asia as prospective purchasers of their weapons.

Meanwhile, Japan had sought through its Defense Agency to acquire nuclear weapons. By 1976 it had both the technical and financial capabilities to make such weapons within two years, though there is no official record that Japan has nuclear weapons. But by late 1976, the U.S. delegation to the Joint Japan–United States Committee on Trade and Economic Affairs noted that the U.S. would continue to sell enriched uranium to Japan to supply its power facilities. Secretary of State Rogers added that the U.S. was quite willing to discuss the sale of classified U.S. technology for the use of the gaseous diffusion process to enrich uranium, provided the enterprise using the process was "multinational" and that certain safeguards were observed. Under this program, in fact, Japan obtained both uranium and the technology that were prerequisites to begin the mass production of nuclear weapons. In the following years, Japan may have done so, though, again, there is no official evidence suggesting this.

There is peripheral evidence of Japan's intent, however.

Though Japan signed the 1970 Nuclear Nonproliferation Treaty, Nippon withheld ratification for fear of making itself a "second-class nation" among the powerful. And with the U.S. military defeat in Vietnam and an expressed U.S. desire for an eventual departure from South Korea, Japan began preparing to step into a future military vacuum. As a close associate of Prime Minister Miki told the press in Tokyo in August 1975, a formal U.S. withdrawal from South Korea would be Japan's signal to replace the Americans with comparable military capability — implying that Japan had nuclear backup for its conventional arms.

Thirteen years later, in 1988, plutonium that had originated in the U.S. and had then been used by Japan was being purified of wastes in Europe for shipment back to Japan under U.S. controls. Japan and the U.S. were negotiating a treaty that permitted the plutonium to be shipped only by air; and in March 1988, a Pentagon study had cited "several basic problems with sea shipment," — including security at ports, the long period required for shipment, the dangers of passage through the Panama Canal or Suez Canal, the relative ease of attacking a ship, and the cost of providing naval escorts, estimated at $2.8 million per voyage. Congress had to approve any changes in the method of shipment, and certain senators and representatives opposed any changes. "The lawmakers said ocean shipping would be susceptible to attack by terrorists who might try to seize the plutonium, which is *suitable for use in nuclear weapons,*" a *New York Times* reporter disclosed.[6] Hence the question was immediately raised about Japanese use of this weapon-grade plutonium to offset the nuclear threat posed by the Soviet Union and China.

Balancing Class Support for Arms

The delicate balance among different social classes within Japan was also changing, making large-scale rearmament a distinct possibility by the mid–1970s.

Former members of the World War II cabinet were again at the center of promilitary sentiment. Kishi Nobusuke and Kaya Okinori, both having served as ministers in Tojo's military cabinet, had again risen to prominent posts. Kishi became prime minister from 1957 to 1960, and Kaya justice minister from 1963 to 1964. A long list of organizations and leaders also advocated nationalism and imperial expansion. Many wanted to repudiate the "blue-eyed," U.S.-imposed constitution that limited Japan to its own military defense; to reassert Japan's spiritual roots; to thereby provide national stability; and to increase the nation's defenses and, if necessary, expand by force throughout Asia.

Included in this group were men like Kodama Yoshio and Sasagawa Ryoichi, World War II militarists and fascists, who, by the mid–1970s, had become exceptionally wealthy financiers of the LDP and of dozens of right-wing and fascist splinter parties and groups. Sasagawa used his cash and ideological zeal to back prime ministers Sato and Tanaka. Both Kodama and Sasagawa offered support to thousands of well-disciplined followers in such austere organizations as *Seirankai* ("Blue Storm Society"), a right-wing group of legislators who have taken a blood oath to fight any drift to the political Left.

All right-wing activities meanwhile came under an umbrella group called the *All Japan Council on Patriotic Organizations,* which at its 1975 Council Convention called for the reestablishment of Japan's historic traditions through a new "Greater Japan Imperial Constitution," the rearmament and militarization of the nation, and a return to the prewar educational system that stressed obedience to the nation under the emperor's authority. The entire Right also sought state support for the *Yasukuni Shrine,* which honors all of Japan's soldiers who died while fighting for the emperor since 1869, including those killed during World War II.

In the 1980s, nationalists, including many senior government officials, continued to worship these war dead at the *Yasukuni Shrine;* they made this *honden* a symbol of their militant reverence justifying Japan's occupation of Asia in the 1930s. Prime Minister Nakasone broke the taboo on Shinto military enshrinement in 1985, by visiting *Yasukuni* in his official capacity. China viewed this gesture as part of a militarist revival, and pressured Nakasone to forego further visits if he wished to maintain diplomatic and economic relations with China.

Again, in 1988, renewed attempts were made to legitimize State Shintoism. The Japanese Supreme Court vindicated the Japanese Defense Agency in allowing a veterans' group to enshrine the soul of a dead soldier — despite the fact that his religion was unknown and the enshrinement was carried out against the strong objections of his Christian wife. The court ruled in a fourteen to one decision that the veterans' group had a religious right to practice enshrinement, and that the "marginal" involvement of the Defense Agency did not violate the constitutional protections of religious freedom and church-state separation. To uphold the Christian wife's argument, the justices said, would violate the religious liberties of those living veterans wishing to enshrine the spirit of her dead husband. "I did not want my husband's death to be used for glorifying war," she had explained. She also mentioned her concern over the growing tendency among top government officials to make formal visits to the *Yasukuni* and other Shinto shrines.

The great majority of Japan's contemporary 121 million population are wedded to a philosophy of nationalist "Japanism," centered on man, yet adhering to a practical merger of Shintoism and Buddhism in a way that accommodated both religions. Japan has only 1.7 million self-described Christians, but 92 million Buddhists overlapping with 115 million Shinto followers. Thus, the court's ruling was "quite appropriate, based on existing cultural and social realities in Japan," said Kamei Shizuka, leader of the right-wing bloc of the LDP.

The case thus helped shift Japan's political spectrum to the right. A prominent scholar took the view that the court was insensitive and reflected "the strong pressure of totalitarianism and the standardization of thought and religious belief." The court ruling suggested that the minority could be disregarded or suppressed. The wife involved in the case received threatening letters and was denounced for being "un–Japanese."[7]

Regional Defense

Internal conflicts about Japan's foreign policy did not subside in the 1970s and 1980s. By the mid–1970s the nation's voters clearly preferred welfare over defense spending, but government officials nonetheless continued to strengthen Japan's military forces in the pursuit of such goals as the need to defend Japan's maritime pathways off Taiwan and through the Malacca Strait that connects the South China Sea with the Indian Ocean. They reasoned that about 90 percent of the oil necessary for Japanese industries was shipped through the Malacca Strait, so that if any nation interfered militarily with Japanese tankers and stopped the flow of oil,

Japanese production, employment, and sales—the whole economy—would be undercut in one month.

After President Nixon was forced to resign, it was an open question whether the *Nixon Doctrine* would continue in force. During 1974 and 1975 Japan took the initial steps toward developing an independent foreign policy. Japan pursued direct talks with Arab governments to guarantee her oil supply. By August 1975, Prime Minister Miki was pressing President Ford and Secretary of State Kissinger to guarantee Japan's access to Middle East oil. Prime Minister Miki also instructed his foreign policy advisers to update his plan for an "Asian-Pacific Community"; this plan postulated a withdrawal from Asia that would oblige Japan to set up a "new cooperative arrangement" among nations of the Pacific basin—including Australia, New Zealand, and Canada.

The plan seemed essential for Japan, because in the mid-1970s Iran was the most important source of Japan's Middle Eastern oil supplies. Since Iran had outflanked the Russians and assumed control of the Persian Gulf as an important waterway for the shipment of petroleum, Japan undertook direct negotiations with the Iranian shah, backed up by a U.S. military presence. Because the Malacca Strait curled around Indonesia, Japan also sought influence with that archipelago. Japanese officials also believed that the Soviet presence in the Indian Ocean was not adequately offset by U.S. forces at Diego Garcia Island, and they began to plan to build up the Japanese navy.

Regional defense was also a theme of Japan's military revanchism. The 38th parallel that divides North Korea and South Korea was seen as Japan's "first defense line" against communism. In November 1969 a U.S.-Japanese communique recognized that both South Korea and Taiwan were important to Japan's security. President Nixon and Prime Minister Sato reaffirmed under the *Nixon Doctrine* that the *Japan-U.S. Security Treaty* encompassed areas bearing on the "security" of both Taiwan and South Korea. Japan's militarists interpreted the provision to mean that Japan was irrevocably committed to "regional defense." Prime Minister Miki also took steps to reduce tensions between North Korea and South Korea, and indicated that the U.S. should end its United Nations command there once a permanent truce was worked out. On conclusions of a U.S. withdrawal, some officials said, Japan might occupy South Korea with its own forces.

Regional defense was also the basis for Japan's conditional repossession of the Ryukyu Islands in 1972, lost to the U.S. after World War II. Japan had to allow the U.S. to maintain bases and other facilities there, including its nuclear and poison gas arsenal. On Okinawa, the largest island, a full 12 percent of the whole land area was a military base. Japan began expanding her Self-Defense Force there, side-by-side with the U.S. military establishment. Still lacking sufficient military forces of its own, Japan made concessions to the U.S. as part of the deal for repossessing the Ryukyus. Shimoda Takezo, Japanese ambassador to the U.S., explained that "It would not be a responsible way of negotiating the return of Okinawa to seek the same [non-nuclear] status for U.S. military installations as those on the [Japanese] mainland." For home consumption the Japanese government added that "It is only natural for Japan to defend the islands in accordance with the nation's [Japan's] right of self-defense."

Not satisfied with the Ryukyus, Japan has also laid claim to the U.S.-controlled Senkaku Islands, situated between Okinawa and Taiwan. Located above a vast pool of oil under the continental shelf, these islands were also claimed by Taiwan and Mainland China. Both China and Japan made preparations to control the oil that lay beneath, but these plans remain unfulfilled to this date.

Japan also made plans to repossess the Kurile Islands to the north from the Soviet Union, which had seized them from Japan at the close of World War II. Japanese leaders reasoned that control over these islands would provide a strategic advantage over both shipping and fishing in the northern Pacific.

Two Routes to Expand: Free Trade Versus Armed Might

Each step in Japanese expansion brought Japan closer to the Chinese mainland.

After 1969, U.S. barriers to Japan's trade had made Nippon more dependent on Asian markets and resources, though China did not yet fit into Japan's immediate future. But the U.S. political rapprochement with China in 1971—without engineered and announced consultation with Japan, as promised—made Nippon acutely conscious of the need for its own Asian policy.

In a replay of Nippon logic of the 1930s, Japan again felt threatened with encirclement by Western powers in a hostile Asia. Giant Western petroleum companies and the Organization of Petroleum Exporting Countries seemed bent on raising the price of imported fuel and threatened to cut off the source of Japan's oil energy unless certain political conditions were met. All these measures made Japan's ruling circles uneasy and led to their determination to quickly expand their sphere of influence in Asia and to make peace with Peking. The ruling Liberal Democratic Party split into two factions: *free traders* and *those advocating expansion by force*.

The free traders at first held the upper hand. They wanted Japan to win by peaceful penetration of the Co-prosperity Sphere she had tried, but had failed to conquer by force of arms between 1931 and 1945. By the mid-1960s Japan's sales to Southern Asia were already 50 percent in excess of her purchases. To offset the balance, Japanese industrialists and the government had exported investment capital and aid—hoping to stimulate the development of new sources of raw materials and manufacturing using cheap labor. By 1968 Japan's favorable balance with Asia was $1,822 million; it rose to $2,300 million the following year; increasing quarterly, by the end of the first quarter of 1971, Japan's reserves of foreign currencies had swelled to over $5,000 million, empowering her to switch roles from being a mere commodity exporter to becoming a major capital exporter as well.

Japan then began to export more capital than she imported, so that her overseas investments appeared to catch up with foreign investments in Japan. In the 1950s a one-way flow had seen foreign capital coming into Japan. From 1961 to 1969, Japan had exported some $1,110 million in capital, and imported about half as much ($570 million) in foreign capital. Yet the cumulative flows of capital movements during the 1950s and 1960s still weighed against Japan—by 1968 Japan had $2,600 million invested abroad, while foreigners owned $5,520 million in Japanese business assets. By 1973, however, the relation with the foreign investors and Japan had changed: Japan had $10,400 million invested in the U.S. and elsewhere overseas, but U.S. investments in Japan were just over $2,200 million.[8]

"Looking ahead," said *Barclays Bank Review* at the close of the 1960s, "it seems inevitable that Japan will play an important role in the development of Asia as the influence of Britain and, probably, the United States decline in relative terms, leaving Japan the dominant commercial power in the area." Asia was already exchanging its primary commodities and materials that Japan lacked for Nippon's manufactured goods, equipment, and capital. *Barclays* noted that Japan's trade with Southeast Asia had already grown to 30 percent of the total, and indicated that the potential for future growth was strong.

"One day the U.S. will pull out of Asia and Japan must recognize its responsibility for the security of Asia and the development of Asia," Japanese Affairs Minister Fukuda then foretold.

This responsibility was also a theme of Emperor Hirohito's 1971 trip to the U.S. and Europe. His journey, President Nixon said, helped "to symbolize Japan's growing position in world affairs. This is true, of course, in the economic sphere, where Japan has developed one of the world's fastest growing and most dynamic economies. It is true in the political sphere, where Japan has been increasingly active in international councils which are helping to shape the future of Asia—and of our entire planet. And it is true also in the cultural sphere, where Japanese art and literature and music and science have won growing acclaim throughout the world."[9]

This American vision fit into Japan's plans. Japanese *free traders* had hoped to create an Asian monetary area dominated by the yen to act as "a bridge to link Asia and Pacific nations," as one Japanese minister explained. For Japan not only needed to import raw materials and 98 percent of her petroleum supplies, but required foreign markets and investment zones that would negotiate and keep their balances in yen. This yen area, it was hoped, would emerge from Japan's central role in the Asian

Parliamentarians Union, whose purpose was to tighten economic relations with its members: South Korea, Taiwan, Thailand, Laos, Malaysia, the Philippines, and Indonesia.

As a first step, a proposal for an "Asian currency" was designed to boost interregional trade and reduce dependence on hard currencies controlled by the United States and Great Britain. Once this Asian currency succeeded, the membership of the Union was to be expanded to include India, Ceylon (Sri Lanka), Cambodia, Singapore, Australia, and New Zealand. "The sterling area" for the Commonwealth, the "dollar zone" in the Americas, and an expected single-unit currency for the Common Market in Western Europe, provide working models for an Asian currency. The Asian Parliamentarians Union through its General Assembly might give the plan full approval in the near future.

In shaping Asia's future, Japan also enlarged her role in a variety of other regional groups. Emulating what she had done in the 1930s, for example, Japan once again encouraged foreign students to study in Japan. She became the central member in the Asian Productivity Organization (APO), which drew together commercial students from thirteen Asian nations: Ceylon, Taiwan, Hong Kong, India, Indonesia, Iran, South Korea, Nepal, Pakistan, the Philippines, Singapore, Thailand, and South Vietnam (during the war between Vietnam and the United States). These business students attended Japan's Productivity Center which, with the cooperation of private industry, offered authentic in-plant practice in business methods and the use of technology. Each year, the APO recruited highly qualified experts from the U.S. to conduct lectures with Japanese instructors, with the last portion of the course involving field practice in another APO member nation. By the mid-1970s, South Korea, India, and Hong Kong had been used as APO laboratories, standardizing the dissemination of Japanese business techniques and technological methods.

Meanwhile, the U.S. not only pressured Japan to expand economically, politically, and culturally in Asia, but militarily as well. Japanese revanchists were in tune with this thinking in the early 1970s. Japan's military leaders and conservative politicians viewed China as Japan's most probable future enemy, followed by the Soviet Union. Japan's Defense Agency calculated that by 1976, China would have eighty to one hundred intermediate-range ballistic missiles, plus about ten intercontinental ballistic missiles, and that Japan was not militarily prepared to defend itself from such firepower.

Indeed, by the late 1970s, China had already surpassed both Britain and France as the world's third largest nuclear power. By the mid-1980s China had built a complete nuclear triad with a "survivable" retaliatory force. By 1988, the U.S.–Soviet treaty that eliminated intermediate-range nuclear missiles gave China a near-monopoly on ballistic missiles with ranges of 300 to 3,000 miles, which China made available for sale to oil-rich Middle Eastern customers.[10]

As Japan could not equal such firepower, Nippon leaders realized they would have to pacify China with words. Thus they apologized to China for Japan's brutal invasion during World War II, and regularized diplomatic relations and trade.[11] This Japan did in the following decade, while commercially expanding step-by-step into other parts of Asia.

Arms, Economic Influence, and Aid in the Late 1980s

Once Japan had firmly established its position as a preeminent manufacturing nation with a positive trade balance of $52 billion in 1988, it could no longer resist its desire to exert economic pressure and political influence over the nations it dealt with either directly or indirectly. It still relied on the U.S. military shield in Pacific Asia, the Persian Gulf, and the Indian Ocean. Yet, Japan could not at once secure the advantages of U.S. military protection for its oil resources passing through the Straits of Malacca and Hormuz and refuse to back up U.S. requests to extend its aid resources to nations of the Middle East. It could not move investment capital into the Philippines, still secured militarily by the U.S., and neglect to enlarge its loans and grants to establish an infrastructure for commerce. It could not hope to extend trade to Southern Europe or Euro-Asia without providing aid to back up the U.S. military presence or grants to Portugal, Turkey, Pakistan, and Afghanistan.[12]

U.S. Defense Secretary Carlucci pressured Japan to back U.S. military positions, speaking in terms of fear and security, warning Japan that the Soviet Union had greatly strengthened its air and naval forces in East Asia and that it presented "a very substantial military threat." He argued that Japan's $10 billion 1988 economic assistance for overseas development would advance the U.S.–Japanese "overall security." And with the Japanese Self-Defense Forces receiving about $30 billion a year (equivalent to 1 percent of the GNP) and Japan annually subventing 40 percent ($2.5 billion) for stationing 55,000 U.S. troops in Japan, the U.S. also hoped to shift part of its annual $3.5 billion outlay to Japan.[13]

Japan refused to be lectured about which nations to aid or the proportion of Japanese resources to be alloted for aid. The United Nations might target aid at 0.7 percent of the GNP of the leading nations, but Japan's Finance Ministry opposed any strict formula that was unrelated to Japan's overall policies. Japan had offered more aid in terms of dollars as the yen scaled upward in value starting in the 1985/86 fiscal year, increasing such aid from $5.6 billion, to $7.4 billion (1986/87), then to $10 billion (1987/88). But this increase represented appreciated *dollars,* not yen as a share of national wealth. Foreign expectations of slightly more than 0.3 percent of Nippon's GNP would have put it ahead of the U.S., at 0.22 percent, yet still behind the 0.36 percent average of the industrialized West.[14]

Aid and Collective Military Security

Nippon also resented America's bombastic attempts to push Japan to spend its tax resources for a purpose the U.S. had designed. The U.S. had spread 500,000 troops abroad, more than the British empire at its zenith; devoted 60 percent of its defense budget to funding its foreign presence; and, concentrated almost as many troops in Japan as throughout the entire Mediterranean Sea, Pacific Ocean, Indian Oceans, and the Persian Gulf, areas.[15]

So it was not unexpected that the U.S. would pressure Japan to assume a portion of both the military and aid burden to maintain Japan's own sphere of influence.

Suffering from yearly budgetary and trade balance crises, the U.S. since the early 1980s had planned to shift to others the burdens of its international obligations by decreasing its overseas military expenditures, as well as aid and loans to the third world. In Europe, the U.S. signed a historic pact with the Soviet Union to reduce short- and intermediate-range missiles, and pressured West Germany to cover a greater share of the cost of Allied military forces.

Though the U.S. Congress voted overwhelmingly in 1987 to urge Japan to triple its defense spending to 3 percent of its GNP, the 1988 Japanese defense budget accounted for 1.013 percent of GNP. In 1988 U.S. Defense Secretary Carlucci said he was not pressing for "dramatic leaps" in Japanese defense spending, but he did indicate that he wanted Nippon aid to be expressly linked to U.S. military backup.[16] In Asia, the U.S. forced the issue. America made peace with China, pressured Taiwan and South Korea to finance a greater share of their own defense, and urged Japan to increase its economic aid to "nations whose political and economic health is vital to our collective security."

This approach earned Japan's bitter enmity in June 1988. Yet, though the conservative LDP that held power had quietly boosted the Diet's military advance to upwards of $40 billion in expenditures (1988), it minimized its position in the global military equation, railed against making any connection between foreign aid and martial enterprises, and justified its military forces as purely in the interest of self-defense.

"Politically, he [the U.S. Defense Secretary] made a great mistake," a Foreign Ministry official pointed out to a group of Western reporters. For a foreign official to link aid to security, he testily continued, was "very difficult for Japan to digest," because the constitution limited Japan to defend itself alone. "In practice," he explained, "we have to take into account our own security when we give aid, but other's security—it's very delicate."[17]

Meanwhile, Japan's Self-Defense Forces were being enlarged. Plans for the five-year rebuilding program from 1985 to 1990 called for 180,000 troops, three times the U.S. number on Japanese soil, as well as 1,205 tanks, 163 F-15 fighter planes, 100 antisubmarine warfare planes, and 16 submarines. Japan also intended to possess more frigates than Britain. And all this firepower was supposedly designed to repel a "limited attack" and act as a critical line of defense until U.S. forces could arrive.[18]

But the chances of the U.S. arriving in the future were fast diminishing. In Tokyo, in July 1988, Secretary of State George Shultz acknowledged that Washington might never again have a balanced trade relationship with Japan. American officials could only watch as Japan began to translate its economic might into political influence in a way the U.S. could no longer afford. Japan stunned the six-nation Southeast Asia Nations' meeting in 1988 when Foreign Minister Uno Sosuke announced a plan to create and pay for an international peacekeeping force for Cambodia. Japan also offered to help finance postwar reconstruction in Iran and Iraq, to send civilians to help the United Nations monitor a cease-fire in the Iran-Iraq war, and to participate in a United Nations peacekeeping force in Afghanistan.[19]

The New Dual Mandate

Since at least the early 1970s trade, a military presence, and aid were different aspects of the Dual Mandate Japan and the Western nations had fastened on the third world. The system provided third world nations with relatively small amounts of aid while extracting larger and larger payments in the form of raw materials, debts, and political helotry.

After the United States and Western Europe had drained revenues from the third world for four decades. Japan stepped into the picture. The need of African and Palestinian peoples, Southeast Asians and Latin Americans was becoming increasingly critical. And by mid-1988, Michel François-Poncet, chairman of the holding company for one of France's major banks, was saying that the global capital movements that once went primarily from the Northern to the Southern Hemisphere were then flowing "within the Golden Triangle of London, New York, and Tokyo" — so that debtor, developing nations "now finance the rich countries to the tune of some $10 billion" a year.[20]

To reverse the flow, Japan became the Western nations' choice of donors, thrusting on it the mantle of power and increasing spheres of influence. Japan promised to spend a little more than $50 billion on foreign aid over five years, starting 1 April 1988, but refused to adopt a GNP-based target that might require higher spending if Japan's GNP grew faster than expected. Because the target would be expressed in dollars rather than yen, if the yen continued to strengthen, the target could be accomplished with a lower yen outlay.[21] Japan thus projected itself into the trade and politics of the Middle East and Asia.

Japan hoped to play a double game in the Middle East. Japan intended to largely heed the Arab boycott of trade with Israel in order not to upset its heavy dependence on Arab oil. It would provide $1 billion to back up U.S. military forces in Saudi Arabia in the contest with Iraq over the latter's conquest of Kuwait. Yet Japan also intended to appease Israel in hopes of extending Japan's trade there in the future by fostering an aid program for the Palestinians that Israel refused to finance.

Japan's official position was that Israel should withdraw to its pre-1967 boundaries, giving up all of the West Bank and East Jerusalem. Israel's official position was that trade with Japan was welcome, as was potential cooperation in science, culture, and politics. Foreign Minister Uno Sosuke made an official visit to Israel on 26 June 1988, in order, he said, to atone for its partial responsibility for World War II by assuming the responsibility to work for peace in the Middle East. Toward this end, Japan planned, with Prime Minister Itzhak Shamir's approval, to aid Palestinian refugee districts on the West Bank.[22]

In Asia, too, Japan viewed the connection of economic and military aid as falling in the same realm. One Japanese military official explained that Japan had promised more "economic aid" to Southeast Asia and the Pacific to help reduce the region's dependence on the United States. Japan's top military official, Kawara Tsutomu, discussed such aid with Singapore's Prime Minister Lee Kuan Yew and Defense Minister Goh Chok Tong on 3 July 1988. Mr. Kawara officially stated that though Japan could not take over the United States role in protecting the region, it could provide more financial assistance.[23]

It was this and comparable assistance that would help set the frame of the changing scenarios of prowess for Japan, the U.S., and Western Europe.

Chapter 19

Scenarios of Prowess

> *Isolation is continuously encouraged by the way in which the Japanese are governed. Isolation follows from the way in which the emergence of a bourgeois has been halted; from the way in which the middle class has been incorporated into the hierarchy of business firms; from the way in which the school system, rather than educating citizens for Japan, produces administrators and salarymen for predetermined levels of the System's hierarchies.* —Karel van Wolferen[1]

> *Politics is the only area left where the rules are those of the old feudal warlords. Of course, the weapons are not swords, but influence, loyalties and money.* —Government official expressing amazement at continuing political rivalries in the National Diet[2]

> *In an age when Japan has vaulted to the top in trade and finance, the ambition, even the vanity, of the Tokyo Globe project is somehow fitting. "It says something about Japan," said Michael Pennington, joint artistic director of the English Shakespeare Company, the British troupe that performed the War of the Roses cycle. ... "If you imagine an expensive new theater opening in the middle of London and the first companies invited are two Kabuki companies and then Ingmar Bergman," he said, "eyebrows would be raised."* —Susan Chira[3]

At the focal point of great wealth and potential world influence, Japan has raised eyebrows in the West. It has consolidated its own economy by combining traditional cultural and religious beliefs with the pressures of state regulations imposed by armies of administrators, as well as by social pressures to conform in personal habits, work, and community life. It has created the forms of constitutional freedoms and parliamentary democracy, but has used one-party government comprised of leaders of leading factions and interest groups vying to buy political power wholesale and trade off benefits retail. It has created a pliant political opposition that expects, and receives, rewards for its subservient obedience — masked by a pretense of public watchfulness. It has, moreover, exercised its authority to tame the press, create an oppressive police system, and undermine the rule of law. It has used government agencies as privatized ministries, with their bureaucratic functionaries expected and obliged to use state funds to subsidize, secure, and aid major enterprises, as well as to insulate them from the vicissitudes of domestic financial risks and foreign competitors. And these administrators' own loyalties and obligations to one another position them to design the content of education and culture, to repress individual initiative at every social juncture, to establish community standards that emerge as "self-enforced" conformity, and to keep up a constant call for personal sacrifices to upgrade the nation's leading enterprises and economic strength.

Some writers have fleshed out these administrators' networks of mutually interdependent relationships and obligations by tracing their origins to peer groups graduating from Tokyo University, alleging they have become a "ruling class" that can manipulate the ministries and, through them, giant enterprises and the political world of contributions and legislative favors.[4] There is some small truth in this, as illustrated in the 1989 disarray of the "lame duck" Prime Minister Takeshita government, the permanent civil service bureaucracy continuing to act "independent" of the misdeeds of political leaders. But the real power lay elsewhere: in the mythologies of the past; in fear of rejection by peers and neighbors; in the material power of the great enterprises and financial groups; in pressures and community expectations demanding personal sacrifice for family, employer, and country.

Drawing and relying on these deep beliefs in filial obligations to one's family, respect for one's neighbors, community and teachers, and a strong belief in service to one's employer and nation, Japan's political leaders have today shaped the nation as an international power. Playing upon, and reinforcing, the nation's narrow ethnocentric outlook, they have directed and monitored a vast productive and financial apparatus empowering its great companies and financial institutions to acquire the resources of others — not by conquest, but through the gridlock of global economic relations.

Stretching its economic might by the close of the 1980s, Japan moved into key Western industries and was again building an Asian co-prosperity sphere that was based as much on trade and investments as on the politics of peacekeeping. True, the United States and Western Europe had once established comparable relations with Asia and between themselves, expecting that certain practices and rules wold be followed by all competitors.

But once Japan began to use different standards and to live by a different set of rules, placing Western economies at a disadvantage, they, too, tried to follow Nippon's unconventional ways. To some degree, West Germany successfully did so. But the other Western Powers lacked the social ethos and national consensus for using a centralized government apparatus to emulate Japan or West Germany — with disastrous effects on their economies. They literally became the shock absorbers of the reorganization of the economies of the others — especially that of Japan.

These patterns were accentuated by Japan's new efforts to create a powerful, domestic consumer market beginning in 1988, as well as by other autarchic forces: the high-pressure movement to consolidate the Western European Common Market by 1992, plans for an American super-state to subsidize the rebuilding of the U.S. economy, and the likely integration of Eastern Europe into the sphere of the Western market place. Though Japan's centralized state capitalist structure was already reorganizing its production base and market, the United States and Western Europe lagged behind in trying to build a comparable central control center to regulate financial and material resources, as well as to expand investments and markets. And Eastern European promised to draw Western investment capital before the West had consolidated its own productive forces that might release the West from its crisis of uncompetitiveness.

Neomercantilist Scenarios

Each of these reform movements was bound up in plans for self-sufficiency. And each was based on establishing a transnational, neomercantilist market with an ancillary sphere of influence.

Japan had taken the lead. Pursuing self-sufficiency, the state moved to transform its domestic production apparatus and market. Initiating its Third Industrial Revolution, the government-directed reorganization of technology and realignment of the domestic work force required the export of the technologies and work roles of Japan's earlier industrial revolutions. And in exporting these technologies, Japanese companies sought *direct control* over foreign workers, resources, and distribution systems.

Japan also operated by increments. Its initial 1988 state plan to spur domestic demand to fuel both production and GNP exceeding 4 percent called for increased exports to keep unemployment low, at about 2.5 percent, with minimum inflation. If successful, this scheme would have minimized imports from the U.S., so that the U.S. would maintain or enlarge its negative trade balance with Japan, not reduce it — as actually occurred.

Nor would Japan voluntarily give up its decided trade advantage. By mid-1988, Japan's economy was not only the second largest in the world among industrialized democracies but, with a little more than half the population of the United States, *Number One* on a per capita basis.

Growing enormously wealthy and self-confident, Japan held the resources to double its foreign aid to $50 billion over the future half decade (1988–92), excuse one billion dollars in interest payments on $5.5 billion in debt the poorest nations owed it, and become an accepted, decision-making member of the world community. "The important thing is not to criticize or be criticized," said Haraguchi Koichi, a member of the Japanese delegation at the seven-nation Toronto economic summit in June 1988. "The important thing at summits is to find ways to cooperate so the world economy will go in a harmonious way."[5]

Yet harmony Japanese-style challenged the traditional authority of Western nations. The new Japanese harmony involved expansion in Asia and establishing a presence in the U.S. dollar sphere in the Americas, as well as in the Common Market and its associated overseas nations. Japanese harmony also completely reversed the *free trade/fair trade* logic the Western powers advocated; Japan viewed Asia as its own preserve, continued to block American and European attempts to open Japan as a market for their goods, and created seemingly unresolvable economic and political problems for the United States and Europe in their own respective spheres. The West now had no defense short of a thorough reorganization of its industry.

Looking Back/Looking Forward

Even in the mid-1970s, Japanese business leaders justified their nation's autarchic leanings, expressing the feeling of being "surrounded" by Western competitors. "The atmosphere is just like that on the eve of World War II, when America, Britain, China and Holland surrounded Japan in the Pacific and tried to squeeze Japan by pressing on its supply of raw materials," said one Japanese diplomat. Nonetheless, even then, Japan's government was still determined to maintain an ostensible posture of flexibility in its dealings with the United States, the Common Market, and Pacific Basin nations.[6]

During the following decade, however, Japan prepared for enhanced self-sufficiency by tightening state controls over production and the labor force at home, systematically appropriating foreign technologies, securing long-term supply contacts for raw materials from Asian and Pacific Basin nations, and dumping manufactures in the West. State-directed, corporatized, and regimented production within Japan was also extended worldwide as Japan's leaders strengthened Japan's links for trade, investment, and raw materials supplies with other nations, concentrating their energy on the United States and East Asia.

In dealing with America, Japan easily overcame U.S. protectionist pressures by investing in the television (since 1972) and automobile industries (since 1982). Locating mainly in the low-wage Sunbelt, and on the

West Coast, these plants sought efficient, undisturbed production. The Japanese kept racial conflict to a minimum by siting their plants away from minority populations and openly excluding non–Japanese employees from certain higher-level positions under the 1953 *Friendship, Commerce and Navigation Treaty* between the U.S. and Japan.[7]

In some cases, U.S. firms locked into economically declining areas had sold out to Japanese companies looking for a pool of inexpensive labor. But in almost all cases, Japanese firms influenced the local economic milieu. The Japanese kept labor costs low; often drew more rural, poorly educated, young men from out-of-state areas than they required; and paid them wages so low that growth in per capita personal income lagged behind population growth in the counties where these firms operated. But it must be admitted that employment rose in many of these company town areas, with wages being spent on more housing space, leading to more personal security and a decided lowering of criminal activity.[8]

But amenities like medical services were often lacking. Japanese labor-saving techniques kept new job offerings at a minimum. Imported Japanese automobile parts slipped under the special trade zone status the U.S. offered to American-located Japanese auto plants — meaning less production and employment in the U.S. auto parts industry.[9]

Japan also entered the most advanced technological fields, drawing on Western methods and products, then "re-tooling" or "reverse-engineering" them under the guiding cooperation of government and private firms, finally reaching the point of "take-off" onto a higher plane of development. These patterns repeated themselves in the semiconductor industry — from equipment suppliers to device makers and chip users — and in biotechnological research and development.[10]

With the emergence of information-intensive research and development delivered by high-tech telecommunication systems, the mode of competitive posturing itself had changed, so much so that Japan's Byzantine bureaucracies at the MITI and other agencies also had to concentrate and specialize the locus of administrative power.[11] The breakup of the Bell system intensified the telecom wars. Competitive companies in the U.S., Japan, and France scrambled to design their own telecommunication networks, adopting an assortment of innovative technologies, and thriving under the protective policies of their respective governments, all of which promoted *nationally oriented* development.[12]

Outdistancing state intervention in both the U.S. and France, the Japanese state mobilized its resources, bureaucracies, and autocratic methods to bolster the corporatized economy. Japan fostered exports to others, but imported little of their goods; invested in assets and resources abroad, but stringently limited investments in Japan; secured copyrights and patents on the inventions of others both within and outside Japan, but made foreigners' patents and copyrights in Japan both worthless and a mechanism for further Japanese appropriation.

Western nations thus came to fear Japan, distrusting what they viewed as a "two-faced" policy. By 1988, Japan had overwhelmed the U.S. in trade, offset its positive balance with extensive investments in key areas of the American economy, and become a major commercial and investing power in Asia. It exported advanced manufactured goods to other nations, imported raw material from nonindustrialized nations, and also imported low-price manufactures from the West and the newly industrialized nations of Asia. It not only granted financial aid to other states, but tied such aid to purchases from Japan and the building of an infrastructure to facilitate Japan's import of raw materials and other necessities and export of investment capital.

Peace or War

Japan thereby created a nonegalitarian trade and investment link with the West and built the frame for a new sphere of influence in Asia. Yet Japanese leaders downplayed military ambitions for expansion, also minimizing Nippon's past invasion of China and role in World War II.

A quiet replay of the 1930s Shintoist practices by leading government officials and the military meanwhile went forward. The government would neither fund the peace movement nor, at first, adequately provide for the survivors of the nuclear bombs dropped on Hiroshima and Nagasaki, though Christian thinkers like Kagawa Toyohiko had pleaded with the U.S. Occupation Forces to relieve the suffering in the bombed cities.[13] Japan had lacked the resources and medical personnel to care for its indigenous victims immediately after the war. A handful of the badly burned had been sent to the U.S. for plastic surgery due to the efforts of *Saturday Review* editor Norman Cousins. Yet it was not until 1957 that the Diet passed the *Survivors Medical Law* that provides health benefits for those within a radius of forty kilometers of the detonation of the bomb or who entered Hiroshima or Nagasaki within five days of the nuclear explosion.[14]

A cenotaph at Hiroshima was also erected to atomic victims, and is now regularly visited by two million visitors each year. The memorial is enscribed "Rest in peace. We shall not repeat the mistake." But who does this "We" represent, and who made what "mistake"? Did Japan make the "mistake" by starting the war in the Pacific or did the U.S. make the "mistake" of using nuclear weapons to end it?

Would the imperially minded perpetrators of the war be ostracized in Japan? Lacking knowledge of their own history, present generations of Japanese have developed a blindspot — acceptance of the nation's economic expansion, sociopolitical domination, and strengthened military structure — that can be attributed to their felt need to be accepted by their peers and to be true to their nation and its goals. Rewriting their history books, the Japanese now call their country's World War II aggression in

Asia an "advance." In 1981, the minister of education determined that it was not appropriate for prints of Maruki Iri and Toshi's *Hiroshima Murals*—powerful expressions of the effects of the atomic bomb—to appear in school textbooks.[15]

In May 1988, cabinet member Okuno Seisuke, director of the National Land Agency, justified Japan's invasion of China. Though Seisuke was forced to resign, demonstrations and many letters to the newspapers openly supported his view. Without a sense of guilt about Japan's wartime depredations in Asia, says Filipino writer Sionil José, Japan promotes a self-image of superiority: "Japan acts not on the basis of humanistic principles, but on the basis of self-interest, its euphoric narcissism. . . . It is not Confucianism that has made the Japanese a prosperous nation. Their pragmatism, their work ethic and harsh history and environment has [sic] tempered them."[16]

Confucianism Japanese-style has historically been based on a hierarchical system of work and order. Japanese Confucianism lacks empathetic compassion for others or their needs. The Japanese perception of their own superior ethnic identity has always been strong. Even in 1983, a survey revealed that 81 percent of those polled believed in Japan's racial supremacy and 74 percent believed in the nation's political supremacy:

Table 19.1
Japanese Perception of Their
Ethnic Identity and Political System

Responses	*Racial Supremacy*		*Political Supremacy*	
Best	320	(27.9%)	181	(15.7%)
Better	617	(53.7)	675	(58.7)
Medium	179	(15.6)	243	(21.1)
Worse	19	(1.6)	29	(2.5)
Worst	3	(0.2)	6	(0.5)
D.K/N.A	12	(1.0)	16	(1.4)
Total	1,150	(100)*	1,150	(100)

* The figure is based on the survey on November 1983 in Tokyo, Japan.

Source: "Frequencies for Question 25, 26," in *Jumin-Ishiki no Kano-sei,* edited by Kokichi Shoji (Tokyo: Azusa Publisher, 1986), 360.

Fearing a new militarism and a revival of state Shintoism, Japan's peace faction had meanwhile grown more vocal. "Men must not kill other men," warned holocaust muralist Maruki Toshi. He appealed to a nation whose leaders were again building a technological military force. Though many of the nuclear survivors had avoided anything that reminded them of the atomic bombing in 1945, a vigil at the Hiroshima cenotaph took place every August 6th, with peoples from all over the world participating. In 1988, the lobbying of Japan's peace faction intensified. At the United Nations Conference on Disarmament in New York City, Morimoto Shoko, a Hiroshima *Hibakusha,* or A-bomb survivor, told the press her story, which represents the anguish of all survivors of 6 August 1945:

> On that day forty-three years ago, my mother and I experienced the hell-like nightmare of Hiroshima. I was four years old then. From that day on, mother suffered from poor health, and after nineteen years of pain, she died of leukemia, not knowing the disease arose from having been A-bombed. Weapons that give no external or visible injury but undoubtedly give us death, these are what nuclear weapons are. A death is surely coming to me as it did to my mother, and I can't turn away from the fear of the death. We 386,000 people should be the first and the last *Hibakusha,* not one more added to our number. We can't co-exist with nuclear weapons. The very existence of these weapons, even if they are not used, threatens our lives. The greatest duty of the grown-ups who are living now is to leave a beautiful earth and a peaceful future to our children and grandchildren.
>
> We really wish for the day when all nuclear weapons are abolished from this world. We hope it comes soon. I believe this wish can come true if we try hand in hand and help each other.
>
> No more Hiroshimas, no more Nagasakis, no more *Hibakusha.* [17]

In 1988 the United States and the Soviet Union successfully concluded disarmament talks to abolish short- and intermediate-range nuclear weapons. The U.S. wished to reduce its own military burden. The U.S. demanded that Japan enhance its military power.

The U.S. government meanwhile finally planned to offer recompense to Japanese-American residents, who had been humiliated in internment camps from 1942 to early 1946. More than 120,000 Japanese-Americans had been sent to these internment camps under President Roosevelt's 1942 order empowering the War Department to designate military areas from which people could be excluded. Military orders had then excluded all people of Japanese ancestry from California, Washington, and Oregon, and some in Hawaii. The orders affected 77,000 United States citizens and 43,000 legal and illegal resident aliens, all of whom were taken to prison camps in the Western states. For forty-two years, since the closing of the last camp in January 1946, the issue of indemnity and apology had lingered. The House of Representatives on 4 August 1988 finally passed legislation apologizing to the victims and ordering $20,000 tax-free payments to the 60,000 living internees at the camps. "It is a time for apology and reunification," offered Minnesota Republican Representative William Frenzel. [18]

Such sentiments were transparently linked to U.S. efforts to allay Japan's fears of American racism — and to abnegate U.S. political obligations in South and East Asia, trying to foist extended conventional military commitments in the region on Japan. "The constant clamor from Capitol Hill for Japan to 'do more' on defense is almost deafening," reported New York Democratic Representative Stephen J. Solarz, chairman of the House subcommittee on Asia. "Never mind that Japan has increased defense expenditures by about 5% a year since 1981. Never mind that by next year Japan will have the third-largest defense budget in the world. The calls for greater Japanese burden-sharing persist."[19]

Fearing a reduction of U.S. armed forces and apprehensive of Chinese military ambitions, Japan moved powerfully to block the shipment of military-related technology to China, arresting Japanese violators, banning Toshiba's 1987 exports, and scrutinizing other technology exports, despite senior Japanese officials' assurances to Beijing that Tokyo was willing to push for reduced Western restrictions on technology sales to China. In mid-1988, MITI accused Kyokutu Shokai Co. of illegally exporting to China five digital memories, a sampling oscilloscope, and a signal analyzer, and charged Shinsei Koeki Co. with shipping two digital memories; the MITI explained that this equipment could be used in testing nuclear explosions, fine tuning radar, and detecting submarines.[20]

In a 1988 poll, most Japanese indicated that the military's primary role should be rescue work rather than defense. "The self-defense forces have always been unpopular; some people don't want to be reminded that they are needed," reported Aoyama Gakuin University international relations professor Sakanaka Tomohisa. Tomohisa was speaking aboard a nearby Japanese destroyer on the afternoon of a collision between a submarine and a fishing boat in Tokyo Bay in late July 1988. The accident left thirty people dead and touched off fierce criticism of Japan's armed forces. "The mood in Japan," he said, "is definitely turning against the military because of this incident."

Following traditional Confucian respect for authority, the matter was to be laid to rest and atonement offered. At a meeting of party executives on 29 July a powerful member of the Liberal Democratic Party warned against an "emotional defense" of the military and suggested that "the captain of the submarine might be charged with criminal responsibility." Speculation was that the director of the armed forces would take personal responsibility for the accident and resign after an investigation was completed. But it was unlikely that the military budget — already edging above the previous unspoken ceiling of 1 percent of Japan's gross national product in 1987 — would be cut as Japan was placed under increasing pressure from the U.S. and Western Europe to make a larger military contribution.[21]

The Nonnuclear Story Line

Japan's assumption of America's military burden was for conventional warfare. Yet, as other great nations and their people were relatively silent in the face of the potential military shift, the possibility of a future Nippon nuclear force posed a worldwide hazard, especially if Japan could produce its own nuclear arsenal and threaten nations in south and east Asia.

In the past, Japan had banned the introduction of nuclear weapons. Most Japanese were led to believe that the United States refrained from bringing nuclear weapons close to Japan. But American ships carrying nuclear weapons had arrived in Japan for years. The Japanese government was well-practiced at overlooking the arrival of U.S. ships carrying such weapons into port.

More than 50 percent of the U.S. base area in Japan was located in Okinawa. Nearly one-fifth of the island's land area was covered by U.S. bases, housing 60,000 American troops, and their dependents. Okinawans liked neither the U.S. nor Japan. In 1898 Japan had conquered them, conscripted their men, undermined their culture, and corrupted their language and women. In the wartime 1940s, Japan forced civilians to relocate at the island's southern end, where they would take the brunt of any U.S. invasion. While Japanese forced them to commit *harakiri,* U.S. flame-throwers, bombs, and hand grenades wiped out 120,000 to 150,000 civilians. Okinawa then became a U.S. neocolony. The U.S. military presence led to the development of bars and red-light districts. One authority says that "the closing of certain central roads during United States firing practice and the knowledge that the United States maintains nuclear weapons and nuclear-capable craft at the center of their homeland raises deep frustration in the Okinawans. Reversion to Japan in 1972 and enforced inclusion as the 47th prefecture without a glance back at Japan's military harm to the islands has led to growing Okinawan self-consciousness and desire for a better, different relationship."[22]

Although Okinawa was returned to Japan, the U.S. military remained in charge. The military failed to disclose that on 6 December 1985 a one-megaton hydrogen bomb was lost when a A-4E Skyhawk strike aircraft with the bomb aboard rolled off the elevator of the aircraft carrier *Ticonderoga,* fell into the Pacific, and sank with its pilot. U.S. experts contended that the hydrogen bomb had burst under intense water pressure at more than 16,000 feet and could not be recovered. The accident spread radioactive plutonium in the hydrosphere but had "no environmental impact," according to the Pentagon.

It was a great story, but practically no one believed it. "What is extraordinary," said author William M. Arkin at the Institute of Policy Studies, "is at the time these ships were engaged in the Vietnam War, they were armed with nuclear weapons." What is more extraordinary is that the Japanese authorities were aware of the nuclear weapons, lied to their own people about nuclear weapons in Japanese ports then, and is likely lying still. Okinawans protested the nuclear accident, held a 10,000 strong anti-military rally on 15 May 1989, accused the U.S. of covering up the incident by classifying the matter, denounced the navy, and called for an immediate investigation into the incident and recovery of the lost weapon.[23]

Some Japanese warned America of the broader implications of nuclear production, including civil uses. Sato Yumiko of Fukushima appealed:

I am a mother of two children, concerned about their health. I fear the possibility of a nuclear power plant accident, and want to stop the operation of all nuclear power plants in Japan. Thirty-six plants operate here. Despite radiation leaks caused by pinholes, which often happen, the Ministry of International Trade and Industry is planning to extend maximum continuous operation of nuclear plants. The government and electric power companies, ignoring protests by residents, prepare to construct a nuclear fuel-reprocessing plant and a spent-fuel storage facility.

In Japan, more than 80 percent of the people are concerned about the dangers, but the news media hardly ever report on the anti-nuclear-power movement. We don't have the appalling experience of Hiroshima and Nagasaki, but don't seem to care about radioactive contamination of food. Nuclear power is not a problem of one country, but a matter for all people of the world.[24]

Japan was moving toward an independent nuclear industry with both civilian and military sides. Nuclear power was not simply the economic framework of self-sufficiency in cheap energy. Nor was its development a pure infrastructural solution to reprocessing nuclear fuel in Japan to break free from U.S.–controlled plutonium regulations for reprocessing in Western Europe and delivery to Japan by indirect air routes that did not cross U.S. territory. For now great power aspirations again shaped the thoughts of many Japanese leaders.

Gunboat Diplomacy and Great Power Aspirations

Did America's military scenario foresee an offense-oriented Japanese armed force and a renewed co-prosperity sphere?

Having secured privileges for American industry and servicemen for nearly four decades, the U.S. military was about to lose them in the face of congressional cries for Japan to assume its own regional defense. "One would have thought, therefore, that Japan's desire to buy the Aegis battle management system would have played well on Capitol Hill," said Representative Solarz. He argued for sales of this proprietary military technology. "Aegis would help the Japanese Maritime Self-Defense Forces deter a full-scale Soviet naval attack, and it would increase the inter-operability of the U.S. and Japanese navies."[25]

The politics of production and sales were also involved. Because Japan had not bought a foreign-built ship in nearly a century, a lobby of special interests and congressmen had written into the Defense Department spending bill a provision barring the sale of four $526 million Aegis systems to Japan unless they were installed on U.S.–built ships. Japan refused to buy the ships, and the Senate reluctantly removed the stipulation on the Aegis — in an effort to make a significant sale, create jobs, and fulfill the Reagan administration's goal of having the Japanese take more responsibility for protecting the air and sea lanes in the northwestern Pacific Ocean.

Alaskan Republic Senator Ted Stevens had argued that "Providing the technology to Japan alone would weaken our competitive position with them and with other nations in shipbuilding."[26] But the Senate majority thought otherwise. "It is estimated that one Aegis for Japan will result in 5,400 man-years of U.S. labor, and that the U.S.-built Aegis-capable hulls would bring 2,700 more," Representative Solarz reported. "Thus, for every shipbuilding job we insist on, we risk losing two jobs in the electronics industry."

"Japan is both an ally and a democracy," he continued. "Its leadership is bucking pacifist public opinion and the imperatives of fiscal austerity to assume a larger burden of the common defense. An effort to squeeze even more out of the Japanese only undermines our own interests and demeans our most important bilateral relationship."[27]

The Latest Military Technologies

In fact, Japanese companies wanted the latest Western technologies, seeking to turn out products involving nuclear power, electronics, aerospace, and advanced composite materials that were critical for military purposes and had wider uses. American defense and high-technology producers justifiably feared commercialization of their products for distribution in Japan.

Many of these American manufacturers held classified government contracts that prevented disclosure of secret technologies to others. The U.S. Patent Office offered security for some 5,000 Pentagon-designated, high-tech patents. To gain comparable security for U.S. military patents in Japan required that the U.S. patent holder obtain Japanese patent protection comparable to that required by the Pentagon in the U.S. Without such a guarantee of secrecy, the U.S. applicant was prevented by the Pentagon from filing for a Japanese patent.

For more than thirty years Japan could not guarantee such secrecy for U.S. applications because of domestic laws giving the public access to the files in the Japanese patent office. But in April 1988 a U.S.-Japanese accord was signed to allow U.S. companies to seek Japanese patents for militarily valuable technology. Such sensitive patents would be kept in a confidential file at the Japan Defense Agency until the Pentagon freed them for public view.[28] The avenue was thus opened for U.S. companies to obtain Japanese patents for production of commercial technologies with a military connection.

Despite patent protection, there was nothing to prevent Japanese companies from using reverse engineering to discover the secrets of American products—and then applying for their own use-specific patents in Japan. Nor was there any way that MITI could be stopped from expediting this effort through organizing and funding consortia as part of its grand design for deploying the most advanced technological equipment to upgrade

Japanese production. The Japan Defense Agency might offer assurances of secrecy to the Pentagon for military-related technologies, but this agency was subject to the pressure of MITI's army of bureaucrats and of the ruling Liberal Democratic Party's politically influential legislators in the Diet.

Military calculations were also involved. For an even greater danger for the West was that, in an effort to involve Japan in its military strategies, the United States might empower Japanese corporations to secretly sell military technology to the Soviet Union. Worse, Japan itself might use this secret military know-how—and deploy it against China or the Soviet Union, drawing the West into a war in the Far East.

Atomic Fuel/Atomic War

The U.S. had foreseen such risks. Recognizing that atomic material used for peaceful purposes could also be put to military use, the U.S. established strict controls on Japan's use of atomic materials.

This was physically possible because Japan possessed no uranium deposits of its own and had only limited capacity to enrich the mineral for use as nuclear fuel. Under the Atomic Energy Act, moreover, the U.S. was to regulate U.S.-owned plutonium used or processed by others; and over several decades Japan became America's largest single foreign customer for enriched uranium. Indeed, the U.S. accounted for about one-half of Japan's needs by 1988.

Even today, because there are still few sources of crude uranium— Canada, the United States, and South Africa are the largest—Japan is dependent on long-term supply contracts with these nations. Japan is also dependent on the U.S. as its main processing supplier.[29]

For such processing, the U.S. has imported as much as one-third of its own crude uranium supply from South Africa. Most South African powdered uranium is shipped in liquid or gaseous form to the U.S. for enrichment—i.e., for separation into its fissionable and nonfissionable forms, and conversion into the pellets that Japanese users later insert into nuclear fuel rods.

By 1988 Japan depended on nuclear energy for more than a quarter of its electrical needs. The four largest Japanese utilities expected $40 billion in revenues from nuclear energy. The nation held long-term contracts for about 203,000 short tons of uranium, including 22,000 from South Africa.

The political consequences were obvious: with most processing to take place in the U.S. Japan had to accommodate itself to U.S. policies.

Congress meanwhile moved to maintain U.S. processing hegemony by openly suggesting that, even if Japan turned to Europe for reprocessing of its spent nuclear plutonium, the U.S. might not give blanket thirty-year approval, thereby regulating Japan's access to a critical source of industrial energy. Because U.S.-owned plutonium was being extracted by companies in Europe from nuclear fuel exhausted in Japan, the U.S. monitored both Europe and Japan as the focal points for production and use. U.S. Senate approval in March 1988 of an agreement between the U.S. State Department and Japan thus allowed Japan to use nuclear fuel made from plutonium that, under international safeguards, was controlled by the United States. And the clear implications were that the U.S. would remain in control.

Even Japan's switch in uranium suppliers would not undermine U.S. hegemony. Japan planned to drop its 11 percent uranium dependence on South Africa by increasing purchases from the U.S., Canada, and Australia. With long-term contracts for purchasing South African uranium expiring in 1989 and international pressure on Japan to boycott South Africa increasing, the switch was logical.[30]

The U.S. also enforced certain conditions on France and other European nations that reprocessed U.S.–owned uranium spent in Japan: that Japanese nuclear shipments by air could neither be refueled at U.S. airports nor cross U.S. or Canadian territory. And the Japan–U.S. agreement specified that, without passing over Canada or the United States, aircraft carrying plutonium from Europe to Japan would be equipped to fly directly by a polar route. The main concern of the Congress seemed less to be Japan's access to U.S. plutonium for potential military use, but access by others. As Brooklyn Congressional Representative Stephen J. Solarz said, those who questioned the agreement with Japan focused on three objections that had been satisfied — that the shipments could be unsafe, that terrorists might obtain the plutonium, and that the agreement would permit the spread of materials that could be used in nuclear weapons.[31]

To break free of U.S. restrictions, the Japanese government and Japanese electric power companies set up a pilot reprocessing plant, imported from France.[32] They also prepared to construct a major nuclear fuel-reprocessing plant and a spent-fuel storage facility.[33] Thus, Nippon is already moving toward an independent nuclear industry — both civilian and military.

Secretly Selling Military Technology

Strong disagreements existed between the U.S. and Japan over the problem of Japanese countries taking and selling U.S. military technology. This "contraband" trade in technology was taking place in two highly charged contexts: the politically intense competition between the Eastern socialist nations and Western capitalist powers, and the economically intense rivalry between Japan and the United States.

The frame was global competition. To simultaneously cut government budgets and relieve overproduction at home, both the U.S. and Japan had moved politically and economically to promote détente and thereby capture markets in socialist nations. As the Cold War had given way to a new level of détente, a process was begun to shift more of the U.S. military burden to its allies. Since 1961 at least the U.S. had believed its defensive, second-strike nuclear forces were more powerful than a Soviet first-strike surprise attack. President Eisenhower had seen the advantage of limiting military outlays by a comprehensive test ban.[34] A decade later, President Nixon's 1971 efforts to promote détente in the East and shift the military burden of Pacific defense to Japan gave encouragement to Japanese military industries. West German Chancellor Schmidt thereafter set the frame for the deployment of U.S.-controlled intermediate-range missiles in Europe.

In the Reagan years, the pressure to cut and shift military outlays intensified as the U.S. military budget grew by 53 percent from 1981 to 1985, procurement of military equipment more than doubled, and spending authority for research, development, testing, and evaluation increased by more than 80 percent. Though the military budgetary authority to commit funds for the future was reduced 12 percent a year from 1985 to 1988, from 1981 to 1988 $2 trillion was spent on defense.[35]

Such spending aggravated the U.S. deficit, reduced the already-low national savings rate, and further undermined national competitiveness. With an eye on rebuilding U.S. competitive positions in the world marketplace for the rest of the century and into the next, both corporate and congressional leaders thus hoped to switch some of the costs to its allies, especially West Germany and Japan.

The U.S. was footing most of the military bill in the nonsocialist world. In the calendar year 1986, some 6.8 percent of the U.S. gross domestic product and one-third of the federal government's budget went to military spending. By comparison, West German expenditures were 3.1 percent of its gross domestic product and Japanese outlays 1 percent. But neither Japan nor West Germany wanted to absorb more of the U.S. burden. In May 1989 West German President Richard von Weizsäcker reaffirmed Bonn's demand that the Atlantic Alliance open negotiations with the East on reducing short-range nuclear missiles, most of which were stationed in the two Germanys.[36]

Washington had also begun to pressure the Nakasone government to enlarge military spending beyond the post–World War II limit of 1 percent of its gross national product. This pressure led to an initial resurgence in Japan's aircraft and space industry, with Kawasaki, Mitsubishi, and others seeking profitable government defense contracts to subsidize research and production facilities for developing both military and commercial air planes.

Arms technology and trade had been linked throughout the 1980s. Both Japan and the U.S. were continually at one another's jugular. Each exhibited a nationalist military pathology, initially concentrating on limiting the absorption of national wealth in military outlays, then leveling accusations that the other nation was extending its military sales markets and other markets by jeopardizing their respective security interests. Japan thus accused the U.S. of contraband sales to its war-time enemy China, claiming Japanese scientists had discovered advanced U.S. electronic equipment being used to direct Chinese medium-range missiles. Dresser Industries was also pointed to for having sold critical oil drilling equipment to the Soviets.

Then in 1987 the U.S. and Japan traded invectives over which goods could be exported to the Soviet Union — each side contending that it should hold authority over the definitions of legitimate and contraband trade. Centering on the case of the Toshiba Corporation's sale of propeller milling machine technology to the Soviet Union, the struggle of the U.S. and Japan to sell military and other commodities resolved itself into two nationalist claims. The U.S. Pentagon depicted the sale as one involving forbidden technology. Pentagon charges led to the resignation of Toshiba's top officials, but the resignations did not prevent the U.S. government from restricting Toshiba's access to U.S. technology and the U.S. market. Many of Japan's business leaders viewed congressional sanctions as U.S. pressure to stop Japan's manufacturers from independently building a new tactical fighter plane, called the FSX. They saw Toshiba's executives as unlucky pawns in the wider commercial struggle between the U.S. defense establishment and Japan's industrial giants, referring to their resignations and apologies in major newspapers as forced suicide.

American methods were transparent. The Pentagon had sought to pressure the Japanese government to agree to its proposal that the new FSX fighter aircraft be developed jointly with U.S. defense contractors, rather than follow the lobbying efforts of Japan's military manufacturers for independent development. And U.S. Defense Secretary Weinberger's 1988 arrival in Tokyo corresponded with the Senate vote to impose sanctions on Toshiba, so that his urgings for joint FSX development "miraculously" won over Prime Minister Nakasone.

Japanese big business had reluctantly recognized U.S. definitions of "contraband" goods. Yet, in response to the Toshiba Affair, in late July 1987, the then-led Nakasone Liberal Democratic Party opposed its own leader's submissiveness to the Reagan administration's insistence on Japanese guilt. Reflecting the views of all sectors of Japan's big business community, the Ministry of Trade and Industry openly criticized Nakasone and the Foreign Ministry for acceding to the U.S. charges without questioning the U.S. Defense Department's interpretation of the security threat posed by the Toshiba sale: were not the submarine propeller lathes Toshiba sold no longer state-of-the-art technology?

Other nationalist pressures meanwhile emerged. Nakasone's Liberal Democratic Party was heavily pressured by the U.S. to initiate legislation to tighten Japan's Foreign Exchange and Trade Control Law. At the core of the disagreement was the U.S. definition of "contraband" items that Japan was commercially interdicted from exporting to socialist countries.

Japan's fear of subservience to America and Japan's need for an independent, multilateral trade and commercial policy added heat to the issue. As America moved to control a part of Japan's exports, even the Socialist nations called for "free trade" and multilateral commerce, without restrictions from either Japan or America.[37]

From Japan's perspective, the U.S. terms were degrading. If Nippon hoped to continue receiving U.S. military-related equipment and know-how, it would have to drop plans for developing its own fighter aircraft. The Western nations would oversee and stop Japan from exporting "critical" technologies to the Soviet Union and other Communist countries.

Japan's independence was being compromised and Japanese leaders were infuriated. As this discourse in the politics of technology and exports disintegrated, reasoned discussion was replaced by power plays and moderation was seen as akin to betraying one's nation's purposes.

FSX as X-Rated High Tech

The conflict was intensified by the 1988–89 U.S.–Japanese military agreement about manufacturing Japan's future generation of jet fighters. The new fighters, code-named FSX—"Fighter Support Experimental"— were expected to feature advanced avionics, stealth technology to stop radar detection, and the latest weapon systems for attacking naval vessels and ground targets. The U.S. Defense Department had pressured the Japan Defense Agency to base its design on the American-gauge, F-16 made by the General Dynamics Corporation, a highly maneuverable single-engine craft, which was then the best U.S. plane for air combat with enemy planes. But Japan had its eye on developing its own civilian and military aerospace industry, ultimately becoming competitive with U.S. superiority. Japan thus rejected an American offer to sell F-16 fighters, saying the plane was unsuitable to Japan's defense needs.

Japan, which had already profited enormously by shouldering so small a share of its own defense costs from 1945 to 1989, Senate Finance Committee chair Lloyd Bentsen criticized, should have seized the opportunity to buy American F-16 fighter planes to help ease the trade imbalance with the U.S. "If we spent 1% of our gross national product on defense," Bentsen complained, "our budget deficit would disappear overnight and their economy would be in chaos, deprived of the oil our nation [has] escorted out of the Persian Gulf."

As a compromise, the Reagan administration then negotiated for joint planning of the FSX, thereby supporting General Dynamics Corporation's lobby for potential benefits of $1.2 billion in development costs and perhaps some share of the multibillion dollar production costs.[38]

Scheming to learn the nuances of aeronautical technology, the Japanese government meanwhile planned to experiment—to spend its military money on learning the intricacies not only of the FSX but, building on these, of U.S. advanced avionics. "The less efficiently Japan spends on its own defense, the more of its defense burden falls on the United States," the *New York Times* editorialized. "So why does Japan insist on a deal that apparently makes no military or commercial sense for either partner? Because it seeks to build its own civil aviation industry. The experience of developing and making fighter planes would surely help in that ambition, even if little of the technology were directly transferable to civilian aircraft."[39]

Dovetailing with this plan, Japan sought to keep all aspects of FSX production at home. The scandal-ridden Takeshita government prematurely awarded the prime developer of the FSX, Mitsubishi Heavy Industries, an $86 million contract from the then-expiring 1989 fiscal year budget — even before Japan reached a formal agreement with the U.S.[40] The Japanese Defense Agency argued that the U.S. demand for billions of dollars' worth of FSX production by General Dynamics was unreasonable because the plane was only in an experimental stage. And Japan did not want to provide America with its alleged newly developed materials for plane wings and computerized radar systems. On these points, though, Japan was forced to concede to the new Bush Administration in Washington.[41]

The initial agreement between both government defense agencies had looked to be about $6.5 billion in design and procurement costs. Japanese aircraft makers were to be put in charge of some 60 percent of the project, including radar and other electronic devices, leaving the U.S. subcontractors to deal mainly with the aircraft engines. Though the underlying American inducements for Japan's Air Self-Defense Force outlay of $6.5 to $7 billion for 100 to 130 aircraft were kept secret, published reports indicated that the U.S. would bear one-third of the cost and Japan two-thirds. Under an ancillary bilateral agreement to transfer Japan's defense technology, the aircraft could also be built under license in the United States.[42]

Under the detailed terms of the agreement, moreover, the United States would transfer designs of the F-16 developed by General Dynamics to Mitsubishi Heavy Industries, the Japanese prime contractor. Japan would only pay the U.S. $480 million for the F-16 technology that cost U.S. taxpayers five to seven billion dollars![43]

General Dynamics would also be a big winner: it would handle 40 percent of the joint program to build 130 FSX aircraft without the usual developmental outlays, as the plane was based on the company's own F-16, altered for a larger wing span, improved engine performance, a longer nose, and other modifications. Through 31 December 1988, General Dynamics had already sold 3,095 F-16 planes, so the new FSX's would generate additional profits to the existing F-16's share of 61 percent of the company's 1988 $318 million operating income.[44]

With such private inducements, the deal was completed without much congressional input. Congress already had limited power on agreements negotiated by the executive branch that went into effect automatically unless blocked by both houses within thirty days. Resolutions to block the FSX program had been introduced in both the House and the Senate. Because the General Accounting Office verified that the U.S. would only obtain technology already known to the American aircraft industry, the U.S. was effectively giving away its advanced technology for political expediency. But, with the contract in his hip pocket, General Dynamic's vice-president Dain M. Hancock disagreed, saying his firm would not transfer technology to Japan: "The technologies in the F-16 are not going to be the set of technologies that will make the next generation of airplanes competitive."[45]

On approving the $7 billion Fighter Plane Technology Agreement, a nonbinding "sense of the Senate" measure called for the U.S. to get 40 percent of the production work, including work on spare parts, which could ultimately be worth two or three times the initial cost of the plane. The Senate also prohibited the transfer of certain jet engine technologies to the Japanese and prohibited the Japanese from selling or transferring FSX technology to third parties.

The computerized "source codes" electronically used to help fly the plane were *not* to be supplied, but those to direct the fighter's weapon system would be. Many still feared Japan would use this technology to develop its own civilian aerospace industry, and wanted to ensure that Japan would have to write its own source code to drive the other functions of the weapon's computer relating to navigation, radar, and so on.

Under the aegis of America's Strategic Defense Initiative—aka the "Star Wars" project—Japan and the U.S. also agreed in July 1987 to cooperate in the Western Pacific section of the space-based program. But Pentagon-granted contracts were only to be awarded to private companies, thereby excluding Japanese government participation. From the U.S. side, contract participants would include the Science Applications International Corporation and the Hughes Aircraft Corporation, a unit of the General Motors Corporation. From Japan, the participants would include its leading weapons makers, Mitsubishi Heavy Industries, Mitsubishi Electric Corporation, the NEC Corporation, Fujitsu Ltd., and Hitachi Ltd.[46]

The way was now open for new weapons competition and cooperation.

Japan's Military Apprehensions

Japan's relations with the Soviet Union had remained unaltered since the close of World War II. The two nations had never signed a peace treaty because of a contest over land rights. For more than four decades Japan insisted that the Russians were wrongfully occupying four islands that Japan regarded as its territory. Known in Japan as the *Northern Territories,* consisting of Kunashiri, Etorofu, Shikotan, and the Habomai group, the islands stretched northeast from the northernmost Japanese island of Hokkaido. The Soviet Union had acquired these islands in the Allied division of Japanese-held territory after World War II, and considered them part of its own Kurile Island chain. Japan had refused to sign a peace treaty unless these islands were returned, despite the reestablishment of diplomatic relations in 1956 and an almost evenly balanced bilateral trade between the two nations by the late 1980s—the Russians selling raw materials, and the Japanese yesterday's technology.

Responding to the Toshiba scandal, in 1988 the Japanese government began a close watch on all technology shipped to Communist countries. Yet the Soviet Union was insistent that what it wanted from Japan was more of the latest technological equipment. "We don't need the technology of yesterday or the day before yesterday," said Tokyo-based Soviet embassy counsellor Georgi Komarovsky. "We need tomorrow's technology."

To get it was a difficult Soviet problem. In a period of plentiful oil and low energy prices, Japan had lost much of its drive to institute joint ventures with the Russians to explore Siberian coal reserves and natural gas deposits off Sakhalin Island. Japan did not trust Russia, viewed Soviet *perestroika* as strictly an internal restructuring that did not affect Japanese-Soviet relations, and feared the Russians militarily. Indeed, the Soviets had treated the Japanese with the utmost contempt in the past, concentrating on its military weakness and, until the late 1980s, paying insufficient attention to its economic might.[47] What would happen if Japan purposely kept the Soviet Union in a stage of technological inferiority and used the most up-to-date equipment and know-how to prepare its own military for repossession of the Northern Territories?

Short of a resurgent bilateral trade between them, there was no short-run way for the Soviets to get the full benefits of modern technology—whether made in Japan or surreptitiously transferred from the United States. The U.S. had partially blocked such indirect trade with its 1988 *Omnibus Trade Bill;* this bill had placed stringent curbs on Toshiba Corporation because its subsidiary had sold sensitive technology to the Soviet Union from 1982 to 1984. The Minister of MITI, the Foreign Minister, and the president of Toshiba together condemned Congress' decision as foolish and regrettable. The Tokyo District Court gave Toshiba a slap on the wrist with a $16,000 fine, and suspended prison sentences for two former Toshiba executives.[48]

Nothing had been resolved, and once more the U.S. and Japan moved along diverging, nationalist pathways in high-tech science, preparing for autarchical production and unfettered trade.

Bombast, Brothels, and Blindness

The foundations for autarchy ran deep, having been laid by the postwar trilateral link between the U.S., Japan, and the rest of Asia. America had opened the door for Japan in the Orient. Unfettered, Japan then extended its trade and investments, both East and West. By the 1980s, Japanese-controlled production plants employed inexpensive workers throughout East Asia, imposing Nippon standards, antiunion practices, and new burdens.

"Now, the Japanese are again in our part of the world—the second coming—using trade and aid in a more subtle way," writes Filipino journalist Sionil José. "They are convinced that our part of the world is the next growth area, that they will dominate it.... A visit to any Southeast Asian capital illustrates how pervasive the Japanese presence is: cars in the streets, appliances in the home, glittering neon signs advertising 'made in Japan,' even the special brothels that cater only to the Japanese."[49]

U.S. critics and students studying abroad might have been America's eyes and ears recording the social dimensions of these shifts and attitudes. But in 1985–86 80 percent of U.S. students going abroad still went to European nations; only 5.4 percent went to south and east Asia, and half of these were destined for Japan.[50]

There were other reasons the West should have been more outspoken about Japan's drive for accumulation and racial supremacist policies. For Nippon's trading muscle relied on power, not principle. At the very time the U.S. antiapartheid movement had pressured the U.S. House of Representatives to vote 244 to 132 to impose a near-total embargo on trade with and investments in South Africa, Japanese exports to South Africa had jumped more than 45 percent to $1.14 billion in the half-year 1988 compared with the same period in 1987.

Certain Japanese companies did cut trade with South Africa due to its apartheid policy. Ito-Yokado Company disclosed that its chain of 133 supermarkets had quit selling South African canned peaches and other products.[51] But this was the exception, not the rule.

With the 1988 Pretorian government still refusing to grant full political rights to twenty-six million black people, Japan's MITI—then directing the total realignment of the Japanese corporate economy—offered the most facile rationale for continuing to expand trade with South Africa. "There is no law against exports," a MITI spokesman said of the lack of plans to impose limits or conditions on exports to Pretoria. "If exports increased 50% this year, then we could think about taking some measures, but we could not comment on that at the moment."[52]

The U.S. Congress held power under the Trade Act of 1974 to use Section 301 to deny access to the U.S. market to any Japanese company that took commercial advantage of American companies because of a U.S. export embargo on specific goods. In 1985 the U.S. had itself banned American exports of computers or related software to some South African government agencies—at the very time Hitachi was selling computer products to the South African police![53] Yet by June 1989 the U.S. had done nothing to embargo proapartheid Japanese companies from dumping on United States markets.

Lack of trade restrictions here and elsewhere in the West also bred ignorance about how both America and Japan conducted themselves in Africa and the East. "I would hope there will be a growing interest in the developing world," said Institute of International Education president Richard Krasno. "For us to remain globally competitive, we have to understand other people, other markets."[54]

Yet, it was this lack of American involvement, understanding, and reporting that abetted the future shift of sections of African and south and east Asian commerce from U.S. hands to Japan. This calculated ignorance, before the turn of the 21st century, might also allow the U.S. to quietly shift advanced arms technology to Japan's Self-Defense Forces and again empower Nippon to assume many of the unrestricted military functions once held by the United States.

Keeping Them Uninformed

Meanwhile, Japan had kept its population ignorant of the underlying ambitions of its foreign service, overseas corporations, and militarists.

At home, the press provided the barest criticism of the government, or anything else, save obvious scandals. Most *men* were kept quiet and in place by ambition and obligations to their employers at home or abroad, *women* by repressed independence and obligations to the head of the family.

Most adult men also consciously sought to keep women uninformed and part of a lowly labor force, on the job and in the home. In the 1980s young working women lived with their parents under their father's tutelage, performing domestic chores. On the job, they faced undisguised discrimination: extra chores, lower wages, and fewer promotions. They had to come to work earlier than men to arrange the office, serve tea, train new staff assistants without extra pay, and take less pay for comparable work than men, who often exhibited less ability and knowledge.

Disappointment and lack of upward mobility in the workplace combined with pressure to marry. Through courting or arrangement *(omiai),* they were then expected to marry, have one or two children, raise them to become good Japanese, become the guardians of both family and a clean and peaceful home, and take care of all domestic affairs as a backstop to ensure their husbands' success in the workplace.

It was not ignorance that kept them back, but social custom. Many Japanese women were well-educated. The waste and exploitation of Japan's female workforce as a low-wage stratum became increasingly obvious in the 1980s. Some 33 percent of female high school graduates went on to higher institutes of learning; 61 percent of these moved on to two-year junior colleges, and the other 39 percent to four-year colleges.

Yet, women graduates were discriminated against on the job. Some 63 percent of companies excluded women from certain positions. Women earned an average of 42.8 percent (1960) to 51.8 percent (1984) of what men earned. Women doing six to eight hours of daily work were classified as "part-time" workers because they were "temporary" labor in medium- and small-size companies (which employed more than half of all female workers, who in most cases were not organized) or remained at home doing piecework, and as part-time workers were paid less and had no fringe benefits, received no bonus, and had no job security.

Because large companies with more than five hundred employees employed predominantly male workers who were more often organized, the wage gap of female full-time workers making 60 percent of that of full-time male workers was reduced to 40 percent for female part-time workers and 20 percent for women working piece-rate at home.[55]

Only a few women with access to financial resources could escape to the urban universities in such cities as Tokyo, Osaka, and Kyoto, or abroad to the U.S. But students who went abroad were often condemned by Japanese society for initial deviance at home (going away to school, dropping out of the job and marriage market) and emigration (dropping out of society by living abroad).

Government ministries and corporations also ostracized their personnel posted to overseas jobs — either wanting to keep them there or keep them quiet if they returned home. Returning to Japan, they were often socially isolated, relegated to less prestigious jobs, ignored within their organizations, and treated as outsiders who were no longer entitled to the confidence of being in the inner circle of those who were "Japanese." Their families were also considered tainted by their absence from Japan. Leaving Japan interrupted their web of connections with the community and undermined the staid predictability of Japan's alleged homogeneous society. They were to remain quiet about the world beyond, until they could be reintegrated into Japanese society and its way of thinking.

Their children were to be debriefed, forced to undergo "readjustment education," and set on the path of the "Examination Hell" that would determine their futures. Not only were educational prospects and careers downgraded, but wives were cross-examined to test their faithfulness to Japanese ways and their attitude toward threatening foreign cultures.[56]

Some educational "reform" was attempted to accommodate the children of Japanese managers sent abroad. In the U.S. Japanese companies pressured the Japanese government to create ten Japanese elementary and junior high schools, accredited by the Japanese Ministry of Education, Science and Culture, to keep their youngsters in step with nationalist sentiments and their educational requirements untainted by U.S. standards. With more than seventy Japanese-owned companies with plants and offices in Tennessee and more than two hundred in neighboring Georgia, the pressure for a separate Japanese high school led the Tokyo Meiji Gakuin (a 112-year-old university founded by U.S. Presbyterian Church missionaries) to set up an affiliate in Sweetwater, Tennessee. Graduates of the Tennessee branch wishing to attend any Japanese university would receive the same consideration as graduates from Meiji Gakuin high schools in Japan.

Accreditation was the key. Because Japanese government requirements demanded that all teachers be Japanese, even in the school's English classes, the children of Japanese temporarily assigned to jobs in the U.S. would obtain the Japanese reading and writing language skills they needed to pass the rigorous entrance examinations for Japanese universities. This would allow Japanese families to remain together, rather than have wives, high school students, and younger siblings return to Japan for high school attendance to assure these youngsters college admission.[57]

In these ways, Japan kept its insularity, built a curtain of ignorance around itself, repressed those who understood its place and role in the world, and used the school system for educational introspection—not to educate its children as global citizens, but to produce administrators and salary workers to unquestionably stand in place for predetermined levels in the system's hierarchies.

Perhaps, though, change is on Japan's doorstep. Will it come through a future labor shortage; the need for a wider distribution of revenue to stimulate the domestic market; a social movement, or another factor? These might foster changes in the level of popular awareness of the needs of other peoples, the right of Japan's own consumers to a greater share of product of their labor, and a recognition of the status of women as the exploited backbone of Japan's successes—to make Japanese women equal in struggle to women in the West, who have also sought to win economic and political equity in a grudging, male-dominated world order.

Chapter 20
Out of Sync . . .
with Destinies Entwined

> *Several foreign journalists have pointed out*
> *that Shinto worship seems out of date and*
> *wholly incongruous in "high-tech Japan."*
> *They may be missing an important point.*
> *Japanese nativism has often thrived precisely*
> *in times of swift change and uncertainty.*
> *Japan may be enjoying unprecedented eco-*
> *nomic success, but, partly as a result, it is*
> *deeply uncertain about its relations with the*
> *outside world and about where the nation is*
> *headed. The attempt to revive native values in*
> *Japan, as in other countries, is usually a sign*
> *of crisis.* — Ian Buruma[1]

Out of Sync, Part 1

Future egalitarian social changes in Japan will likely increase the nation's labor cost of production and expand the wages Japanese, especially Japanese women, spend on consumer items in the domestic market. The nation is on the doorstep of a vast expansion of production to fill this emerging demand. But meanwhile the West remains unprepared to respond to Japan's growing economic power and methods, foreign policies, and ethnocentric beliefs. Instead, Western leaders have blithely blamed Japan for their own domestic failings and argued for *free trade, fair trade* and an *open door* for investments — policies Japan is not organized to pursue.

The development of the American economy has been decidedly out of sync with the central control mechanisms Japan relies on to regulate its internal and external economy. In the past, Japan never had a domestic market economy, only a highly regulated, oligopolized production apparatus and near-monopsonistic distribution system. It never provided adequately funded college opportunities for its youth nor social security for its retired workers, forcing them to save for their children's education and their own retirement rather than spend today to raise their living standards. The government then channeled these forced savings through the banking apparatus into industrial investments. (Comparative per capita savings deposits in 1986 U.S. dollars were: Japan $27,303; West Germany $12,288; United States $9,733; France $6,207; United Kingdom $5,818.)

Japan also never had a free labor force or an independent trade union movement. Labor cooperated with management to establish job categories, but did nothing about work rules that could stop speedups and thereby restrict maximum production. Japan's employers controlled labor's annual pay for each given job, making wages a fixed cost while increasing output per worker and reducing unit production costs.

Japanese workers not only worked intensely under standards set by their employers, but they felt an obligation to their co-workers to perform an equal share of labor — even to the point of denying themselves paid vacations which they could neither turn into cash nor carry over to future years. Thus there was great continuity of Japanese production. Gauged by the number of working days lost for every one thousand employees a year, Japan's loss was tiny by U.S. or British standards (though greater than that in West Germany, where workers had won significant benefits in the past).[2]

Japan's peer pressures kept work hours long, production intensive, and vacations short or unused. In 1987 there was a rise in the number of hours Japanese actually worked, despite a new law aimed at gradually reducing the nation's forty-eight-hour work week to forty hours in an effort to reorganize the labor force, reduce production in certain export-oriented industries, and fuel consumer spending. Labor Ministry statistics showed the Japanese workers took only half of the fifteen days of paid holidays that most companies, on average, offer each year. This finding reflected the habit of most Japanese of taking time off only when everyone else did: at the three yearly national holidays of New Year's, the spring break known as Golden Week, and the summer holidays that coincide with O-Bon, a festival commemorating the dead. Companies usually shut down for at least part of these holidays, which can total three weeks.

One out of three workers never took a vacation longer than three consecutive days, a 1988 survey by the Leisure Development Center disclosed. And though the Labor Ministry called for limiting the work week to five days, as of 1987 only 6.2 percent of Japanese companies declared Saturdays to be holidays, though some 50.9 percent had already moved toward a five-day week, allowing employees to take off some Saturdays. Eventually, the new program to cut work hours without reducing wages might fit in with U.S. pressures on Japan to reduce production for export and stimulate domestic demand. The deciding factor will be the state as the focal point of power: "We Order You to Take One Week of Vacation," a 1988 Labor Ministry poster proclaimed, adding the words "Hotto Week," a pun on the English word "hot" and a Japanese word for relaxation.[3]

The large producers and trading firms had never competed in world markets without the aid of government subsidies for research, development, technological advances, production, and exports. In terms of both researchers and expense, the government coordinated the university system and research institutes to create an infrastructure and support system for corporate projects in the natural sciences — meanwhile largely neglecting the social sciences and humanities. State-funded university and research institutes maintained as many or more researchers than corporations from 1980 to 1986. But total corporate research spending was 58 percent of the total of all research institutions in 1980, 63 percent in 1984, 65 percent in 1985, and 73 percent in 1986. University and research institute investigators, equal in number to corporate researchers in 1986, accounted for only 27 percent of all research expense — presumably their pay scales were proportionally lower than corporate researchers. Finally, all corporate research was in the natural sciences, and none in the social sciences — an indication of the orientation of an economy with the singular ethos of accumulation.[4]

The government also held the central role in shaping both production and competition; it intervened to reorganize old industries in decline or to promote the development of new technological industries.[5] Corporate Japan followed these government guidelines, filling them out in the interest of transforming both technology and realigning production and the work force.

In the midst of the reorganization of the technical base of the economy, in 1985 and 1986, corporations were the center of research and development of new technologies, products, and processes. Corporations continued to concentrate on research in manufacturing at the same time they elevated their outlays on electronics and chemicals. True, university departments provided far more research personnel and resources than did junior colleges and affiliated research institutes, but private and corporate research institutes spent one-third more on research than did federal and public research institutes.[6]

Meanwhile, backed by the government, Japanese manufacturers and exporters had no qualms about capturing foreign market shares by pursuing dumping: absorbing *all* fixed costs, including labor, in high domestic prices, and selling goods in foreign markets *at or even below* the variable costs of raw materials, energy, and transportation.

Out of Sync, Part 2

By contrast, in the West there was no comparable unity of national purpose for a labor speedup, subsidized production, and market dumping. There was no continuity of output, no social contract, no labor-management recognition that fewer job categories, work restrictions, and work rules could increase total output per worker for a given annual wage.

Rather, the logic of production was rooted in the traditions of confrontational relations between organized labor and large-scale employers. Confrontation was replicated in smaller enterprises with nonunion labor, the main difference being that in the large firms there were more rigid work classifications—and thus more carefully delineated labor functions—at different pay scales. Workers performed similar tasks in both work places, but in unionized plants work rules and job categories meant that the detailed, narrow tasks of one worker could not be transferred to any other worker. A single worker assigned a particular task could thus slow operations, the continuity of production, and total output. If the worker was absent, late to work, took an unauthorized break, got sick, or was injured, the entire work process could be delayed, though wages for all workers would still have to be paid—effectively reducing production volume while maintaining wages, and forcing up the unit labor cost of production, often above that of competitors.

The employers had conspired to create this system of work by insisting on paying labor by job functions, classifying the tasks each worker was to perform, and embodying this penny-pinching ethos in the contract signed with the unions. "The vehicle for work rules and job restrictions is, of course, the labor contract," management expert Peter F. Drucker has explained. "But don't just blame the unions. Managements are equally at fault. One major reason for proliferation of work rules and job restrictions is the narrow focus on dollars per hour with which Western managements conduct labor negotiations—and their tunnel vision is shared by economists, politicians, the press, and the public. As a result, managements accepted, often eagerly, tighter work rules and more restricted job classifications in exchange for a few pennies less wage per hour. Companies that all along paid attention to the *total cost* of work done rather than solely to immediate wage dollars per hour—IBM is one example—do not, it seems, suffer from a 'productivity gap' either in their American or in their European plants."[7]

The *comparative annual labor payment, allocated to total output, as the cost per unit*—the critical factor through which Japanese companies pay workers a yearly fixed sum by the job regardless of the level of sped-up output—was almost completely ignored in the U.S. Thus Japan could pay workers relatively more, drive labor to increase output in a given time, narrow the gap with America for yearly manufacturing hours per worker—from U.S. 1,930 hours and Japan 2,252 hours in 1970 to U.S. 1,966 hours and Japan 2,133 hours in 1968[8]—and still the U.S. did not lower *unit labor costs* below those in Japan.

Moreover, the government reorganization of the Japanese economy and the Japanese system under which employers were obligated to retrain, subsidize, and relocate displaced workers was rarely followed in the U.S. In Japan, this reassembly of the means of production and the work force during its Third Industrial Revolution led not only to higher economic growth, but also to a fall in its rate of unemployment to 2.4 percent in June

1988—its lowest level in five years and seven months.[9] But in America, market forces set the frame for the so-called decay of basic industry between 1973 and 1987, the decade-long reorganization and (from the employers' point of view) cheapening of the labor force, the new technological advances that became the core of America's Third Industrial surge, and the ultimate drop in unemployment to 5 percent, the lowest level in more than a decade.[10]

There were also distinct differences in the organization of government for contouring the economy and balancing social groups and classes. Japanese state programs under the Liberal Democratic Party promoted the interests of big business and farmers in Japan. But the U.S. federal government was partitioned into conflicting centers that traditionally acted as "checks and balances" on one another. U.S. government agencies respond to the desires of innumerable, often conflicting economic factions, social groups, and classes. The American system makes a concerted national effort nearly impossible. Big business successfully lobbied to shift taxes to individuals and consumers. Labor pressured government for costly fringe benefits and job security. Environmentalists demanded limits on giveaways and pollution of land, water, and air. The elderly sought higher Social Security payments and health care. The representatives of the young wanted child care, health facilities, etc. And the military wanted a greater chunk of national output, the federal budget, and America's resources. The contests between claimants dissipated national energies and prevented the construction of a single national plan to guide the economy.

The fiscal powers meanwhile fell into one hand, so to speak, the monetary policies into another, making the American economy one of incalculable and gyrating Stop/Go cycles. And the more agencies that were created to resolve these problems, the more piecemeal were the "solutions" proposed and tried—and the deeper became America's economic malaise.

Thus, if America threatened to expand industrially and unemployment declined too much, wage and fringe benefit increments might increase domestic production costs faster than output, thereby raising prices and encouraging lower-price imports. There would be no place either to market high-price excess output abroad or to sell to a Japan or a Common Market that blocked out U.S. goods.

As domestic U.S. production and demand went up, for example to 3 percent a year, manufacturers operating at close to full capacity would experience higher costs and low-price imports might undercut U.S. producers, worsening the balance of trade. In turn, this situation could force the dollar lower, with two contradictory effects: import prices would be raised and U.S. export industries would be pushed to their capacity. But inflationary cost pressures might also force the Federal Reserve to push U.S. interest rates upward, inducing a domestic recession, draw foreign investment capital leading to slower growth elsewhere (especially in Canada and Western Europe), raise the interest service charges on variable third world loans, and put liquidity strains on financial markets.[11]

Only Japan might benefit by expanding its domestic production for home consumption and dumping abroad; building up its balance of trade to be offset by the export of investment capital and closely linked aid; and generally growing more wealthy while others, especially the U.S., suffered a crisis of profit realization in the marketplace, leading to capital disaccumulation.

The way around the American dilemma seemed to be tariffs and other restrictions on trade. The basic program — to stimulate U.S. exports, but limit imports — became the subject of the 1988 *Omnibus Trade and Competitiveness Act,* which gave the president added powers to defend the nation's trade interests and retaliate against "unfair" foreign trade practices. The executive as granted the power to respond on an ad hoc basis to trade issues. The new law seemed to put the U.S. on the road to neomercantile, bilateral trade relations with other nations — the very pathway followed by Japan.

Claiming it sought free trade, America not only threatened Japan with 100 percent duties if Japan did not open its telecommunications market (in accordance with the 1984 cartel agreement), but Western Europe as well. "We are starting to see an immense amount of bashing of our trading partners" that could lead to a "trade war," said chairman Boskin of the President's Council of Economic Advisers, citing the biggest risk facing the growing U.S. economy in May 1989.

The great trading nations were at each other's markets, with each feeling the pressure to retaliate by punishing the others with tariffs, duties, and trade restrictions. Washington cited Japan, India, and Brazil as "unfair traders" on 25 May 1989, then relented when Japan and Brazil partly opened some markets in 1990.

The broader structural problems that linked economic issues with national security and foreign relations issues were capped by U.S. charges of Japanese pricing practices involving high cartel prices at home and dumping abroad; domestic distribution monopolies that excluded foreign-made products; bid-rigging on construction; other anticompetitive practices; and the high Japanese savings rate that prevented spending on both imported and Japanese-made goods — thus requiring Japan to seek export markets. Facing a firestorm of demands on Capitol Hill, the president cited Japan as an unfair trader under "Super 301" of the act — specifically for the refusal of its public authorities to purchase America commercial satellites and supercomputers, and for stringent import requirements that kept out American manufactured forest products worth an estimated $1.2 billion a year. In 1990 Japan gave way, promising to import supercomputers and manufactured wood products.

Japan saw America's unilateral action as unfair, so much so that if Washington proceeded to punish Japan with 100 percent duties on selected imports under the 1988 *Trade Act,* Japan threatened to pass further restrictions on U.S. exports, blocking items like U.S. cosmetics. "European and Asian cosmetics firms doing business in Japan would lose no time in taking full advantage of any difficulties encountered by U.S. cosmetic firms," offered Leonard A. Lauder, the chief executive of Estée Lauder Inc., warning that a nationalist backlash of Japanese consumers was possible if Japanese cosmetics were put on America's retaliatory list.[12]

Short-Run Growth Traps

Trade barriers, neomercantilist practices, and new markets for dumping to back up autarchic production were the obvious escape routes from the "growth traps" that had sprung up in both the United States and West Germany, the second and third most prosperous capitalist economies. The U.S. looked to Canada, Mexico, and the newly liberated zones of Eastern Europe; West Germany sought to join with East Germany in a uniform currency union that would facilitate new investment and trade relations with the rest of Eastern Europe.

The U.S. weakness was periodic stagflation: its lack of precision state controls over production exceeding marketing capacity *and* excess domestic demand for goods that was not filled from high-cost domestic production, which caused domestic production cutbacks and an inflationary spiral, and encouraged low-price imports. West Germany's major failing was its failure to deploy centralized power to flexibly increase domestic demand to fuel enlarged production and employment.

Without greater central government authority to set unified goals, the U.S. had no way to restrain domestic demand to reduce imports, or to bolster savings to stimulate technological investments that, in turn, might increase production capacity to lower costs and stimulate exports. The result, the Bank for International Settlements reported, had been and would continue to be domestic inflation.

Just as harmful it said, was the "growth trap" fostered by West Germany's weak domestic demand, which discouraged capital formation, hence the growth potential for output, employment, tax revenues, and expansionary government policy measures. Just as in the U.S., such West German decay had harshly hit the work force, with unemployment edging up by mid–1988—even though the labor force had not grown.[13]

Rather than encourage investment at home to stimulate production and employment, the Bundesbank was determined to stop "overproduction" that could neither be sold at home nor exported. West German exports were already at the highest level in the world in both 1986 and 1987, but imports were small by comparison, leaving a huge trade balance. The $294 billion in 1987 exports overwhelmed the $228 billion in imports, with the $66 billion balance available to fund capital exports.[14]

In 1988 the West German market was not only saturated with too many well-made goods, but the population of consumers was rising more slowly than that in major competitor nations and the nation's transport systems, office buildings, and housing were largely postwar and did not need renewal. Moreover, 50 percent of German exports already went to, and overwhelmed competitors in, the European Community. And unionized, high-price labor and the government's failure to eliminate restrictions on German capital markets sent investment finance scurrying abroad.

German capital had long since been exported to set up subsidiaries in the U.S. and other European countries. In preparation for the 1992 lifting of all trade and investment barriers, cash-rich German companies could bide their time waiting — to release an avalanche of takeovers never before seen in Europe.

To stimulate capital exports, the Bundesbank concentrated on preventing inflation by keeping interest rates below those prevailing in world financial markets. But in 1988 it refused to cut them more or to pump up a budget deficit that already represented a higher percentage of the West German economy than the U.S. deficit — because these measures would stimulate production and lead to what the Bundesbank and the business community saw as a dreaded inflationary spiral. The result was a continual drop in domestic investments — from 9 percent of output in the mid-1970s to 5.5 percent in 1985, and to an approximated 5 percent in 1988; 8 percent unemployment from 1983 to 1988; and the highest wages in Europe for the shortest hours.[15]

Following these cues, German financiers concentrated on international markets. Germany became the entrepôt of global capital flows — importing foreign finance paid on the nation's positive trade balance and monies earned on overseas investments and services, and exporting more capital than it imported. German financiers borrowed at low interest rates and then sent their capital abroad in search of higher interest rates, with some $27 billion of capital being exported in the first six months of 1988 alone. More would follow in an effort to sidestep a January 1989 German 10 percent withholding tax on interest on domestic West German savings accounts and bonds.[16] Though the withholding tax on interest on domestic West German savings was reversed on 1 July 1989, German capital continued to pour overseas, with both Luxembourg and Britain also opposing any Common Market withholding tax that would stop the considerable inflow from West German investors.[17]

West Germany had thus become a global investment economy, opportunistically reacting to the needs of the moment, with the foresight that comes from the second largest accumulation of finance capital in the world — waiting to place vast sums into an economically consolidated Western Europe, into East Germany that was soon to merge with it as one nation, and in the rest of Eastern Europe.

And yet West Germany and the United States suffered from economic uncertainties. Their short-term vision faced Japan's long-term outlook for growth till the end of the century. The European Common Market had mapped the future of a consolidated continental enterprise, but was not yet a single political entity that could supplant national legislatures, nor anything approximating an egalitarian marketplace. German and French farmers worried about losing subsidies. Labor unions worried about losing jobs to countries like Spain and Portugal where wages were lower. Smaller industries worried about being overwhelmed by larger ones. Britain repeatedly flaunted its independence, its parliamentary self-determination, its lower value-added tax and agricultural subsidies, its own currency system, and an independent Bank of England; England wanted no part of the European Monetary System or a central European bank transferring Britain's "fundamental economic decisions to another country," as conservative Prime Minister Thatcher said.[18]

True unity was still something to be achieved in the far distant future. Why else would Willy de Clercq, the EC's top trade official, insist that agricultural subsidies could *never* be eliminated![19] "It is not possible to have a United States of Europe," Prime Minister Thatcher ominously added on 27 July 1988. "What is possible is for the twelve countries of Europe steadily to work more closely together on things we do better together, so we can trade better together."[20]

The U.S. sociopolitical apparatus was disjoined and could not easily foster tranquility or long-run assurances of production continuity or access to markets. United States political structures, that ensured a switch of priorities with the election every two years of a new Congress and the election every four years of a president, could not equal Japan's Liberal Democratic Party that had repeatedly rebalanced its forces to continue in power for decades. Assessing such American short-term calculations, MIT Professor Rudiger Dornbusch told the Senate Banking Committee in July 1988: "For election reasons and as a result of the failure to unwind the inappropriate policy mix" — an investment-stimulative fiscal policy relying on deficit spending, and a relatively restrictive, tight-money Federal Reserve monetary policy to raise interest rates and curtail investments — "the U.S. economy is heading in the wrong direction: inflation is going up, and so is the dollar. Unless the incoming administration addressed squarely and effectively the fiscal problem, interest rates, the deficit and the unemployment rate are all bound to go up, too."[21]

Even if this prognosis might not be totally fulfilled, it relayed an undeniable central truth: the U.S. would suffer from continual bouts with stagflation, a lack of savings, too little new investment in the latest technology, runaway industries, and loss of capital to markets abroad. The uncoordinated U.S. polity was no match for Japan's centrally directed state economy, that itself was rooted in Shinto beliefs in Japanese superiority, Confucian practices of respect for and subservience to authority, extended *zaibatsu* and other conglomerated enterprises wielding hierarchical

controls, ancillary government agencies coordinating research, development, production and marketing, and the strong and growing economic
and political interests of the Self-Defense Forces.

"Island Psychology," Diversities, and Destinies Entwined

The future destiny of Japan was undoubtedly linked to the destiny of
America and Western Europe, but would be a common destiny only in the
sense that a certain equality and strength was established in each to enable
mutual accommodations to one another's needs. Both the West and Japan
would have to bend, show flexibility, and establish comparable institutions
and standards. Yet it would not suffice to promote and finance cultural
understanding to resolve disagreements rooted deeply in different economic
and political systems.

Japan's facile, one-dimensional "productive-efficiency" approach to a
world in turmoil had awarded its controlled economy an advantage in the
domain of production and trade. But the world did not appreciate the blind
eye Japan turned toward its own problems. Japan placed itself at a tremendous global disadvantage through its ethnocentric self-image of racial
superiority and — following its own Confucian logic — its lack of empathy
for others. Shintoism stressed unquestioning duty to the emperor, not
ethical compassion. Most Japanese leaders simply did not comprehend the
nature of an America characterized by many ethnic groups and races, in
constant turmoil, fighting the tides of uniformity, shared assumptions, and
rigid discipline. Such social differences and pressures seemed not only
foreign to Japan, but Japanese society suppressed its own diversity and
drew much of its identity and security from shared assumptions and predictability.

It seemed futile to tell the Japanese that living within their own islands
were 700,000 Korean nationals, 120,000 naturalized Koreans, an unknown
number of Japanese citizens born of Korean-Japanese marriages, and
10,000 to 100,000 illegal Korean immigrants. These one million or more
ethnic Koreans (comprising over 80 percent of all foreign nationalities living in Japan) suffered the degradations of passport registration with the
police and discrimination in the workplace, in housing, for loans, and
social rights. In 1947 Japan, the government had ordered all Koreans to
register as foreign residents, denying them basic rights accorded Japanese
nationals. Five years later, Koreans in Japan were officially deprived of
their Japanese nationality (originally forced on them during Japan's imperial control of Korea), taking away their remaining protective legal
status. Thereafter, some 60 to 80 percent of the Koreans in Japan were
classified as "foreign residents" who lacked Japanese nationality, though
the vast majority were second-, third-, and fourth-generation born in

Japan, had never seen Korea, and intended to permanently remain in Japan!

Until 1984, to become Japanese through naturalization required that Koreans discard their non–Japanese name and adopt a Japanese ethnic name—thereby giving Japan the superficial appearance of ethnic uniformity and national oneness. But as the civil rights movement among young Koreans in Japan emerged in the 1970s, the issue of equating ethnicity with nationality was raised. Seeing themselves as an ethnic minority in Japan, they hoped to sway thinking in both Japan and Korea that the Korean people living in Japan were Japanese nationals with a Korean ethnic identity, customs, and traditions; that, like America, Japan could also be a national "melting pot" of different ethnic groups.[22]

Of the remaining "foreigners" with restricted rights in Japan, almost 10 percent are Chinese involved in trade; more than 2 percent are Filipino workers; and others are from the U.S., England, and West Germany. All of these people have restricted legal rights and social privileges in Japan.[23]

Japan's own people, the descendants of its Caucasian aborigines, *Ainu,* of its historic tanner and butcher workers, the *Burakumin,* and *Hibakusha,* the atomic bomb victims (viewed as tainted physically, genetically and morally) are discriminated against in education, employment, marital alliances, and social rights.

A March 1987 survey of the *Burakumin* put their number at over one million; they comprise 0.9 percent of Japan's 121,672,000 people.[24] According to the Japanese government, 1,166,000 Burakumin lived in 4,603 Buraku districts throughout Japan in 1987. But there may be as many as three million Burakumin, many of whom are impoverished, receive no governmental assistance, and experience a cycle that keeps them impoverished. The cycle begins with discrimination that places the Burakumin in unskilled and unstable jobs where they perform dangerous and heavy work, which leads to low income, which in turn breeds poverty and household instability—further leading to an inferior educational environment and finally to unskilled labor again.

As of 1988, a *blacklist* was still being published, continuing more than a decade of discrimination, designating the names and populations of Buraku districts throughout Japan. For years the Yasuda Trust Bank and other great companies had hired detective agencies to check the family background of prospective employees—to find out if the applicant was a Burakumin or a naturalized Korean. "The corporations used this publication to make sure that they would not hire any Burakumin, and if they already had Buraku employees, to deny promotions to them," said Professor Noguchi Michihiko of the Research Institute of the Dowa Problem.

In marital alliances, too, the Burakumin were not considered acceptable partners. "Marital discrimination by the Japanese is sustained by their wish to conform to other people's ideals and general social attitudes," Noguchi explained. "This is why they carefully investigate the family background and status of marriage partners." Noguchi's poll of women in their forties in Osaka showed that 60 percent would be opposed if one of their children wanted to marry a Burakumin, fearing such a marriage would become an obstacle for the marriage of their other children, and would hurt relatives and the children of such a marriage. Even if the Burakumin emigrate to the United States, if they want to marry a Japanese, marital discrimination has continued among the *Issei* (first generation), *Nisei* (second generation), and *Sansei* (third generation).[25]

Overt discrimination and a less-than-homogeneous population exists within Japan. Prime Minister Nakasone could issue denials, insisting in the Diet on 21 November 1986, that "no minorities in Japan who hold Japanese citizenship are discriminated against."[26] But this was untrue regarding both Ainu and Burakumin citizens, and also for both citizen and noncitizen Koreans and others. Minorities in Japan protested that Nakasone totally disregarded their status and plight. Formal protests were lodged by the Ainu through their Kanto Utari Association and Hokkaido Utari Association, which were joined by the Japan Catholic Council for Justice and Peace.[27] On 10 December 1986 the largest minority organization in Japan, the Buraku Liberation League, joined forces with Ainu and resident Koreans for the first time to protest Japanese human rights violations at the International Human Rights Day rally.[28]

Ignorant of what the world considered offensive, Prime Minister Nakasone had also emphasized on 22 September 1986 that Japan consisted of a unified ethnic race that was highly educated and intelligent, while America's black and Hispanic populations lowered that nation's average intelligence "level."[29] In response to an outpouring of U.S. criticism, Nakasone later "apologized," but still claimed that "the United States is a multinational society and in some fields, such as education, there are points that they have not reached."[30]

A joint statement denouncing Nakasone's derogatory remarks was issued by the Tokyo-based Japan Pacific Resource Network and Japan Watch International, a multinational ecumenical organization that defended Koreans and other foreigners who refused to be fingerprinted. In Tokyo, the Reverend Jesse Jackson demanded Nakasone's further explanation and declared the solidarity of Americans with the rallying groups.[31]

But many in Japan thought that Nakasone should not have apologized. These people believed that he spoke forthrightly of the lower educational achievements of U.S. black and Hispanic populations. An open contest then emerged. U.S. civil rights groups were outraged. Reverend Jackson called for an international boycott of selected Japanese firms that discriminated against minorities,[32] and the issue was even considered by executives of Matsushita U.S.A. Meanwhile, Liberal Democratic Party leader Watanabe Michio insisted that U.S. blacks had no qualms about absolving their debts through personal bankruptcy, while Japanese would rather commit *harakiri* than become debtors. Japan's characterization of

American blacks as Little Black Sambo figures had long been the case of black store mannequins with exaggerated racial features. Such mannequins were not removed until protests by U.S. black organizations in 1989. Japanese emphasis on Caucasians as the typical American young children — pink-skinned, blond, and cherubic — showed little appreciation of America's ethnic diversity.

These misunderstandings will not easily be corrected by remaking Japan's "island psychology" or elevating Americans' awareness of Japan's cultural attributes. Chairman Nagamura Toshio of the California First Bank, a subsidiary of the Bank of Tokyo, tried to increase American understanding of Japan by raising $125 million in Japanese money for a new Pavilion for Japanese Art at the Los Angeles County Museum of Art in 1988. He told Japanese executives that "We have to communicate with the American people, not only politically and economically but also culturally. Japan has great art — to show such great art will help promote better feeling."[33] Yet better feeling alone is not likely to resolve the tensions between the two economic superpowers.

To reduce such tensions, one possibility is that Western nations in crisis will attempt to approximate Japan's system of centralized, governmental control over their population and economy, and establish their own, exclusive common markets, associative relations, and spheres of influence with ancillary nations. Yet, thereby, democratic rights would be withdrawn or limited at home, and the metropoles and peripheries of the past will be recreated, not in the form of empires and colonies controlled by armies, but as politically independent nations that are bound economically in a common market.

Another possibility is that Japan will alter its institutions, mores, and ethos of the marketplace to accommodate the West. Japan has always made great internal changes in the face of threats and crises in the past. The emperor, expecting bellicose foreigners, had dispersed his militant, resisting *daimyo* in 1864, no longer requiring that they take residence every year at Edo. The Meiji Revolution transformed social relations, took up the commercial and military practices of the West, and unhinged traditions that might stop Japan's advance in the face of the Western threat.

The Reemergent Imperial State

After World War I, Japan's imperial state became increasingly rigid. The modern Japanese state had emerged from feudal divisions only under the threat of warships sent by the commercial Western Powers, with the Meiji Emperor rallying his people by exhortation and inspection tours, acting as an agent of modernization and national unity. But the Meiji era ended in 1912, and was followed by Japan's *Twenty-One Demands* to oust Western interests in China in 1915. Japan sided with the victors of World

War I and won a seat as a power broker at Versailles. The ruin of the empires previously held by Turkey, Russia, Germany, and China meant the balance of power had shifted. Japan's subservience to the Western Powers came to a close.

To strengthen itself, Japan required domestic tranquility and the popular subservience of its population. The sovereign would have to command new powers and play a different role: the emperor became aloof, distant, more sacrosanct, acting as both a symbol of conformity that defined nationality and a barrier against social change. Under the new symbolic emperor, differing political views concerning the way to expand abroad emerged, with the military and fascist vision gradually prevailing. Japan gave up its long-standing association with Great Britain in the 1920s; signed the Washington Pacts' illusive, and transient, peaceful trading arrangements with Western Powers; then openly allied itself with Germany and Italy in the 1930s in the hope of winning regional hegemony.

For these ends, the Japanese variety of Confucianism and Shintoism was domestically paraded as a shield against the destructive aspects of Western materialism and individualism. But both Japanese Confucianism and Shintoism were lacking in feeling for others. It set forth a rationale of imperial expansion based on Japan's self-images as a superior race and a superior culture. These feelings merged with the military goals of state industrial planning and regional dominance in Asia. The Japanese High Command advocated displacement of the Western empires. As we have seen, the Imperial Way faction — which relied on the spirit of the Imperial Army *(Kogun)* — was first defeated by, and then mobilized by, the High Command's Control School that, in turn, believed the material base of war imperialism was state management of industry, a military dictatorship, and a mass party based on complete, popular conformity.

Meanwhile, Western anti–Japanese feelings ran high; the West passed tariffs against Japanese exports and negotiated secret embargoes on oil and other resources critical to Japan; and the fascist assertion of Japanese superiority muffled the voices of both political moderates and business interests pursuing positive trade balances through *free trade*. Seeking an exit from unresolvable domestic crises, the right-leaning parties and military fascists inflamed popular sentiments against the West and promoted belief in Japan's *rights* to Manchuria as the equivalent of the Western empires and the U.S. Monroe Doctrine in Latin America. At the emperor's insistence, domestic opposition was no longer tolerated; the High Command crushed the Tokyo military revolt of 1936, strengthened Japan's divisions in Manchuria and on the China front in 1937, and moved to strengthen Japanese forces against Soviet forces on the Manchurian-Siberian border in 1938–39.

Is this pure history, or are there links between Japan's imperial past and the present? In the past Japan emulated German state-guided capitalism and authoritarian institutions—not so different from today's MITI guidance of the national economy and the internal state police apparatus that ensures domestic deference to authority. In the past Japan's laws granted family heads authority over each member; these familial hierarchies in which fathers commanded respect, work, and commitment were replicated in the government of local and regional communities, and, on a national level, in the role of the divine emperor as a venerated father-figure. Today the male-dominated family and employer-regulated work force are the command posts, discouraging self-assertion and demanding corporate and national devotion, effort, and service. In the past propagandistic notions of racial superiority made the state-family link a nationalist enterprise, while today complaints about Western arrogance and unfairness turn on a similar government-familial framework to regenerate Japan's xenophobia and register new calls for the national greatness of a superior people. In the past Western moves to strengthen nationalist autarchy, helotries, and spheres of influence led to Japan's economic entrapment, its political jealousies, and its military ambition to create its own comparable empire, while now Japan has responded to Western market spheres by securing its own neomercantile trade and investment area through a grinding production system at home, the appropriation of foreign technologies, unfair trading, dumping, and financial maneuvering.

The linkages between Japan past and present are both material and ideological. A powerful bond has sustained the individual obligation of social conformity, lasting through Tokugawa Ieyasu's authoritarian, 17th-century military and bureaucratic régime, the Meiji era, two world wars, and the postwar U.S. "democratization" that purged only the most notorious military leaders, businessmen, and politicians, leaving the government bureaucracy largely untouched. The traditions of "Japanism" reemerged to neutralize and undermine U.S.-promoted reforms. The social obligations of conformity empowered the bureaucracy to use the same methods employed in the wartime economy to mobilize the nation's labor force, resources, and patriotism for production, exports, and economic supremacy.

Japanism again turned to Shinto practices. Increasing numbers of Japanese went to Ise to worship the sun goddess as the divine ancestor of the emperor and the Japanese race. "Japan's national character was formed before history was recorded," argues the noted social critic Kase Hideaki. "When Japan was born, the Emperor was already a high priest and head of the state. The imperial family cannot be separated from Japanese mythology. The myths are identical to the birth of Japan. The Emperor is sacred because of his blood ties with the gods that created our nation."[34]

The emperor, the benign patriarch at the apex of the hierarchical family-state, was meanwhile being *politically* elevated by a sense of sacred communion between man and gods, linking the state and religion. This tie was expressed in the national anthem that evoked the unbroken imperial line. Its social dimension was characterized by popular subservience to imperial will. It was enforced by the 1989 Ministry of Education directive requiring that the flag be raised, that school children sing the old imperial anthem, and that they be taught respect for the emperor.

Dissent was again becoming suspect, dissenters socially isolated. Right-wing organizations began using weapons just as they had in the 1920s to terrorize people and to keep them in line, again attacking nonconformists, including journalists (two of whom were shot in 1988). With the Showa Emperor Hirohito's death, Shinto ritual and state ceremonies on the same sacred grounds — unwittingly attended by the heads of leading world powers who might otherwise oppose the rebirth of authoritarian State Shintoism — politically reaffirmed Japan's spiritual culture of blind obedience and action according to imperial will.[35]

Danger/Opportunity

Once again State Shintoism, mass conformity, and an ethnocentric fixation on race superiority has fortified Japanese leaders to mobilize the nation in the myopic quest for a self-sufficiency a resource-poor nation can never attain; neomercantile markets that may one day close; investment and financial spheres that may reject Nippon's narrow calculations in the 1990s; foreign technologies that may be cut off; and military alliances that are already in jeopardy.[36]

These limitations and risks will persist despite a change in the nation's outlook. Japan has changed its basic vision and blurred its lens more than once. Overturning its earlier mindset that, whatever the nation's will, events would enclose Japan and set the frame of its destiny, postwar occupation and economic resurgence demanded material calculations, more pragmatism, and less metascience.

Japan quickly recognized its advantage, as the U.S. sought to use it strategically to maintain America's commercial and military sphere of influence in Asia. By the 1950s Japan was already a major military supplier for U.S. forces in Korea. In the 1960s Japan's renewed neomercantilist policies were winning its industries unfettered markets abroad and access to inexpensive raw materials in the same Southeast Asia it has so recently sought to control by arms. As rising production then demanded full employment, workers with wages and unmet needs extended the still-limited domestic market for both consumer goods and the capital equipment needed to produce them. And as production boomed, the domestic market was easily filled, export markets were secured under U.S. sponsorship of Japan's entrance into international bodies, and Japan became America's principal trading partner after Canada — again making it dependent on U.S. acceptance of its neomercantile ways.

But Japan also worried that the U.S. might one day desert it militarily and cut off its critical resources. Japan lacked the petroleum, other raw materials, and foods it required to keep its industrial apparatus alive and well. The Arab-Israeli war of 1973 and the ensuing oil crisis proved that Japan would have to secure its own future requirements of almost 100 percent of its oil and 80 percent of its total energy needs. The island nation would thus have to rely on nuclear power as an alternative source of energy, and establish better ways to deal with nuclear pollution in a densely populated urban domain, twelve-to-twenty times more geographically concentrated than in the U.S.

The sudden 1973–74 inaccessibility of cheap petroleum, foods, and resources sharply elevated the domestic cost of production and raised the price of Japanese exports at the very time that America was closing some markets to Japanese goods. Japan then defended itself with more encompassing state controls and regulations—as well as by designing its own foreign policy. Japan thus followed the U.S. into China, going even further than America by reversing its relations with both Taiwan and Beijing. In 1974 Prime Minister Tanaka wooed the nations of Southeast Asia. Appealing to these regional states at the 1977 Manila Conference, Prime Minister Fukuda attempted to regularize diplomatic and economic relations. In 1978 the Japan-China Treaty of Amity was signed, marking the official end to wartime hostilities and establishing commercial ties. As its own "China policy" emerged, Japan implicitly recognized that the future resolution of its problem with the U.S. might well reside on the Asian mainland.

Yet, so long as China's market remained relatively underdeveloped, Japan would continue to stretch the limits of America's political and economic patience. Government subsidies to production and trade spurred export-dumping and limited imports of the manufactured goods of others. Japan began building up monumental trade surpluses, with a full 25 percent of all exports going to the U.S. in the 1970s—just as the U.S. lost its 1970 place of 30 percent on Japan's market, retaining only 18 percent by 1977. Yet America refused to *officially recognize* that Japanese neomercantilism necessarily meant the size of this bilateral imbalance would enlarge.

Building on a past qualitative linkage, by the 1980s the situation had quantitatively changed. Japan still demanded the complete benefits of neomercantilism: unbridled access to foreign technology and a U.S. military shield in Asia. It was unlikely that it would ever willingly permit an open market at home because Japan feared that an open market would undermine both class relations and domestic order.[37] It had outflanked the U.S. Congress to secure advanced aircraft technology, while preferring Japan Airlines and All Nippon Airways (both unable to purchase new planes very quickly) to deny American airlines the right to expand services—claiming that Japan was out of runway space and other facilities and would not be able to satisfy demand for several years, at the very time when air travel between the U.S. and northeast Asia was growing at 10 percent a year.[38] True, it could not yet become either a regional or global policeman. And it also lacked inventive resources.

But Japan's genius remained: it easily adopted the technologies of others, adapted them to Japanese standards for production, and marketed them worldwide. Though Nippon's credibility as a free-trade or fair-trade nation was fast eroding, the rise of its power seemed both relentless and limitless.

Yet Japan's entire system rested on an implicit arrogance—a plan for imperial "self-sufficiency" that, in truth, could not be sustained without foreign resources, markets, and investment opportunities. Japan held seeming material assurances for continuity. It *seemed* that state-directed production under the reign of large-scale manufacturing and mass marketing would continue in Japan. It also *seemed* that the *domestic* market would be extended to accommodate enlarged output and to temporarily relieve Japanese dumping pressure on Western markets. It *seemed* that there would be short-term disruptions in old industries reorganized by the state, but long-term full employment in new industries in Japan. It *seemed* that Nippon would come to realize that it was an island physically, but reliant on the successes of the United States and Western Europe economically. And it seemed that Japan would recognize that the only alternative to the "war" of the marketplace and competition to capture spheres for global investments might be China and the rest of Asia—as well as a cooperative plan to stimulate production in each nation and provide for adequate distribution of output to maintain full employment and domestic prosperity.

This would offset the neomercantilist logic that Japanese and Asian manufactures must hold sway in world production and markets. Such dominance became increasingly unlikely in the early 1990s as Japanese capital invested directly in production facilities moved to the NICs, the third world, the U.S., and Western Europe. Japan's new efforts to stimulate domestic consumption eventually might also reduce exports as a percent of the nation's total output, generate imports, reduce the positive trade balance, and wean Japan from many of its neomercantile ways.

Whether and when this would transpire is still unknown in the early 1990s, for neither Japan nor the West seem inclined to agree to such a cooperative solution.

Rather, fears and accusations call attention to underlying economic conflicts, and rationalized national motives in language bordering on racial stereotypes and irrational prejudice. Socioeconomic implosions intensify in each nation. While inherently contradictory production and trade problems between Japan and the West call for resolution. These are being publicly presented in illogical ways that give renewed life to old emotions, state patriotism, thinly veiled racism, and atavistic hatreds. And yet, given their mutual need for unfettered production, full employment, expanding markets, and fields for exportable capital, the common destiny of America and Japan might logically lead to future accommodations—or, failing these, a warren for unresolvable crises.

Notes

Part 1

1. Kaneyoshi Nakayama, ed., *Pictorial Encyclopedia of Japanese Culture: The Soul and Heritage of Japan,* trans. Richard Delapp (Tokyo: Gakken Co., 1987), 6.

Chapter 1

2. Taoism was sometimes called "Suntaoism" in ancient China, and some historians claim that Shintoism can be regarded as a disguised version of Taoism. But this linkage occurred, if at all, before the introduction of Chinese characters to Japan. No extant written records reveal what Shintoism was in its pure and primitive form. See Koji Fukunaga, Ueda Masaaki, and Ueyama Shunpei, *Dokyo to Kodai no Tennosei (Taoism and the Ancient Imperial System)* (Tokyo: Tokuma Shoten, 1978); and Marius B. Jansen, *Japan and Its World: Two Centuries of Change* (Princeton: Princeton University Press, 1980), 71–72.

3. Seiichi Mizuno, *Asuka Buddhist Art: Horyu ji,* trans. Richard L. Gage (New York: Weatherhill; Tokyo: Heibonsha, 1974), 150–57, 169.

4. David L. Snellgrove, ed., *The Image of the Buddha* (Paris: Kodansha International/UNESCO, 1978), 400.

5. Nakayama, 37, 44.

6. Michio Morishima, *Why Has Japan "Succeeded"?* (London: Cambridge University Press, 1982), 3–7.

7. Jansen, 41–42; **also see** Kate Wildman Nakai, "The Nationalization of Confucianism in Tokugawa Japan: The Problem of Sinocentrism," *Harvard Journal of Asiastic Studies* 40, no. 1 (June 1980): 159–99.

8. Jansen, 70–71.

Chapter 2

1. Nakayama, 36–37.
2. Nakayama, 38.
3. Nakayama, 52–53.
4. Nakayama, 56.
5. Nakayama, 66–67.
6. Nakayama, 64–65.
7. E. Herbert Norman, *Japan's Emergence as a Modern State: Political and Economic Problems of the Meiji Period* (New York: Greenwood, 1946), 15–16.

8. Norman, 17; G.B. Samson, *The Western World and Japan* (New York: C.E. Tuttle, 1950), 240–41.

9. Norman, 17.

10. Karel van Wolferen, *The Enigma of Japanese Power: People and Politics in a Stateless Nation* (New York: Alfred A. Knopf, 1989).

11. Jansen, 16–18.

12. Nakayama, 60–61.

13. Nakayama, 50–51.

14. Nakayama, 62–63.

15. Edward Emerson, Jr., *A History of the Nineteenth Century Year by Year* (New York: P.F. Collier and Son, 1900), 2: 1175–76.

16. Emerson, 3: 1254.

17. Emerson, 3: 1255.

18. Emerson, 3: 1255–56; Iwao Seiichi, *Biographical Directory of Japanese History* (Tokyo: Kodansha International, 1978), 192.

19. Emerson, 3: 1256.

20. Emerson, 3: 1260–61.

21. Emerson, 3: 1299–1300.

22. Conrad D. Totman, *The Collapse of the Tokugawa Bakufu: 1862–1868* (Honolulu: University Press of Hawaii, 1980), xx–xxii; Emerson, 3: 1339–41.

23. Samson, 189; Norman, 49.

24. Emerson, 3: 1340–41.

25. Emerson, 3: 1446.

26. Emerson, 3: 1462.

27. Emerson, 3: 1468.

28. Richard Krooth, *Japan: Five Stages of Development and a Look at the Nation's Future* (Santa Barbara, Calif.: Harvest, 1976), Chapter 1; Edwin O. Reischauer, *Japan, Past and Present* (New York: Alfred A. Knopf, 1946), passim; Jansen, passim.

29. Krooth, *Japan,* Chapter 1; Reischauer, *passim;* Jansen, *passim.*

30. Emerson, 3: 1482–83.

31. Emerson, 3: 1530–31; Norman, 50–52.

32. H. Kohachiro Takahashi, "La Place de la Revolution de Meiji dans l'histoire agraire du Japon," *Revue Historique* (October–November, 1953): 248.

33. Emerson, 3: 1530–31.

34. Michihiko Noguchi, *Japan's Minorities: Discrimination and the Buraku,* Research Paper Series, Research Institute of the Dowa Problem, Osaka City University, Osaka, Japan, March 1989; Emerson, 3: 1531.

35. Krooth, *Japan,* Chapter 1; Reischauer, *passim;* Jansen, *passim.*

36. Emerson, 3: 1535–36; Marius B. Jansen and Gilbert Rozman, eds., *Japan in Transition: From Tokugawa to Meiji* (Princeton: Princeton University Press, 1976), 248–52.

37. Emerson, 3: 1660.

38. Norman, *passim;* Krooth, *Japan, passim.*

39. Krooth, *Japan,* Chapter 1; Norman, 94–95, *et passim.*

40. Emerson, 3: 1566–67.

41. Norman, 131–32; Krooth, *Japan,* Chapter 1; Reischauer, *passim.*

42. Norman, 131, *et passim;* Krooth, *Japan,* Chapter 1; Reischauer, *passim.*

43. Emerson, 3: 1586–87; Norman, *passim.*

44. Emerson, 3: 1621; Norman, *passim.*

45. Emerson, 3: 1648.

46. Emerson, 3: 1659–60.

47. Emerson, 3: 1696.
48. Emerson, 3: 1712-13.
49. Norman, *passim;* Krooth, *Japan, passim.*
50. Krooth, *Japan,* Chapter 2.
51. Krooth, *Japan,* Chapter 2.
52. Krooth, *Japan,* Chapter 2.
53. Norman, *passim;* Krooth, *Japan, passim.*
54. Emerson, 3: 1551.
55. Emerson, 3: 1556.
56. Emerson, 3: 1628.
57. Emerson, 3: 1648.
58. Emerson, 3: 1659.
59. Emerson, 3: 1769.
60. Emerson, 3: 1771-73.
61. Emerson, 3: 1773-75.
62. Emerson, 3: 1777-79.
63. William Manchester, *The Arms of Krupp: 1587-1968* (New York: Bantam, 1970), 246.
64. Emerson, 3: 1771.
65. Emerson, 3: 1799.
66. Emerson, 3: 1891-94.
67. Krooth, *Japan,* Chapter 2.
68. Krooth, *Japan,* Chapter 2.
69. Krooth, *Japan,* Chapter 2; Andrew J. Crozier, *Appeasement and Germany's Last Bid for Colonies* (New York: St. Martin's Press, 1988).
70. *War Supplement to Compton's Pictured Encyclopedia* (Chicago: F.E. Compton & Company, 1939), 20, 32.
71. Krooth, *Japan,* Chapter 2.

Chapter 3

1. General Harold R., L.G. Alexander, *Current Bibliography* (London: Macmillan, 1942), 13.
2. W.J. Hinton, "Economic Occasions of Conflict in the Far East," in *The Causes of War* (London: Macmillan, 1932), 225-26.
3. *War Supplement to Compton's Pictured Encyclopedia,* 24-25.
4. Krooth, *Japan,* 4.
5. Hinton, "Conflict in the Far East," 227.
6. Reischauer, *Japan,* 148-49.
7. Krooth, *Japan,* 7; **also see** Arthur Tiedemann, *Modern Japan: A Brief History* (New York: D. Van Norstrand Company, 1955), *passim.*
8. Krooth, *Japan,* 7; **also see** Helen Mears, *Mirror for Americans* (Boston: Houghton Mifflin, 1948), *passim.*
9. B.G. Ghate, *Asia's Trade* (New Delhi: Indian Council of World Affairs, Oxford University Press, 1948), 142; "Supplement on Japan," *The Times* (London), November 22, 1965; The Foreign Capital Research Society, *Japanese Industry, 1965* (Tokyo: F.C.R.S., 1966), 18; G.C. Allen, *A Short History of Modern Japan* (New York: Frederick A. Praeger, 1963), 217, Table 26 A.
10. Krooth, Japan, 5; G.A. Johnson, "Industrial and Labor Influences," in *The Causes of War* (London: Macmillan, 1932), 35-36.
11. Richard Storry, *A History of Modern Japan* (London: Penguin Books, 1960), 172.

12. "The Tanaka Memorial," *China Critic* (Shanghai), 24, no. 9 (1931): 923–924.

13. "The Tanaka Memorial," 923, 927–28, 932.

14. Krooth, *Japan,* 5; "The Tanaka Memorial."

15. See Mears, *passim;* Takashi Oka, "Saionji and the Manchurian Crisis," *Harvard Papers on China* (Cambridge: Harvard University Committee on International and Regional Studies, 1954).

16. Storry, 271.

17. Tiedemann, 64–65.

18. Krooth, *Japan,* 5; **also see** Tiedemann, *passim.*

19. Storry, 173, 177–78.

20. Tiedemann, 64–70; Storry, 177–81; Hosea Ballou Morse and Harley Farnsworth MacNair, *Far Eastern International Relations* (New York: Riverside Press, 1931), 771; Nobutaka Ike, trans., *Japan's Decision for War: Records of the 1941 Policy Conferences* (Stanford: Stanford University Press, 1967).

21. Storry, 200.

22. See Morse and MacNair, 760; O. Tanin and E. Yohan, *When Japan Goes to War* (New York: International Publishers, 1936), 13–54, 95–100, 208–10, 251–52; Ghate, 142; William W. Lockwood, ed., "Japan's New Capitalism, in *The State and Economic Enterprise in Japan* (Princeton: Princeton University Press, 1965), 476–78.

23. Reischauer, *Japan,* 161–62.

24. Reischauer, *Japan,* 165–66.

25. Tiedemann, 134–35.

26. Krooth, *Japan,* Chapter 3.

27. Saburo Hayashi and Alvin D. Coox, *Kogun: The Japanese Army in the Pacific War* (Quantico: Marine Corps Association, 1959), 8.

28. Reischauer, *Japan,* 70; Tiedemann, 74–75.

29. Tanin and Yohan, 250–51.

30. Tanin and Yohan, 250.

31. T.A. Bison, *Japan's War Economy* (New York: International Secretariat, Institute of Pacific Relations, 1945), 29.

32. Bisson, 92–105, *et seq.*

33. Bisson, 27–30, 101–6, 140–61, 199–206; Brian Power, *The Puppet Emperor* (London: Universe Books, 1987).

34. *Japan-Manchukuo Yearbook, 1940* (Tokyo, A.Y.I., 1941); Bison, *passim;* Tain and Yohan, *passim.*

35. See Mears, *passim;* Andrew J. Grajdanev, "Manchuria: An Industrial Survey," in *Pacific Affairs* (New York: PA, 1945); Krooth, *Arms and Empire: Imperial Patterns Before World War II* (Santa Barbara, Calif.: Harvest, 1980), chapters 1 and 2.

36. Hayashi and Coox, 2.

37. See Hayashi and Coox, 17; Morse and MacNair, 772; Storry, 207–8.

38. Hayashi and Coox, 18.

39. *War Supplement to Compton's Pictured Encyclopedia,* 24–25.

40. *War Supplement to Compton's Pictured Encyclopedia,* 55.

41. *War Supplement to Compton's Pictured Encyclopedia,* 55.

42. V. Avarin, "Manchuria as a Japanese Base of Attack on the Soviet Union," *New Times* (Moscow), 15 August 1945.

43. Masaki Kobayashi, director, *The Human Condition, a Trilogy: No Greater Love; Road to Eternity; The Soldier's Prayer* (Berkeley, Calif.: Pacific Film Archives).

44. **See** J.H. Landman and Herbert Wender, *World Since 1914.* 10th ed. (New York: Barnes and Noble, 1958), 319; Tiedemann, 77–79, 136–39; Hayashi and Coox, 23–24; Reischauer, 178–81.
45. Hayashi and Coox, 29–30, 33.
46. Reischauer, 182–85.
47. Krooth, *Japan,* 8–10.
48. Krooth, *Japan,* 9; Wilfried Loth, *The Division of the World, 1941–1955* (New York: St. Martin's Press, 1988); **also see** Martin E. Weinstein, *Japan's Postwar Defense Policy, 1947–68* (New York: Columbia University Press, 1971).
49. "Text of Secretary Byrnes's Message," *New York Times,* 12 August 1945.
50. "Text of Directive," *New York Times,* 23 September 1945.
51. "White House Directive," *New York Times,* 23 September 1945.
52. "Text of Directive," *New York Times,* 23 September 1945.
53. Krooth, *Japan,* 10.
54. Sidney Shalett, "Japan Body Meets Without Russians," *New York Times,* 7 November 1945.
55. "Foreign Interests in Japan," Associated Press, Tokyo, 6 November 1945.
56. Krooth, *Japan,* 10; **also see** Edwin O. Reischauer, *The Japanese* (Cambridge: Harvard University Press, 1977).
57. Philip Jaffe, *New Frontiers in Asia: A Challenge to the West* (New York: Random House, 1945); Andrew Roth, *Dilemma in Japan* (Boston: Little, Brown, 1945); Reischauer, *Japan, passim;* Reischauer, *The Japanese, passim;* Weinstein, *passim.*
58. Sidney Shalett, "Japan Commission Halts for Russia," *New York Times,* 31 October 1945.
59. Shalett, "Japan Body Meets."
60. "Japan's Steel Production Capacity," Associated Press, Tokyo, 7 December 1945.
61. Ichiro Nakayama, *Industrialization of Japan* (Tokyo: Center for East Asian Cultural Studies; Honolulu: East West Center Press, 1963), 9–10; **also see** Weinstein, *passim.*
62. Nakayama, *Industrialization,* 19–20.
63. Nakayama, *Industrialization,* 10.
64. Nakayama, *Industrialization,* 14; Krooth, *Japan,* 11; **see** Weinstein, *passim.*
65. Nakayama, *Industrialization,* 14–15; **see** Lockwood, *passim;* Hugh Patrick and Henry Rosovsky, eds., *Asia's New Giant: How the Japanese Economy Works* (Washington, D.C.: Brookings Institution, 1976); Weinstein, *passim.*
66. Robert Guillain, *The Japanese Challenge,* trans. Patrick O'Brian (Philadelphia and New York: J.B. Lippincott, 1970), 313–14.
67. Guillain, 314.
68. Guillain, 312.
69. Guillain, 312.
70. Krooth, *Japan,* 11; **see** Reischauer, *The Japanese, passim.*

Part 2

1. Krooth, *Japan,* 12.

Chapter 4

2. Krooth, *Japan,* 14; Jansen, 101–4.

3. Economic Planning Agency, *Work and Leisure* (Tokyo: Ministry of Finance, 1988), 106–26.

4. Economic Planning Agency, *Work and Leisure,* 1988, 141.

5. Economic Planning Agency, *Work and Leisure,* 1988, 142–45.

6. Satoshi Kamata, *Japan in the Passing Lane* (New York: Pantheon Books, 1982), 1–38.

7. Dumping was *also* made possible by the internal resources of the conglomerated groups that approximated the monied cliques of the pre–World War II era. "From 1985 to 1987 Japanese producers lost between $3 billion and $5 billion in their push [read, investment and/or dumping] for supremacy in chip production," said Michael Borrus, deputy director of the Berkeley Roundtable on International Economy at the University of California, Berkeley. "That kind of loss could not be sustained without cross subsidies from other company divisions, guaranteed long-term purchases from divisions of the same corporate 'family' and an atmosphere of patience from financial institutions — also with close corporate and family ties. Japanese companies could not have made their gains so efficiently without close links to affiliated suppliers." See, for example, Michael Borrus, "How to Beat Japan at Its Own Game," *New York Times,* 31 July 1988.

8. Small and Medium Enterprises Agency, *White Paper on Small and Medium Enterprises* (Tokyo: Ministry of Finance, 1988), 58.

9. Small and Medium Enterprises Agency, "Survey of Manufacturing Sectors in December 1987," in *White Paper on Small and Medium Enterprises* (Tokyo: Ministry of Finance, 1988).

10. Small and Medium Enterprises Agency, 58–71.

11. Small and Medium Enterprises Agency, 61–62.

12. Small and Medium Enterprises Agency, 33.

13. Small and Medium Enterprises Agency, 61–65.

14. Ministry of Labor, *Survey of Incorporated Systems of Working Hours* (Tokyo: ML, 1988).

15. Morishima, 178–180.

16. Kenichi Ohmae, *The Mind of the Strategist* (New York: McGraw-Hill, 1982).

17. Edgar H. Schein, "Does Japanese Management Style Have a Message for American Managers?" *Sloan Management Review* (Fall 1977): 1–20.

18. For the two decades 1963–83, Japan's rising labor productivity averaged about 2.2 percent per year. Even in hard times on a global scale, Japan's gross national product continued to scale upward — a 2.40 percent rise from 1985–86, 4.20 percent from 1986–87, 4.25 percent from 1987–88, and an estimated 3.75 percent from 1988–89. See, for example, Organization for Economic Cooperation and Development, *Forecasts* (Paris: O.E.C.D., May 1988); International Monetary Fund, *Monthly Statistics* (New York: IMP, May 1988).

19. Ohmae, *The Mind of the Strategist, passim;* Schein, 1–20; Dore, "Introduction," *Japan in the Passing Lane* (New York: Pantheon Books, 1982), xxix–xxx.

20. Kamata, 34, 59.

21. Kamata, 37.

22. Dore, "Introduction."

23. Robert H. Hays, "Why Japanese Factories Work," *Harvard Business Review* 55 (July/August 1981), 57–66.

24. See Richard T. Pascale and Anthony G. Athos, *The Art of Japanese Management* (New York: Simon and Schuster, 1981).

25. T.A. Bisson, *Japan's War Economy* (New York: International Secretariat, Institute of Pacific Relations, 1945).

26. Harris, 36.

27. Kamata, 5–85.

28. Kamata, 49.

29. Kamata, 26.

30. Kamata, 29–32, 33–34.

31. *Kyodo News Service* (Tokyo), 23 July 1988.

32. Dore, "Introduction"; Ohmae, *The Mind of the Strategist;* Schein, 1–20.

33. Tsuneari Fukuda, *Japan and the Japanese* (Tokyo: Kodansha, 1957).

34. Dore, "Introduction," xxxi.

35. Bernard Wysocki, Jr., "In Japan, Breaking Step Is Hard to Do," *Wall Street Journal,* 14 December 1987.

36. Masao Maruyama, *Thought in Japan* (Tokyo: Iwanami Shoten, 1961).

37. Wysocki, "In Japan."

38. Michael R. Sesit, "Japanese Executive Defies Convention in Preferring U.S. Management Style," *Wall Street Journal,* 26 July 1988.

39. See Robert B. Reich, *The Next American Frontier* (New York: Times Book, 1983), 108–9, 166, 259–60.

40. Kamata, 57.

41. Ronald Dore, *British Factory, Japanese Factory: The Origins of National Diversity in Industrial Relations* (Berkeley and Los Angeles: University of California Press, 1973).

42. See Yoichi Oyama, ed., *Labor and the Large Enterprise: A Study of the Toyota Motor Company* (Tokyo: Ochanomizu Shobo, 1985).

43. Reich, 259.

44. Kamata, 58–80.

45. Christopher Lasch, *The Culture of Narcissism: American Life in an Age of Diminishing Expectations* (New York: Warner Books, 1979), 108.

46. Susan Chira, "Motto for a New Breed: Less Work, More Play," *New York Times,* 25 January 1988.

47. Buraku Liberation Research Institute (Buraku-Kaiho Kenkyu-jo), *Buraku Problems, Materials, and Explanations* (Osaka, Japan: Liberation Publishing [Kaiho-Shuppan-Sha], 1988).

48. Susan Chira, "In Japan, the Land of the Rod, an Appeal to Spare the Child," *New York Times,* 27 July 1988.

49. Economic Planning Agency, *White Paper on Japanese National Life (Kokumin Seikatsu)* (Tokyo: Ministry of Finance, 1988), Figure II-1-26.

50. Susan Chira, "In Student Game Plan, College Is a Racquet," *New York Times,* 29 June 1988.

51. Economic Planning Agency, *White Paper on Japanese National Life,* Figure I-2-7.

52. Economic Planning Agency, *White Paper on Japanese National Life,* Figure I-2-4.

Chapter 5

1. Kamata, 5–31; also see Ronald Dore, *Japanese Factory, passim.*

2. See Richard Krooth, *The Great Homestead Strike of 1892* (Palo Alto, Calif.: Ramparts, 1990); Manchester, *passim.*

3. Kamata, *passim.*

4. Richard Krooth, *The Great Homestead Strike, passim;* Kamata, 57, 61; Dore, *British Factory, passim;* Yoichi Oyama, ed., *Labor and the Large Enterprise: A Study of the Toyota Motor Company* (Tokyo: Ochanomizu Shobo, 1985), chapters 4–6.

5. Kamata, 12–13.

6. Dore, "Introduction," xxxii.

7. Ohmae, *The Mind of the Strategist, passim;* Schein, 1–20; Kamata, 16, 22, 25, 26; Dore, *British Factory, Japanese Factory, passim.*

8. See Paul Lansing and Kathryn Ready, "Japanese Women and the Professions," *California Management Review* 30 (Spring 1988): 112–27.

9. Kamata, 28.

10. Kamata, 10–16.

11. Kamata, 48.

12. Reich, *The Next American Frontier,* 259; Kamata, *passim.*

13. Dore, "Introduction," xx–xxi.

14. See Oyama, chapters 4–6.

15. Kamata, 60.

16. Kamata, 9, 12, 31, 46, 60.

17. Kamata, 9.

18. Kamata, *passim.*

19. Richard Krooth, "The Nature of Labor in the Production Process: A Historical Account," in *The Dynamics of Enterprise in the American Milieu* (Berkeley, Calif.: CIM, 1988); Reich, 260.

20. Reich, 260.

21. *Japan Economic Institute,* cited by J. Ernest Beazley, in "In Spite of Mystique, Japanese Plants in U.S. Find Problems Abound," *Wall Street Journal,* 22 June 1988.

22. Beazley, "In Spite of Mystique."

23. See Jeffrey Broadbent, *Social Networks as Transmitters of Social Control in Local Japanese Politics,* a paper delivered at the 77th Annual Meeting of the American Sociological Association, San Francisco, 6–10 September 1982; Oyama, *passim;* Michihiko Noguchi, "Interview," Osaka City University, Osaka, Japan, 22 April 1988.

Part 3

1. Krooth, *Arms and Empire, passim;* Fusao Hayashi, *Pleading for the Great East Asian War* (Tokyo: Bungei Shunju, 1964); Fusao Hayashi, *A New Plea for the Great East Asian War* (Tokyo: Bungei Shunju, 1965).

2. Eshun Hamaguchi, *Rediscovering Japanese Uniqueness* (Tokyo: Yuhikaku, 1977).

3. Yasusuke Murakami et al., *'Le' Society as a Civilization* (Tokyo: University of Tokyo Press, 1979).

4. Yasusuke Murakami, *The Age of New Middle Masses* (Tokyo: University of Tokyo Press, 1984).

5. Masakazu Yamasaki, *The Birth of Soft Individualism* (Tokyo: Chuo-Koron-Sha, 1984).

6. Kokichi Shoji, "Rising Neonationalism in Contemporary Japan: Changing Social Consciousness of the Japanese People and Its Implications for World Society," unpublished paper, University of Tokyo, 1988.

7. Shigenobu Kishimoto, *Fantasy of the Middle* (Tokyo: Foreign Press

Center, 1978); Ezra F. Vogel, *Japan's New Middle Class* (Berkeley and Los Angeles: University of California Press, 1963).

Chapter 6

8. Ken'ichi Tominaga, ed., *Stratification Structure in Japan* (Tokyo: University of Tokyo Press, 1979).

9. Kamata, 19.

10. See Prue Dempster, *Japan Advances* (London: Methuen, 1967); Patric and Rosovsky, *passim;* Vogel, parts 2 and 4.

11. Kishimoto, *passim.*

12. Kishimoto, *passim.*

13. Krooth, *Japan,* 15; Lockwood, *passim.*

14. Krooth, *Japan,* 16.

15. Krooth, *Japan,* 16; S. Ogawa, "Banking in Japan," in H.W. Auburn, ed., *Comparative Banking,* 3d ed. (Dunstable, England: Waterlow and Sons, 1966), 105–9.

16. Ogawa, 105–9; U.N. Department of Economic and Social Affairs, *International Social Development Review, no. 1: Urbanization: Development Policies and Planning* (New York: United Nations, 1968), 10.

17. Krooth, *Japan,* 16; Ogawa, 105–9; "Supplement on Japan," *Times* (London), 22 November 1965; Foreign Capital Research Society, *Japanese Industry* (Tokyo: FCRS, 1965).

18. Krooth, *Japan,* 17; Ghate, 142; "Supplement on Japan," *Times* (London), 22 November 1965; The Foreign Capital Research Society, 18; G.C. Allen, *A Short History of Modern Japan* (New York: Praeger, 1963), 217, Table 26A.

19. Consultative Committee, *The Colombo Plan: Tenth Annual Report,* October–November 1961 (London: Her Majesty's Stationery Office, 1962), 193–94.

20. Herman Kahn, *The Emerging Japanese Superstate: Challenge and Response* (Englewood Cliff, N.J.: Prentice-Hall, 1970).

21. Krooth, *Japan,* 18.

22. Kahn, *passim.*

23. Krooth, *Japan,* 19.

24. Krooth, *Japan,* 20.

25. Krooth, *Japan,* 23.

26. Krooth, *Japan,* 23–24.

27. See Ministry of International Trade and Industry, *The Vision of MITI Policies in the 1980s* (Tokyo: MITI, 1980); Barry Meier, "Chemical Giants Are Turning to New Materials," *Wall Street Journal,* 24 June 1966; Marc Aaron Cohen, *The United States Fiber Optics Industry: Japanese Challenge, International Competitiveness, and Public Policy,* master's thesis, John F. Kennedy School of Government, Harvard University, microfiche, 1982; Calvin Sims, "Advances in Conductivity," *New York Times,* 21 January 1987; Jan Wong, et al., "Robots: Next Step for Garment Maker," *Wall Street Journal,* 7 August 1986.

28. See Japanese Ministry of International Trade and Industry, *The Vision of MITI Policies in the 1980s;* Richard Krooth, *High-Tech in Crisis: Decay as an Historical Dilemma* (Berkeley, Calif.: CIM, 1987); Bernard Wysocki, Jr., "Venture Capitalists: Japanese Start Buying U.S. Firms Stressing Latest in High Tech," *Wall Street Journal,* 8 August 1986; Nicholas D. Kristof, "Surge in the Yen Spurs Japanese to Invest in U.S.," *New York Times,* 9 August 1986.

29. Clyde Haberman, "Japan's 20,000 Unwelcome 'Guests,'" *New York Times,* 17 November 1987.

30. Foreign workers also faced poverty and the Yakuza, Japan's organized crime syndicate, which controlled the day-labor market in the construction industry. To mediate between the two forces, the day-labor union was mobilized by the Reverend Watanabe Hidetoshi of the United Church of Christ. His volunteer network to stop human rights abuses was directed to care for the immigrants. Yet, fear of deportation prevented the immigrants from going to the police for help if they were abused or defrauded. Some were sick, injured, or out of work. There were unconfirmed reports of foreign workers starving to death in Chiba Prefecture. One clam packer commended his Ghanian employee for his hard work and following orders, but his wife worried that: "He wants to send his money to his old parents. But what will he live on? What if he gets sick?" See, for example, Michael Shapiro, "In Japan, Tyson's Impact Is Powerful and Perplexing," *New York Times,* 9 March 1988.

31. Kathryn Graven, "Japan Isn't Ready for Illegal Aliens, But It Has 100,000," *Wall Street Journal,* 23 June 1988.

32. Leonard Koren, "Great Ideas of Eastern Man," *California,* March 1988, 56–57.

33. "If developing countries are not to be left further behind," said Overseas Development Council president John Sewell, "their national scientific and technical capacity must be increased. Currently, many of their products and processes are not suitable for industrial countries." He found that "many developing countries, already experiencing crippling unemployment, face a difficult choice: If the new labor-saving technologies are introduced, many fewer jobs will be created. But if the technologies are not used, their products will not be competitive in international markets."

The division of third world nations by tiers of usefulness or exploitation thus became likely. Sewell explained that "new technologies already are making some developing countries less attractive to foreign investors. As trained workers and sophisticated communication networks become more important than low-cost, unskilled labor, developing countries have less to offer the multinationals, which are important sources of capital and technology. These new technologies mean that existing barriers to entry into world-class industry are becoming higher. Third world countries that are already more advanced will benefit most from further technological advances, while others — the vast majority — will be perhaps permanently disadvantaged by the scale and pace of industrial change." With tremendous financial resources and advanced technologies, Japan was particularly well suited to determine which third world nations fit into its global scheme. **See,** for example, John W. Sewell, "The Development Gap," *New York Times,* 22 May 1988.

34. Krooth, *Arms and Empire,* 14.

35. Krooth, *High-Tech in Crisis, passim;* Kiyohiko Fukushima, *Memo on the Transfer of Technology from Japan to the Less Developed Countries* (Tokyo: Nomura Research Institute, 30 April 1988); Kristoff, "Surge in the Yen," *passim;* Lewis H. Young, "The Corporate Links Abroad," *New York Times,* 6 August 1986.

36. Compare Krooth, *High-Tech in Crisis;* and Eleanor M. Hadley, *Japan's Export Competitiveness in Third World Markets* (Washington, D.C.: Georgetown University Center for Stratetic and International Studies, 1981).

37. Compare Krooth, *High-Tech in Crisis;* and Organization of Economic Cooperation and Development, *International Investment and Multinational Enterprise: Supporting Documents* (Paris: OECD, 1980, 1981, 1985, 1986).

38. Kamata, 9, 18, 28ff.

39. Masayoshi Kanabayashi, "More Time Off, Not Wages, Emphasized in Japan's Labor Bargaining This Year," *Wall Street Journal,* 23 February 1988.

40. Compare Organization of Economic Cooperation and Development, *International Investment and Multinational Enterprise;* and Bureau of Industry Analysis, Department of Commerce, *Survey of Current Business* (January 1981, December 1981, *et seq.*).

41. Peter F. Drucker, "Beyond the Japanese Export Boom," *Wall Street Journal,* 7 January 1987.

42. Henry F. Meyers, "Will Mergers Help or Hurt in the Long Run?" *Wall Street Journal,* 2 May 1988.

43. Krooth, *High-Tech in Crisis, passim.*

44. Louise Uchitelle, "Overseas Spending by U.S. Companies Sets Record Pace," *New York Times,* 20 May 1988.

45. Drucker, "Beyond the Japanese Export Boom."

46. Clyde Haberman, "American Lawyers Land on Their Feet in Tokyo," *New York Times,* 22 May 1988.

47. Finance Ministry, *Direct Japanese Investments, Fiscal Year 1988* (Tokyo: Finance Ministry, 31 May 1988).

Chapter 7

1. "Japanese Widen U.S. Merger Role," *New York Times,* 28 July 1988.

2. Economic Planning Agency, *White Paper on Japanese Economy,* 1988, Table I-2-15.

3. Small and Medium Enterprises Agency, *White Paper on Small and Medium Enterprises,* 1988, Figure 2-1-26.

4. Small and Medium Enterprises Agency, *White Paper on Small and Medium Enterprises,* 1988, Figure 2-1-25.

5. Economic Planning Agency, *White Paper on Japanese Economy,* 1988, Table I-2-17.

Chapter 8

1. William M. Burkeley, "Frontiers of Science," *Wall Street Journal,* 10 November 1986.

2. See Peter Drucker, "A Crisis of Capitalism," *Wall Street Journal,* 30 September 1986.

3. Yoshi Tsurumi, "Forum: Explaining the 'Japanese Paradox,'" *New York Times,* 16 November 1986.

4. See Jean-Jacques Servan-Schreiber, *The American Challenge* (New York: Antheneum, 1976); George Guilder, "The New American Challenge," *Wall Street Journal,* 3 November 1986.

5. Krooth, High-Tech in Crisis, *passim.*

6. National Science Foundation, *Statistical Resources* (Washington, D.C.: N.S.F. Research Department, 1986).

7. Seth H. Lubove, "The Old College Tie," *Wall Street Journal,* 10 November 1988.

8. Lubove, "The Old College Tie."

9. Burkeley, "Frontiers of Science."

10. Barnaby J. Feder, "Technology," *New York Times,* 12 June 1986.

11. Meier, "Chemical Giants Are Turning to Raw Materials."

12. Brenton R. Schlender, "Unpopular Science," *Wall Street Journal,* 10 November 1986; Lester C. Thurow, "A Briefing for the Next President," *New York Times,* 21 August 1988.

13. Wong, et al., "Robots: The Next Step."

14. Richard Krooth, *Empire: A Bicentennial Appraisal* (Santa Barbara, Calif.: Harvest, 1975).

15. United Technologies, "High Tech, High Trade," *New York Times,* 5 November 1986.

16. Leonard Silk, "Economic Scene," *New York Times,* 12 November 1986.

17. Bernard Wysocki, Jr., "Venture Capitalists," *Wall Street Journal,* 8 August 1986; Akio Morita and Shintaro Ishihara, *Japan That Can Say No* (Tokyo: Kobunsha, 1989).

Chapter 9

1. Krooth, *Bicentennial Appraisal, passim.*

2. See Thornstein Veblen, *The Theory of Business Enterprise* (New York: New World Library, 1952); Peter T. Kilborn, "Treasury Official Assails 'Inefficient' Big Business," *New York Times,* 7 November 1986.

3. See Tsurumi, "Forum"; Clyde Farnsworth, "Washington Watch," *New York Times,* 18 November 1986; Cynthia F. Mitchell, "Coming Home," *Wall Street Journal,* 14 November 1986; Lewis H. Young, "Economic Scene," *New York Times,* 6 August 1986.

4. Richard Krooth, "Tour of Freemont Plant," Freemont, Calif., April 1987.

5. Robert C. Christopher, "Don't Blame the Japanese," *New York Times Magazine,* 19 October 1986; Douglas R. Sease, "Yen's Rise Said to Spur Japanese Dumping," *Wall Street Journal,* 6 October 1986.

6. Sease, "Yen's Rise"; Clifford M. Hardin, "Trade War Follies," *New York Times,* 21 August 1986.

7. This is why the *locale* of production, sale, and accumulation is a great concern of academic economists, and its contours and social dimensions are increasingly the object of sociological investigations. These investigators have said that America's social dilemma is that jobs are lost due to: U.S. capital invested abroad in search of lower costs; the unrestricted drive to apply U.S. technology to displace labor; the diversity of locating production near markets, extending the possibilities for multiprice listings to gain sales advantage, and thereby maximum profits. Most academic researchers also point to the combined effects of capital exports on production, employment and wage levels at home, some arguing they are unavoidably decreased in basic industries, others that this displacement will be offset by the emergence of new technological industries. See Christopher, "Don't Blame the Japanese"; and David Halberstram, *The Reckoning* (New York: William Morrow, 1986).

8. John B. Schnapp, "Shock Waves from Korea Reach Northwood, Ohio," *Wall Street Journal,* 13 November 1986.

9. Schnapp, "Shock Waves"; Tsurumi, "Forum"; Peter H. Lewis, "Satellites Let Executives Be Two (or More) Places at Once," *New York Times,* 10 December 1986.

10. Quick, Finan, and Associates, Inc., *The U.S. Trade Position in High Technology: 1980–1986,* a Report Prepared for the Joint Economic Committee of the United States Congress, Washington, D.C., October 1986.

11. Economic Planning Agency, *White Paper on Japanese Economy,* 1988, Table I-2-17.

12. Cynthia J. Mitchell, "Coming Home," *Wall Street Journal,* 14 October 1986.

13. Bernard Wysocki, Jr., "Venture Capitalists," *Wall Street Journal,*

8 August 1986; Nicholas Kristof, "Surge in Yen Spurs Japanese to Invest in U.S.," *New York Times,* 9 August 1986.

14. Timothy Egan, "Japanese Plunge into U.S. Realty," *New York Times,* 23 November 1986.

15. James Sterngold, "Dollar Plummets to Postwar Low Against the Yen," *New York Times,* 18 March 1986.

16. Tsurumi, "Forum."

17. Quick et al., *The U.S. Trade Position, passim.*

18. Robert B. Reich, "Making a Rust Bowl of Silicon Valley," *New York Times,* 12 October 1986; Andrew Pollack, "A Sober Silicon Valley Is 'Changed Forever,'" *New York Times,* 5 October 1986; Kristof, "Surge in the Yen."

19. "Fujitsu to Buy U.S. Chip Unit," *New York Times,* 24 October 1986; Brenton R. Schlender, "Schlumberger Ltd., Fujitsu to Merge U.S. Chip Units," *Wall Street Journal,* 24 October 1986, and "U.S. Chip Makers See New Japan Threat," *Wall Street Journal,* 27 October 1986.

20. United Technologies, "High Tech, High Trade."

Chapter 10

1. David E. Sanger, "Japan Yields to U.S. on Chips," *New York Times,* 31 November 1986.

2. Michael W. Miller, "Korean Focusing on Personal Computers: Nation Is Challenging Japan in U.S. Market," *Wall Street Journal,* 6 November 1986.

3. Art Pine and Peter Waldman, "Japan to Press Its Chip Makers to Hew to Pact," *Wall Street Journal,* 19 November 1986.

4. Art Pine, "U.S. May End Microchips Pact with Japan," *Wall Street Journal,* 13 November 1986.

5. Sanger, "Japan Yields to U.S. on Chips."

6. See Art Pine, "U.S. Considers Challenging the Merger of Schlumberger and Fujitsu Chip Units," *Wall Street Journal,* 31 October 1986; "Fujitsu to Buy U.S. Chip Unit," *New York Times,* 24 October 1986; Schlender, "Schlumberger Ltd."

7. Schlender, "Schlumberger Ltd."

8. John Diebold, "A New Track to High-Tech Growth," *New York Times,* 2 November 1986.

9. Laurie P. Cohen, "Companies Rush to Sell Their Properties Because of Tax Law, Japanese Interests," *Wall Street Journal,* 6 November 1986.

10. Cohen, "Companies Rush to Sell Their Properties."

Chapter 11

1. Stephen Kreider Yoder, "Japanese Banks on Cooled Computer Circuits," *Wall Street Journal,* 22 October 1986.

2. Yoder, "Japanese Banks."

3. Sanger, "Japan Yields to the U.S."

4. Yoder, "Japanese Banks."

5. Yoder, "Japanese Banks."

6. Barnaby J. Feder, "The Computer as Deal Maker," *New York Times,* 14 August 1986; **also see** "A Special Report: Technology in the Workplace," *Wall Street Journal,* 10 November 1986; Marshall Schuon, "Automation That's Flexible," *New York Times,* 2 October 1986; Alan Bayless, "Technology Reshapes North America's Lumber Plants," *Wall Street Journal,* 16 October 1986.

7. Stephen Kreider Yoder, "Automating Software," *Wall Street Journal,* 10 November 1986.

8. Yoder, "Automating Software"; Stephen Kreider Yoder, "Hitachi, Fujitsu Link in Microprocessors," *Wall Street Journal,* 28 October 1986.

Chapter 12

1. Quick et al., *The U.S. Trade Position,* 2.

2. Quick et al., *The U.S. Trade Position,* 4.

3. Quick et al., *The U.S. Trade Position,* 13.

4. Quick et al., *The U.S. Trade Position,* 11, 32.

5. Quick et al., *The U.S. Trade Position,* 17.

Chapter 13

1. "Cowboys and Japanese," *New York Times,* 8 March 1988.

2. Quick et al., *The U.S. Trade Position,* 33–35.

3. Lawrence M. Fisher, "Seagate Trips, Industry Cringes," *New York Times,* 23 August 1988.

4. Quick et al., *The U.S. Trade Position,* 51 fn.

5. Theodore P. Perros, "U.S. Heads Down the Road to Scientific Dotage," letter to the editor, *New York Times,* 8 December 1986.

6. Reuters (Tokyo), 24 May 1988.

7. "Capital Inflows Called Helpful," *New York Times,* 25 May 1988.

8. Daniel Patrick Moynihan, "Debunking the Myth of Decline," *New York Times Magazine,* 19 June 1988.

9. Krooth, *Empire: A Bicentennial Appraisal,* 13.

10. Secretary of Labor's Task Force on Economic Adjustment and Worker Dislocation, *Economic Adjustment and Worker Dislocation in a Competitive Society* (Washington, D.C.: U.S. Department of Labor, 1986), 3.

11. Ken Slocum, "The Sun Belt Gains Manufacturing Jobs as Nation Loses Them," *Wall Street Journal,* 1 April 1988.

12. Ralph E. Winter and Gregory Stricharchuk, "Weaker Dollar Saves Many Small Concerns from Imminent Death," *Wall Street Journal,* 25 July 1988.

13. Susan Chira, "A New Pride Changes Japan's View of the U.S.," *New York Times,* 30 June 1988; Morita and Ishihara, *passim.*

14. Chira, "A New Pride," *passim.*

15. Lawrence H. Summers, "Good News on the Trade Deficit, But," *New York Times,* 20 May 1988.

16. Peter T. Kilborn, "Key U.S. Shift Seen to Job Protection from Free Trade," *New York Times,* 29 April 1988.

17. Kilborn, "Key U.S. Shift Seen."

18. Leonard Silk, "Economic Scene," *New York Times,* 3 December 1986.

19. Salomon Brothers, cited in *New York Times,* 27 July 1988.

20. Sarah Bartlett, "Big Banks Shift from 3rd World," *New York Times,* 27 July 1988.

21. Robert E. Taylor, "Greenspan Notes Pressure on Banks to Increase Rates," *Wall Street Journal,* 13 May 1988.

22. R. Dan Brumbaugh, Jr., and Robert E. Litan, "The Banks Are in Big Trouble, Too," *New York Times,* 21 August 1988. Calculated with assistance from the Financial Institutions Group at Drexal Burnham Lambert Inc.

23. Michael R. Sesit, "U.S. Is Urged to Take Action Against Deficit," *Wall Street Journal,* 7 June 1988.

24. *Acquisitions Monthly,* cited in *New York Times,* 11 July 1988.

25. Steve Lohr, "Wall Street Rethinks Its Global Plans," *New York Times,* 11 July 1988.

26. Franklin D. Roosevelt, "Anti-Inflationary Order," *New York Times,* 9 April 1943.

Chapter 14

1. Damon Darlin, "Japan Firmly Resists U.S. Pressure on Rice," *Wall Street Journal,* 12 November 1986.

2. Masayoshi Kanabayashi, "Japan's Biggest Steel Companies Swing to Losses," *Wall Street Journal,* 12 November 1986.

3. Bernard Wysocki, Jr., "Japanese Are Suffering Unemployment Rise in a Shifting Economy," *Wall Street Journal,* 6 November 1986.

4. Sanger, "Japan Yields to the U.S."

5. Sanger, "Japan Yields to the U.S."

6. Susan Chira, "Fujitsu, a Match for IBM, Making Further Inroads in U.S., *New York Times,* 3 November 1986; Yoder, "Hitachi, Fujitsu Linᴵ⁻ in Microprocessors."

7. Silk, "Economic Scene."

8. "Software Group Picks Site," *New York Times,* 23 August 1988.

9. John Marrkoff, "IBM and a University Plan Swift File Network," *New York Times,* 23 August 1988.

10. See Ramchandran Jaikumar, "Postindustrial Manufacturing," *Harvard Business Review* 6 (November-December, 1986): 69–76; Chira, "Fujitsu, a Match for IBM"; Schuon, "Automation That's Flexible."

Chapter 15

1. Albert Scardino, "Deal Maker Thriving on U.S.-Japan Gap," *New York Times,* 6 June 1988.

2. Kenichi Ohmae, *Beyond National Borders* (Tokyo: McKinsey and Co., 1985).

3. Damon Darlin, "'American Train' Will Toot Its Way Through Japan, Hawking U.S. Goods," *Wall Street Journal,* 9 June 1988.

4. "All Aboard the American Train!" *Wall Street Journal,* 30 June 1988.

5. MITI, *Estimated Trade Figures, Fiscal Year Report, 1988*-1989 (Tokyo: MITI, 1988), fax edition.

6. Jeremy Mark, "Narrowing of Japanese Trade Surplus Accelerates as Import Boom Continues," *Wall Street Journal,* 10 June 1988.

7. Marshall Robinson, "Household Debt," *New York Times Magazine: Business World,* 12 June 1988, 8, 12.

8. Ministry of International Trade and Industry, *White Paper on International Trade* (Tokyo: MITI, Trade and Policy Bureau, 1988).

9. Robert D. Hershey, Jr., "Foreign Stake in U.S. Rose to Record in '87," *New York Times,* 1 July 1988.

10. "From Superrich to Superpower," *Time,* 4 July 1988, 28.

11. Hershey, "Foreign Stake in U.S."

12. "Europe in New Japan Inquiry," *New York Times,* 4 June 1988.

13. Paul R. Sullivan, "Strategies for Playing the Global Game," *New York Times,* 26 June 1988.

14. "From Superrich to Superpower," 29.

15. "Japan Trade Surplus Cut," *New York Times,* 6 June 1988.

16. Clyde V. Prestowitz, Jr., *Trading Places: How We Allowed Japan to Take the Lead* (New York: Basic Books, 1988); *Corporate Focus: Are We Giving Our Economic Future to Japan?* A paper presented to the World Affairs Council and the Japanese Society of Northern California, San Francisco, Calif., 23 June 1988.

17. Sullivan, "Strategies for Playing the Global Game."

18. "Japan Rejects U.S. Chip Plea," *New York Times,* 17 June 1988.

19. William Celis et al., "Pressure Builds to Seek More Sanctions Against Japan After Chip Talks Collapse," *Wall Street Journal,* 6 November 1988.

20. "Electronics Industry Talks," *New York Times,* 8 June 1988.

Chapter 16

1. Quoted in "Foreign Criticism of U.S. Trade Bill Rejected by Yeuter," *Wall Street Journal,* 11 August 1988.

2. *Foreign Affairs,* June 1988.

3. Quoted in Walter S. Mossberg and John Walcott, "U.S. Redefines Policy on Security to Place Less Stress on Soviets," *Wall Street Journal,* 11 August 1988.

4. See Ellen L. Frost, *For Richer, for Poorer: The New U.S.-Japan Relationship* (Washington, D.C.: Council on Foreign Relations, 1987).

5. Krooth, *Arms and Empire, passim.*

6. See Benjamin Duke, *The Japanese School* (New York: Greenwood Press, 1986).

7. See Boye De Mente, *Made in Japan: The Methods, Motivations, and Culture of the Japanese, and Their Influence on U.S. Business and All Americans* (Washington, D.C.: National Textbook, 1987).

8. See Prestowitz, *Trading Places, passim.*

9. See Edward T. Hall and Mildred Reed Hall, *Hidden Differences: Doing Business with the Japanese* (New York: Anchor Press/Doubleday, 1987).

10. Nakayama, 52.

11. For a purely cultural interpretation, see John Condon and Keisuke Kurata, *In Search of What's Japanese About Japan* (Tokyo: Tuttle, 1974); John C. Condon, *With Respect to the Japanese: A Guide for Americans* (Yarmouth, Maine: Intercultural Press, 1988).

12. See Hall and Hall, *passim.*

13. Krooth, *Empire: A Bicentennial Appraisal,* 3.

14. Marcus W. Brauchli, "Japan May Face Some Pressure to Raise Rates," *Wall Street Journal,* 11 August 1988.

15. Wyatt Co. H.K., *Ranking 191 Equity-Unit Funds, 1983–87* (Hong Kong: Hong Kong Unit Trust Association, 1988), fax edition.

16. John Valentine, "Platinum Soars on Japanese Demand, Followed by Increases in Gold, Silver," *Wall Street Journal,* 1 June 1988.

17. George Milling-Stanley, *Annual Gold Review* (London: Consolidated Gold Fields PLC, May 1988).

18. Kathryn Graven, "Stock Market May Help Japanese Banks Meet International Capital Standards," *Wall Street Journal,* 14 June 1988.

19. David E. Sanger, "Insider Trading: A Japan Tradition," *New York Times,* 10 August 1988.

20. "Japan Dealers Consider New Insider-Trading Rules," *Wall Street Journal,* 2 June 1988.

21. *Asahi Shinbun* (Tokyo), 6 and 23 July 1988.

22. Urban C. Lehner and Masayoshi Kanabayashi, "Japanese Aides Tied to Scandal on Stock Sales," *Wall Street Journal,* 7 July 1988.

23. Steven R. Weisman, "Takeshita Resigns as Japan's Premier Over Gift Scandal," *New York Times,* 25 April 1989.

24. Susan Chira, "Japan 'Money Politics' Rears Its Head," *New York Times,* 8 August 1988.

25. Thomas E. Ricks, "Foreign Brokerages Appear Frequently in Insider-Trading Reports, Study Says," *Wall Street Journal,* 6 June 1988.

26. Clyde H. Farnsworth, "U.S. and Japan Ponder a Free Trade Proposal," *New York Times,* 12 August 1988.

27. Clyde H. Farnsworth, "Gain Seen in U.S.–Japan Farm Talks," *New York Times,* 18 June 1988.

28. Monica Langley, "America First: Protectionist Attitudes Grow Stronger in Spite of Healthy Economy," *Wall Street Journal,* 16 May 1988.

29. Farnsworth, "U.S. and Japan."

30. Ernest H. Preeg, "Next, a Free-Trade Pact with Japan?" *Wall Street Journal,* 12 August 1988.

31. Langley, "America First."

32. Clyde H. Farnsworth, "The Industrialized World Shows Its Love for the Farm," *New York Times,* 26 June 1988.

33. James Bovard, "Farm Subsidies Stifle Agriculture," *New York Times,* 29 May 1988.

34. Farnsworth, "Gain Seen in U.S.–Japan Farm Talks."

35. William Robbins, "A Meatpacker Cartel Up Ahead?" *New York Times,* 29 May 1988.

36. Marj Charlier, "IBP Wants Cattlemen to 'Do Something' About Contracts with Rival Meatpackers," *Wall Street Journal,* 26 July 1988.

37. Marj Charlier, "Few U.S. Producers See Early Gains from U.S.–Japan Pact on Beef, Citrus," *Wall Street Journal,* 21 June 1988.

38. "Beef Market in Japan Cited," *New York Times,* 26 May 1988.

39. "U.S. Cautions Japan on Delay of Import Issue," *Wall Street Journal,* 19 May 1988.

40. John T. Norman, "U.S. Study Ordered of Japanese Curbs on Orange Imports," *Wall Street Journal,* 25 May 1988.

41. Krooth, *Japan,* 12; also see Patrick and Rosovsky, *passim.*

42. "U.S. Cautions Japan," *Wall Street Journal,* 19 May 1988.

43. Koichi Kato, "Making Internationalists Out of Domestic Politicians," *Wall Street Journal,* 16 May 1988.

44. "U.S. Cautions Japan," *Wall Street Journal,* 19 May 1988.

45. Damon Darlin, "U.S., Japan Are Said to Reach an Accord on Tokyo's Imports of Some Farm Goods," *Wall Street Journal,* 6 January 1988.

46. "Japan Is Firm on Rice Ban," *New York Times,* 23 February 1988.

47. "Japanese Plan Less U.S. Grain," *New York Times,* 12 January 1988.

48. Farnsworth, "Gain Seen in U.S.–Japan Farm Talks."

49. Charlier, "Few U.S. Producers See Early Gains."

50. Susan Chira, "U.S. and Japan Clear a Trade Hurdle," *New York Times,* 21 June 1988; Gary Klott, "A Doubling of Some Exports Is Seen," *New York Times,* 21 June 1988.

Chapter 17

1. Prime Minister's Select Panel, *Maekawa Report: Five Year Economic Plan, 1988–1992 (Summary of Economic Problems and Their Planned Resolution)* (Tokyo: Economic Planning Agency), fax edition, 23 May 1988.

2. Economic Planning Agency, *White Paper on Japanese National Life,* 1988, figure I-2-9.

3. Economic Planning Agency, *White Paper on Japanese National Life,* 1988, figure I-2-10.

4. Susan Chira, "Takeshita Stakes Prestige on Tax Plan," *New York Times,* 30 July 1988.

5. Susan Chira, "The New Effort in Japan to ChangeTax System," *New York Times,* 15 June 1988.

6. Former Finance and Trade Minister Watanabe also explained this as racially determined: "among those guys over there are so many blacks and so on, who would think nonchalantly: 'We're bankrupt, but starting tomorrow we don't have to pay anything back. We just can't use credit cards any more.'" See *Nihon Keizai Shinbun* (Tokyo), 24 July 1988.

7. Using a complex logic that neglected to focus on *how* Japanese consumers actually accumulated their savings, McKinsey and Co.'s managing director, Kenichi Ohmae, calculated that from 1981 to 1985, the Japanese savings rate measured on a financial asset base was about 14.4 percent compared with the U.S. rate of 19.6 percent. The Bank of Japan updated these figures for mid-1988 to a Japanese savings rate of 16.7 percent (due to appreciation in Tokyo stock prices, etc.) and a U.S. savings rate of 14.7 percent. See Kenichi Ohmae, "Americans and Japanese Save about the Same," *Wall Street Journal,* 14 June 1988.

8. Clyde McAvoy, "Making an Honest Dollar in Japan," *Wall Street Journal,* 13 June 1988.

9. "Tokyo Lifts Stock Margins," *New York Times,* 3 June 1988; "Tokyo Stock Exchange Lifts Margin Rule to 70%," *Wall Street Journal,* 3 June 1988.

10. Economic Planning Agency, *Preliminary Quarterly Report, 1988* (Tokyo: EPA, June 1988), fax edition.

11. Computed from "Sumitomo and Nissho Iwai Post Profit Gains for Year," *Wall Street Journal,* 16 June 1988.

12. Through continual upgrade of its industrial technology, by 1987 the average age of Japan's industrial base was already ten years compared with the U.S. average of seventeen years. See, for example, Farnsworth, "Gain Seen in U.S.–Japan Farm Talks."

13. Kenneth H. Bacon, "Rebuilding America: Start at the Factory," *Wall Street Jorunal,* 16 May 1988.

14. "Saturday Closings Planned," *Wall Street Journal,* 1 June 1988.

15. MITI, *Preliminary Report of the Semi-Annual Meeting of Leading Companies, Fiscal Year March 31, 1988* (Tokyo: MITI, 1988), fax edition.

16. Prime Minister's Select Panel, *Maekawa Report.*

17. Karl August Wittfogel, *History of Chinese Society* (New York: Macmillan, 1949); *Oriental Despotism* (New Haven, Conn.: Yale University Press, 1957).

18. Stephen Kreider Yoder, "Like Noah of Old, Japanese Consider Building Some Arks," *Wall Street Journal,* 25 May 1988.

19. "Japan Asks End to Builder Ban," *New York Times,* 27 May 1988.

20. "Japan Asks End to Builder Ban," *New York Times,* 27 May 1988.

21. Japan Central Bank, *Quarterly Survey and Diffusion Index of 7,635 Companies* (Tokyo: JCB, June 1988), fax edition.

Notes—Chapter 18, Chapter 19 273

22. Bank for International Settlements, *Annual Report* (Basel: BIS, June 1988).

23. McAvoy, "Making an Honest Dollar in Japan."

24. Masayoshi Kanabayashi, "Foreign Investment in Japan Is Growing, Helped by Nation's Economic Expansion," *Wall Street Journal,* 14 June 1988.

Chapter 18

1. Quoted in Walter S. Mossberg and John Walcott, "U.S. Redefines Policy on Security to Place Less Stress on Soviets," *Wall Street Journal,* 11 August 1988.

2. Quoted in Mossberg and Walcott, "U.S. Redefines Policy."

3. Congressional Economic Leadership Institute, *Choate Report on Foreign Direct Investment* (Washington, D.C.: Congressional Research Institute, 27 July 1988); International Monetary Fund. Cited in Mossberg and Walcott, "U.S. Redefines Policy."

4. Krooth, *Japan,* 31–32.

5. U.S. Department of State, *The Nixon Doctrine* (Washington, D.C.: State Department, December 1971).

6. John H. Cushman, Jr., "Moving Plutonium by Sea Is Assailed," *New York Times,* 6 August 1988.

7. Clyde Haberman, "Shinto Back on the National State," *New York Times,* 7 June 1988.

8. Krooth, *Japan,* 25.

9. Krooth, *Japan,* 26–27.

10. Chong-Pin Lin, "China: Nuclear Wild Card," *New York Times,* 29 July 1988.

11. Krooth, *Japan,* 26–27.

12. Susan Chira, "Japan Is Entering Talks in a Position of Strength," *New York Times,* 18 June 1988.

13. Clyde Haberman, "Carlucci Seeks Aid on Bases in Japan," *New York Times,* 7 June 1988.

14. Organization for Economic Cooperation and Development, Official Government Aid Figures (Paris: O.E.C.D., June 1988).

15. Gregory Tarpinian, "U.S. Outdoes British Empire in Troops Abroad," letter to the editor, *New York Times,* 14 June 1988.

16. "From Superrich to Superpower," *Time,* 4 July 1988, 31.

17. "From Superrich to Superpower," *Time,* 4 July 1988, 31.

18. "From Superrich to Superpower," *Time,* 4 July 1988, 31.

19. Elaine Sciolino, "Some Kind Words in Asia Do Not Dispel a Sense of Waning U.S. Influence," *New York Times,* 24 July 1988.

20. Michael R. Sesit, "U.S. Is Urged to Take Action Against Deficit," *Wall Street Journal,* 7 June 1988.

21. "Japan Cabinet Sets $50 Billion of Foreign Aid," *Wall Street Journal,* 14 June 1988.

22. Joel Brinkley, "Japanese Official in Visit to Israel," *New York Times,* 27 June 1988.

23. "Japan Vows Aid to Asia," *New York Times,* 4 July 1988.

Chapter 19

1. Karel van Wolferen, *The Enigma of Japanese Power: People and Politics in a Stateless Nation* (New York: Knopf, 1989).

2. Steven R. Weisman, "Infighting Paralyzes Japan's Quest for New Leader," *New York Times,* 18 May 1989.

3. Susan Chira, "Shakespeare Plays the Globe Theater, in Tokyo," *New York Times,* 31 May 1988.

4. van Wolferen, *passim.*

5. Peter T. Kilborn, "Japan Asserts American-Style Clout in Toronto," *New York Times,* 20 June 1988.

6. Krooth, *Japan,* 24.

7. This favoring of Japan's nationals was done in the name of providing a stable environment for private international investments. Only on 26 February 1982 did Japan's Ministry of Foreign Affairs and the U.S. Department of State finally agree that, if a Japanese company wholly owned a U.S. corporation, it was not a "Japanese company" under the FCN Treaty and thus was not protected by the treaty in allowing discriminatory employment in the U.S. The same year, the U.S. Supreme Court affirmed this judgment, so that Japanese firms could no longer arbitrarily employ executive and managerial personnel "of their choice" in violation of the 1964 U.S. Civil Rights Act (Title VII). Discrimination nonetheless continued in the name of the Supreme Court's dicta that U.S. nationals would not be on an equal footing if they could not speak Japanese and were not familiar with the culture, customs, and business practices of that country. Yet in two subsequent lawsuits, involving C. Itoh Co. and Sumitomo Shoji, the requirement of equal employment practices for managerial level employees was reaffirmed. **See** Hiroshi Kashiwagi, *Employment Discrimination at Japanese Firms in America: A Case Study of EEOC Lawsuits,* Working Paper No. 4 (Berkeley, Calif.: Japan Pacific Resource Network, April 1988).

8. Tomoji Ishi, *Japanese Automobile and Television Assembly Plants and Local Communities: County Demographic Correlates* (Berkeley, Calif.: Japan Pacific Resource Network, 1988).

9. "U.S. Auto Jobs: The Problem Is Bigger Than Japanese Imports," *UAW Research Bulletin* (June 1986); U.S. General Accounting Office, *Foreign Investment: Growing Japanese Presence in the U.S. Auto Industry* (Washington, D.C.: GAO/NSIAD, March 1988).

10. See Jay Stowsky, *The Weakest Link: Semiconductor Production Equipment, Linkages, and the Limits of International Trade* (Berkeley, Calif.: Berkeley Roundtable on the International Economy, Working Paper no. 27); Akihiro Yoshikawa, *The Japanese Challenge in Biotechnology: Industrial Policy* (Berkeley, Calif.: Berkeley Roundtable on the International Economy, Working Paper no. 29).

11. Chalmers Johnson, *MITI, MPT, and the Telecom Wars: How Japan Makes Policy for High Technology* (Berkeley, Calif.: Berkeley Roundtable on the International Economy, Working Paper no. 21).

12. Francois Bar and Michael Borrus, *From Public Access to Private Connections: Network Policy and National Advantage.* (Berkeley, Calif.: Berkeley Roundtable on the International Economy, Working Paper no. 28).

13. Robert Schildgen, *Toyohiko Kagawa: Apostle of Love and Social Justice* (Berkeley, Calif.: Centenary Books, 1988).

14. *Remembering the Bomb,* a documentary broadcast on KQED, San Francisco, 5 April 1988; *Black Rain,* a documentary directed by Shohei Imamura, based on the novel by Masuji Ibuse, 1969.

15. *Hellfire, a Journey from Hiroshima,* a film documentary broadcast on KQED, San Francisco, 4 August 1988.

16. F. Sionil Jose, "After Hiroshima, the Second Coming," *New York Times,* 6 August 1988.

17. "No More Hibakusha," *The Co-Op News* (Berkeley, California), 20 July 1988.

18. James M. Markham, "NATO Compromise Seems to Rule Out Tactical Arms Ban," *New York Times,* 31 May 1989; "Bill Apologizing to War Interns Goes to Reagan," *New York Times,* 5 August 1988.

19. Stephen J. Solarz, "Foes of Aegis Sale to Japan Miss the Boat," *Wall Street Journal,* 1 August 1988.

20. "Three Japanese Executives Charged in Illegal Exports," *Wall Street Journal,* 18 May 1988.

21. David E. Sanger, "Japanese Ask Which Side Navy Is On," *New York Times,* 30 July 1988.

22. Robert W. Northup, "Okinawa Is an Island That Lost Its Culture," letter to the editor, *New York Times,* 13 May 1989.

23. David E. Sanger, "U.S.–Japan Ties Worsen on News That Warhead Was Lost in 1965," *New York Times,* 9 May 1989; David E. Sanger, "U.S. Says the Bomb Lost Close to Japan Scattered Radiation," *New York Times,* 16 May 1989.

24. Yumiko Sato, "Japanese Mother Makes an Antinuclear Plea," Letter, *New York Times,* 12 August 1988.

25. Solarz, "Foes of Aegis Sale," *passim.*

26. "Senate Clears Way for Japan to Buy Anti-Missile Systems," *Wall Street Journal,* 8 August 1988.

27. Solarz, "Foes of Aegis Sale," *passim.*

28. "U.S., Japan Sign Pact on Patents, Resolving Sensitive Technology," *Wall Street Journal,* 18 April 1988.

29. Solarz, "Foes of Aegis Sale."

30. **See** David E. Sanger, "Utilities in Japan to Shun Uranium from South Africa," *New York Times,* 2 November 1988.

31. John H. Cushman, Jr., "New Rules on Atomic Fuel to Japan," *New York Times,* 3 June 1988.

32. Sanger, "Utilities in Japan to Shun Uranium."

33. Sato, "Japanese Mother Makes an Antinuclear Plea."

34. Charles R. Morris, *Iron Destinies, Lost Opportunities: The Arms Race Between the U.S.A. and the U.S.S.R., 1945–1987* (New York: Bessie Book/Harper & Row, 1988).

35. See Ruth Leger Sivard, *World Military and Social Expenditures, 1985* (Washington, D.C.: World Priorities, 1985); U.S. Arms Control and Disarmament Agency, *World Military Expenditures and Arms Transfers, 1985* (Washington, D.C.: ACDA Publication 123, August 1985); Leonard Silk, "The New Guns-and-Butter Battle," *New York Times,* 22 May 1988.

36. Silk, "The New Guns"; Serge Schmemann, "Germany's President Upholds Country's Assertive Stance," *New York Times,* 25 May 1989.

37. "More to Toshiba Affair Than Meets the Eye," *JPRN Bulletin 6,* no. 2 (Winter 1987): 1, 6.

38. Steven R. Weisman, "Japanese Say Bush Plan to Revise Pact on Jet Leaves 'Serious Scar,'" *New York Times,* 28 March 1989.

39. "The Pentagon Handout to Japan," *New York Times,* 12 February 1989.

40. David E. Sanger, "Japan to Let Contract on Disputed Jet Project," *New York Times,* 30 March 19898.

41. Steven R. Weisman, "Reaction in Japan Mixed on Jet Deal," *New York Times,* 30 April 1989.

42. "U.S.–Japanese Deal on Fighter," *New York times,* 31 May 1988; "Japan to Lead Plane Project," *New York Times,* 4 June 1988.

43. Clyde H. Farnworth, "Japan Deal Questioned by G.A.O.," *New York Times,* 3 May 1989.

44. Thomas C. Hayes, "FSX: Icing on the Cake for General Dynamics," *New York Times,* 2 May 1989.

45. Hayes, "FSX: Icing on the Cake."

46. Farnsworth, "Japan Deal Questioned by G.A.O."; "Mitsubishi Star Wars Contract," *Nihon Keizai Shinbun* (Tokyo), 14 May 1988.

47. Clyde Haberman, "For Russians and Japanese, How Near Is a Warming in Their Relations?" *New York Times,* 19 May 1988.

48. Clyde Haberman, "Japanese Protest Curbs on Toshiba," *New York Times,* 2 April 1988.

49. Jose, "After Hiroshima, the Second Coming."

50. Institute of International Education, *Survey of American Colleges and Universities, 1985–86* (Washington, D.C.: IIE, 1988).

51. "Import Boycott in Japan," Associated Press, Tokyo, 17 June 1988.

52. "Japan's Sales to Pretoria," *New York Times,* 13 August 1988; "Pretoria Says New U.S. Sanctions Could Jeopardize Namibia Plans," *New York Times,* 13 August 1988.

53. Nathaniel C. Nash, "Washington Watch: A New Twist for Trade Law," *New York Times,* 11 August 1986.

54. "Foreign Study Growing with Stronger Goals," *New York Times,* 3 August 1988.

55. Yumiko Miyano, *In Search of a New Life: Profiles of Japanese Newcomer Women in California,* Working Paper No. 2 (Berkeley, Calif.: Japan Pacific Resource Network, March 1987); Jane A. Condon, *A Half-Step Behind: Japanese Women of the 80's* (New York: Dodd, Mead and Co., 1985), 144–45; Kazuyo Yamoto, "Women's Life-Long Education: Present Conditions and Related Themes," *Feminist International,* no. 2 (June 1980); Etsuko Kaji, "Herded into the Labor Market," *AMPO Japan-Asia Quarterly Review* 18, nos. 2-3 (1986): 36–37.

56. Merry White, *The Japanese Overseas: Can They Go Home Again?* (New York: The Free Press, 1988).

57. Katy Koontz, "Japanese High School Opens in Tennessee Town," *New York Times,* 11 May 1989.

Chapter 20

1. Ian Buruma, "After Hirohito What Remains Sacred," *New York Times Magazine,* 28 May 1989.

2. Institute of the German Economy, *Labor Dispute: Working Days Lost Per Year Per 1,000 Workers* (Bonn: Research Department, I.G.E., 1988).

3. Susan Chira, "Tokyo Journal: It's Official! Vacations Really Aren't Un-Japanese," *New York Times,* 7 August 1988.

4. Statistics Bureau, *Statistics Handbook of Japan* (Tokyo: Management and Coordination Agency, 1988), table 409.

5. Laura D'Andrea Tyson and John Zysman, *Politics and Productivity: Developmental Strategy and Production Innovation in Japan* (Berkeley, Calif.: Berkeley Roundtable on the International Economy, Working Paper no. 30).

6. Statistics Bureau, *Statistics Handbook of Japan* (Tokyo: Management and Coordination Agency, 1988), table 409.

7. Peter F. Drucker, "Workers' Hands Bound by Tradition," *Wall Street Journal,* 2 August 1988.

8. Institute of the German Economy, *passim.*

9. Management and Coordination Agency, *Seasonally Adjusted Unemployment Rates* (Tokyo: MCA, 29 July 1988), fax edition.

10. U.S. Labor Department, *Monthly Labor Statistics* (Washington, D.C.: USLD, July 1988).

11. **See** Leonard Silk, "Economic Scene: Looking for a Way to Fight Inflation," *New York Times,* 29 July 1988; Organization for Economic Cooperation and Development, *World Economic Outlook* (Paris: OECD, June 1988).

12. Peter T. Kilborn, "Warning on Trade Retaliation," *New York Times,* 2 May 1989; Clyde H. Farnsworth, "U.S. Cites Japan, India and Brazil as Unfair Traders," *New York Times,* 26 May 1989; Clyde Farnsworth, "Cosmetics Industry Criticizes Duties," *New York Times,* 25 May 1989.

13. Steven Greenhouse, "Central Bankers Warn of Further Instability," *New York Times,* 13 June 1988.

14. International Monetary Fund, *Monthly Trade Statistics* (New York: IMF, July 1988).

15. Philip Revzin, "Treading Water: Rich and Comfortable, West Germany Also Is Ominously Stagnant," *Wall Street Journal,* 1 August 1988.

16. Michael Farr, "German Lombard Rate Is Raised to Curb Dollar," *New York Times,* 29 July 1988.

17. Ferdinand Protzman, "Ten Percent Withholding Tax Abolished by Germany," *New York Times,* 28 April 1989.

18. James M. Markham, "Britain, Not Exactly a Joiner, Still Favors a Few Barriers," *New York Times,* 31 July 1988.

19. Walter S. Mossberg, "Outlook: Europe Could Become the New Trade Villain," *Wall Street Journal,* 1 August 1988.

20. Neal S. Lipschutz, "European Scene: Looking for a Way to Fight Inflation," *New York Times,* 29 July 1988.

21. Quoted in Leonard Silk, "Economic Scene: Looking for a Way to Fight Inflation," *New York Times,* 29 July 1988.

22. Chang Kuk Cho, *Ethnic Identity and Political Movement: A History of the Korean Minority in Japan,* Working Paper No. 3 (Berkeley, Calif.: Japan Pacific Resource Network, 1987).

23. Statistics Bureau, *Statistics Handbook of Japan* (Tokyo: Management and Coordination Agency, 1988), table 14.

24. Buraku Liberation Research Institute, *Buraku: Its Materials and Explanations* (Osaka: BLRI, 1988).

25. Michihiko Noguchi, "Interview," Research Institute of the Dowa Problem, Osaka City University, Osaka, Japan, 16 August 1988.

26. *Kashu Mainichi* (Los Angeles), 24 October 1986; *Asahi Shinbun* (Tokyo), 22 October 1986.

27. *Kashu Mainichi* (Los Angeles), 26 September 1986.

28. *Tong-Il Ilbo,* 10 December 1986.

29. *Chuo Koron* (Tokyo: Chuo-Koron-Sha, November 1986), 146–162.

30. *Washington Post,* 24 September 1986.

31. *New York Times,* 9 December 1986; *San Francisco Chronicle,* 9 December 1986; *Kashu Mainichi* (Los Angeles), 9 December 1986.

32. *Kashu Mainichi* (Los Angeles), 4 February 1984.

33. Robert Reinhold, "A Japanese Banker's Bid to Cement U.S.-Japanese Ties," *New York Times,* 31 July 1988.

34. Buruma, "After Hirohito What Remains Sacred."

35. Buruma, "After Hirohito What Remains Sacred."

36. van Wolferen, *passim.*

37. van Wolferen, *passim.*

38. David E. Sanger, "Japan Seen Hedging on Airline Deal," *New York Times,* 18 May 1989.

Bibliography

Acquisitions Monthly. Cited in *New York Times,* 11 July 1988.

Alexander, General Harold R.L.G., *Current Bibliography.* London: Macmillan, 1942.

"All Aboard the American Train!" *Wall Street Journal,* advertisement, 30 June 1988.

Allen, G.C. *A Short History of Modern Japan.* New York: Praeger, 1963.

Anders, George. "Daiwa Securities Launches Fund to Buy Bonds." *Wall Street Journal,* 10 May 1988.

Avarin, V. "Manchuria as a Japanese Base of Attack on the Soviet Union." *New Times* 15 August 1945. Moscow: NT Publishers.

Bacon, Kenneth H. "Rebuilding America: Start at the Factory." *Wall Street Journal,* 16 May 1988.

Bank for International Settlements. *Annual report.* Basel, Switzerland: BIS, June 1988.

Bar, François, and Michael Borrus. "From Public Access to Private Concessions: Network Policy and National Advantage." Working Paper #28. Berkeley, Calif.: Berkeley Roundtable on the International Economy.

Bartlett, Sarah. "Big Banks Shift from the Third World." *New York Times,* 27 July 1988.

Bayless, Alan. "Technology Reshapes North America's Lumber Plants." *Wall Street Journal,* 16 October 1986.

Bean, Ed. "Federal Express Gets Extension for Tokyo Service." *Wall Street Journal,* 31 May 1988.

Beazley, J. Ernest. "In Spite of Mystique, Japanese Plants in U.S. Find Problems Abound." *Wall Street Journal,* 22 June 1988.

"Beef Market in Japan Cited." *New York Times,* 26 May 1988.

Berg, Eric N. "Japanese Turn More Cautious on U.S. Realty." *New York Times,* 2 June 1988.

"Bill Apologizing to War Interns Goes to Reagan." *New York Times,* 5 August 1988.

Bison, T.A. *Japan's War Economy.* New York: International Secretariat, Institute of Pacific Relations, 1945.

Borrus, Michael. "How to Beat Japan at Its Own Game." *New York Times,* 31 July 1988.

Bovard, James. "Farm Subsidies Stiffle Agriculture." *New York Times,* 29 May 1988.

Brauchli, Marcus W. "Japan May Face Some Pressure to Raise Rates." *Wall Street Journal,* 11 August 1988.

Bray, Nicholas. "Spain Is Flooded by Japanese Investment." *Wall Street Journal,* 24 May 1988.

279

Brinkley, Joel. "Japanese Official in Visit to Israel." *New York Times,* 27 June 1988.

Broadbent, Jeffrey. *Social Networks as Transmitters of Social Control in Local Japanese Politics.* A paper presented at the 77th Annual Meeting of the American Sociological Association. San Francisco, Calif., Sept. 6–10, 1982.

Brown, Ralph H. *Likeness of the Eastern Seaboard.* New York: De Capo, 1968.

Brumbaugh, R. Dan, Jr., and Robert E. Litan. "The Banks Are in Big Trouble, Too." *New York Times,* 21 August 1988.

Burgess, John. "International Reaction to Nakasone." *Washington Post,* September 24, 1986.

Buraku Liberation Research Institute (Buraku—Kaiho Kenkyu-jo), *Buraku Problems, Materials, and Explanations.* Osaka, Japan: Liberation Publishing [Kaiho—Shuppan-sha], 1988.

————. *Buraku: Its Materials and Explanations.* Osaka, Japan: B.L.R.I., 1988.

Burkeley, William M. "Frontiers of Science." *Wall Street Journal,* 10 November 1986.

Buruma, Ian. "After Hirohito What Remains Sacred." *New York Times Magazine,* 28 May 1989.

"Capital Flows Called Helpful." *New York Times,* 25 May 1988.

CBS. "American Game/Japanese Rules." *Frontline.* Broadcast 2 May 1988.

Celis, William, et al. "Pressure Builds to Seek More Sanctions against Japan After Chip Talks Collapse." *Wall Street Journal,* 6 June 1988.

Charlier, Marj. "Few U.S. Producers See Early Gains from U.S.–Japan Pact on Beef, Citrus." *Wall Street Journal,* 21 June 1988.

————. "IBP Warns Cattlemen to 'Do Something' About Contracts with Rival Meat Packers." *Wall Street Journal,* 26 July 1988.

"Chicago Board in Japan Pact." *New York Times,* 6 June 1989.

"Chiku, Junko no Bunpu (Districts and population distribution)." In *Buraku Mondai-Shiryo to Kaisetsu (The Buraku problem, its materials and explanation),* 2d ed. Tokyo: B.L.R.I., 1988.

Chira, Susan. "Fujitsu, a Match for IBM, Making Further Inroads in U.S." *New York Times,* 3 November 1986.

————. "In Japan, the Land of the Rod, an Appeal to Spare the Child." *New York Times,* 27 July 1988.

————. "In Student Game Plan, College Is a Racquet." *New York Times,* 29 June, 1988.

————. "Japan Is Entering Talks in a Position of Strength." *New York Times,* 18 June 1988.

————. "Japan 'Money Politics' Rears Its Head." *New York Times,* 8 August 1988.

————. "Japan's New Goal: U.S. Companies." *New York Times,* 27 April 1988.

————. "Motto for a New Breed: Less Work, More Play." *New York Times,* 25 January 1988.

————. "New Effort in Japan to Change the Tax System." *New York Times,* 15 June 1988.

————. "New Pride Changes Japan's View of the U.S." *New York Times,* 30 June 1988.

————. "Shakespeare Plays the Globe Theater, in Tokyo." *New York Times,* 31 May 1988.

————. "South Korea Swept by Labor Unrest." *New York Times,* 3 June 1988.

————. "Takeshita Stakes Prestige on Tax Plan." *New York Times,* 30 July 1988.

————. "Tokyo Journal: It's Official! Vacations Really Aren't Un-Japanese." *New York Times,* 6 August 1988.

————. "U.S. and Japan Clear a Trade Hurdle." *New York Times,* 21 June 1988.

Cho, Chang Kuk. *Ethnic Identity and Political Movement: A History of the Korean Minority in Japan.* Working Paper no. 3. Berkeley, Calif.: Japan Pacific Resource Network, 1987.

Christopher, Robert C. "Don't Blame the Japanese." *New York Times Magazine,* 19 October 1986.

Cohen, Laurie P. "Companies Rush to Sell Their Properties Because of Tax Law, Japanese Interests," *Wall Street Journal,* 6 November 1986.

Cohen, Marc Aaron. "The United States Fiber Optics Industry: Japanese Challenge, International Competitiveness, and Public Policy." Masters thesis, microfiche edition. John F. Kennedy School of Government, Harvard University, 1982.

Condon, Jane A. *A Half-Step Behind: Japanese Women of the 80s.* New York: Dodd, Mead and Co., 1985.

Condon, John C. *With Respect to the Japanese: A Guide for Americans.* Yarmouth, Maine: Intercultural Press, 1984.

Condon, John C., and Keisuke Kurata. *In Search of What's Japanese about Japan.* Tokyo: Tuttle, 1974.

Congressional Economic Leadership Institute. *Choate Report on Foreign Direct Investments.* Prepublication press edition. Washington, D.C.: Congressional Research Institute, 27 July 1988.

Consultive Committee. *The Colombo Plan: Tenth Annual Report, October–November 1961.* London: Her Majesty's Stationery Office, January 1962.

"Cowboys and the Japanese." *New York Times,* 8 March 1988.

Crozier, Andrew J. *Appeasement and Germany's Last Bid for Colonies.* New York: St. Martin's Press, 1988.

Cushman, John H., Jr. "Moving Plutonium by Sea Is Assailed." *New York Times,* 6 August 1988.

————. "New Rules on Atomic Fuel to Japan." *New York Times,* 2 November 1988.

Darlin, Damon. "American Train Will Toot Its Way through Japan, Hawking U.S. Goods." *Wall Street Journal,* 9 June 1988.

————. "Japan Firmly Resists U.S. Pressure on Rice," *Wall Street Journal,* 12 November 1986.

————. "U.S., Japan Are Said to Reach an Accord on Tokyo's Imports of Some Farm Goods." *Wall Street Journal,* 6 January 1988.

"Demand to Abolish Fingerprinting." *Kashu Mainichi* (Los Angeles), December 9, 1986.

De Mente, Boye. *Made in Japan: The Methods, Motivations, and Culture of the Japanese, and Their Influence on U.S. Business and All Americans.* Washington, D.C.: National Textbook, 1987.

Dempster, Prue. *Japan Advances.* London: Metheun, 1967.

Department of Commerce, Bureau of Industry Analysis. *Survey of Current Business.* Washington, D.C.: Department of Commerce, January 1981 et seq.

Diebold, John. "A New High Track to High-Tech Growth." *New York Times,* 2 November 1986.

Dore, Ronald. Introduction to *Japan in the Passing Lane* by Satoshi Kamata. New York: Pantheon Books, 1982.

————. *British Factory, Japanese Factory: The Origins of National Diversity in Industrial Relations.* Berkeley and Los Angeles: University of California Press, 1973.

Drucker, Peter F. "A Crisis of Capitalism." *Wall Street Journal,* 30 September 1986.

————. "Beyond the Japanese Export Boom." *Wall Street Journal,* 7 January 1987.

————. "Workers' Hands Bound by Tradition." *Wall Street Journal,* 2 August 1988.

Duke, Benjamine. *The Japanese School.* New York: Greenwood, 1986.

"EC Sets Duties on Printers from Japan." *Wall Street Journal,* 27 May 1988.

Economic Planning Agency. "Changes in Dollar Exchange Rate: February 1985 through April 1987." *White Paper on the Japanese Economy.* Tokyo: Economic Planning Agency, 1988.

————. "Content and Transitions of Long-Term Capital Investments." *White Paper on the Japanese Economy.* Tokyo: Economic Planning Agency, 1988.

————. "Income Gains and Capital Gains: 1970 through 1986." *White Paper on Japanese National Life (Kokumin Seikatsu Hakusho).* Tokyo: Ministry of Finance, 1988.

————. "Preliminary Quarterly Report, 1988. Tokyo: Economic Planning Agency, Fax Edition, June 1988.

————. "Structural Changes in Japanese Money Market and Assets." *White Paper on Japanese National Life (Kokumin Seikatsu Hakusho).* Tokyo: Ministry of Finance, 1988.

————. "Survey Report: Japanese Consumers' Perception on the Price of Imported Goods, February 1987." *White Paper on Japanese National Life (Kokumin Seikatsu Hakusho).* Tokyo: Ministry of Finance, 1988.

————. *White Paper on the Japanese Economy.* Tokyo: Economic Planning Agency, 1988.

————. *Work and Leisure.* Tokyo: Economic Planning Agency, 1988.

Egan, Timothy. "Japan Plunge into U.S. Realty." *New York Times,* 23 November 1986.

"Electronics Industry Talks." *New York Times,* 8 June 1988.

Emerson, Edward, Jr. *A History of the Nineteenth Century Year by Year.* 3 vols. New York: P.F. Collier and Son, 1900.

ENA. New York: McGraw-Hill, 1–7 June 1988.

"Europe in New Japan Inquiry." *New York Times,* 4 June 1988.

Farnsworth, Clyde H. "Cosmetics Industry Criticizes Duties." *New York Times,* 25 May 1989.

————. "Gain Seen in U.S.–Japan Farm Talks." *New York Times,* 18 June 1988.

————. "Industrialized World Shows Its Love for the Farm." *New York Times,* 26 June 1988.

————. "Japan Deal Questioned by G.A.O." *New York Times,* 3 May 1989.

————. "U.S. and Japan Ponder a Free Trade Proposal." *New York Times,* 12 August 1988.

————. "U.S. Cites Japan, India, and Brazil as Unfair Traders." *New York Times,* 26 May 1989.

————. "Washington Watch." *New York Times,* 18 November 1986.

Farr, Michael. "German Lombard Rate Is Raised to Curb Dollar." *New York Times,* 29 July 1988.

Feder, Barnaby J. "Technology." *New York Times,* 12 June 1986.

————. "The Computer as Deal Maker." *New York Times,* 14 August 1986.

Finance Ministry. *Direct Japanese Investments, Fiscal Year 1988.* Tokyo: Finance Ministry; Fax Edition, 31 May 1988.

Fisher, Lawrence M. "Seagate Trips, Industry Cringes." *New York Times,* 23 August 1988.

"Flying Tiger Files Japan Complaint." *New York Times,* 16 July 1988.

Foreign Capital Research Society. *Japanese Industry 1965.* Tokyo: F.C.R.S., 1966.
"Foreign Criticism of U.S. Trade Bill Rejected by Yeutter." *Wall Street Journal,* 11 August 1988.
"Foreign Holdings Up." *New York Times,* Tokyo: Associated Press, 6 November 1945.
"Foreign Interests in Japan." Tokyo: Associated Press, 6 November 1945.
"Foreign Study Growing with Stronger Goals." *New York Times,* 3 August 1988.
"From Superrich to Superpower." *Time,* 4 July 1988.
Frost, Ellen L. *For Richer, for Poorer: The New U.S.–Japan Relationship.* Washington, D.C.: Council on Foreign Relations, 1987.
"Fujitsu to Buy U.S. Chip Unit." *New York Times,* 24 October 1986.
Fukuda, Tsuneari. *Japan and the Japanese.* Tokyo: Kodansha, 1957.
Fukunaga, Koji, Ueda Masaaki and Ueyama Shunpei. *Dakyo to Kodai No Tenno-sei (Taoism and the Ancient Imperial System).* Tokyo: Tokuma Shoten, 1978.
Fukushima, Kiyohiko. *Memo on the Transfer of Technology from Japan to the Less Developed Countries.* Tokyo: Nomura Research Institute; Los Angeles Fax Edition, 30 April 1988.
Funahashi, Yoichi. "Congress Could Denounce Nakasone." *Asahi* (Tokyo), October 7, 1986.
Furumori, Yoshihisa. "Japanese Media Covers Nakasone." *Mainichi* (Tokyo), September 30, 1986.
Ghate, B.G. *Asia's Trade.* New Delhi: Indian Council of World Affairs, Oxford University Press, 1948.
Grajdanev, Andrew J. "Manchuria: An Industrial Survey." *Pacific Affairs* (New York), December 1945.
Graven, Kathryn. "Japan Isn't Ready for Illegal Aliens, but It Has 100,000." *Wall Street Journal,* 23 June 1988.
———. "Stock Market May Help the Japanese Banks Meet International Capital Standards." *Wall Street Journal,* 14 June 1988.
———, and and Susan Moffat. "Japan, Korea Seek a Windfall in Gulf Peace." *Wall Street Journal,* 25 July 1988.
Greenhouse, Steven. "Central Bankers Warn of Further Instability." *New York Times,* 13 June 1988.
———. "Europeans Adopt Plan to End Curbs on Capital Flows." *New York Times,* 14 June 1988.
———. "Making Europe a Mighty Market." *New York Times,* 22 May 1988.
Guilder, George. "The New American Challenge." *Wall Street Journal,* 3 November 1986.
Guillain, Robert. *The Japanese Challenge.* Translated by Patrick O'Brian. Philadelphia and New York: Lippincott, 1970.
Haberman, Clyde. "American Lawyers Land on Their Feet in Tokyo." *New York Times,* 22 May 1988.
———. "Carlucci Seeks Aid on Bases in Japan." *New York Times,* 7 June 1988.
———. "For Russians and Japanese, How Near Is a Warming in Their Relations?" *New York Times,* 19 May 1988.
———. "Japan's 20,000 Unwelcome Guests." *New York Times,* 17 November 1987.
———. "Japanese Protest Curbs on Toshiba." *New York Times,* 2 April 1988.
———. "Pricey Japan." *New York Times Magazine,* 8 May 1988.
———. "Shinto Back on the National Stage." *New York Times,* 7 June 1988.
Hadley, Eleanor. *Japan's Export Competitiveness in Third World Markets.*

Washington D.C.: Georgetown University Center for Strategic and International Studies, 1981.

Halberstram, David. *The Reckoning*. New York: William Morrow, 1986.

Hall, Edward T., and Mildred Reed Hall. *Hidden Differences: Doing Business with the Japanese*. New York: Anchor Press/Doubleday, 1987.

Hamaguchi, Eshun. *Rediscovering Japanese Uniqueness*. Tokyo: Yuhihaku 1977.

Hardin, Clifford H. "Trade War Follies." *New York Times,* 21 August 1986.

"Hawaii Airline Parent, HAL, to Sell Holdings to Unit of Japan Air." *Wall Street Journal,* 31 May 1988.

Hayashi, Fusao. *A New Plea for the Great East Asian War*. Tokyo: Bungei Shunju 1965.

_____. *Pleading for the Great East Asian War*. Tokyo: Bungei Shunju 1964.

Hayashi, Saburo, and Alvin D. Coox. *Kogun: The Japanese Army in the Pacific War*. Quantico, Va.: Marine Corps Association, 1959.

Hayes, Robert H. "Why Japanese Factories Work." *Harvard Business Review,* (July-August 1981), 57–66.

Hayes, Thomas C. "FSX: Icing on the Cake for General Dynamics." *New York Times,* 2 May 1989.

Hershey, Robert D., Jr. "Foreign Stake in U.S. Rose to Record in '87." *New York Times,* 1 July 1988.

Hinton, W.J. "Economic Occasion of Conflict in the Far East." In *The Causes of War,* edited by Arthur Porritt. London: Macmillan, 1932.

Holusha, John. "Mixing Cultures on the Assembly Line." *New York Times,* 5 June 1988.

"Hyundai Motors Suspends Production in Ulsan Plant." *Wall Street Journal,* 2 June 1988.

Ichikawa, Kon. Director. *Nobi (Fires on the Plain)*. Based on the novel by Shohei Ooka. Berkeley, Calif.: Pacific Film Archives, 1988.

Ike, Nobutaka, trans. *Japan's Decision for War: Records of the 1941 Policy Conferences*. Stanford: Stanford University Press, 1967.

Imamura, Shohei. Director. *Remembering the Bomb*. A documentary broadcast on KQED, San Francisco, 5 August 1988.

_____. Director. *Black Rain*. A documentary broadcast on KQED, San Francisco, based on the novel by Masuji Ibuse, 1969.

"Import Boycott in Japan." Tokyo: Associated Press, 17 June 1988.

Ingrassia, Paul, and Joseph B. White. "GM Mulls Tough Call in Toyota Venture." *Wall Street Journal,* 10 June 1988.

Institute of International Education. *Survey of American Colleges and Universities, 1985–86*. Washington, D.C.: I.I.E. Study Group, 1988.

Institute of the German Economy. "Labor Disputes: Working Days Lost per Year per 1,000 Workers." Bonn: I.G.E. Research Department, 1988.

International Monetary Fund. *Monthly Trade Statistics,* 1980–88. New York: IMF.

_____., "Monthly Statistics." May 1988 et seq. New York: IMF.

Ishi, Tomoji. *Japanese Automobile and Television Assembly Plants and Local Communities: County Demographic Correlates*. Berkeley, Calif.: Japan Pacific Resource Network, 1988.

"Jackson Boycott Plan." *Kashu Mainichi,* February 4, 1986.

Jaffe, Philip. *New Frontiers in Asia: A Challenge to the West*. New York: Random House, 1945.

Jaikumar, Ramchandran. "Post-Industrial Manufacturing." *Harvard Business Review* (November-December 1986), no. 6: 69–76.

"JAL's Pretax Profit Soars on Unconsolidated Basis." *Wall Street Journal,* 1 June 1988.
Janesway, Eliot. "Forum: It's a Bad Time to Cut Consumption." *New York Times,* 15 May 1988.
Jansen, Marius B. *Japan and Its World: Two Centuries of Change.* Princeton, N.J.: Princeton University Press, 1980.
————. "Monarchy and Modernization." *Journal of Asian Studies* (August 1977).
————, and Gilbert Rozman, eds. *Japan in Transition: From Tokugawa to Meiji.* Princeton: Princeton University Press, 1986.
"Japan Asks End to Builder Ban." *New York Times,* 27 May 1988.
"Japan: Business Survey." *Wall Street Journal,* 14 March 1988.
"Japan Cabinet Sets $50 Billion of Foreign Aid." *Wall Street Journal,* 14 June 1988.
Japan Central Bank. *Quarterly Survey and Diffusion Index of 7,635 Companies.* Tokyo: JCB; Fax Edition, June 1988.
"Japan Dealers Consider New Insider-Trading Rules." *Wall Street Journal,* 2 June 1988.
"Japan Is Firm on Rice Ban." *New York Times,* 23 February 1988.
"Japan Rejects U.S. Chip Plea." *New York Times,* 17 June 1988.
"Japan to Lead Plane Project." *New York Times,* 4 June 1988.
"Japan Trade Surplus Cut." *New York Times,* 6 June 1988.
"Japan Vows Aid to Asia." *New York Times,* 4 July 1988.
Japan-Manchukuo Yearbook, 1940. Tokyo: HYI.
Japanese Ministry of International Trade and Industry. *The Vision of MITI Policies in the 1980s.* Tokyo: MITI, 1980.
"Japanese Plan Less U.S. Grain." *New York Times,* 12 January 1988.
"Japanese Vehicle Exports to the U.S. Fall." *New York Times,* 8 June 1988.
"Japanese Widen U.S. Merger Role." *New York Times,* 28 July 1988.
"Japan's Sales to Pretoria." *New York Times,* 13 August 1988.
"Japan's Steel Production Capacity." Tokyo: Associated Press, 7 December 1945.
Johnson, Chalmers. *MITI, MPT, and the Telecom Wars: How Japan Makes Policy for High Technology.* Working Paper no. 21. Berkeley, Calif.: Berkeley Roundtable on the International Economy.
Johnson G.A. "Industrial and Labour Influences." In *The Causes of War,* edited by Arthur Porritt. London: Macmillan, 1932.
José, F. Sionil. "After Hiroshima: The Second Coming." *New York Times,* 6 August 1988.
Kahn, Herman. *The Emerging Japanese Superstate: Challenge and Response.* Englewood Cliffs, N.J.: Prentice Hall, 1970.
Kaisetsu, Shiryo to. *Buraku Mondai (Buraku Problem: Its Materials and Explanation),* 2nd ed. Osaka: 1988.
Kaji, Etsuko. "Herded into the Labor Market." AMPO *Japan-Asia Quarterly Review,* 18, nos. 2-3, 1986 36–37.
Kamata, Satoshi. *Japan in the Passing Lane: An Insider's Account of Life in a Japanese Auto Factory.* Translated by Tatsuru Akimoto. New York: Pantheon Books, 1982.
Kanabayashi, Masayoshi. "Foreign Investment in Japan Is Growing, Helped by Nation's Economic Expansion." *Wall Street Journal,* 14 June 1988.
————. "Japan's Biggest Steel Companies Swing to Losses," *Wall Street Journal,* 12 November 1986.
————. "Local Demand and Yen's Impact on Costs Fuel a Recovery by Japanese Companies." *Wall Street Journal,* 16 May 1988.

————. "More Time Off, Not Wages, Emphasized in Japan's Labor Bargaining This Year." *Wall Street Journal,* 23 February 1988.

————. "Tokyo Stock Market Nears Record Highs as Traders Prepare for New Fiscal Year." *Wall Street Journal,* 31 March 1988.

Kashiwagi, Hiroshi. "Employment Discrimination at Japanese Firms in America: A Case Study of EEOC Lawsuits." Working Paper no. 4. Berkeley, Calif.: Japan Pacific Resource Network, 1988.

Kato, Koichi. "Making Internationalists Out of Domestic Politicians." *Wall Street Journal,* 16 May 1988.

Keizai-Kikaku-Cho. *Kokumin Seikatsu-hen.* Tokyo: Ministry of Finance, 1988.

Kilborn, Peter T. "Japan Asserts American-Style Clout in Toronto." *New York Times,* 20 June 1988.

————. "Key U.S. Shift Seen to Job Protection from Free Trade." *New York Times,* 29 April 1988.

————. "Treasury Official Assails 'Inefficient' Big Business." *New York Times,* 7 November 1986.

————. "Warning on Trade Retaliation." *New York Times,* 2 May 1989.

Kishimoto, Shigenobu. *Fantasy of the Middle.* Tokyo: Foreign Press Center, 1978.

Kissinger, Henry A., and Cyrus R. Vance. "Bipartisan Objectives for Foreign Policy." *Foreign Affairs* (Summer 1988), Vol. 16, no. 5, 899–921.

Kleinman, Dena. "Bacon Joins Borscht at Catskill Tables." *New York Times,* 21 June 1988.

Klott, Gary. "A Doubling of Some Exports Is Seen." *New York Times,* 21 June 1988.

Kobayashi, Masaki. Director. *The Human Condition, A Trilogy: No Greater Love; Road to Eternity; The Soldier's Prayer.* Berkeley, Calif.: Pacific Film Archives, 1988.

Koontz, Katy. "Japanese High School Opens in Tennessee Town." *New York Times,* 11 May 1989.

Koren, Leonard. "Great Ideas of Eastern Man." *California,* (March 1988), Los Angeles: California Magazines, 56–57.

KQED Special. *Hellfire, a Journey from Hiroshima.* Film documentary. San Francisco: KQED, 4 August 1988.

Kristof, Nicholas D. "Surge in the Yen Spurs Japanese to Invest in the U.S." *New York Times,* 9 August 1986.

Krooth, Richard. *Arms and Empire: Imperial Patterns before World War II.* Santa Barbara, Calif.: Harvest, 1980.

————. *Empire: A Bicentennial Appraisal.* Santa Barbara, Calif.: Harvest, 1975.

————. *Great Homestead Strike of 1892.* Palo Alto, Calif.: Ramparts Press, 1990.

————. "High-Tech in Crisis: Decay as a Historical Dilemma." In *The Dynamics of Enterprise in the American Milieu, Vol. 1.* 3rd ed. edited by Richard Krooth. Berkeley, Calif.: CIM, 1988.

————. *Japan: Five Stages of Development and the Nation's Future.* Santa Barbara, Calif: Harvest, 1976.

————. "Nature of Labor in the Production Process." In *The Dynamics of Enterprise in the American Milieu,* Vol. 1, 3rd ed. edited by Richard Krooth. Berkeley, Calif.: CIM, 1988.

————. "Tour of the Freemont Plant." Freemont, California, April 1987.

Kukunaga, Koji, Ueda Masaaki, and Ueyama Shunpei. *Dokyo to Kodai no Tennosei (Taoism and the ancient imperial system),* Tokyo: Tokuma Shoten, 1978.

"Kumagai Gumi's Link to Turner." *New York Times,* 4 June 1988.

Kurosu, Satomi. "Rural Disintegration and Suicide in Japan." A paper presented at the 84th Annual Meeting of the American Sociological Association, August 10, 1989. San Francisco, CA.

Kyodo News Service. Tokyo, 23 July 1988.

Landman, J.H., and Herbert Wender. *World since 1914.* 10th rev. ed. New York: Barnes & Noble, 1958.

Langley, Monica. "America First: Protectionist Attitudes Grow Stronger in Spite of Healthy Economy." *Wall Street Journal,* 16 May 1988.

Lansing, Paul, and Kathryn Ready. "Japanese Women and the Professions." *California Management Review* (Spring 1988), Vol. 30: 112–127.

Lasch, Christopher. *The Culture of Narcissism: American Life in an Age of Diminishing Expectations.* New York: Warner Books, 1979.

Lehner, Urban C. "World Clamors for an Increase in Japanese Foreign Aid." *Wall Street Journal,* 10 June 1988.

_____, and Masayoshi Kanabayashi. "Japanese Aides Tied to Scandal on Stock Sales." *Wall Street Journal,* 7 July 1988.

Lewis, Peter H. "Satellites Let Executives Be Two (or More) Places at Once." *New York Times,* 10 December 1986.

Lin, Chong-Pin. "China: Nuclear Wild Card." *New York Times,* 29 July 1988.

Lipschutz, Neal S. "European Central Bank Creation Hinges on British Participation, Analysts Say." *Wall Street Journal,* 1 August 1988.

Lockwood, William E., ed. *The State and Economic Enterprise in Japan: Essays in the Political Economy of Growth.* Princeton, N.J.: Princeton University Press, 1965.

Lohr, Steve. "The Big Dividends of a Gulf Peace." *New York Times,* 13 August 1988.

_____. "Wall Street Rethinks Its Global Plans." *New York Times,* 11 July 1988.

Loth, Wilfried. *The Division of the World, 1941–1955.* New York: St. Martin's Press, 1988.

Lubove, Seth H. "The Old College Tie." *Wall Street Journal,* 10 November 1986.

Lueck, Thomas J. "Japanese Interest in Harlem, Megaprojects Create Hope — and Fear." *New York Times,* 17 April 1988.

McAvoy, Clyde. "Making an Honest Dollar in Japan." *Wall Street Journal,* 13 June 1988.

McCain, Mark. "Japanese Invest in Manhattan Condos." *New York Times,* 31 March 1988.

Management and Coordination Agency. *Seasonally Adjusted Unemployment Rates.* Tokyo: MCA; English Fax Edition, 29 July 1988.

Manchester, William. *The Arms of Krupp: 1587–1968.* New York: Bantam, 1970.

Mark, Jeremy. "Narrowing of Japanese Trade Surplus Accelerates as Import Boom Continues." *Wall Street Journal,* 10 June 1988.

Markham, James M. "Britain, not Exactly a Joiner, Still Favors a Few Barriers." *New York Times,* 31 July 1988.

_____. "NATO Compromise Seems to Rule Out Tactical Arms Ban." *New York Times,* 31 May 1989.

Markoff, John. "IBM and a University Plan Swift File Network." *New York Times,* 23 August, 1988.

Maruyama, Masoa. *Thought in Japan.* Tokyo: Tokuma Shoten, 1961.

Mears, Helen. *Mirror for Americans.* Boston: Houghton Mifflin, 1948.

"Media and Nakasone." *Asahi* (Tokyo), September 27, 1986.

Meirer, Barry. "Chemical Giants Are Turning to Raw Materials." *Wall Street Journal,* 24 June 1986.

Meyers, Henry F. "Will Mergers Help or Hurt in the Long Run?" *Wall Street Journal,* 2 May 1988.

Miller, Michael W. "Korean Focusing on Personal Computers: Nation Is Challenging Japan in U.S. Market," *Wall Street Journal,* 6 November 1986.

Milling-Stanley, George. *Annual Gold Review.* London: Consolidated Gold Fields PLC, May 1988.

Ministry of Finance. *Overseas Investments, Fiscal Year April 1, 1987–March 31, 1988,* Tokyo: MF; Fax Edition, June 1988.

―――――. *Estimated Trade Figures, Fiscal Year Reports, 1988–1989.* Tokyo: MITI; Fax Edition, June 1988.

Ministry of International Trade and Industry, *Preliminary Report on the Semi-Annual Meeting of Leading Companies, Fiscal Year March 31, 1988,* Tokyo; MITI; English Fax Edition, 1988.

―――――. *White Paper on International Trade.* Tokyo: MITI Trade and Policy Bureau: Fax Edition, 3 June 1988.

―――――. *White Paper on International Trade.* Tokyo: MITI Trade and Policy Bureau: Fax Edition, 7 June 1988.

Ministry of Labor. *Survey of Incorporated Systems of Working Hours.* Tokyo: ML, 1988.

Minor Enterprises Agency. "Content of Japanese Overseas Investments." *White Paper on Minor Enterprises.* Tokyo: Ministry of Finance, 1988.

―――――. "History of Japanese Enterprise Overseas Investment: 1978–1987." *White Paper on Minor Enterprises.* Tokyo: Ministry of Finance, 1988.

―――――. "Reasons for Japanese Overseas Investment." *White Paper on Minor Enterprises.* Tokyo: Ministry of Finance, 1988.

"Minorities Protest." *Japan Times* (Tokyo), October 18, 1986.

"Minority Rights." *Kashu Mainichi* (Tokyo), September 26, 1986.

Mitchell, Cynthia F. "Coming Home." *Wall Street Journal,* 14 November 1986.

―――――. "Pentagon Eases Stand against Foreign Stakes in U.S. Defense Firms." *Wall Street Journal,* 28 April 1988.

"Mitsubishi Star Wars Contract." *Nihon Keizai Shimbun.* Tokyo: Nihon Keizai Shimbun, 14 May 1988.

Miyano, Yumiko. "In Search of a New Life: Profiles of Japanese Newcomer Women in California." Working Paper no. 2. Berkeley, Calif.: Japan Pacific Resource Network, March 1987.

Mizuno, Seiichi. *Asuka Buddhist Art: Horyu ji.* Translated by Richard L. Gage. New York: Weatherhill; Tokyo: Heibonsha, 1974.

Mobile Corporation. "Karl Marx Meet Adam Smith." *New York Times,* advertisement, 2 June 1988.

"More to Toshiba Affair Than Meets the Eye." *JPRN Bulletin,* 6 No. 2 (Winter 1967): 1, 6.

Morimoto, Shoko. "No More Hibakusha." *The Co-op News.* Berkeley, Calif., 20 July 1988.

Morishima, Michio. *Why Has Japan "Succeeded"?* London: Cambridge University Press, 1982.

Morita, Akio and Shintaro Ishihara. *Japan That Can Say No.* Tokyo: Kobunsha, 1989.

Morris, Charles R. *Iron Destinies, Lost Opportunities: The Arms Race Between the U.S.A. and the U.S.S.R. 1945–1987.* New York: Bessie Book/Harper & Row, 1988.

Morse, Hosea Ballou, and Harley Farnesworth MacNair. *Far Eastern International Relations.* New York: Riverside Press, 1931.

Mossberg, Walter S. "Outlook: Europe Could Become the New Trade Villain." *Wall Street Journal,* 1 August 1988.

_____, and John Walcott. "U.S. Redefines Policy on Security to Place Less Stress on Soviets." *Wall Street Journal,* 11 August 1988.

Moynihan, Daniel Patrick. "Debunking the Myth of Decline." *New York Times Magazine,* 19 June 1988.

Murakami, Yasusuke. *The Age of New Middle Class Masses.* Tokyo: University of Tokyo Press, 1984.

_____, et al. *"Le" Society as a Civilization.* Tokyo: University of Tokyo Press, 1979.

Nakai, Kate Wildman. "The Nationalization of Confucianism in Tokugawa Japan: The Problem of Sinocentrism." *Harvard Journal of Asiatic Studies.* 40, No. 1 (June 1980), 159–197.

"Nakasone, United Nations, Human Rights." *Asahi* (Tokyo), October 24, 1986: 17–20.

Nakasone, Yasuhiro: Text of Speech to Training Session, Liberal Democratic Party." *Chuo Kobon* (Tokyo), November 1986, 146–152.

"Nakasone Statement to Diet," Oct. 31, 1986. *Kashu Mainichi* (Tokyo), Oct. 24, 1986.

Nakayama, Ichiro. *Industrialization of Japan.* Tokyo: Center for East Asian Cultural Studies; Honolulu: East West Press Center, 1963.

Nakayama, Kaneyoshi, ed. *Pictorial Encyclopedia of Japanese Culture: The Soul and Heritage of Japan.* Trans. by Richard Delapp. Tokyo: Gakken Co., 1987.

Nash, Nathaniel C. "Washington Watch: A New Twist for Trade Law." *New York Times,* 11 August 1986.

National Science Foundation. *Statistical Resources.* Washington, D.C.: N.S.F. Research Department, 1986.

Nihon Keizai Shimbun. Tokyo: Nihon Keizai Shimbun, 24 July 1988.

"Nikko Plans to Invest in Foreign Nations' Issues." *Wall Street Journal,* 10 May 1988.

Noguchi, Michihiko. "Interview." Osaka, Japan: Research Institute of the Dowa Problem, Osaka City University, 22 April and 16 August 1988.

_____. *Japan's Minorities: Discrimination and the Buraku.* Research Paper Series. Research Institute of the Dowa Problem, Osaka City University, March 1989.

Norman, Herbert E. *Japan's Emergence as a Modern State: Political and Economic Problems of the Meiji Period.* New York: Greenwood, 1946.

Norman, John T. "U.S. Study Ordered of Japanese Curbs on Orange Imports." *Wall Street Journal,* 25 May 1988.

Norman, Peter. "Kleinwort Set to Sell Stake in Unit to Fuji." *Wall Street Journal,* 10 May 1988.

Northup, Robert W. "Okinawa Is an Island that Lost Its Culture." Letter to the editor. *New York Times,* 13 May 1989.

Ogawa, S. "Banking in Japan." In *Comparative Banking,* 3rd ed., edited by H.W. Auburn. Dunstable, England: Waterlow and Sons, 1966.

Ohkawa, Kazushi, et al. *Patterns of Japanese Economic Development.* New Haven: Yale University Press, 1979.

Ohmae, Kenichi. "Americans and Japanese Save About the Same." *Wall Street Journal,* 14 June 1988.

_____. *Beyond National Borders.* Tokyo: McKinsey, 1985.

_____. *Mind of the Strategist.* New York: McGraw-Hill, 1982.

Oka, Takashi, *Saionji and the Manchurian Crisis.* Harvard Papers on China. Cambridge: Harvard University Committee on International and Regional Studies, 1954.

Okabe, Kazuaki. "Nakasone Hatsugen to Taminzoku Shakai." *Sanzenri.* Winter 1986, 147–153.

Organization for Economic Cooperation and Development. *International Investment and Multinational Enterprise; Supporting Documents.* Paris: O.E.C.D., 1980, 1981.

_____. *Forecasts.* Paris: O.E.C.D., May 1988.

_____. *Official Government Aid Figures.* Paris: O.E.C.D., 1986, 1988.

_____. *World Economic Outlook, Semi-Annual Report, June 1988.* Paris: O.E.C.D., June 1988.

Oyama, Yoichi, ed. *Labor and Large Enterprise: A Study of the Toyota Motor Company.* Tokyo: Ochanomizu Shobo: 1985.

Pascale, Richard T., and Anthony G. Athos. *The Art of Japanese Management.* New York: Simon and Schuster, 1981.

Patrick, Hugh, and Henry Rosovsky, eds. *Asia's New Giant: How the Japanese Economy Works.* Washington, D.C.: Brookings Institute, 1976.

"Pentagon Handout to Japan." *New York Times,* 12 February 1989.

Perros, Theodore P. "U.S. Heads Down the Road to Scientific Dotage," letter to the editor, *New York Times,* 8 December 1986.

Pine, Art. "Foreign Takeovers Stir Fear from Main St. to Congress." *Los Angeles Times,* 5 June 1988.

_____. "U.S. Considers Challenging the Merger of Schlumberger and Fujitsu Chip Units." *Wall Street Journal,* 31 October 1986.

_____. "U.S. May End Microchips Pact with Japan," *Wall Street Journal,* 13 November 1986.

_____, and Peter Waldman. "Japan to Press Its Chip Makers to Hew to Pact." *Wall Street Journal,* 19 November 1986.

Pollack, Andrew. "A Sober Silicon Valley Is 'Changed Forever'." *New York Times,* 5 October 1986.

Power, Brian. *The Puppet Emperor.* London: Universe Books, 1987.

Preeg, Ernest H. "Next, a Free-Trade Pact with Japan?" *Wall Street Journal,* 12 August 1988.

Prestowitz, Clyde V., Jr. *Corporate Focus: Are We Giving Our Economic Future to Japan?* A paper presented to the World Affairs Council and the Japanese Society of Northern California, San Francisco, Calif., 23 June 1988.

_____. *Trading Places: How We Allowed Japan to Take the Lead.* New York: Basic Books, 1988.

"Pretoria Says New U.S. Sanctions Could Jeopardize Namibia Plans." *New York Times,* 13 August 1988.

Prime Minister's Select Panel, Gaishi Hiraiwa, Chairman. *Maekawa Report: Five Year Economic Plan, 1988–1992 (Summary of Economic Problems and Their Planned Resolution).* Tokyo; (Diet) Naikaku, Economic Planning Agency, English Fax Edition, 23 May 1988.

Protzman, Ferdinand. "10% Withholding Tax Abolished by Germany." *New York Times,* 28 April 1989.

Quick, Finan, and Associates. *The U.S. Trade Position in High Technology: 1980–1986, A Report Prepared for the Joint Economic Committee of the United States Congress.* Washington, D.C.: J.E.C., October, 1986.

Quint, Michael. "Japan's About-Face on Mergers, Acquisitions." *New York Times,* 1 August 1988.

_____. "Yamaichi-Lodestar Deal Is Part of a Growing Trend." *New York Times,* 28 July 1988.

Recruit, U.S.A. "Seminar." Berkeley: University of California, 25 September 1988.

Reich, Robert B. *The Next American Frontier.* New York: Times Books, 1983.
_____. "Making a Rust Bowl of the Silicon Valley." *New York Times,* 12 October 1986.
Reinhold, Robert. "A Japanese Banker's Bid to Cement U.S.-Japanese Ties." *New York Times,* 31 August 1988.
Reischauer, Edwin O. *Japan, Past and Present.* New York: Knopf, 1964.
_____. *The Japanese.* Cambridge: Harvard University Press, 1977.
Report of the Secretary of Labor's Task Force on Economic Adjustment and Worker Dislocation. *Economic Adjustment and Worker Dislocation in a Competitive Society.* Washington, D.C.: U.S. Department of Labor, December 1986.
Revzin, Philip. "Treading Water: Rich and Comfortable, West Germany Also Is Ominously Stagnant." *Wall Street Journal,* 1 August 1988.
"Rev. Jesse Jackson's Support." *Tong. Il Ilbo* (Seoul), December 10, 1986.
Ricks, Thomas E. "Foreign Brokerages Appear Frequently in Insider-Trading Reports, Study Says." *Wall Street Journal,* 6 June 1988.
Robbins, William. "A Meatpacker Cartel Up Ahead?" *New York Times,* 29 May 1988.
Robinson, Marshall. "Household Debt." *New York Times Magazine: Business World, Part 2,* 12 June 1988.
Roosevelt, Franklin D. "Anti-Inflationary Order, April 8, 1943." *New York Times,* 9 April 1943.
Roth, Andrew. *Dilemma in Japan.* Boston: Little, Brown, 1945.
Salomon Brothers. Cited in "Shedding Loans to Developing Nations." *New York Times,* 27 July 1988.
Samson, G.B. *The Western World and Japan: A Study in the Interaction of European and Asiatic Cultures.* New York: C.E. Tuttle, 1950.
Sanger, David E. "Insider Trading: A Japan Tradition." *New York Times,* 10 August 1988.
_____. "Japan Seen Hedging on Airline Deal." *New York Times,* 18 May 1989.
_____. "Japan to Let Contract on Disputed Jet Project." *New York Times,* 30 March 1989.
_____. "Japan Yields to the U.S. on Chips." *New York Times,* 31 November 1986.
_____. "Japanese Ask Which Side Navy Is On." *New York Times,* 30 July 1988.
_____. "U.S. Says Bomb Lost Close to Japan Scattered Radiation." *New York Times,* 16 May 1989.
_____. "U.S.-Japan Ties Worsen on News that Warhead Was Lost in 1965." *New York Times,* 9 May 1989.
_____. "Utilities in Japan to Shun Uranium from South Africa." *New York Times,* 2 November 1988.
Sato, Yumiko. "Japanese Mother Makes an Antinuclear Plea." Letter to the editor, *New York Times,* 12 August 1988.
"Saturday Closing Planned." *Wall Street Journal,* 1 June 1988.
Scardino, Albert. "Deal Maker Thriving on U.S.-Japan Gap." *New York Times,* 6 June 1988.
Schein, Edgar H. "Does Japanese Management Style Have a Message for American Managers?" *Sloan Management Review* (Fall 1981), 1-20.
Schildgen, Robert. *Toyohiko Kagawa: Apostle of Love and Social Justice.* Berkeley, Calif.: Centenary Books, 1988.
Schlender, Breton R. "Schlumberger Ltd., Fujitsu to Merge U.S. Chip Units." *Wall Street Journal,* 24 October 1986.

————. "Unpopular Science." *Wall Street Journal,* 10 November 1986.

Schmemann, Serge. "Germany's President Upholds Country's Assertive Stance." *New York Times,* 25 May 1989.

Schnapp, John B. "Shock Waves from Korea Reach Northwood, Ohio." *Wall Street Journal,* 13 November 1986.

Schrager, James E., and Julian Gresser. "Going Public, Japanese Style." *Wall Street Journal,* 2 May 1988.

Schuon, Marshall. "Automation That's Flexible." *New York Times,* 2 October 1986.

Sciolino. Elaine. "Some Kind Words in Asia Do Not Dispel a Sense of Waning of U.S. Influence." *New York Times,* 24 July 1988.

Sease, Douglas, R. "Yen's Rise Said to Spur Japanese Dumping." *Wall Street Journal,* 6 October 1986.

————, and Michael R. Sesit. "An Appraisal: Foreign Investors Wait for Progress on U.S. Deficit." *Wall Street Journal,* 14 December 1987.

————. "Economic Scene: Looking for a Way to Fight Inflation." *New York Times,* 29 July 1988.

Secretary of Labor's Task Force on Economic Adjustment and Worker Dislocation. *Economic Adjustment and Worker Dislocation in a Competitive Society.* Washington, D.C.: U.S. Department of Labor, December 1986.

Seiichi, Iwao. *Bibliographical Directory of Japanese History.* Tokyo: Kodansha International, 1978.

"Senate Clears Way for Japan to Buy Anti-Missile System." *Wall Street Journal,* 8 August 1988.

Servan-Schreiber, Jean Jacques. *The American Challenge.* New York: Atheneum, 1976.

Sesit, Michael R. "An Appraisal: Japanese Appetite for U.S. Stocks May Be Growing." *Wall Street Journal,* 9 May 1988.

————. "Fuji Bank Buys Stake in Kleinwort Unit, Gaining Toehold as Primary U.S. Dealer." *Wall Street Journal,* 24 May 1988.

————. "Japanese Executive Defies Convention in Preferring U.S. Management Style." *Wall Street Journal,* 26 July 1988.

————. "Nissan's Earnings Rebound Culminates Long Struggle to Overcome Strong Yen." *Wall Street Journal,* 3 June 1988.

————. "U.S. Is Urged to Take Action against Deficit." *Wall Street Journal,* 7 June 1988.

Sewell, John W. "The Development Gap: Help the Third World Catch Up." *New York Times,* 22 May 1988.

Shalett, Sidney. "Japan Body Meets Without Russians," *New York Times,* 7 November 1945.

————. "Japanese Commission Halts for Russia," *New York Times,* 31 October 1945.

Shapiro, Michael. "In Japan, Tyson's Impact Is Powerful and Perplexing." *New York Times,* 9 March 1988.

Shoji, Kokichi. *Jumin-Ishiki no Kano-sei.* Tokyo: Azusa Publisher, 1986.

————. "Rising Neonationalism in Contemporary Japan: Changing Social Consciousness of the Japanese People and Its Implications for World Society." Unpublished paper, University of Tokyo, June 1988.

Shuchman, Lisa. "Japan Increases Imports from Four Asian Countries." *New York Times,* 25 April 1988.

Silk, Leonard. "Economic Scene." *New York Times,* 12 November 1986.

————. "Economic Scene." *New York Times,* 3 December 1986.

_____. "Economic Scene: Looking for a Way to Fight Inflation." *New York Times,* 29 July 1988.

_____. "New Guns-and-Butter Battle." *New York Times,* 22 May 1988.

Sims, Calvin. "Advances in Conductivity." *New York Times,* 21 January 1987.

Sivard, Ruth Leger. *World Military and Social Expenditures 1985.* Washington, D.C.: World Priorities, 1985.

Slocum, Ken. "The Sun Belt Gains Manufacturing Jobs as Nation Loses Them." *Wall Street Journal,* 1 April 1988.

Small and Medium Enterprise Agency. *White Paper on Small and Medium Enterprises.* Tokyo: SMEA, 1988.

_____. *Survey of Manufacturing Sectors.* Tokyo: SMEA, December 1987.

Smith, E.J. *The New Trades Combination Movement.* London: Rivingtons, 1899.

Smith, Guy-Harold and Dorothy Good. *Japan: A Geographical Survey.* New York: American Geographical Society, 1943.

Snellgrove, David L., ed. *The Image of Buddha.* Paris: Kodansha International/ UNESCO, 1978.

"Software Group Picks Site." *New York Times,* 23 August 1988.

Solarz, Stephen J. "Foes of Aegis Sale to Japan Miss the Boat." *Wall Street Journal,* 1 August 1988.

"Solidarity Statement." *Hokubei Mainichi* (Tokyo), November 19, 1986.

Solomon, Anthony M. "Checking the Spread of a New Xenophobia." *New York Times,* 31 May 1988.

"South Korea Estimates Iran-Iraq Building Orders." *Wall Street Journal,* 11 August 1988.

"State Department Accepts Nakason Remarks." *Los Angeles Times,* September 25, 1986.

Statistics Bureau. *Statistical Handbook of Japan.* Tokyo: Management and Coordination Agency, 1988.

Sterngold, James. "Dollar Plummets to Postwar Low against the Yen." *New York Times,* 18 March 1986.

Storry, Richard. *A History of Modern Japan.* London: Penquin Books, 1960.

Stowsky, Jay. *The Weakest Link: Semiconductor Production Equipment Linkages, and the Limits of International Trade.* Working Paper no. 27. Berkeley, Calif.: Berkeley Roundtable on the International Economy.

Sullivan, Paul R. "Strategies for Playing the Global Game." *New York Times,* 26 June 1988.

"Sumitomo and Nissho Iwai Post Profit Gains for Year." *Wall Street Journal,* 16 June 1988.

Summers, Lawrence H. "Good News on the Trade Deficit, But...." *New York Times,* 20 May 1988.

"Supplement on Japan." *The Times* (London), 22 November 1965.

Takahashi, H. Kohachiro. "La Place de la Révolution de Meiji dans l'histoire agraire du Japon." *Revue Historique* (October-November, 1953): 248. Paris. Statistics by M. Yamada.

"Tanaka Memorial." *China Critic.* (Shanghai) 24, no. 9 (September, 1931): 923–932.

Tanin, O., and E. Yohan. *When Japan Goes to War.* New York: International Publishers, 1936.

Tarpinian, Gregory. "U.S. Outdoes British Empire in Troops Abroad." Letter to the editor, *New York Times,* 14 June 1988.

Taylor, Robert E. "Greenspan Notes Pressure on Banks to Increase Rates." *Wall Street Journal,* 13 May 1988.

"Text of Secretary Byrnes's Message." *New York Times,* 12 August 1945.

"Three Japanese Executives Charged in Illegal Exports." *Wall Street Journal,* 18 May 1988.

Thurow, Lester C. "A Briefing for the Next President." *New York Times,* 21 August 1988.

Tiedemann, Arthur. *Modern Japan: A Brief History.* New York: D. Van Norstrand Company, 1955.

"Tokyo Lifts Stock Margins." *New York Times,* 3 June 1988.

"Tokyo Stock Exchange Lifts Margin Rule to 70%." *Wall Street Journal,* 3 June 1988.

Tominaga, Ken'ichi, ed. *Stratification Structure in Japan.* Tokyo: University of Tokyo Press, 1979.

"Top-Ranked Takeover Advisers." *Acquisitions Monthly.* Cited in *New York Times,* 11 July 1988.

Totman, Conrad D., *The Collapse of the Tokugawa Bakufu: 1862–1869.* Honolulu: University Press of Hawaii, 1980.

Townsend, Alair, and Ronald Shelp. "Japan's Money Helps Build America." *New York Times,* 5 June 1988.

"Trade Zone." *Automotive News* (Detroit), August 17, 1987.

Tsurumi, Yoshi. "Forum: Explaining the 'Japanese Paradox'." *New York Times,* 16 November 1986.

"Twenty-Five Largest Banks." *American Banker,* 19 July 1988, centerfold.

Tyson, Laura D'Andrea, and Zysman. *Politics and Productivity: Developmental Strategy and Production Innovation in Japan.* Working Paper no. 30. Berkeley, Calif.: Berkeley Roundtable on the International Economy.

"Union Construction Labor." Kashu Mainichi (Tokyo), November 18, 1986.

United Technologies. "High Tech, High Trade." advertisement *New York Times,* 5 November 1986.

United Nations, Department of Economic and Social Affairs. *International Social Development Review,* no. 1: *Urbanization: Development, Policies and Planning.* New York: United Nations, 1968.

"U.S. Auto Jobs: The Problem Is Bigger than Japanese Imports." *UAW Research Bulletin* (June 1986), 1ff.

"U.S. Cautions Japan on Delay of Import Issue." *Wall Street Journal,* 19 May 1988.

"U.S. Chip Makers See New Japan Threat." *Wall Street Journal,* 27 October 1986.

Uchitelle, Louis. "Overseas Spending by U.S. Companies Sets Record Pace." *New York Times,* 20 May 1988.

U.S. Arms Control and Disarmament Agency. *World Military Expenditures and Arms Transfers, 1985.* Washington, D.C.: ACDA Publication 123, August 1985.

U.S. Commerce Department. *Preliminary Report on Foreign Direct Investment, 1987.* Washington, D.C.: Commerce Department, 31 May 1988.

_____. *Survey of Current Business.* Washington, D.C.: Bureau of Industry Analysis, January 1981, December 1981, *et seq.*

U.S. Department of State. *The Nixon Doctrine.* Washington, D.C.: State Department, December 1971.

U.S. General Accounting Office. "Foreign Investment: Growing Japanese Presence in the U.S. Auto Industry." Washington, D.C.: GAO/NSIAD, March 1988.

U.S. Labor Department. *Monthly Labor Statistics.* Washington, D.C., 1985–88.

"U.S.–Japan Deal on Fighter." *New York Times,* 31 May 1988.

"U.S., Japan Sign Pact on Patents, Resolving Sensitive Technology." *Wall Street Journal,* 18 April 1988.

Valentine, John. "Platinum Soars on Japanese Demand Followed by Increases in Gold, Silver." *Wall Street Journal,* 1 June 1988.

Van Wolferen, Karel. *The Enigma of Japanese Power: People and Politics in a Stateless Nation.* New York: Knopf, 1989.

Vartan, Vartanig G. "Market Place: Japanese Stocks Build Momentum." *New York Times,* 18 March 1988.

Veblen, Thornstein. *The Theory of Business Enterprise.* New York: New World Library, 1952.

Vogel, Ezra F. *Japan's New Middle Class.* Berkeley and Los Angeles: University of California Press, 1963.

Wald, Matthew L. "Foreign Investors Step into More Active Roles." *New York Times,* Real Estate Report: Commercial Property, 25 May 1988.

Wallace, Anise C. "Market Place: End-Year in Japan Could Affect U.S." *New York Times,* 15 March 1988.

War Supplement to Compton's Pictured Encyclopedia. Chicago: F.E. Compton & Company, 1939.

Weinstein, Martin E. *Japan's Postwar Defense Policy, 1947–1968.* New York: Columbia University Press, 1971.

Weisman, Steven R. "Infighting Paralyzes Japan's Quest for New Leader." *New York Times,* 18 May 1989.

_____. "Japanese Say Plan to Revise Pact on Jet Leaves 'Serious Scar'." *New York Times,* 28 March 1989.

_____. "Reaction in Japan Mixed on Jet Deal." *New York Times,* 30 April 1989.

_____. "Takeshita Resigns as Japan's Premier Over Gift Scandal." *New York Times,* 25 April 1989.

"White House Directive." *New York Times,* 23 September 1945.

Winder, David. "Japan and South Korea Work at Making Peace." *Christian Science Monitor,* 17 September 1984.

Winter, Ralph E. "U.S. Manufacturers Are Expanding Capacity of Plants." *Wall Street Journal,* 7 June 1988.

_____, and Gregory Stricharchuk. "Weaker Dollar Saves Small Concerns from Imminent Death." *Wall Street Journal,* 25 July 1988.

Wittfogel, Karl August. *History of Chinese Society.* New York: Macmillan, 1949.

_____. *Oriental Despotism.* New Haven: Yale University Press, 1957.

Wong, Jan, et al. "Robots: The Next Step for Garment Makers." *Wall Street Journal,* 7 August 1987.

WTTW/Chicago & Central Independent Television. "Japan." Jane Seymour, Producer. Broadcast 2 May 1988.

Wyatt Co, H.K. *Ranking 191 Equity-Unit Funds, 1983–87.* Hong Kong: Hong Kong Unit Trust Association, May 1988, Fax edition.

Wysocki, Bernard, Jr. "In Japan, Breaking Step Is Hard to Do." *Wall Street Journal,* 14 December 1987.

_____. "Japanese Are Suffering Unemployment Rise in a Shifting Economy," *Wall Street Journal,* 6 November 1986.

_____. "Venture Capitalists: Japanese Start Buying U.S. Firms Stressing Latest in High Tech." *Wall Street Journal,* 8 August 1986.

Yamaichi Securities Company. "Mergers and Acquisitions." Tokyo: Yamaichi, 1988.

Yamasaki, Masakuzu. *The Birth of Soft Individualism.* Tokyo: Chuo-Koron-sha, 1984.

Yamoto, Kazuyo. "Women's Life-Long Education: Present Conditions and Related Themes." *Feminist International,* no. 2 (June 1980): 9.

Yates, Ronald E. "Nakasone Apology." *San Francisco Examiner,* September 30, 1986.

"Yes, Big Science, but Which Projects." *New York Times,* editorial, 20 May 1988.

Yoder, Stephen Kreider. "Like Noah of Old, Japanese Consider Building Some Arks." *Wall Street Journal,* 25 May 1988.

_____. "Automating Software." *Wall Street Journal,* 10 November 1986.

_____. "Japanese Banks on Cooled Computer Circuits." *Wall Street Journal,* 22 October 1986.

_____. "Hitachi, Fujitsu Link in Microprocessors." *Wall Street Journal,* 28 October 1986.

Yoshikawa, Akihiro. *The Japanese Challenge in Biotechnology: Industrial Policy.* Working paper no. 29. Berkeley, Calif.: Berkeley Roundtable on the International Economy.

Young, Lewis H. "The Corporate Links Abroad." *New York Times,* 6 August 1986.

_____. "Economic Scene." *New York Times,* 6 August 1986.

Index

297

M

N